Paul Broca

Oil portrait of Paul Broca, probably in his thirties,
at the Mairie of Sainte Foy. (Artist unknown.)
(Courtesy of Photo André, Sainte-Foy-la-Grande.)

Paul Broca

Founder of French Anthropology, Explorer of the Brain

Francis Schiller

Oxford University Press
New York   Oxford

Oxford University Press

Oxford   New York   Toronto
Delhi   Bombay   Calcutta   Madras   Karachi
Kuala Lumpur   Singapore   Hong Kong   Tokyo
Nairobi   Dar es Salaam   Cape Town
Melbourne   Auckland

and associated companies in
Berlin   Ibadan

Copyright © 1992 by Oxford University Press

First published in 1979 by University of California Press
2120 Berkeley Way, Berkeley, California 94720

First issued as an Oxford University Press paperback, 1992

Produced by arrangement with the University of California Press

Oxford is a registered trademark of Oxford University Press

Library of Congress Cataloging-in-Publication Data
Schiller, Francis, 1909–
[Paul Broca, founder of French anthropology, explorer of the brain]
Paul Broca, explorer of the brain / Francis Schiller.
Originally published : Paul Broca, founder of French anthropology,
explorer of the brain. Berkeley, Calif. : University of California
Press, c1979.
p.   cm.   Includes bibliographical references and index.
ISBN 0-19-507496-3 (pbk)
1. Broca, Paul, 1824–1880.
2. Anatomists—France—Biography.
3. Anthropologists—France—Biography.
4. Surgeons—France—Biography.
I. Title.
[DNLM: 1. Broca, Paul, 1824–1880. 2. Anthropology—biography.
3. Neurology—biography. WZ 100 B863Sa   1979a]
QM16.B76S33   1992
612.8'2'092—dc20   [B]   DNLM/DLC   92-16433

2   4   6   8   10   9   8   7   5   3   1
Printed in the United States of America
on acid-free paper

Contents

Foreword

$\mathscr{P}$aul Broca, born in 1824, participated in a most exciting chapter in history in general and in the history of science in particular. He was a near contemporary of Queen Victoria (born 1819), Lord Lister (born 1827), Herbert Spencer (born 1820), Cyrus Field and Walt Whitman (both born 1819), Louis Pasteur and Gregor Mendel (both born 1822), and R. Virchow and H. Helmholtz (both born 1821). Broca, in his many-sidedness and inventiveness, was hardly second to any of them. It seems almost incredible that this is the first scientific biography of Paul Broca in any language. Hospitable and friendly California seems destined to fill the gaps of French historiography of science. It was also in California that J. Olmsted a few decades ago wrote the first books on Magendie, Claude Bernard, and Brown-Séquard.

Broca's accomplishments in his short fifty-six years of life are almost immeasurable. Even non-historians know about his work in surgery on cancer and aneurysm; in neuroanatomy, neurophysiology, and neuropathology on the speech center and the limbic lobe; in anthropology on the founding of the discipline in France and formation of its contents, methods, School, and Society. Yet more important perhaps than any single detail is Broca's role in the emergence of modern scientific medicine, so-called "laboratory medicine," around 1860. And Broca accomplished this in a country in which the finest medical traditions were not favorable and which was in danger of being outdistanced, not only politically but intellectually, by an awakening Germany! Just as Claude Bernard could and did see himself rightly as an equal to Helmholtz, Broca could and did feel the same way concerning Virchow, who, by the way, respected him highly. Both men show many common traits, including general biological orientation and strong interest in pathological microscopy, anthropology, and politics.

Francis Schiller—after many smaller contributions to the history of neurology—has with unequaled devotion, skill, and tenacity given us this portrait of a great and good man. He deserves our highest admiration and gratitude.

Zürich   ERWIN H. ACKERKNECHT
May, 1978

Acknowledgments

$\mathcal{A}$t the time of writing no one who knew Paul Broca was alive. Some friendly persons who immeasurably helped my efforts by giving me information (through anecdote or document), advice, and encouragement, survive only as memories. Here is the list (incomplete, I fear): Doctor Philippe Monod-Broca, M. Alain Peyromaure-Debord-Broca, and other members of the Broca family; Professor Henri Vallois; Professor Pierre Huard; Professor Delmas; Professor Alajouanine; M. Mahieu (Archives Nationales); M. Candille (Assistance Publique); Mlle. de Ferron (Consistoire, Eglise Réformée de France) — all in Paris; M. Jean Corriger, Sainte-Foy-la-Grande; M. & Mme. Peyros and the Mayor of Luzarches; Professor Earl Count, Hamilton College, Clinton, New York; Professor Owsei Temkin, Baltimore, Maryland; Professor J. B. de C. M. Saunders, Professor Gert Brieger, University of California; Professor Herbert Phillips; Mrs. Hutchinson-Merritt; Mrs. Ruth Straus (Kaiser Foundation-Permanente Medical Group); Mr. Ernest Callenbach (University of California Press) — all of the San Francisco Bay Area; innumerable librarians in Paris and San Francisco; and the United States taxpayers through USPHS Grant R.G. 9890.

Most insistent and instrumental in reducing the manuscript to its present length has been Professor Erwin Ackerknecht of Zürich. To him, first and last, I dedicate these pages, as well as to the readers who will share them; and to all the other helpers, my warmest thanks.

Introduction

$\mathscr{P}$aul Broca was a French surgeon-anthropologist who more than a hundred years ago identified a certain area on the convoluted surface of the human brain, approximately a square inch in size, as the central organ for speech. It is known as "Broca's area", and its destruction causes "Broca's aphasia."

Broca explored a multitude of other "areas" as well. An imposing figure, a tremendously energetic activist, a promoter of science, he stood at that busy intersection of historical crosscurrents where progress clashed with tradition.

Paris still has its Hôpital Broca and its Rue Broca. The medical dictionaries add, to Broca's area and aphasia, Broca's center, convolution, and fissure; Broca's band and limbic lobe; Broca's formula, plane, pouch, and space. Yet Broca's life has not been written, nor has an analysis been done of his writings on surgery, comparative anatomy, neurology, pathology, statistics, hypnosis, blood transfusion, anthropology: well over 500 titles plus two volumes of privately published letters.

Statements about him are sometimes contradictory: "Nothing he ever wrote was mediocre,"[1] and "the genius of the great Broca . . . no one could associate with him without catching a portion of the sacred flame,"[2] wrote some contemporaries. Modern critics have commented: "Broca, a French anthropologist with a broad skull, wrote five volumes to prove that the broader the head the better the brain, and the French had particularly broad heads,"[3] and "had the wheel of fortune

1

turned differently, Broca would have lived out his career as a pedestrian practitioner of surgery with an interest in craniometry."[4] Garrison's standard text of medical history has a confused comment about Broca, the anthropologist.[5] But toward the end of Broca's life, by the time he had become Senator, he ranked with Pasteur and Claude Bernard in French biological science.[6]

The subtractions and additions of a century have modified his stature. But no matter what our distance and desire to focus on the forest rather than the trees, the impression that remains is one of diversity, a diversity that has eluded casual historians. They have been apt to single out one aspect of his work; failing to see its place in a most remarkable composite, some of them concluded his success was due to circumstance. No doubt Broca had a flair for the untilled, fertile field; no doubt he brought to a great many of those fields the proper plough and backbreaking labor. He belonged to a breed of naturalists gradually becoming extinct under the pressure for specialization. None of the conventional pigeonholes accommodate Broca.

How are we to summarize the significance of a mind whose "transcendent capacity of taking trouble,"[7] whose memory and drive, whose resolving and combining power were such as to make him anatomist, surgeon, biologist and neurologist, all at once? We are faced with a man's extraordinary compulsion to grasp, embrace, hold, and deliver diverse knowledge. A glutton for information, a lover consumed with science, Broca was as generous as a donor as he was successful as a collector. His mind held constant open house, as though driven by a claustrophobia of the closed argument, the unqualified absolute, the established rule and system. He fought absolutism everywhere as contrary to his nature and contrary, he felt, to nature itself. Empiricist and pragmatist, he distrusted the unifying formula, scorned homogeneity, rejected monogenism. In politics as in science, authority meant prejudice, the evasion of justice. Truth, never to be decreed, must submit to questioning. Justice must be done to the facts, evidence pieced together, yet judgment suspended where the evidence, as usual, was incomplete. He denied the simple answer to the complex problem, denied others the right to impose rules to which they felt entitled, by birthright, custom, or expediency. As the member of a minority and a dissenter even from that dissenting group, he was sensitive to the pressures by majorities or by powerful minorities—aristocracy, clergy, and the moneyed bourgeoisie—or simply by tradition in science. This made him support the oppressed friend and the suppressed idea. In accordance with his upbringing, religious in spirit only (he had early spurned the latter) and Voltairian,

2

he became in nearly every pursuit, champion as well as investigator of a cause. In putting his questions to nature, he seemed motivated by the suspicion that dogma rather than nature was hiding the facts. And so, to practice microscopy was to propagate the microscope against the clinicians' resistance; to localize speech in the brain was to open up Gall's lost case. In curare, hypnotism, muscular dystrophy, the analytical method in assessing vascular surgery, the resuscitation of organisms, Brown-Séquard's experiments on conduction in the spinal cord,[8] the transformation of species,[9] the Celtic myth, the value judgment attached to the cranial index, the linguistic fallacy in racial classification, Cro-Magnon Man[10]—in all his multitudinous efforts, there are few where the pioneer is not joined by the crusader.

Yet much in Broca's approach was traditional. When he embarked on his major study in comparative anatomy of the brain—a subject not apt to fire popular imagination in his or our own time—Broca had to defend himself against the reproach of hanging on to an old-fashioned line of research. The great "vivisectionist" and inaugurator of experimental physiology, Claude Bernard himself, had written in 1865: "What can we say about fishes' brains, for instance, until experiment has clarified the question? . . . Anatomical deduction has yielded what it can. To linger in this path means lagging behind the progress of science . . . a relic of scholasticism . . . "[11] But this "relic" of comparative anatomy has become a towering if little understood classic: Broca's "great limbic lobe."[12]

Together with (though almost in opposition to) his aggressive crusading was Broca's territorial defense, his insistence that alien elements—religion, philosophy, politics—should stay out of the scientist's way and, as a corollary, that scientists ought to refrain from applying their method to religious beliefs. This was far from obvious. In his review of a book entitled *Medical Miracles of the Gospels* (1855), he criticized the author's attempt at mixing religious faith and medical fact.[13] Whichever of the two might give the mixture its taste, it was bound to be bad, he said, adding that the same holds for philosophy. There is an amazing similarity between Claude Bernard's dictum, "I can no more accept a philosophy which tries to assign boundaries to science, than a science which claims to suppress philosophic truths . . . outside its own domain," and Broca's even more forceful statement: "Any philosophical system that enslaves science, no matter how opposed it may be to religious dogma, is just as objectionable as that dogma."[14]

Science has its own ethics, its own methods to establish the truth. We also must remember that a long line of moral reasoning stretching from the Middle Ages has equated "error" with "sin." To this day, for scientists to be deceived by their own bias has remained a moral as much as an intellectual shortcoming. A good deal of science as Broca saw it was, and to some degree still is, concerned with the eradication of bias.

"Let scientists," he is quoted as saying, "be interested in the affairs of the world, let them get excited about philosophy or religion, about social or humanitarian matters: nothing could be better. But when they go back to their studies and laboratories, they must remain independent and never bow to party discipline." So far, so good: science in pure culture, as it were. But he supposedly went on to this conclusion: "An august goddess, Science thrones above humanity . . . Only of her it may be said that she is made to command, not to obey."[15]

He may or may not have spoken or written these exact words, or he may have later regretted their tone for being open to interpretations that are far from the liberal humanitarianism for which he stands. But quite possibly he was carried away to utter this Victorian hyperbole; its scientism was still revolutionary in his day.

Mutual stimulation, however, was acceptable, even desirable, between the specialties in medicine and anthropology. In that age of growing specialization, it was a healthy move, half retrospective and half forward-looking, to merge some of those specialties in the superspecialty called anthropology. Interdisciplinary discourse was also at work in Broca's aphemia, which gave precision to Gall's idea of hybridizing a behavioral with an anatomical fact.

Achievement in the biological sciences was no longer based on "vision" alone: laboratory precision was added. Broca contributed to this development when he created so much of the methodology — together with the Society, the Laboratory, the School, and the Institute — of Anthropology. He will be remembered for his vision and precision, always precariously balanced; ideas, ground rules, and innumerable practical measuring devices and factual details; rigorous critical watch against imposing ideas that may vitiate the facts; criticism of the facile, often dishonest nationalist or racialist conclusions. An ardent believer in statistics,[16] he was called not only "one of the great anatomists of the last century," but also "one of the first men to introduce probabilistic concepts into biological research," by E. Schreider, who used Broca's thousands of unpublished skull measurements for his own up-to-date correlative statistical evaluation.[17] More recently, A. Leguèbe has pointed to Broca as the first after Quételet to have championed, since 1860, the statistical method to accommodate the treacherous variability of biological characteristics.[18]

In providing the working basis for all future cerebral localization, he naturally had forerunners, but their revival by latter-day historians is essentially owed to Broca's eminence in the field of aphasia. Its clinical importance and theoretical consequence made his fame, while his admirable concept of the great limbic lobe — another cortical system hardly appreciated before — merits greater attention now than ever.[12]

Broca appeared in French medicine at the end of its most brilliant period as a clinical school, a half-century that established as the hallmark of the good physician the search for "physical signs" in the patient and the corresponding post-mortem changes. It also was the time when the German universities began to steal a march on Parisian complacency. If French medicine nevertheless maintained the highest repute, it was only thanks to men like Bernard, Pasteur, and Broca, who, by their criticism and their achievement, spurred the profession to apply "basic science" in their practice; clinical methods alone had ceased to be good enough for making a good doctor.

After Claude Bernard's death, Broca was the first choice to represent science in the Senate, and (like Virchow, his great German counterpart) he plunged into social legislative work. Unlike Claude Bernard, however, and unlike also a good number of lesser men in France, Broca was not a member of the Institut, of the Académie des Sciences; he stood for issues that were rather controversial, represented rather scattered fields, and he died relatively young. "Bertillot" (senior, the statistician), it was said, "might bring all this down to a single statistical question in mortality."[19]

But a list of titles, civic and scientific, no matter how long and significant, does not by itself convey a man's impact. More perhaps than any one or all of the innumerable facts or the tools for finding them that he added to knowledge, it was his attitude itself to the process of finding, reporting, and disseminating such facts that distinguishes Broca, the investigator and teacher. Hence, his impact is largely one of morals and methods. These foundations he helped to lay down did not rest on the faith and certainty of past centuries. Broca's science, modern science, and its claim to our trust are founded on a confession of uncertainty; its integrity is based on honest doubt. But methods and discoveries, even ethical precepts — old hat — are passed on, taken for granted, cemented into the body of knowledge and practice: Science with a capital S, even the science of and for man, has become part of our everyday lives. Many, though, still see reasons for looking upon this as the work of the Devil, and upon scientists as rather inhuman. Extraordinary some of them certainly are —

extraordinarily devoted and successful, just as are some statesmen or artists. Whatever their field, we value most their integrity, the quality of the integrated whole. *Le style c'est l'homme*: slightly misquoted, from an acceptance speech in the Académie, it was surprisingly uttered by a zoologist. Buffon in his *Discourse on Style*, 1753, said: "The quantity and detail of a man's knowledge, even the novelty of his discoveries, are no certain guarantee for his immortality ... Such things are outside the man. The style is the man himself (*le style est l'homme même*) ... The beauty and the composition of ideas have a truth of equal usefulness, and perhaps greater value for the human mind, than you will find in the mere essence of the subject matter."

Buffon's literal and literary meaning lends itself to the current wider interpretation of "style." Broca's special measure as a man lies in the manner in which he embodied each chosen field, the heat and radiation of his personal involvement, the style of his humanity, and his humor.

I

Sainte-Foy-la-Grande

"Before your immense devotion my
gratitude must remain silent . . ." "Now
you are gasconading!" "All right, you do
not care for frills and flourishes; thanks,
then, for passing on to me your taste for
things positive."

*L*es Bouhets is a hamlet a few miles from Sainte-Foy-la-Grande in
the southwest of France. Scattered among the rows of vines running
up and down the old province Guyenne-et-Gascogne, occasional
farmhouses with little round red-roofed turrets for the pigeons interrupt the gentle green monotony.

There is a hill and on it a dark grove of oak and cypress. You enter
its shade unhindered by wall or fence and find a group of ten flat rough
granite slabs embedded in the grass. On one of them, moss outlines
the lettering:

LEONTINE BROCA,
BORN ON THE 3RD SEPTEMBER 1822,
DECEASED ON THE 9TH JULY 1840.
FLESH WAS SHE SOWN CORRUPTIBLE.
IN GLORY WILL SHE RISE.

READ CHAPTER XV FIRST EPISTLE CORINTHIANS.

This was Paul Broca's elder sister, and had she not died at the age of
eighteen, perhaps he would not have taken up medicine.

Also in the small cemetery is "Aunt Jourdit," who lived to be
ninety-three, her name presumably that of the place where she was
born. There are Paul's parents, Uncle Pierre Broca, who lived to be
ninety, two grandparents, and two other maiden aunts. There is Pierre

7

Private cemetery of the Broca family, Les Bouhets, near Sainte-Foy-la-Grande, Gironde. (Courtesy of Photo André, Sainte-Foy-la-Grande, 1962.)

Léon, a brother who died when five months old in the year before Léontine was conceived. Paul is not among them.

The now-silent group is united in a privacy that may seem puzzling. The Brocas, a Huguenot family, Calvinist Protestants in Roman Catholic France, had some land and a modest summer dwelling among the vineyards of Les Bouhets. But Sainte Foy was their main residence, and Sainte Foy has a large cemetery. When one of the Brocas died there, the funeral procession must have rambled for hours up the uneven roads to a grave on that hill. Sealed into the tombs is the memory of a past when Protestants could not bury their dead in public graveyards, of a segregation during and after life.

Calvinism was always concentrated in the south and southwest of France.[1] The hopes of the rising Reformed Church for dominating the country were crushed when Henry IV, a Protestant, reverted to Catholicism on ascending the throne. His Edict of Nantes of 1598 granted formal religious freedom but, in fact, sealed the fate of Calvinists as a minority, an anomaly, and, finally, a poisonous menace.

Under Louis XIV, new laws to wipe out the "heresy" would forbid anything the Edict of Nantes had not expressly allowed. Could Protes-

8

tants bury their dead? Certainly, but not in daytime. Baptize and wed? Surely, but the party must not exceed a dozen. Pray in their own temples? Yes, if they had been built before 1598, the year of the Edict. Teach in their own schools? Just the three R's. Money rewards were given for conversions, children above the age of seven were induced to renounce the religion of their fathers. Civil service, medicine, the law, even the grocery business[2] were closed to Protestants. Hospitals would keep neat registers "indicating the name and occupation of patients who have renounced the heresy of Calvin."[3] Then there were the famous *dragonnades* — royal dragoons, "missionaries in boots," billeted in Protestant homes, with privileges as in occupied territory; several hundred conversions easily followed in any small town after a single night of terror. With impeccable logic, Louis XIV concluded from the mass conversions so achieved that hardly any Protestants worth tolerating were left. He revoked the Edict: from 1685 on, no more gatherings of the R.P.R. (an early acronym: "Religion Pretending [to be] Reformed"); demolition of their temples; marriages, baptisms, and education only for Catholics; exile for pastors; the galleys and later death for everyone else leaving the country; a 3000-pound fine and a whipping for repeaters of the crime of helping them escape. Hence all those emigrants for the Protestant world: England, Denmark, Holland, Prussia. At home, too, Calvinism survived underground and with it, in every Huguenot family, some of the bitterness against the Establishment. Internal exiles, the members of the "Church of the Desert" gathered to read the Bible under the skies, under the threat of ruin and death. The Revolution restored tolerance,[4] but by 1787, in the Edict of Versailles, Louis XVI was again legalizing non-Catholic marriages. At Sainte Foy, with a community, then as now, of some 3500 to 4000 souls, the Marriage Register of 1789 lists 735 newly wed couples within eight months: most of them had been living in officially imposed sin.

To distinguish it from other small towns dedicated to the memory of Santa Fides or Santa Fe, the martyred fourth-century adolescent, Sainte Foy added "la Grande" as a suitable epithet. The Gasconading touch was redeemed by the number of outstanding men born and educated there.

This citadel was built in 1255 in one piece—not unlike places that nowadays are put on the map for military or industrial purposes—fewer than 100 blocks on some 15 streets, all of which, except the capricious Rue des Amours, intersect at right angles, unlike in the typical medieval town.

Thoroughly Protestant at the time of Henry IV, it was host to the king on several occasions, so that Montaigne could speak of "all this

Court of Sainte Foy." It was spared none of the bloody indignities of the Counter-Reformation, until Calvinism again flourished there throughout the nineteenth century among about one-third of the population.[5]

"Broca" is not a common name. Its derivation from *brouca*, Gascon for a place covered with *broc*, i.e., with thorns, brush, or heather, suggests, not improperly, a certain ruggedness.[6]

As early as 1569, during the wars of the Reformation, a pastor named Gilles de Broca came to Sainte Foy. Perhaps an ancestor of the family, he had once escaped after being arrested for his beliefs and was sentenced to a whipping and banishment *in absentia*. He lived and died at Sainte Foy and was instrumental in the construction of the Protestant temple.[7]

Great-grandfather Jacques, born one hundred years before Paul, was a *Sergeant du Roy* and *huissier* (bailiff) at Pujols, a little town in the vicinity. "By and large one can say," a late member of the family wrote, "that for generations Paul Broca's ancestors belonged to the so-called 'enlightened' bourgeoisie. While they were either in public service or had liberal professions—rather modest ones, incidentally—they remained attached to the native soil."

They included several non-conformists. Paul's paternal grandfather, Jean, volunteered and died fighting the counter-revolution in 1793. "Rebels beaten on all sides," read his laconic last letter from the front in the Vendée, "hope to return with friends soon." He was not to come home to his wife, his seven children, his small business, and to the "Society of Friends for the Constitution," which he had founded together with Paul's other grandfather in support of the great revolution.

"VICTIM OF THE TERROR" says the gravestone over Paul's maternal grandfather, Pierre Thomas. The "terror" was of the "white" variety, a royalist revenge after the downfall of Napoleon I for the "red terror" of the Revolution. The inscription refers to an occurrence in 1820, when the sixty-year-old man was banished for several months to a small village a hundred miles away from Sainte Foy. Mayor of Bordeaux during the Revolution and, during Napoleon's reign, pastor at Sainte Foy forty miles away, his record was that of a "moderate" *sansculotte*.[8]

Around 1817, he gave away his daughter Annette to Doctor Jean Pierre, called Benjamin, Broca, the young local physician, a son of the late secretary of the "Society of Friends for the Constitution." They lived on the arcaded main square, in a two-story house, together with the doctor's two maiden sisters, whose store on the ground floor contributed substantially to the family's income.

10

House where Paul Broca was born and raised, 1824 to 1841. Sainte-Foy-la-Grande, corner of Rue Louis Pasteur and Rue J.L. Faure (formerly Rue de l'Union and Rue Sainte-Foy), an angle of the main square surrounding the Mairie, with roomy arcades. (Courtesy of Photo André, Sainte-Foy-la-Grande, 1962.)

Their third child, Pierre Paul Broca, was registered June 29, 1824, as "born yesterday," No. 27, in the Register of Births in the Canton and Commune of Sainte-Foy-la-Grande, Arrondissement (County) of Libourne, Départment Gironde.

This was the year Lord Byron died, the decade that produced such promising infants as Baudelaire, Flaubert, and Dostoyevski, Ibsen and Jules Verne, Thomas Huxley, Pasteur, and Johann Strauss, Princess Victoria and Bismarck, Dickens and Karl Marx. Darwin, Richard Wagner, and Chopin were children or adolescents; Pushkin, Victor Hugo, and Balzac in their twenties, Walter Scott in his fifties, Goethe in his seventies. It was the decade following the end of Napoleon's empire and 150 years of French supremacy; an Indian Summer also for ultra-reactionary feudal Europe, restored but harrassed on the

11

continent by romantic conspirators, unable to forget the Revolution. Less rigid British liberalism, capitalism, colonialism, and men's fashions impressed themselves on the world, and 1824 marked the English workers' gain of the right to associate and strike. In the Western Hemisphere, the Spanish settlers and Creoles were staging successful revolts from their long-enfeebled mother country. James Monroe, in 1824, was serving his last year in the White House. Puffing and whistling here and there for a few miles, a steam-powered train, brought up in the coal mines, a younger cousin of the steam boat, slower than a horse, desperately pushed by inventor and promoter, raised hopes, alarm, or ridicule in the Old World and the New.

A raconteur with a ready wit, Paul Broca's father may have tired out an occasional listener with endless stories of his part in the Spanish wars and the Battle of Waterloo.[9,10] An awe-inspiring mutilated index finger "eternally covered by a tight sheet of black silk" bore witness to an injury incurred while attending to a wounded man.[10] He was the doctor of the poor, of which his clientele abounded, and he reputedly paid for their medicines, while treating the rich for a song.[11] "Coi ré"—"it's nothing" in the Gascon patois—was his favorite reassuring phrase, whether the patient's condition warranted it or not. "Father Coi ré" they called him, and he was loved by all.

From this pleasant if volatile man, Paul learned or inherited a kind and cheerful, if restless disposition, love of nature and good companionship, and the rudiments of natural history as he accompanied him on some of his rounds. In print we have his 28-page doctor's dissertation on lymph nodes and their diseases.[12]

A more serious strain was derived from mother. Annette Broca, busy in home, vineyard, and "office," had all the virtues of a militant Calvinist pastor's daughter and seems to have molded Paul's ideal of a wife. More than the good things in life, she seems to have insisted on the right ones. Righteousness was well paired with humility and an unforgetting, intransigent sense for truthfulness, tempered by tolerance. Very well educated, a true child of the Revolution, she probably found Voltaire prefectly compatible with Scripture and parsimony with charity. While Calvinists are not quite Puritans or Wesleyans and pleasure as such is not considered ungodly, all activity must be fruitful, and man's duties as well as his rights must be rigidly defined and enforced. Annette Broca was a perfectionist, perhaps given to depressions; there is a good deal of anxiety in her unceasing demand for letters from absent members of the family, also a certain querulousness, some of which she may well have passed on to her son together with her excellent qualities.[11, 13]

Even in the latter part of the nineteenth century, life at Sainte-Foy-la-Grande rather resembled the period of Charlemagne, according to Jean Louis Faure, a distinguished gynecological surgeon, one of its native sons.[14] It could boast of a Calvinist college for boys, famous in the Protestant world, conferring on the place the importance of a little Geneva. All the great names of the nineteenth-century Protestant revival in France—Monod, Coquerel, Pressensé—were its professors, boarders, or students. On the more mundane side were such well-known-men-to-be as Professor Pozzi, who became a gynecologist after serving as Broca's intern, his anthropological collaborator, and finally his biographer and bibliographer. Pozzi's father, who came from the neighboring Bergerac (of Cyrano fame) taught at the Collège. Also educated there and natives of Sainte Foy were the five brothers Reclus, famous, respectively, as a communist philosopher and director of the Bibliothèque Nationale in Paris (Elie); two geographers (Elisée, also a militant anarchist, and Onésime); a surgeon who co-invented local anesthesia and was one of Broca's pupils and obituarists (Paul); and the first and basic, if unsuccessful, planner of the Panama Canal (Armand).[8]

Broca entered this Collège as an externist at the age of eight, after three years of elementary school. For the next seven years it became the center of his life, the stage of his early triumphs. Founded in the year of his birth, it remained an object of his interest and survived him by only ten years.

"A charming child ... a scholar at the age of eleven," says a former classmate, "admired for his prodigious memory, quick understanding, and self-assurance."[9] "He got any problem by some sort of intuition," says another. "He was as good at classical and modern languages as at mathematics and all the rest. His drawings were perfect. He played the horn quite agreeably—the achievement he was most proud of—and he took it up again much later to accompany his daughter when she played the piano . . . ."[14]

Naturally, he also wrote poetry. Like some of his colleagues, he kept up the writing of rhymed verse during his maturity as an occasional form of self-expression, too intimate for the spoken word. Never art for art's sake, most of this writing to let off steam is satirical and epigrammatic; love poems occur only in the years between seventeen and twenty-nine. Probably only one (of the satirical kind) ever appeared in print; several reached his family, friends, and colleagues. Yet he was not a man to throw things away. Some forty-five items in manuscript were kept in a small, neatly leatherbound volume, as No. 1913 of his large library.

Aside from his activity in school politics and as a substitute teacher in mathematics, he also gave history lessons.[15] "We considered him as one of us—he answered our questions willingly and without pedantry or condescension; the profit was mutual. . . . We were some twenty boys assembled around the seat of our young professor. He was talking—and I see myself sitting there—of the origins of history and mankind. This, he showed, was going back to an immeasurable antiquity. He criticized the Benedictine monks and the great Cuvier and attempted a new classification of races, looking mostly for influences by the environment; he opened our eyes to a vast and deep horizon of prehistory. On our occasional excursions we loved to explore natural caves, to dig in every little recess, and when we discovered some old bone, some instrument from ages past, he made them bear witness to his words and compelled us to dream . . . the dreams one only has between ten and twenty."[15]

Imaginary or real, the kind of objects Broca had seen, and mainly read about, was to make famous not only the Dordogne country—one of the world's richest paleontological areas as it turned out—but his own name. He was then familiar with the eighteenth-century writers on man and some of the early nineteenth-century paleontologists as well. In 1840, he presumably heard of the stir made by Boucher de Perthes' discoveries of flint implements.

But although the study of history, and with it that of prehistory[16,17], saw a steep rise in those days, our amateur anthropologist's main efforts were directed toward mathematics. Paul also was relatively immune to the period's effusive sentimentality. The romantic movement, while creating a fashion, never engulfed France as much as its eastern neighbors. The religious revival in both Roman Catholic and Protestant circles (supplying also one of the main streams to the rise of socialism) did not take hold in a young man brought up as a skeptical rationalist.

Secretly—his father wanted him to be a physician—he prepared himself for the Ecole Polytechnique in Paris, that school of higher learning which has given France the dashingly uniformed students who become her military and civil engineers. Entrance meant working, to start with, for a bachelor's degree in mathematics. Openly, however, he studied for a bachelor's degree of letters (history, literature) and received it in August, 1840. He then was in a position to persuade his father to let him travel to Toulouse to take his mathematics degree. When he again returned with flying colors, it was agreed that he might compete for admission to the Ecole Polytechnique. He studied differential calculus at night while teaching school during the day. Because of his age he had to wait until the next year to be accepted.

Grief over the death of Paul's sister Léontine overshadowed all these successes of a crowded summer. It is tempting, though it may be quite wrong, to conclude that this gifted girl who could draw and play the organ was, or had reasons for being, unhappy at home, where she may have been growing up in the shadow of an even more promising younger brother.[13] An acute appendicitis presumably killed her.

The wish that his parents would not have to stay all by themselves, together with some direct parental pressure, made Paul give up the engineering plans that would have taken him too far afield. By studying medicine, he could return home eventually and take over the country practice of his aging father. It was not an easy decision. Once made, however, it did not seem to dampen Paul's spirits. "He could have succeeded in literature, industry, business, or law."[9] His attitude was practical, self-assured, gasconading. Almost anything would do, as he would do well in almost anything: hard work seemed all that was required. Why not be a medical student?[15]

As he was only seventeen, the question arose of where he should stay in Paris during his medical studies. What might be the best place both to protect a young boy from the perils of the metropolis and to save expenses? Might not the ability he had shown as a teacher be turned to advantage? The Collège of Sainte-Barbe had a wide reputation. Situated on the Mont Sainte-Geneviève, near the Panthéon, its history went back to the fifteenth century. It had sheltered great men: among others Ignatius Loyola, the founder of the Society of Jesus, possibly also Calvin.[18] Its teaching assistants, *ushers* in England, were called *pions*, with a rather derogatory connotation. Cousin Elie Broca, ten years older and a teacher himself, made all the arrangements. Paul, then, would be a *pion* at the same time as *carabin*, a medic, (after the *carabins de St. Côme*), the surgeons' mates in the French armies of a distant past. (St. Cosmas, third-century Syrian physician-martyr, is the patron saint of surgeons.)

His friend Poyen and a number of Protestant families with affiliations to Sainte Foy lived in Paris. On the journey between Paris and Sainte Foy, M. Cadars, a friend of the family, would hold the pursestrings, and look after the potentially homesick and very young man, with "a high, broad, and open forehead, an observant and penetrating eye, a fine and sincere smile, pleasant and firm features, and a conversation ... well-nigh bubbling over."[9]

≈II≈
Carabin

"I am not much of a letter writer."

By the *diligence* from Bordeaux, Paul Broca reached the Quartier Latin in October 1841. "Latin" it was by its old learning, and its narrow, messy streets were a reflection of the Middle Ages; it was also traditionally young and brilliant, an explosive nucleus of Paris society, bristling with poverty as much as gaiety, with hard work as well as jealousies.

He became one of approximately 875,000 inhabitants, a contributor to the bulk of 20,000 letters sent out daily from Paris.[1] On horse-drawn carts, the mail to Sainte Foy took three days on the average; many of Broca's letters also went by travelling friends.[2] The telegraph, though invented, would not be in common use for another decade or two; photography was an exciting novelty.

To us Broca's letters disclose the anatomy of his young mind: a sharp eye, a thin skin, and an unyielding backbone. He needed love and security—and above all, an audience. Writing home meant maintaining a lifeline. Such maintenance, and the establishing of new anchorages in the strange big city, exacted occasional heavy dues. Some of the Protestant community of Paris had ties with coreligionists at Sainte Foy. These Broca was to visit for "his own good"—not always evident to him. First, and again, he went to the Monods, a family of pastors (later surgeons), a pillar of French Protestantism.[3]

"At two o'clock I put on my Sunday best and was off to pay visits. I walked! I walked! My shoes were pinching—after all, you have to be a dandy ... get blisters on your feet visiting people who will not receive visitors!"[4]

16

Some of his mother's admonitions to visit Protestants influential in medicine were respectfully scorned. "Persecution again about this visit of mine to Professor Marjolin. . . . He was infinitely more occupied with his little dog than with me. Humility is an excellent thing, but I have not reached the stage of considering myself less than a little dog, no matter how nice."[5]

The friendship that was soon to link him to General and Mme. Subervie started out by, "Dash it, I don't know how to introduce myself, he has seen me only once, a year ago, and is certainly not going to recognize me."[6]

There were compensations. Old friends at home, fellow students, arrived by November. Like immigrants resisting the melting pot, his circle of friends was for a few years recruited "only from the plain of the Dordogne." They met Sunday nights "for tea and *gâteaux* worth 40 sous, and play a game of chess, whist, piquet, etc—for love only. . . ."[15] Another balm of the soul arrived by mail: "Yes, I did enjoy getting my horn. Locked with it in my tiny room, I started to laugh and jump around like a madman."[14] Nothing could have been more exhilarating than the nostalgic romances of the period, nothing more soothing than this most sentimental of instruments—if not for the neighbors: "A police commissar came this morning to impose silence on me in the name of the King [between 9 p.m. and 6 a.m.] 'You are lucky,' he said, 'that we do not confiscate it.' "[7]

Along with running a hundred errands for the people at home, these were his distractions. What about work? In one of his earliest letters, he gives his expected weekly schedule, the courses at the School of Medicine:

Anatomy	Breschet	Tuesday, Thursday, Friday, 10:30 to 12 noon
Medical Chemistry	Orfila	The other days — idem
Legal Medicine	Adelon	Noon; my dinner.
Surgical Pathology (Surgery)	Marjolin Gerdy	Monday, Wednesday, Friday, 3 p.m.
Medical Pathology (Internal Medicine)	Duméril or Piorry	The other days, 4 p.m. (I am occupied with recreation time.)
Idem & General (Therapeutics)	Andral	Tuesday, Thursday, Saturday, 3 p.m.
Operations & Instruments	Blandin	Same (I am busy after school on Thursday)

Hospital Clinics	Roux, Cloquet, Velpeau, Chomel, at Hôtel-Dieu. La Pitié, etc., Rostan, Paul Dubois, Fouquier—from 8 to 10 a.m. (I go there sometimes)
Courses at the Sorbonne	Pouillet, Physics—Tuesday, Saturday 10:30 Dumas, Chemistry—Idem, 12 noon, my dinner
Collège de France	These courses take place from 10 a.m. to 3 p.m., a time when I am always occupied.[8]

To this galaxy of famous names he adds: "You seem worried about not seeing me work. But I am not wasting my time. In the moments left over between the School and the Sorbonne, I am doing some osteology by myself, from Boyer, and with some bones I am getting.... As I progress I realize more and more the immensity of the study of medicine ... it seems impossible ever to reach the end: one man's life just is not long enough for everything. But I am far from being discouraged, quite the contrary, I feel that all this stimulates me...."[9]

Grandiose and brave words after two or three weeks' exposure, in his first of fifteen trimesters. There were five examinations, one for each of these five years, and a final doctor's dissertation. "I have been twice to the dissecting room. I saw the students in their blue smocks bent over the corpses, cutting, snipping, clipping, and probing the human flesh, plunging their hands into it and withdrawing them all covered with blood and pus! All this is too awful to think about, and as I entered I expected promptly to have to get out again. At present, the main point is cleared up, the great obstacle lifted, and I can become a physician without inconvenience."[10]

There also was the Collège of Sainte Barbe and his unpalatable job of a *pion*, to pay for his up-keep. After a week or two of this "I think by now I have no more illusions about my work at Sainte Barbe. I am not an assistant teacher, not even a supernumerary, less than that; I am the executioner, the hangman. My job is to administer punishment and to watch the pupils who are kept after school, in addition, to supervise their evening gym lesson ... on the average this amounts to two or two and one-half hours a day. I wish it to go on. In addition to Sundays, I am free from 8 a.m. to noon and twice a month from 2 to 4 p.m. Instead of having breakfast at 8 I take it at 6 a.m."[11]

As to his morals, he had good news: "... My dear aunt Mariette, thanks for your advice. What really should reassure you is that, stick-in-the-mud that I am, I could not get into trouble if I wanted to. Actually when do the carabins go on a spree? At night, and at night I am tied up."[12]

Collège Sainte-Barbe. (From C. Simond: *Paris de 1800 à 1900*, Vol. II, 1830-1870, Paris: Plon, 1900, p 380.)

    "the wan and flickering light of the street lamps . . . reflected in the black-ish water running through the center of a muddy pavement . . ." (Eugène Sue: *Les mystères de Paris*, 1844).

Experimental science opens its wonders: "What fun to work with our professors! Orfila performs beautiful experiments! The other day he made water freeze in a crucible heated to 1000 degrees . . ."

The first New Year away from home was greeted soberly, all too modestly: "Thanks, mother dear, for the New Year's gift which you offer me: however, I probably won't take advantage of it. . . . It never occurs to me to buy what is in the shop windows. . . . My presents are the music lessons and the firewood I bought this morning."[13]

As the winter went on, his reports became even less cheerful. For a while he found congenial neither his studies nor his job, which took him away from them. "At present I study the skull. I do not find osteology very amusing. Besides being a drudgery, it has the disadvantage that one forgets it so quickly. A nuisance to be gone through . . ." writes the future craniologist.[14]

And at Sainte Barbe, "They incessantly dig up some new jobs for me, which more and more chop up my time and nail me down. During the first fortnight, I now notice, M. Guérard was kind and considerate only out of calculation. When I say he was afraid I'd leave, it is no presumption. . . . With the pupils, I have not had the slightest difficulty, despite my lack of a beard. But to change a teacher means a lot of trouble . . . and particularly for them to get somebody without paying him a salary. That fashion dates only from this year; last year they paid 400 frs. As Élie had even offered to pay for my keep, M. Guérard began to treat me like a broom stick. . . ." Reprimands he felt were undeserved. Eventually Broca wrote M. Guérard a tough note. "Since then M. Guérard takes off his hat when he sees me; when he writes me a note he asks if I would be so kind . . . etc., and I am perfectly satisfied with what I have done."[15] Dismal Sainte Barbe became impossible in the long run. After six months, in a series of letters, Paul explained that with 75 francs more per month (he now received 300) he could live on his own and be a self-supporting interne after three years. But to prepare for this, he had to cease being a pion.[16]

He was not exaggerating. The competition certainly was fierce at all levels. In order to rise to any official position, French aspirants were — and are — forced through a fine meshed sieve: the concours, an examination in which a candidate must beat a large number of competitors in addition to knowing the subject well. This was not necessary for the doctor's degree but for the coveted position of externe des hôpitaux (for one year) followed by one to four years as interne des hôpitaux — the longer the better, not in order to be allowed to practice medicine, but to cut a figure in the medical world.

In contrast to the intern in the United States, the French *interne* serves while he is still an undergraduate, but the duties are fairly identical. He is housed, partly fed, and paid. These wonderful positions were controlled by the local government or *département*, not the medical school. In France to this day the public hospitals are run by a departmental charitable institution, called Assistance Publique. For the higher echelon of service this organization confers, by concours, the titles of *Chirurgien* and *Médecin des hôpitaux*. The *Faculté de Médecine*, on the other hand, is the medical school as a whole, not only its teachers as the American usage of "faculty" might imply. *École* is the school building. The *Faculté* is a direct charge of the Minister of Education, who also confirms appointments to the staff. But whereas a full professor is elected by the Academic Council, the *Professeur agrégé* is the product of another *concours* set by the Faculté.

Assistance Publique and Faculté are independent in theory, but some of the titled physicians officiate as examiners in the concours held by both institutions. There is collaboration between the two but also conflict.

Preparing for a career in medicine was a full-time occupation; the concours, an obsession. After those six months at Sainte-Barbe — an experience out of a Dickens novel — can one doubt the dénouement? "How am I to thank you, my dear parents, for this new proof of your affection . . . for this sacrifice which you are taking upon yourself for the sake of my happiness!"[17] Ah, to be able to give one's private address: "Rue du Battoir-Saint-André, Number 20 . . . merging into Rue Serpente [to which it was to lose its name] half a minute from the School . . . launched on my life as a bachelor, *in my own room*, for the first time in my life, sitting in front of my own fire, my writing accompanied by the sound of boiling water from *my own* kettle, making myself à tisane for my cold. . . ."[18]

His was only a March cold. But his friend Poyen, with whom he used to discuss God and the universe under the lamppost in the school yard of Sainte Foy, was less fortunate. How were such cases taken care of in those days? There was optimism at first. "Poor unfortunate Poyen has been in bed since nearly a fortnight. He is affected with pericarditis. Already at Sainte Foy he suffered quite a bit from a fast pulse. We are nursing him in turns. Today he is much better and fast on his way to recovery."[18] Hardly escaped from his chores as a *pion*, Broca felt he ought to attend Poyen's classes as well as his own and take notes for him. Bérard's physiology course, he says, made this worth his while. But, "in all my life I have not had so many things on my hands. Three hours of lectures, six hours for copying them, Poyen to look after,

21

visiting ... not much time for breathing...."[19] A few weeks later: "The pericarditis is gone but he has pulmonary pthisis. Imagine our grief; fortunately his brother has arrived."[20] Poyen died in the middle of June.[21]

Meanwhile, a catastrophe had shaken the public. It was a railroad accident between Paris and Versailles, the first in France, where in the 1840's rail construction was relatively behind that of other western countries. "As your solicitude, my dear parents, forbids me to use the steam cars, I shall abstain from them in the future."[22] But two years later the rule could no longer be enforced.

Broca continued to be most attracted by the basic sciences and apparently felt a little guilty about it: "Maybe I had better use the time for medicine which I am now spending on physics ... but I cannot resist attending the course at the Sorbonne. We are doing optics based on the new wave theory. All the phenomena can be mathematically explained with admirable simplicity."[23] This presumably refers to Fresnel's famous work done some 20 years earlier. In botany he is impressed by the classification of Jussieu, and by Professor Achille Richard himself taking his students "on herborization trips to Saint-Cloud or Meudon, Montmorency, Remainville, Nogent-sur-Marne — so far outside Paris that we cannot make them on foot."[23]

Farther afield, he spends his vacations at Sainte Foy, visits innumerable friends in Bordeaux, Montagne, Rochefort, and Tours. Back in the city after several months and three sleepless nights on the *diligence*, he moves with his friend Roudier to a hotel between the Panthéon and the Sorbonne, close to Boulevard St. Michel, then still the narrow Rue de la Harpe. The two rooms at 18 Rue des Grés (Rue Cujas) are lavish: "Mahogany and marble, a clock, sofas, overstuffed easy chairs, drapes with tassels and fringes, etc.... We pay 19 francs each. We make only one fire, we light the same lamp; alas, the bottom of this sheet carries the imprint of the oil...."[24] All costs were shared: the single daily meal, taken in a restaurant on Rue de la Harpe, paid for monthly.

Before the end of that first year, after waiting two weeks for the results, he knew he had passed his preclinical examination by the Faculté. As compensation for having been only "satisfactory" was his admission to the École Pratique as one of "only ninety competitors, most of them in their second year though." He now was an *élève*, a "pupil" in anatomy, a significant development, that might lead, after an "aideship," to a "prosectorship" and possibly an academic career as a surgeon. "I also got the post of voluntary externe at the Hôtel-Dieu, in the surgical ward of Blandin, only for doing dressings, but it's a start.[25]

Paul Broca, age eighteen. "I am sending you my portrait, as a New Year's gift if you like, though I daresay it is odd to make people presents with their own money!" [C.I. p. 110 Dec. 29, 1842] (Oil painting owned by members of the family. Artist unknown.)

... Blandin is a little hard on his externes, especially the new ones, but the work can be handled. He runs the best surgical clinic in Paris and is one of the most skilled surgeons. ... After rounds he gives us the whole history of a disease, using the patients we had seen that day as examples. ... "[26]

Books keep accumulating; Broca reads the standard surgical work by Boyer, the standard physiology text by Richerand. There are no references to theaters, concerts, or fiction, Broca's light reading on one vacation were love-letters about the titillations of virtue, the four volumes of Rousseau's *Nouvelle Héloïse*.[27] Essentially he reads medical books, though, and never has enough money to buy that omnibus work, a freight train really, the *Dictionnaire Encyclopédique des Sciences Médicales* in 25 volumes. And if he takes time off, it is to hear a celebrated rhetorician: "Roudier and I went this morning to hear Ravignand preach at Notre Dame. His eloquence is admirable, but I do not like his dramatic gestures. He is quite the rage, and there are great crowds. If you want a seat you have to queue up for two hours and pay four sous to get in. ... [28]" He went to such a performance as to a recital for the esthetic effect and, maybe, to pick up some technical tricks. As for the religious aspect and his own church, " 'Do you often join the congregation?' — Dearest Aunt, I wish I did not have to answer this question. I am not good at lying, and the truth will not be to your liking. Well, no, I do not. ... When I am at Sainte-Foy I go because I am with you, but you must have noticed that I do not enormously care. I am not devout, which no doubt is a misfortune. But as a misfortune is always good for something, this is all the better for my studies. ... "[29]

An occasional bourgeois dance at a countryman's wedding is duly recorded,[30] but for weeks he does not set foot outside the Quartier Latin. Politics, on the other hand, especially those in his own sphere, attracted this small town boy from the beginning. The rights of the members of his profession and of the public had to be guarded against poorly qualified practitioners of the art. When the revolution and the wars around the turn of the 18th century had reduced the medical corps, a law in 1803 allowed the so-called *officiers de santé* to practice without a doctor's degree. "A petition for abolishing the *officier de santé* by 1844 has been circulated among the medical students. Similar petitions have again and again been presented, and always in vain ... but at least this will be one more demonstration. Every interne, every prosector, and the majority of the students have signed — four hundred signatures, all told. Bouillaud, who is deputy for Angoulême, has undertaken to present and support the petition in the Chambre des

Députés. Despite his eloquence, I must say I am far from believing that it will succeed."[31] A correct guess, for such "health officers" were permitted to practice until 1892.

More important, "a big affair is at present on the student mind. You must have heard about the immense reactionary activity of the clerical party and the new Jesuit organization. With the intention of destroying the present set-up of the University and replacing it by priests as teachers, these gentlemen have, in France and abroad, distributed millions of copies of a pamphlet in which they denounce the public and even the private life of every professor at the Sorbonne and the Collège de France. Michelet and Quinet, the professors of history at the Collège de France, took the cause of progress into their hands, each in his way, recounting the history of the Jesuits and exposing their constitution, while abstaining from any judgment and letting the facts speak for themselves. With the intent to have these courses closed, the Jesuits attended the first lecture in enormous masses, drowning the voice of the lecturer by whistling as soon as he arrived. In order to prevent a similar scandal the students piled into the next lecture by the thousands maintaining order in an admirable spirit of unity. The Jesuit trouble-makers were thrown out, and the lecture remained undisturbed to the end."[32]

Broca's conversion to medicine complete, he has started on his *concours* for the *externat*. The written test was easy, "merely a matter of good writing; the reward goes to those whose sentences are the most correct and methodical."[33] The oral test also demanded the adroitness of the seasoned speaker, applied to a repertoire of countless set pieces. It took six weeks before he could announce "*la Grrrrande nouvelle.*" Fifty-six failed; he was the 52nd of the 109 who made it. "Hence all is for the best in this world, according to the doctrine of Pangloss. Still, you will say, you are the 52nd. True, but I could have been the 53rd. . . . "[34]

Emoluments, if any, amounted to 300 frs per hospital service per year to be divided among the externes, of whom there might be up to half a dozen—enough to have one's shoes resoled a couple of times. One's assignment depended on several factors, some of them quite unforeseeable.

"You are living, I am sure, in a profound illusion regarding my fate," he writes at the beginning of 1844. "Every morning on getting up you say to yourself: At this hour my poor child is at the Necker Hospital or freezing on his way there. Not at all; I am at a hospital in the city. Now you will say: 'That's splendid. Well, I say it's worse. . . .' "

The prospective chief had forgotten to request Broca as promised. "Consequently ... I was put into the Hôpital du Midi, in the service of M. Ricord, a splendid service in its way but, as it is specialized in venereal diseases, I shall not learn a great deal to be of use in my career. I was vexed in the highest degree.... The work begins and ends rather late, the hospital is in the city and so does not give any emoluments to externes." (A petition, initiated by Broca and backed by Ricord, changed this inequity within three months.) "Fortunately the Service is quite amusing ... and, as Ricord says, syphilis does not exempt you from acquiring any other disease.... Of these we are seeing here a great number.... Ricord is very different from other specialists who never get away from their own subject: he is very good in every branch; at the same time, according to general opinion he is the greatest wit among the physicians of Paris.... "[35]

This great observer, who first separated gonorrhea from syphilis, also turned out to be a wonderful chief. "This morning I stayed at the hospital until 10:30 taking notes. Ricord came along. 'Hell,' he said, 'our externe is a distinguished syphilographer; he works so hard that we must do something for him. To start with,' he said, tapping me on the shoulder, 'come to my house tonight, I am giving a party.' I was stiff with surprise. I did not even know how to thank him. Ordinarily he invites his interne; this is the first time that his externe is being admitted to the 'sanctum sanctorum' as the antiquarian said."[36]

Ricord's party "consisted almost exclusively of artists and composers. Adam (*Postillon de Lonjumeau,* etc.) Henrion, Albertini, all famous people were there with their spouses. They were making music until midnight, then everybody started to dance. I did not dare at first to throw myself into this unfamiliar world ... eventually I was dancing like everybody else. At 3 the party broke up. I was about to leave with the rest. Ricord tapped me on the shoulder. 'An externe,' he said, 'must be thirsty at all times and in all places. Stay, we are going to have some punch.'

"Five or ten years of special and concentrated study have allowed him to formulate the new laws of syphilis ... and to clear away the mysterious aura that has surrounded this disease since the Dark Ages. In the ensuing controversy with the majority of the physicians of his time, all the young ones were converted to his theory.... An enormous clientele (100,000 francs a year), his long ward rounds, and the work on a great book, which will presently be published, still leave him time for corresponding with scientific societies abroad. In England and Germany his name is the rage. He gets decorations everywhere but has remained kind and full of fun, is patient with the sick, a pianist and an accomplished singer.... "[37]

The externeship left time for work on the cadavers; in the spring he was proudly doing operative arterial ligatures and other procedures for lacrimal fistula, cataract, and finger amputations. There was enough spare time for spending four exhausting hours running through the Louvre, in preference to seeing the water works in Versailles ("I detest crowds; I have put off this chore").[38] An Industrial Exhibition brought a similar blasé response from this young Parisian: "More exhausting than a six leagues' walk in the mountains. You have no idea of the crowds. All of the 40,000 provincials in Paris were there, milling about. . . . My final word on the Exhibition is the same as when I saw Libourne for the first time: 'Fancy, is that all?'"[39]

Once more, he sighs, the whitewashed walls do not allow "a single sunray to escape . . . ah, Dordogne, Dordogne, when will I throw myself into thy arms. . . . Here comes a soldier of France who has reached the age of serving his country. Another expense: conscription."[40] He was twenty and the thing to do was to buy off his military obligation. Vacation was to be short, because "the concours is at my heels." But again he saw quite a bit of France, by train, river steamboat, and *diligence*.[41]

To prepare for the *concours* for the interneship, the little band of six externes acquired a coach to drill them in the style and polish with which to treat, in a fine ten-minute speech, any one of the 350 known questions taken from every field of medicine. "Free professors," i.e., teachers without an academic title, were legitimately tutoring at the École Pratique. Dr. Martin-Magron "offered to one of us whom he met privately to direct our conferences. In the belief that his was a business trick we asked him what his conditions were. 'Young men,' he replied, 'who in Paris arrange conferences for the *internat* are liable to be good, that is, intelligent and hard-working. I shall enjoy working with you and try to be useful. As a compensation I only ask of you to work hard. My reward will be ample if one or the other among you is accepted as an interne.'"[42] The two men were immediately impressed by one another and remained so; fifteen years later Martin-Magron became the first president of the Société d'Anthropologie.

Attendance at lectures was reduced to a minimum. At this point Broca shared the views of many students and professors: *"Lectures are for me the most secondary thing in the world,"* he underlines, "a way of distracting yourself for an hour from the serious work done in your own room . . . The purpose of a course is to teach you how to study."[43] In particular he ridicules the course in *pathologie interne* (internal medicine), taught by Piorry, "the man with a system, who spends a whole year talking on how to apply his plessimeter to the diagnosis of the diseases of the spleen."[44]

Two weeks before the written test he loses four of those hectic days in which "the whole" of medicine must be rehearsed to an "intestinal upset" and is sick for the first time since he had "la fièvre rouge" (measles, possibly scarlet fever). The four days "might be inscribed as Fast, Broth, Chicken, Chops and Steaks"; he managed to get away with only two purgations and evaded an emetic; Labrunie, his colleague from Sainte Foy, examined him rather than troubling Ricord or Martin-Magron, "who would have hastened to my bedside at the slightest hint." His friends in the quarter were attentive; for two days he was not left alone as long as half an hour at a time.[45]

There were "provisional" as well as regular interne positions to fill, some preference being given to the older students. "There will be about one hundred of us fighting for seven or eight places. . . ."[45]

Under such pressure Broca abandoned his former lofty principles: like everyone else, he realized, he must get some influential support. "If you want to succeed in anything, you have to be a Macaire,"[46] he bitterly rationalizes, invoking a character from a contemporary comedy, a crook made famous by a series of caricatures by Daumier. General Subervie comes to his help with one of the examiners. " 'A recommendation by M. Subervie,' Rostan told me, 'is almighty with me, for I love him dearly. But this year the points are given by majority vote; hence, you need the support of three judges to succeed. In any case, I promise to uphold your rights. I take it upon myself to prevent any foul play against you.' This is already something. . . ."[47]

"Paris, 21 December 1844. Five minutes to midnight." After many lines of trivia: "P.S. This is a postscript à la Walter Scott (Puritan). How is it possible that I forgot to mention what interests you most at this moment: my concours and my second examination? My thoughts are decidedly mixed up tonight. To begin with, my second examination — nothing about it yet. The next week, however, cannot pass without my being called. . .

"Another thing I forgot: my oral test . . . My flair was good enough to guess in the morning the question that emerged from the urn in the evening, but I had no chance of finding even a minute to re-read it. The question: *The first diagnostic sign in various forms of meningitis.*

"Of the ten candidates called that day, six gave up. . . . My total score is 26 points. Calculating the probabilities . . ." he saw his only chance as getting ahead of a single one of the candidates, "but he belongs to the Society of Saint-Vincent-de-Paul and has a most powerful pull. I had only one hope of being nominated: by moving heaven and earth and getting some recommendations, too, I first went to M. Monod to have his brother's pull, but I could not find him. M. Lacroix spoke of me to Vigla, M. Dezeimeris also did, Mr. Georges went to Lenoir, Ricord wrote to Rostan and was impatient to hear of the result of the concours, which was to be made known on December 21st 1844. Well, the 21st December is today; it is midnight past; consequently the result is known . . .

"I wonder how you will be reading this letter . . . 'What a chatterbox this child is! We are roasting on the coals!' Poor parents, you might as well stay there for five minutes. I have been on them for two months. And can you really not guess? Is it possible that you should not have understood? Go ahead, laugh, hug each other, don't you see . . . long live joy, long live the examiners, long live even the King! I am an interne. Instead of being the last one, I am the one before the last. . . . My nomination did not encounter any difficulty; all my efforts to get recommendations were unnecessary, of course. I am no less grateful to those who went out of their way for me."[48]

A week later, his regular examination was "carried off at sword point." The swashbuckling hero had scored the top mark. On December 28th he has "pretty well decided not to touch another book until January 1st." The new position does not exactly fire him with enthusiasm. He is at least by one year the youngest of all the internes of this year's batch, and he must again be content with being posted at a "special" hospital, i.e., not a major surgical or medical service in the city. It was the Bicêtre, where Pinel had first taken the chains off the insane, but it still had a prison within its walls.

The chief of service was Leuret. Broca could not know what this unpalatable appointment, what this psychiatrist and his work on the comparative anatomy of the brain, meant for his future as a scientist. "I shall be in a section for lunatics but it will not prevent me from doing some medicine in the neighboring wards. Bicêtre is 20 minutes from the city barrier on the road to Fontainebleau. It is a town of three or four thousand souls who communicate by several omnibus lines with Paris. . . . Our chief of service is a very friendly and very engaging man. I am lucky in this respect. The emoluments are considerably higher than anywhere else. . . . Evidently I am asking for a diminished contribution from you, but will leave this to your generosity."[49]

"Confronted with these indefinable and incomprehensible maladies I felt momentarily drained of all my strength; a visit to the insane is like a descent to hell of the ancient epic poets. A man's insanity is not only an immense and hopeless misery of the present; it is also a whole tragedy lying in the past. How much torture of superstition and religious fear must have gone into shattering the reason of this Jewish renegade who sees in everyone of us an instrument of

29

celestial vengeance as he incessantly cries: 'Have pity, have pity on me, God of Israel!' How this unfortunate man must have suffered as his father, wife, and only son were carried off by the cholera! And that other who, quite innocently, killed his mother with a pistol shot! Or those two going insane in 1830, one because they had chased away his king, the other because they had blown the lights out of the republic of which he had dreamed!

"April 4, 1845

". . . Like everybody else I admire the power of fascination M. Leuret exerts over our lunatics. There is much to learn from such a chief, and I am quite keen to stay at Bicêtre until September; moreover Spring is back . . . it is so long since I have been out in the country in the Spring. . . .

"Paris, 199 rue Saint-Dominique, Saint-Germain, Sunday, 20 April 1845

"Dear Maman . . .

". . . I earn. 'Oh well, ' says Aunt Mariette, 'is it money he is talking about? Can one make so much fuss about that shabby and base metal?' Being twenty and having both an excellent appetite and a cheerful disposition, I am far from such reasoning.

"I earn 500 francs a month, no more, no less. I am with a Duke, I eat ducal meals. I have at my discretion a fine Bordeaux and cigars a sou apiece. 'Disgusting,' says Aunt Magdeleine, 'I can smell them from here.' Quite possible, dear Aunt, for I must confess I am smoking one at this very moment. And in return for all this I have only the trouble of living in a magnificent mansion in the Faubourg Saint-Germain, of going back to the hospital in an elegant carriage every morning, and loafing the rest of the day in an enormous and peaceful park in this lovely spring sunshine. Last Tuesday, April 15, M. Leuret informed me that the sermons of M. de Ravignan have rendered insane the high and mighty Duke de la T. . . .: that for treatment the lunatic needed the constant attendance of a professional man so as to keep up his morale: and that for this job he had chosen me among his pupils. Moreover, Monsieur le Duc was the owner of an indefinite number of hundreds of thousand livres of income and that he would pay at least 500 francs a month; that, finally, my service at the Bicêtre was not going to suffer in any way, as M. Leuret himself would take me there every morning in his carriage and back to Paris the same way. The conditions were fine, and I thought I ought to accept, but now I am tied up and vastly so. Between six a.m. and midnight I can take off here and there, but most of the time I must stay in the duke's house and always sleep there at night.

"My duke is sequestrated in a private hôtel which he does not know yet and which his parents have rented for that purpose. There are three servants and a major domo to take orders—not his but mine. He is not to see any members of his family; only M. Leuret comes to see him twice a day. His relatives, all dukes and duchesses, with more or less historical names, incessantly drop in for news. Astonishing how stupid two or three of these dukes are. 'All these people,' M. Leuret said to me 'are convinced that because they are good for nothing, they are worth infinitely more than we are. Now, my opinion is precisely the opposite. I insist that you will not let yourself be bullied by them, that you treat them as you would treat your equals, and if anyone is going to be condescending, it will be you.' That is what I have done . . .

"Besides, of all the lunatics I have seen so far, our duke certainly is the most interesting from a scientific point of view. He is afflicted with intermittent religious mania. His crises last 36 hours and recur every 48 — i.e., with only a 12-hour respite. He goes into a rage, has to be tied, put in a straight jacket and shackled; in addition, my men have a tough job to prevent him from getting killed as he throws himself against the bed boards or tries to smother himself under his bed clothes. His delusions are most bizarre. He believes he is God, the devil, damned at one moment and chosen the next; today he thought he was dead. For the last 48 hours he has refused nourishment and even nutrient enemas. An hour ago I had to make him eat with an esophageal tube and a syringe. Needless to say, I am taking meticulous notes. Goodby, poor liberty, not another moment of respite. I can work very well in my room but never go out. Only Sunday when I do not go to Bicêtre I am free until noon. . . .[52]

"My madman was much better for two weeks, now he has relapsed. We pour cold water on his naked body and are fully launched on our moral treatment. . . ."[53]

"At present we are getting along fine with the family. There has been some bickering between them and us. Because of the cold affusions (Papa knows what they are) which we are using to correct him, they got the revolting idea that we were punishing him, one of their own, a duke, and they naively tried to remonstrate with us. You understand how elegantly we put them in their place. Anyway, they had to give up, for what would they do without us?"[54]

Papa, who read the medical journals where Leuret was criticized a good deal for his method, knew indeed what these "affusions" or douches of the chief's *traitement moral* meant. If kind persuasion failed, buckets of cold water would be poured over the patient, held

31

down by servants, every time his answer to a pointed question betrayed that he was still holding on to one of his delusions. This treatment must have been not a little wearing for therapist as well as patient. Surprisingly, the results were sometimes satisfactory, as they are with the more radical, and in some respects more humane, shock methods of today.[55]

"I am going with my patient by post-chaise to Brittany to stay for eight days in one of his châteaux as a means of distraction; during the trip the honorarium will be doubled. I am going on a pass and not on leave, that is to say, M. Leuret will authorize me to disappear without informing the Bureau Central . . ."[54]

Not too unusual for the times and instructive in its way, the assignment proved to be distasteful, distracting, and left no time for studying. We do not know quite how long he stayed with the mad duke (in Dieppe) but soon after his release from this remunerative chore, he decided to leave the Bicêtre too; the work there—the lack or the type of it—was also a waste of his time. But each new hospital position meant playing another rough game of musical chairs. By taking advantage of some confusion among his competitors he was able to announce in July:

"Next Monday I am leaving for the Hôpital Beaujon, to be in the superb surgical service of Laugier, to which has been added that of retired Marjolin senior. . . . But what running around also, and in what heat! . . . At the beginning of the year I would never have done this sort of thing, but now I have lost my restraint, and it pays off. The intrigues around me have been causing me enough trouble in the fight for all kinds of positions, and my conscience is no longer affected as I hit back.

"A more delicate matter was to get M. Leuret's consent, at least so as not to fall out with him. I went to him asking for advice as though I were faced with a sudden and very embarrassing situation and had to make a fast decision, without the opportunity of consulting my parents. At the time he seemed to take it rather well, for he gently replied that in my place he would also leave for the Beaujon. But since that day he has not spoken to me on our morning rounds. . . ."[56]

Nevertheless, six months later, Leuret sent him his New Year's greetings, a most unusual favor. "He seemed to take great interest in me . . . urged me to visit him again and often. Positively he is a man whom I understand less and less"[57]—an allusion to some gossip he had picked up about his former chief, as well as about the duke's subsequent attendant, who let him die of starvation.[58]

Salle de Garde. Living and dining room of internes' quarters in the former Hôpital de la Charité. Painting left top: The surgeon Velpeau in a classical setting, driving out a cancer quack. Row of medallions represent local internes who have "arrived." (Courtesy Musée de l'Assistance Publique, Paris.)

Critical, restless, ambitious, by August, 1845, Broca was interne not only at the Beaujon but also, for the time being, at the Hospice Sainte-Périne, substituting for his friend Faure. By November he had accepted what he had called, not without reason evidently "a filthy hole, a repulsive coop:"[55] "I am definitely living in at the Beaujon. Aside from getting the heating and lighting gratis, there is another consideration: my daily dissecting at Clamart. I shall spend the evening in my room; the candle here will shine as brightly as anywhere, and I shall not have to see the bars."[59]

There could be no further doubt about his penchant for anatomy and surgery. "You are right in supposing that I am busy with my plans concerning the post of Aide in anatomy. In January I was to start work with Malgaigne at the Saint-Louis." But it was too far away. " 'My

33

friend,' Malgaigne said, 'what I shall do is not for your sake but for that of Anatomy. You are registered in my services for 1846, but I let you off so that you may get a position at the Pitié or the Hôtel-Dieu. If you have an opportunity there you will at least be close to Clamart.' "[60]

After a very complicated play of politely broken promises and substitutions involving Piorry as well as Malgaigne and three or more prospective chiefs,[60] Broca did not become the interne of any of these. Praising his lucky star, he joined Gerdy, professor of external pathology (surgery) at the Charité Hospital.

All was well. But if anything surpassed the fickleness and cunning of the internes it was that of the chiefs. It amounted to a vicious circle. "This last incident has wiped out all my conscience regarding the Piorry incident. Let's see. Boyer promised me his position for 1846. He keeps me on tenterhooks and promises it to someone else. Brichetau promises me his position and gives it to a colleague of mine. Moquet, on Leuret's recommendation, gives me great hopes, and one fine day he lets me down. . . . So many chiefs have let me down that I cannot feel sorry for them. . . . What does a chief care whether he is getting this interne or that? The work will always be done by somebody. For the student, on the contrary, it is of the greatest importance whether he does or does not get a certain position. . . . Have I not recently been informed that even Malgaigne, in whom I had such confidence and who had given me every assurance for 1847, filled his vacancy with another fellow, about one month before I got into trouble?"[60]

≈III≈
Upheaval One

The "trouble" that Broca spoke of was personal only; another upheaval of the times affected all of Europe as well. The first is quite insufficiently documented; the second, only too well recorded.

Was Broca's "trouble" the expected great love affair of his youth? No, the young man's amours left few traces, all merely poetical. Across that steady flow of correspondence we see not a single flicker of romance; such things, if mentioned at all, appear only as a cheerful repudiation of gossip. The other references are of impeccable morals and an occasional remark breathing a high tone of Victorian sententiousness: "Is nothing known about the seducer, a thousand times more to blame than she? A few days ago we have unveiled the statue of Molière; unfortunately not all the Tartuffes are dead . . ."[1] In a similar case, the twenty-one-year-old feels compassion for the unfortunate and rather unbelievable waywardness of the weaker sex: "They say passion may lead to anything. But how is a passion for a man so ungainly and insignificant conceivable? The only possible interpretation, it seems to me, is that the poor thing, seduced a long time ago, became pregnant. . . . How will she dare to return. . .? What will happen to her next? The mere thought of it makes me shudder. If only one could find her and persuade her to become a nun. . ."[2]

The romantic cliché of student life of the period is enshrined in Murger's *Vie de Bohème* and Puccini's subsequent opera. A more factual contemporary account of the medic's conventional sweetheart is given in Desprez' *Le Livre des cent et un*, where "*grisettes . . .* naturally a source of anguish to mothers who send their sons as students to Paris . . ." are portrayed as just ordinary girl friends employed in honest bourgeois trades.[3]

A "Demoiselle Eugénie," for instance, was a laundress at the "Convent of St. Benoît," and her further address, given by Broca when he was at Bicêtre, "Nr. thirteen, first floor down from the roof." A

35

Carabin to a Pock-Marked Laundry Maid is a string of smooth verse, some in quite elaborate meters, where he approaches this slightly blighted creature in terms of the pining lover who has to overcome his shyness. "Through living flesh my steady knife I guide—but tell my love? I tremble, terrified. . ."[4] Was this only a literary exercise in the art or a means of amusing the boys, rather than any genuine feeling for the girl?

A few more such items are dated 1841, 1849, and 1853 and addressed to four or five idols. One, undated, to a Madame V., erupts into genuine passion. The lady, he confesses, was not one he would have thought of as an object of his love—not at first, for he used to dream of shy, pale, and sensitive maidens, untouched by the world, for whom he would provide strength and protection, "the egotistic dream of my exalted heart." He is struck rather than awed by a goddess, perhaps too beautiful to love, and off he goes in rapturous praise of this sensuous, sumptuous, fiery, generous, healthy creature, describing her charms in unequivocal detail.[4]

But Broca's "trouble" was of another kind and, at least in his eyes, a serious threat to his career. We do get a good idea of its nature—suspension from his interneship—but are left guessing about the cause. None of his obituarists recalls this break in a virtually straight line of successes. If it was deliberately suppressed, the job was done so poorly that Broca himself could not have had a hand in the suppression. Suppression is indicated by a gap in the correspondence between March 28, 1846, and July 28, 1846, of four months or, at the least of three months, if a letter dated "June, 1847," which seems out of context, is restored to its presumably correct place in June, 1846. His customary interval was one or two weeks.

The first intimation of trouble appears "End of 1845."[5] (Certainly it was not later than spring, 1846, because Broca speaks of prospective interne placements for 1846 and 1847.)

"We have petitioned for our reinstatement, asking for a revision of our conviction—as a favor—and as an act of justice, because we were much less guilty than it was thought." So he was not alone, but what was he convicted of?

There had, for instance, been a clash with the administrator of the Beaujon Hospital, but only a variation on the not-uncommon theme of interne versus administrator, and it involved no other student.[6]

A different incident added to the relief of parting from the filthy Beaujon. To us it looks like a salmonella infection; the victims had another diagnosis: copper poisoning. "To dispel any possible doubt and to refute any allegation of an incidental colic, an interne in Pharmacy took a sample of the night's bouillon, analyzed it and found copper. . . . Surely an administration that does not watch the copper lining of its pots is pretty negligent. . . ."[7]

Despite "violent pains in the bowels, a little fever, and other ill effects which I abstain from mentioning," Broca reported that 1846 began in a most promising way, with plenty of opportunity for dissecting, invitations for dinner, concerts, dancing, and introduction to "M. Coste, the famous professor of comparative embryology at the Collège de France, who promised to show and explain to me in detail his beautiful collection of embryos of all animal species." Lest this "unique opportunity" might be considered a frivolous distraction, he adds, "Perhaps it will help me in the *concours.*"[8]

No source of trouble here. And most important was the association with Gerdy, his new chief at the Charité Hospital, an apprenticeship that developed into a friendship. The professor must have valued his pupil's critical attitudes to society, his violent reactions to insincerity and injustice. Gerdy was not only a fine teacher and thinker, but also as forthright, decent, and bitter as they come. Gerdy did not have to implant such attitudes in Broca, but he certainly strengthened them in his fledgling and more extroverted colleague.

Did intransigence and rebelliousness cause Broca's suspension from his internship? This is what the upheaval in the spring of 1846 amounted to. We must consider his growing political activities during his early twenties, for instance, his participation in a student demonstration for Quinet that he vividly describes complete with *agents provocateurs.* [9]

He also felt the need of contributing his opinions to a rebellious monthly sheet published in 1845 and 1846. *Les Écoles* professed, under the July monarchy, republican principles by the inscription *Liberté, Egalité, Fraternité* on the top of its title page. The publication was "founded and edited by the students of the various Schools of Paris, the Faculties of other Departments and of Foreign Universities." Unsigned but listed in Pozzi's bibliography and unmistakably by Broca, as certain phrases repeated in his letters confirm, his four articles are serious, politely mature, often constructive, sometimes forcefully radical.

He favorably comments on a Medical Congress attended by physicians and surgeons from all over France, held for the first time at the Hôtel de Ville. On one hand, academic medicine was to be kept from falling entirely into the hands of the government; on the other hand, the practitioners were to preserve a modicum of independence from the universities. As one result, the first "free" medical societies, complete with published proceedings, were set up for each *arrondissement* (city district) of Paris.

Although only twenty-one, Broca also supported the installation of a chair for History and Philosophy of Medicine, but he opposed compulsory examination in these subjects. Then would nobody attend the lectures? "The young generation, gentlemen, is more studious than you seem to think," he writes. "Were not Malgaignes' lectures on the history of surgery overcrowded?"[10]

One of his chief targets is Orfila, the powerful Dean of the Medical School. While showing laudable concern for the students of the Faculté, in his position as the only medical man in the Council of Hospitals, Orfila has a pernicious influence on the well-being of the internes. New regulations by the Assistance Publique made the hospital administrators arbiters over the suitability of quarters for internes sleeping out, closed the door on them after midnight, allowed them to receive visitors only until 11 p.m., absolutely excluding all females at all times. "It will please the most exigent *mamans* . . . to see internes made equal to little boys of seven living in boarding schools . . . But it will hit visiting mothers and sisters most—and do nothing for the service to the sick."[11]

Not only Orfila, but also the rich laymen who compose the Council of Hospitals are attacked. They, too, boost the power of administrators, wish to abolish post-mortem examinations, restrict the use of potassium iodide in the treatment of syphilis, because it is relatively expensive, and the use of leeches, because the chief pharmacist who studies annelid worms must get them back from all the hospitals every day by noon. The millionaires in the Council prevent the admission of sick old working men to the Salpêtrière and the Bicêtre in favor of any one of their own retired servants or "any *fainéant* who all his life has done nothing but wear a livery and lower the footboards . . . all because M. le Baron with three stars . . . now refuses to feed a useless mouth." A documented three-quarters of the inmates in these old people's homes were former lackeys.

Another point was the scandalous suspension from a hospital service of several well-known *médecins* and *chirurgiens des hôpitaux*. In Magendie's case, the writer presumes, the reason must have been the great physiologist's courageous stand for Michelet and Quinet, the persecuted liberal historians. But worst of all was the suspension of the Cliniques Libres, a form of bedside teaching provided by *médecins* and *chirurgiens des hôpitaux*. The alleged reason was to prevent discussion at the bedside which might upset the patients—mere pretext, because after the observations were made on the wards, the discussion was held in a lecture room. But it was the lecture rooms they intended to close, forcing the discussion to return to the bedside. When this measure was being debated at the Council, two journals inspired by Dean Orfila were full of praise for his absence from the meeting, ostensibly to manifest his noble indignation. "Small wonder, for M. Orfila is the owner of the *Gazette médicale*, and the editor of the other journal, the *Gazette des hôpitaux*, sees everything through the red ribbon [of the Legion of Honor] which he owes to the Dean's munificence. . . . What does his devious step signify? . . . Is the Dean for or against? . . . His tendency to concentrate all teaching at the École de Médecine is well known, and the suppression of this free form of clinical [hospital] teaching admirably suits his purpose. . . . The permanent committee of the Medical Congress has immediately protested to the Minister of the Interior. . . . We presume that he will not sign this unfair order. . . . But we also would not be sorry to see the protest fail. . . . Swollen by success . . . the Council is sure to issue one inept order after another . . . sure to make itself impossible and sure in the end to collapse like a house of cards. . . . "[12]

Although Broca did not sign these fine pieces of bitter rhetoric, the authorities must have known that he was their author and an agitator. Was the little interne, like the great Magendie, denied access to a hospital service on political grounds?

Shocked, he also tells his parents the grim story of a woman giving birth to a dead fetus on the Quai St. Michel after having been given the run-around by two hospitals because of administrative red tape.[13] Broca did not think any institution ought to get away with inflicting unjustifiable hardship on the vulnerable individual or community, nor the daily press, nor medical publications. These journals were following fast in the footsteps of the dailies, pushing the prosperous spiral of lowered prices, increased circulation, and advertising revenue, often a vicious circle with a decline in standards. The well-known Doctor Fabre, Broca reminds us in some notes, had modeled *Lancette Française* in 1828 on Thomas Wakley's *Lancet* of 1823; it was later called *Gazette des Hôpitaux*.[14] The police had closed a previous venture of this doctor: a sanatorium from which he let escape a certain Calorghi, a convicted rapist of little girls. Calorghi had bribed Dr. Fabre with 30,000 francs; Fabre was fined 20,000. In order to promote *Lancette,* Fabre solicited juicy case histories from internes. As a bribe he slipped tickets to a certain dancing establishment under the wrappers of his weekly, delivered gratis to the internes' quarters. On Broca's initiative, the internes of the Hôtel-Dieu formally refused acceptance of the periodical; their colleagues in other hospitals followed promptly, and Broca addressed him with many jangling stanzas, to a popular tune, such as this:

"Your plasters, bandages, and potions,
Your jellies over pages spread,
Suspensories, false teeth, and lotions
Cause our faces to turn red. (repeat)
From charlatans who pay your prices
There penetrates a hideous smell:
Lancette inoculates but vices;
Take it away, take it to hell!" (repeat)[15]

But in that critical spring of 1846, there was no cause for merriment. He was in serious straits. What could hurt more than being cut off from hospital work and the chance of becoming an eminent clinician? He spent his time with desperate attempts at getting reinstated, and he read. He bought (or coveted) from his century and the last, a translation of Meckel's *Comparative Anatomy* (10 volumes), and Henle's *General Anatomy*, Bichat's works, Halles' book on hygiene, and, of course, Gerdy's *Physiology*. He studied Professor Coste's embryological collections.[16] If the Assistance Publique would have none of him, he might try the other line: an appointment at the Faculté, at least at the École Pratique. After a little hesitation he goes all out to make his mark in the concours for *aide d'anatomie*. The project originated in the Fall of 1845 while he was still at the Beaujon. It was no easy decision. Marjolin senior promised his support — "as he had no one else to push," — but Marjolin junior poured cold water on it: " 'A stepping stone for those who wish to practice in Paris,' he said . . . 'Fiddling, scraping bones, doing expensive injections, making microscopic observations — a waste of time and money. . . . It has been unheard of for any candidate to be nominated whose chief was not one of the examiners. . . . Finally, none of your competitors will fail to say to the judges: I am twenty-eight or thirty, time for me to get somewhere. M. Broca is a charming fellow, a man with a future, and all that stuff, but he is only twenty-two, he will certainly be nominated next year, etc., etc.' "[17] Encouraged by Dr. Martin-Magron, he wrote, though "success seems impossible — the grind goes on."[18]

The letter dated "June, 1847" (erroneously, it seems, instead of 1846) voiced a great deal of strain and irritation. His specimens for the concours at the École Pratique were not progressing; the task was complicated, required many trials and many subjects; subjects were scarce, half decomposed by the summer heat; and the brain he wanted to study had usually been removed elsewhere, sabotage by a colleague.

"Instead of pursuing me with your eternal reproaches could you not talk kindly? You ought to realize that if I suffer it is only because of you, because I know you are suffering. If I were alone in this world, for quite some time I would not have given this matter another thought. . . . I am certain to get back [as interne] next October. This is a formal promise. Will it not be better to get back through M. Thierry and the Subervie family who act without self-interest, than through the Duc Decazes, whose tact you know well and who will keep this business in his portfolio so as to throw it in our face every time I or one of the family will have a disagreement with him. . . . "[19]

But by the end of July, 1846, he was compensated for his ill-luck as an interne. In his *concours* for aide in anatomy, he was first in the written composition (surgery, anatomy, and physiology), the oral test in surgery and in operative medicine, second in all other parts: "Despite this I was almost sunk. M. Denonvilliers did not give me his vote because I was too young, M. Bérard because I know no member of the Institut. . . . M. Cloquet hesitated . . . but was partly converted by M. Leuret. M. Duméril voted for me after first treating me like a dog in a game of skittles. M. Blandin was in my favor through M. Gerdy and fully satisfied by my tests. This morning M. Marjolin told his interne: 'I shall vote for M. Broca but I fear my vote will be lost . . . we were told he was not quite twenty-two.' I beg your pardon: I am twenty-two and one month."[20] Meanwhile, his "affair with the hospitals" was hanging fire. Nevertheless, his spirits were high.

"Before your letter came, I told Roudier: 'It will be in two parts: Papa will be quite proud and not hide it; Maman will be equally proud but hide it just a little so as to guard me against the sin of pride.' Sure enough, she has a whole paragraph directed against this capital sin. Still, without being accused of this sin, I dare say that we may all be proud . . . Aide in Anatomy at twenty-two — no one has ever been that before the age of twenty-three (Chassaignac), and very few got it at the first crack. But all the honor goes to you who sent me to school at six, to the collège at eight; to you who gave me a taste for studying while you were depriving yourself of so much. . . ."[21] He made it clear that he must participate every year in a *concours* for the prosectorship or lose his position as an *aide*.

"Maman is mistaken when she thinks that I enjoy the commotion of the *concours*. Of course, it needs constant struggle, toil, and cunning, but it has the thrill of any sort of fight . . . like a game of chess, and you know how I love to play. But I am just as I was as a little boy: not a good loser. Without that certain starting chance, I would give up the game. . . ."[21]

Suddenly after those bleak months, one day in November, things moved with dramatic speed. Word was received from on high that this was the moment for action. M. Thierry, member of the Municipal Council, a surgeon and a friend, sent Broca and his fellow victim on their way "in a carriage rented by the hour, taking us through practically every street in Paris, seeing every member of the Council whom we could find, with or without a letter of recommendation. By the time we came home it was 8 p.m. . . . Next day at one o'clock we returned to M. Thierry. This excellent man had taken our petition to the Hôtel de Ville and pressed it upon the Prefect of the Seine Department (Head of the Assistance Publique). At 4 p.m. . . . Orfila . . . told us that my memorandum had been extremely well received, our re-entry was endorsed unanimously. I ran to Thierry . . . to M. Cadars where a bottle of champagne was opened . . . I have no obligation either to the Duc Decazes . . . nor to a host of others . . . I am grateful to all who have tried to help me, but the campaign was planned and carried through by a single man: M. Thierry. . . ."[22] No doubt an admirable man, this descendant of the Dumont-de Valdajou-Thierrys—most of them benefactors of the poor and *renoueurs*, i.e., royally appointed bonesetters—had mended this fracture well.[23]

We never learn why Broca, interne again, at the Charonne Hôpital, had been suspended.[22] The story with the makings of a tragedy—at one time his parents even feared he might be facing a duel[24]—had a happy ending. With the usual complications and intrigues, he got Blandin's interneship at the Hôtel-Dieu and was able to write home at the end of 1846: "Who could have told me six months ago that come January 1st I would have the finest surgical service in Paris?"[25] He stayed for two years.[26] At first he was lodged a few hundred yards away from the Hôtel-Dieu across the river, in quarters paid for by the administration. He was sharing this billet, and his days on duty, with his "old pal Bleu," an attachment going back to Bicêtre days, which he calls "most important for my enjoyment of life. . . ."[27]

Then, even more than today, Rue Saint Julien le Pauvre must have been almost uninhabitable and disreputable.[28] After less than three months there, with Paul making 60 francs a months by giving lessons to another student, three hours a week,[27] the two internes moved "into the new street that leads from the Hôtel-Dieu to the Pont d'Arcole: Rue d'Arcole Nr. 7 . . . a bedroom, an alcove with swinging doors and a large salon with two windows . . . all perfectly new, with hardwood floors, decorated with mirrors . . . cost about 160 francs for each. Bleu has his own furniture."[29]

"A new street"; some of the sanitary destruction of the old Paris had begun even before Baron Haussmann, Prefect and city planner of Paris under the Second Empire, carved the Boulevards Saint Germain and Saint Michel through the maze of Left Bank alleys, malodorous with poverty, disease, and crime, and so conducive to the erecting of barricades. Demolition had been in the air ever since the first Napoleon had called Ile de la Cité "a vast ruin, fit at best to house Lutetia's ancient rats."[30]

A total of 25,000 people were gradually evacuated around the gothic twin-mountain of Notre-Dame to enlarge the *Parvis* and make room for the headquarters of the Police, the Law Courts, and, finally a new Hôtel-Dieu Hospital.

The forbidding black block defacing today the north side of the *Parvis* is not Broca's, Blandin's, Dupuytren's Hôtel-Dieu. That stood on the opposite side, some wards spanning the bridge across the river to Quai Saint Michel on the Left Bank. What remains of the old hospital site is a little park with a huge, atrocious equestrian Charlemagne in bronze.

Broca was given some scope in the part of the upheaval that started further up the river on the Right Bank. Military barracks and the wide Boulevard Henry IV now cover the area once owned by a Benedictine order, Les Célestins. It was dissolved in 1785 for immorality and non-conformity, and the monastery soon destroyed by the revolution.[31] Pickaxe and shovel revealed a number of sarcophages and skeletons of great antiquity in the remaining vaults. To take stock of the osseous findings, the Municipal Commission—quite likely on Thierry's recommendation—appointed an able young aide from the École Pratique, one Paul Broca. The report became his first anthropological publication.[32]

Soon there was cause for concern at 7, Rue d'Arcole: "For about two weeks my poor and excellent friend Bleu has been having such serious and repeated hemoptyses that, with his previous history, one cannot hope to see him escape the phthisis that undermines his life. Most unfortunately, he is perfectly aware of the extent of his implacable disease. He knows that any improvement will be only temporary, that he will relapse after a few months and eventually succumb. He is taking the blow with courage, but how awful to see oneself die at this age!"[33]

Bleu had to leave Paris. But some eighteen months later Broca announces his friend's recovery and marriage to a "charming only child

with 150,000 francs immediately and 200,000 later. In exchange . . .
he has a diploma and a library full of books. . . . Since the citizen
Proudhon has been threatening private property, the stock of physicians has gone up!"[34]

Broca's own future in Paris was by no means assured. His appointments at the École Pratique and at the Hôtel-Dieu were no
sinecures. The one involved the yearly trial in anatomy and pathology
with the prosectorship in view; the other, a *concours* in clinical
surgery to retain his interneship for a fourth year. At home the idea of
a prosectorship was resisted. Was the prodigal son not going to return
soon, a doctor's diploma in his pocket, and take over his father's
practice? Or at least, after passing a concours in Bordeaux, come closer
to home? On the contrary, he pointed out to his mother, a Paris
prosectorship would be of great help in Bordeaux. He countered her
misgivings about the fickleness of fate by boasting of his "almighty"
backers, Gerdy and Blandin.[35]

Broca went ahead, and: "Oh bonheur! Broca, first; Follin, second; Richard, third. Far behind, Houel, and all the way down,
Gros!"[35]

"Too bad I have to run after two hares at once . . ." meaning the
concours both for the École Pratique and his fourth, or "lauréate," year
as an interne. But first he had to take over the work of his colleague
Richard, who had a whitlow; next he had an abscess on the back of his
own hand. In people dealing with cadavers, such things were hazardous, quite a few pathologists have succumbed to septicemia. Blandin,
who six weeks earlier had excised one of Broca's abscessed tonsils, now
dealt with "the furuncle, or *anthrax,* because of its large volume" by
making "a large incision on the fourth day." Was this "miserable *bobo*"
(French babytalk for a minor ailment) going to annihilate the efforts
of a whole year? The *concours* for the fourth interne year required an
essay written in advance. "I ran up and down the Quartier Latin . . .
and finally assembled four or five men for dictation. . . ." They were
working in shifts around the clock, increasing their "daily coffee ration
by one or two demi-tasses. . . . All in all I slept six hours out of a
hundred and twenty. . . . but almost without interruption for the following three days. . . . The last half of the memoir and the thirty pages
of case histories are still hardly legible. . . . Put yourself in the place of
the examiners. . . ."[36]

He ended up fourth of the four lauréate internes, with a reassuring "second mention." The minute description of a horse race hardly
equals the five-page report (in print) of this event. At any stage of the

close bout, the field among the competitors changes, while the examiners seem almost as agitated and vociferous as the candidates and tell them afterwards of the scenes that went on behind the scenes. Their warm and indeed heated interest was more than to see a protégé win, but one of their future peers, even a potential successor.[37]

A reference to Baron Rothschild in this report is coupled with the remark that his protégé was a "coreligionist." This may raise some eyebrows but Broca was not brought up in a spirit of anti-semitism and seems to have judged such facts on their own merits. Before coming to Paris he may not have met a Jew; he mentions visiting a synagogue on his trip to Metz, the city with France's largest Jewish community. His friend Bleu, as the name suggests, may have been of Jewish origin; Lebert, of whom we soon shall hear, was a convert to Christianity. Paul also must have been struck by the parallel between the precarious minority position of Protestants in French society and the historical fate of the Jews. Once he had felt it necessary to reassure his family about the company he kept: "I went to two Jewish dances where I was introduced by a Jewish friend of mine who is a rather gifted composer. One occasion was the wedding of the Grand Rabbi's daughter who received her dot from Rothschild. The august banker himself appeared for a moment at the dance. Fine Jewish society is every bit as good as ours; I saw several girls' faces of that Jewish type which is being talked about so much . . ."[38] The delicate features of the incomparable actress Rachel must have set a fashion.

But what are we to make of these examination practices? Condemn them out of hand? Since Napoleon I, the *concours* has controlled official promotion in France. The competitive system has by no means eliminated favoritism and injustice; it burdens the candidate with hardship and frustration; it puts an unjustified premium on rhetoric and rote memory. But, says Guillain in his biography of Charcot, "The issue is much more complex than it appears to the inexperienced eye."[39] The backing of an assistant by his chief is a common manner of selection nearly everywhere. However, because it is too time-consuming, clumsy, and particularly unsuitable for higher appointments, rather than because it offends any moral principle, the *concours* may be on the way out. Its abolition, advocated by ultraconservative elements in Broca's day, was strongly resisted by him; it was, after all, an instrument of democracy. In his experience, "two things are put to the test in a *concours: knowledge and shoe leather. . . .* But as a matter of fact, the wire-pulling is not too effective, except with regard to three or four competitors, and their performances do not differ greatly from one another. . . . All the others do not count; despite the pull on their behalf, several appointments were not extended."[40]

By the end of 1847, Paul's parents realized that he was not cut out to be a humble small town practitioner, that his ambition and his aptitude for an academic career in the capital must not be stifled. To him their sudden resolve was everything. "My dear parents, I am so thankful for this new sign of your utter self-denial and devotion. For over a month I have said nothing about any future *concours*, and now you decide to let me compete for the *agrégation*. Believe me also when I say how well I am aware of my obligations. . . ."[41]

His self-confidence was nearly boundless, his decision rarely regretted. Three years later he happened to be picked up one day to assist at the baptism of Bleu's daughter. "I found my excellent friend as happy as he deserves to be. He has a charming wife, parents as good as mine, and a clientele taken over from his father, which this year has netted him 6000 francs. To realize that without my cursed ambition the equivalent would perhaps have awaited me at Sainte Foy! Unfortunately I do not think I am cut out for this sort of quiet happiness; I must have . . . those steeplechases. Poor human nature! — I stayed for three days because he had an operation to perform . . . he kindly trusted me with the cataract knife. The immediate success was complete. I then put a cannula into a lacrymal fistula and came home last night, a little fatigued from the good food. . . ."[42]

~IV~
Upheaval Two

On February 23, 1848, Broca wrote another reassuring letter to his parents. Thanks to a city ordinance posted on the walls of Paris "with a hundred thousand of the regular troops to lend it weight . . . all heralds a quiet day. The Chambre des Députés was mobbed, they say, and the dragoons d'Orsay had to restore order. In the Champs Elysées there were about a thousand workers. Through the railings of the Hôtel-Dieu we ourselves cannot see a thing except, in the distance, the heads of people massed on the Quai of the Hôtel de Ville. If the riots continue tomorrow there will be casualties, and my place still in the Hôtel-Dieu. . . . It was like that on the 26 July 1830 . . ."[1] The rumors were true, the comparison accurate: it was another revolution.

That same day Paul still has time to get off a second letter, less reassuring: ". . . During the night the Municipal Guard opened fire on some workers in the Rue Transnonain of evil memory. [A massacre of working class people followed a demonstration in 1834.] This morning the people are exasperated. In the streets the National Guard mix with the workers . . . they all shout in unison *Vive la réforme!* . . . But barricades are up . . . and some shooting has started. We are waiting for the casualties to come in. . . . I had to stay with three men all night; two of them have already died.

"This morning there were about thirty dead in Paris. In fact, there must be many more. We do not get outside the colonnade of the hospital yard.

"Adieu, I embrace you on the run."[1]

Two days later he still reassured his parents, but had not slept for three days: "The Republic has been proclaimed. . . ."[2]

Louis-Philippe had lasted over seventeen years. Disappointingly, this would-be "people's king" was unable to live up to the popular idea either of a king or of a democratic leader.[3] In 1847, a third of the one million inhabitants of Paris were dependent on charity; 450,000 per-

Revolution of 1848. "The victorious people fraternizing with the military."
(From C. Simond: *Paris de 1800 à 1900*, Vol. II, 1830-1870, Paris: Plon, 1900, p 316.)
"In the street the National Guard mix with the workers" (Broca, C.II, 2/23/1848 p. 3).

sons received food tickets.[4] The bourgeoisie, too, had ceased to be grateful to their king for having saved them from a workers' revolution in 1830; he had failed to save them from an economic slump in 1847.

Industry had made small strides in France, in contrast to England, where a class-conscious proletariat was rapidly forming apace with the increasing wealth of the nation and the political power of British trade. But here as there the employed were grossly underpaid. Prices had been rising, even in the provinces.[5,6,7] In February, 1847, Broca wrote to his parents: "I am sorry to hear of the disturbances which the price of bread has occasioned in our peaceful countryside. . . ."[8]

In this new mercantile and industrial age, socialism and its extreme, communism, joined liberalism and republicanism. The liberty won in the 1790's, the one law and justice for all, had remained compatible with "have" and "have-not" inequality. Men and women endowed with a sensitive heart, a logical mind, and a desire for self-expression found this difficult to tolerate. Side by side with the religious revival of the day, Comte de Saint-Simon's "New Christianity," a science of economics, called for a new state run by "savants" and "industrialists" as the sole owner of property. Proudhon had coined the famous phrase "property is theft," yet rejected communism as leading to "disgusting" coercion. "Practical" socialists—Owen, in England, Fourier and Cabet in France—and especially Cabet's book *Icaria* gave rise to "communionist" experiments, "Harmonies," and "Phalansteries" in the United States. Karl Marx was in Paris several times between 1843 and 1848. His and Engels' *Communist Manifesto* had just appeared, but it remained without much influence on the French class struggle during the nineteenth century.[9] Broca may have never heard his name.

Social conflagrations frame Broca's and his parents' lives: four of them, leading to three republics, alternating with five monarchies, one Orléans and two Bourbon kings, two Bonaparte emperors (each starting as the head of a republic), aided by a host of social reformers, poets, and professors of history.

Things had gone with such speed that, the fateful last week in February not yet over, Broca marvelled at living in a period "without parallel in history." By comparison the upheaval of 1789, in which both his grandfathers had fought, seemed a slow terror. Now "the face of the country changed as fast as the decor on a stage . . .," and he and his friends were among the fiery actors.

"Last Sunday, at General Subervie's dinner table, we were talking about the necessary reform of abuses in the military administration. 'If I were Minister of War for only twenty-four hours . . .' the general said. Today he is Minister of War. On the same day I was talking with M. Thierry about our skeletal antiquities and mentioned some recent inroads made by the administration of hospitals. 'Let me get my hands on them!' he cried, 'I would make an end to this loathsome robbery!' The same M. Thierry has been given the task of reorganizing the administration. One puff at the house of cards, and today we are sovereign masters of the hospitals.

"Down with the Dean of the Faculty of Medicine! Bouillaud has replaced him. Down with the Council of Public Education! Gerdy has

49

free reign in all matters regarding the lycées (high schools), and I trust Elie will not be sorry."

"The Republic! I often used to dream about it, and in a mere twenty-four hours it has come into being, greater, nobler, stronger than I dared hope. For days I had some terrible fears, and I cried bitterly with disappointment. . . . Where was this movement to stop? Thanks to their courage these men, oppressed from childhood, exploited forever by their united masters, had suddenly become the rulers of a large city. Would they be magnanimous enough to lay down arms and put on once again the yoke of labor? Well, this self-abnegation of which we perhaps would not have been capable, we, the lucky ones in this world who enjoy the benefits of an education—this abnegation of absolute power that no king has ever been willing to show, here was an example of it in the behavior of the people. Noble, noble people, more courageous even at work than on the barricades. No more alarms!"

Ultraradicals and reactionaries, both from within and without, were powerless, he thought.

"Raspail, another Marat, tried to engineer an ultra-revolution, but his *Ami du People* finds no echo, and his attempt falls flat like his camphor industry.

". . . The revolution has quickly reached us internes of the Hôtel-Dieu in general and me in particular. Tuesday (22nd) the quarrels with the administration flared up again. Wednesday they became intolerable. Batel, of the administrative commission, and Perignon, of the general council, were sneering at the wounded as they were brought in . . . and applauding the exploits of the Municipal Guard. A mounted detachment of them had suddenly come out of the Rue d'Arcole and given rein to some incredible cruelty against unarmed workers. A few of these men were taking refuge in the Bureau Central when the Guard forced the door, grabbed the unfortunate men by their hair, and dragged them under the hooves of their horses. Standing along the railings of the Hôtel-Dieu, we watched this loathsome scene of savage brutality. We all shouted: 'Down with the Municipals! Death to the Municipals!' They heard this and made for us, but the railings and our internes' aprons held them in respect; they just gave us some savage looks and their commander shook a threatening fist at us. The administrator, that man Batel, and that fellow Perignon made us a scene, but with the consensus of my colleagues I permitted myself to send them to the devil. You should have heard these gentlemen change their tone the next day, and a day later, when M. Thierry came with his mandate from the provisional government. Ordinarily so

50

The first Hôtel-Dieu, 1852. Note the railings. (Courtesy Bibliothèque École de Médecine, Paris.)

insolent, these people could not do enough to heap flatteries upon our zeal for the wounded. . . ."[10]

Never in his twenty-four years had Broca felt so elated for so long, never in a life full of enthusiasm would he recapture the utter satisfaction of these few weeks where he gave himself whole to the great and still-winning cause. At the same time he coolly advised his parents to hold on to their silver and convert their paper money into real estate.[11]

He thrived on the sensation that "ten existences would not be enough. . . . Ward rounds for four and one-half hours in the morning, one hour in the evening. . . . Ecole and pupils, Garde Nationale (twice a week), electoral assemblies, and clubs. Yes, clubs!" (The English word for the weapon, and originally the symbol for a fighting organization, had been taken over half a century before by the founders of the revolutionary "Club des Jacobins" and "Club des Cordeliers." It still sounded shocking.) "Yes, clubs. . . . During the first six years we have been sufficiently stoned for being honest and faithful republicans. Now we must try . . . to guard the people against both anarchy and counter-revolution. Hence, we are founding a club, the *Club de la Cité* and hold our meetings in the amphitheaters of the hospitals. . . ." A "Society of Freethinkers" promised less chaos: soon only members were allowed to make speeches and to vote.[12]

51

"Clearly our role in the affairs of the country is infinitesimal. . . . But not so in the affairs of the Faculté. The first decree of the Provisional Government was, in Public Education, the indispensable dismissal of Orfila . . . However, the obstetrician of the Duchesse de Berry [whose allegedly illegitimate pregnancy he had publicized for political purposes] did not deem himself beaten; he began to organize a sort of school mutiny. First-year students felt moved by the dean's tears. . . . 'This to me, who always was such a good republican! Adieu, I have no strength to talk to you about potassium!' Emotion in the audience. 'Vive Orfila!' And protests. An address to the Provisional Government was drafted, letters were circulated in the Quartier Latin, deputations went to the Minister of Education. . . . There was a serious question of reinstating him — in the face of an existing Republic! —

"Quickly we arranged a meeting. Our minds were made up fast. It was 6 p.m., the official decision due at 8. Ledru-Rollin, the Minister of the Interior, just happened to visit the wounded.. . . . As he was stepping out into the colonnades, he was faced by sixty aprons in battle formation. One of us, I confess it was myself, addressed him: 'This morning's manifestation was the work of inexperienced students who have come to Paris only three months ago. . . . We old-timers . . . are unanimously grateful to the Provisional Government for our new dean.' Ledru-Rollin thanked us warmly and charged us with sending a deputation to the Minister of Education. We did not fail. The same night M. Bouillaud's nomination was signed into effect.

"At 4 o'clock next day the great amphitheater of the Faculté was full. We took along all our pupils, all our friends . . . twelve hundred of us were stacked one on top of the other. A *concours* was in session and Bouillaud one of the examiners. When it was over we demanded the new dean. Bouillaud got up and took the chair in the midst of frantic applause. He spoke a few words; from this moment it was evident that Orfila was commanding only a negligible minority.

"Today we know why that dean resisted so strongly the decree of the Provisional Government, why this unfortunate man was clinging with tooth and nail to his plank. The Faculté chest has been the scene of the most scandalous defraudations; when funds were running low the thing was fixed. . . ." The pun, *Orfila: l' or fila* — "the gold got away" — is still remembered.

"The Provisional Government has announced that everywhere officials of the old regime will remain in office. I have stopped getting upset over these people. They have been judged by public opinion, and I am not trying to inflict on them the evil things they have done. There appeared a pamphlet enumerating a part of the misdeeds committed by Batel, of our administrative board. I suggested to burn it before reading, and my suggestion was unanimously adopted. My heart is too full of joy for hatred to survive in it, and I deeply wish to preserve this disposition for a long time . . .

"We are being very much spoilt. The cook has been given stern orders from above, and we are now every day fed in a very decent manner. The Administrator — I mean *l'agent de surveillance* — for at present this is his official name — is as meek now as he was arrogant before the revolution. . . .

"What is our little town like these days? The peasant has not had time to think about politics and evidently will be subjected to every possible influence. . . ."[13]

With the revolution in its second month, more or less violent moves from the extreme right and left continued. Broca remained confident, although he had to admit there were "ifs." "A reactionary change is impossible today. . . . If the Legislative Assembly would propose a king, this would be the end, with civil war and no quarters until the last royalist or the last republican is killed. . . ."[14]

"There are socialists in Paris, but there is only a handful of communists, and the clubs who are reputedly indulging in the most inflammatory speeches loudly affirm the principle of respecting private property. . . .

" . . . I was offered the rank of Lieutenant. . . . A powerful group supported my nomination, the whole *quartier* is well disposed to the staff of the Hôtel-Dieu. Of course I refused. I am asking only for one honor: to be a simple soldier. Hence, you need not fear that I am going into politics. My future lies elsewhere. . . ."[15]

"You must have taken me for a madman, an enthusiast ready to fall into all sorts of extravagance . . . but I have been a moderate republican for a long time and known as such by everyone around me; I do not need to act in the exaggerated manner of a recent convert. . . . I want order above all, and you need not fear to see me taking part in disorders if such should occur.

"If the country remains as sensible as Paris, all will be perfectly quiet. As a matter of fact, money is reappearing, credit returning, securities have been up by 10 francs for the last week; everything favors the idea that the financial crisis will soon be completely over.

" . . . I do not go out at all. I have caught my first enthusiasm for the microscope, and in all my moments of leisure I stay in the little cabinet that M. Blandin has just installed in a corner of the Hôtel-Dieu for my microscope. . . ."[16]

In the middle of April an intended coup by the extreme left failed, thanks to the support of the Provisional Government by the National Guard. The ensuing elections had shown that "evidently the large majority of Parisians are adhering to the idea of a comfortable, sensible, and moderate program. . . .

"I even find the results too lukewarm. I would have preferred to see the old deputies of Paris removed from the initial legislature. . . . I would have wanted at least seven or eight working men, but there probably will be only four or five. It would be good to have in the Chambre a few very advanced men to keep a very sharp lookout for the interest of the poor, to act as an advance post of social improvement . . . fast and yet as gradually as possible. . . ."[17]

On May 15, a huge but unarmed crowd of "workers, loafers, and agitators, with more than a vague taste for disorder"[18] marched across Paris. Again they invaded the Chambre des Députés, protested to its reactionary composition, and moved towards the Hôtel de Ville to overthrow the government. This time Broca, on the side of law and order, defended the new National Assembly against the "infamous creatures."[19] Even so, the "order" had turned out more than a shade too conservative for his taste. "By its presence, impact, and moral strength, and without a single drop of blood, the National Guard quelled the revolt, and the leaders of the anarchist party have been arrested. I was up under arms all night. . . ."[19]

In less than four months the whole beautiful impetus of the February days had fallen apart.[20] "I am disgusted with politics. The French are too petty for one's concern. The elections in Paris prove it. There are asses who have elected Louis Napoléon, egoists who have elected Thiers, fools who have elected Lagrange, and swindlers who have nearly elected Girardin. This is Paris, the city of light and progress and intelligence. It hurts to say, but not only is our country unintelligent as a whole, there are not even any intelligent individuals in it. . . . The Chambre, that flower of France, is certainly the silliest of all assemblies, past, present and future. . . . Let the wheel of events turn as it may! Republic on one side, despotism on the other, the constitutional hypocrisy in the middle, and the water that turns the wheel never stops. Turn, turn, turn, I don't care. There'll always be some Englishman here who wants to learn anatomy and some citizens who fracture a leg. . . ."[21]

What finally, under the pressure of the bourgeoisie and the provinces, broke the back of the utopian and divided new order was the fiasco of the "national workshops." They had been invented and organized by Louis Blanc, the man of the famous phrase repeated by Marx: "From each according to his abilities, to each according to his needs." The Minister of the Interior was determined to demonstrate the impracticability of providing paid work to 100,000 unemployed men. No plan existed for using this potential labor force to benefit Paris. On June 21, the government, unable to bear the cost of feeding them, abolished the workshops. Men, women, and children were given the choice of either joining the army in Algeria or building roads in the provinces. Not only was there no transportation to implement such a plan, but these workers, hungry yet self-respecting, provoked and armed, also were not going to have themselves deported so shortly after a victorious revolution. On June 23, they erected barricades over a large area of Paris to join battle with the rest of France. Trying to mediate, the archbishop of Paris was shot to death.[18]

Four days later Broca, in his first moment of respite, reported that Paris was pacified. "But at what price, good God! Never in the memory of men has so much blood been shed in Paris. The insurgents had made it known that they would win or die. They lost, they are dead. [Fourteen hundred and sixty quoted by police, 50,000 quoted by the English press, many murdered in prison, 4000 deported without trial. General Cavaignac, expert in the mass slaughter of Algerian tribesmen as well as an honest republican of the old order, did the job in three days.] Faced with artillery they had to withdraw from the streets; fighting from house to house began. Every door was crashed, blood running in streams. . . .

"The Hôtel-Dieu is full; five hundred wounded, over one hundred dead. The medical wards had to be evacuated and many casualties had to go to the Charité. There is no more room; an *ambulance* [an emergency ward for casualties] had to be installed in the vestibule. Where are we going to put the wounded who will be brought in in great numbers tonight?

"Being neutral ground, the Hôtel-Dieu was the center of operations for all insurgents and soldiers of the Republic. It is the key position for the Cité and the Left Bank. For 36 hours the shooting did not stop and more than one bullet broke our windows, but fortunately nobody inside the Hôtel-Dieu was wounded.

"I spent three days and nights without sitting down. Now I am going to throw myself on the first best mattress."[22] And in reply to the next "desperate letter" from his parents: "There can be no more questions of my *concours*. How could I abandon my patients? And why should I? I could not, even if I did not consider my obligation and my position here binding. Paris is an exhausted town; rebellion is no longer possible; there are no combatants left. All the insurgents are dead, wounded, or in prison . . . the material forces gone . . . As to the moral forces, or rather the money which dirty agents were distributing to liberated criminals and pimps—an inquiry would bring to light a good deal of shameful crime. Russia, England, the royalists, and mostly that man Louis Napoléon have been showering their millions over Paris, instigating this atrocious fight which is without parallel in our revolutionary past. It was to the cry of '*Vive Napoléon*' that groups were forming; it was the pretenders who hired the editors of thirty Bonapartist papers that have soiled the streets of Paris this last fortnight. It was his name, too, that was heard on the barricades. My curses and my repugnance for this ambitious brigand, who had 12,000 Frenchmen killed and more than 20,000 wounded, do not date from today. Yes, it would be terribly painful for me to see my father still attached to that name—glorious once but dishonored today by so much bloodshed. . . . In conformity with the decree that licenses our *légion* (the 9th), I have returned my arms to the Mairie so that in no case could I be apprehended with arms about me and subjected to martial law. . . ."[23]

The let-down was as contagious as the euphoria of the February days had been. Both had spread to a more despotic central and eastern Europe; resistance and hopes were shattered everywhere. France, who has given the civilized world many admirable things (even her revolutionary climaxes have been inspiring), has always fallen on her reactionary feet, and her social progress has been slow. In the resulting political vacuum, the left paralyzed and the royal rule discredited, the republic was merely allowed to exist, soon to wither away. Moderate people withdrew from politics, horrified by the bloodshed. June, 1848, had stunned into passivity any will for action or prevention. In the first month or two of the revolution, Broca could underestimate the power of the reaction; soon he recognized the man who inevitably would step into the vacuum.

Louis-Napoléon Bonaparte, nephew of a great name, had been able to collect the money necessary for what was perhaps the first modern electoral campaign in Europe, conducted with all the tricks of commercial advertising, down to lapel buttons. Had his backers all been English? He knew, too, how to appeal to all the mutually incompatible desires of the citizens at once. In his pronouncements he was able to mix socialism with the defense of capital investment, the legitimacy of his imperial background with liberal sentiment, security with adventure, and pacifism with the militarism which finally led to his country's undoing and his own.[4,18]

By the end of 1848, "Paris is paved with leaflets carrying the name of Bonaparte; two million of them are distributed everywhere, and I am not exaggerating. . . ."

Rather than vote for Louis Napoléon, which was out of the question, or for Ledru-Rollin, who had shifted too far to the left, Broca, perhaps to one's surprise, voted for Cavaignac, the stone-cold general who had massacred the people for the maintenance of the republic and had solved the problem of the rising proletariat by its political annihilation. (Broca blamed Napoléon for inciting that massacre.) Was Broca then not a man of the progressive left? Like most Frenchmen, he occupied a fine line in the political spectrum. Antimonarchist first, disbeliever in the one-man, one-principle rule, he was no tame liberal, because he detested the oppressive aspects of big ownership and regretted the neglect of social legislation. "I find the [election] result too lukewarm," he wrote, yet he considered himself a moderate: "I want order above all," he said. His family saw in him a potential or actual left radical. He expressed satisfaction when "communists" were arrested, because he saw in them an irresponsible element that sacrificed workers while trying—or pretending—to protect their interests.

After a stint in politics with word and rifle (he probably never fired a shot) and after surgical care for some of the bloody results, professional competition had to go on. This had its own traumatic aspects, including a stab in the back by one of his best friends. "Because of the June events," Broca wrote in the middle of July, "the *concours du prosectorat* was postponed for two weeks, and then again it was not . . . . On July 4 . . . I suggested to X, then one of my best friends, to ask for a few days' delay. . . . He eagerly consented. . . . Next day X came to see me. 'Why ask for a postponement . . . why sentence ourselves to two weeks of preparation in this heat? Rather let us agree to prepare one specimen instead of two and explain the reason to the examiners.' . . . We gave one another our word of honor in the presence of two other friends, that we both would prepare only one single piece . . . I started work without undue haste . . . with enough time ahead until July 17. Last Friday, with only four more days to go, I heard that X had two specimens. . . .

"Caught in this trap . . . I had to have two specimens too—but only four days left for dissecting, drying, and painting the second . . . Yesterday I presented my two specimens: one good, one bad. I am not out of the running, but thanks to the loyalty of X, I am completely beaten in one of the most important, if not the most important, test of the *concours*. And yet, after Roudier, X was of all my friends the one whom I would have trusted most blindly. It is a useful lesson. Out of a hundred men ninety-nine are rascals. . . ."[24]

Who was "X"? No one else but Follin, then an interne at the Charité. It is questionable whether the discreet omission of his name — because its mention was too painful — was Broca's; the substitution may have been the work of the editor of the correspondence. Most likely his parents knew the identity. In spite of his duplicity, X continued to be *aide d'anatomie*, and Broca was made prosector.[25]

After the dust had settled and the vacations, with a little surgical practice at Sainte Foy thrown in, were over, "I am seeing X daily at the Ecole Pratique; he really is making up to me. At first I was a little cold; but then how could I be angry with him for having doubled my pleasure when I was made prosector? . . . Soon, maybe, we shall appear to be on terms as good as before. How is the wine harvest? Has the hail done much harm? . . ."[26]

Follin was made prosector in the following year. It seems that one could not for long remain angry with his unusual charm and unusual gifts. Verneuil, the third of the "Young School," and Follin were Broca's seniors by one year, and all three remained close, in friendship and rivalry. When Follin died at the age of 43, Broca said of him: "He has had everything a man could dream of. Now it is only a dream. . . ."[27]

By the end of 1848 Bouillaud, the "red dean" (Broca's term) was dismissed, and Orfila, the embezzler, was cleared by some falsified accounts.[28]

As to Broca, National Guardsman if perhaps not ideal soldier, casualty officer, historian, and participant of 1848, and nearly recipient of the Cross of the Legion of Honor for temporarily replacing the embalmer at the Hôtel-Dieu,[29,30,31] a contemporary remembered him in this way: "You could see him on sentry duty at the entrance of the Hôtel-Dieu, his rifle in one hand, a book in the other — conduct, no doubt, hardly compatible with the regulations, yet how symbolic!"[32]

⚛V⚛
Cancer and the Microscope

⟶ | *"a burning question as you know . . ."*

For nearly two centuries the microscope had been quietly pioneered and perfected by French scientists. But as an arbiter between normal and abnormal human tissues, as a detector of "cancer cells," it was almost forced upon French medical practice by Hermann Lebert, a Prussian Jew turned Protestant, and his disciples: Broca, Follin, and Verneuil.

While still a student of zoology and botany, Lebert had been critical of the "inferiority of method" in medicine, "the healing *art*, unable to earn the title of a healing *science*," its "dominant schools thriving on tradition at the expense of observation."[1] He would concede some outstanding contemporaries in the field; and at the age of twenty-two, one sunny spring day, he set out on a hike from Berlin to receive his instruction in microscopy from Professor Schönlein, a political refugee from Bavaria, in Zürich.

Four years later, in 1839, the cell was finally established as the lowest common biological denominator for vegetable, animal, and man by Theodor Schwann in Louvain, another German disciple of Schönlein (and of Johannes Müller). By that time Lebert was a Swiss cantonal physician near Bex, a fashionable mountain spa. But earlier he had known the Paris of the great luminaries of the day: Dupuytren in surgery and Laennec and Louis in medicine. Soon he was spending his winters in Paris again, and there he settled in the late 1840's. Not unlike the contemporary Duchenne from Boulogne or, earlier, Franz Jos. Gall from Vienna, Lebert was tolerated, even esteemed, as an outlandish if stimulating figure; his quixotic stock-in-trade was the microscope, which he tried to impose on an elegant but die-hard tradition. Had not even Bichat, the rebuilder of anatomy from elemental tissues, characterized that instrument as "the kind of agent from which physiology and anatomy never appear to derive much help, because looking at things in the dark makes everybody see them in his own way and according to how he feels?"[2]

Lebert had no academic position. But in 1845 his controversial *Physiologie pathologique* was published, one of the earliest microscopic treatises on tumors.[1] In the introduction he was able to drop such names as Andral, Velpeau, Cruveilhier, Louis, A. Bérard, Blandin, etc., and to thank them for "the beautiful and rich case material. . . . " But in his autobiography, Lebert had to admit that his life in academic Paris had begun as "a fierce struggle with the young medical elite, the internes, and up to the highest ranks. My research was at first viewed with benevolent suspicion. But when I began an earnest and determined attack on much of the apparently solid doctrines of medicine and surgery, my activity caused a veritable storm—always, I must add, within the limits of the most gentlemanly scientific debate. After two years of campaigning, I emerged victorious. . . . In addition I had gained the friendship and support of the very same young elite. . . . In Germany the French are often criticized for their fickleness in friendship. Nothing could be more unfounded and unjust. Sealed in the hospital wards, the dissecting rooms, and at the microscope, my friendship with such men as Robin, Broca, Follin, Verneuil—Follin having been taken from us all too soon—has remained to this day as secure, close, and unspoiled by success, as it was a quarter of a century ago."

Although Lebert was persona grata and licensed to practice, both under Louis-Philippe and Napoleon III (the latter personality made a deep impression on him, he said) and although he became a respected member of several learned societies, "my social activities, otherwise so pleasant, became tiring through the late hours involved and work starting early in the morning. In Paris a busy young physician cannot withdraw from society. . . . I also did not wish to give up science . . . or my remunerative practice, as the largest part of my income went into my scientific endeavors."[3] This common dilemma made him leave Paris again in 1852 to head the Department of Medicine, first in Zurich, then in Breslau.

Lebert's controversial concept was the uniqueness of the cancer cell, a conviction he shared with Bruch and Vogel, two other Germans.[4] Isolated cancer cells, in smear preparations as they were looked at by Lebert and his school, have only in the last few decades again become an important object of diagnosis. They are now studied in body fluids, but the main difference and the greater reliability of modern cytology lie in the development of staining methods. The slides of Lebert and his school were unstained. Histology—both of tissues cut with the microtome and of cells suspended in liquids and smeared on to slides—was then only beginning to profit from the use of dyes.[5]

Lebert's gross pathology, nevertheless, was rooted in the ideas of Laënnec and the older Paris School. But he criticized the sterile, exclusive anatomical description of lesions: "I soon saw the need for combining clinical, experimental, and microscopic observations."[1] It was the "physiologic" or, as we would say, "dynamic" aspect of disease that endeared this new kind of pathology to the young doctors on both sides of the Rhine. Lebert's "influence on Virchow is undeniable," says Ackerknecht.[6]

Lebert wrote: "I divide tumors into two classes according to their constituent tissues. . . . I call *homomorphous* those tissues which are simply a local development of one of the elements as they normally exist in the organism, either in the permanent or the embryonic stage. I call *heteromorphous* those that are not found in the normal state and represent an entirely new formation. I particularly insist on all the structural details of cancer as the subject most in need of elucidation."[1]

In other words, Lebert conceded to the old school, in a classification similar to Laennec's, that cancer was something utterly *praeter naturam*, something entirely *sui generis*, but there was only one certain criterion for establishing malignancy: the cancer cell as seen under the microscope.

(The trouble with the latter view, which sounds so reasonable, clearly is that "differential diagnosis is very difficult. . . . Errors are made by the most skillful cytologist, especially in the interpretation of single cells. It is evident that this danger is being appreciated more than a few years ago. . . . " A few years plus one hundred, for I quote from an editorial in the August 4, 1962 issue of the *Journal of the American Medical Association*.)[7]

Broca, too, became such a "most skillful cytologist." "The microscope has replaced hypothesis by evidence. . . . Any observation unconfirmed by the microscope must be regarded as null and void," he decreed in one of the aphorisms appended to his doctoral thesis of 1849.[8] In his first year as an interne he had mentioned the microscope as one of the most desirable things money could buy, together with books, a watch with a second hand, and travel.[9] In 1847 he bought his own microscope, with the first self-earned 400 francs—long before the

watch. Although he paid in installments, this far-sighted nonconform-
ist felt a little guilty for spending such a tremendous sum on a "hobby"
and, significantly, forgot to enter it in his account book.[10]

Broca presumably met Lebert, who was eleven years older, either
early in 1846 at the Charité or in 1847 at the Hôtel-Dieu. One may
wonder how close their friendship really was. Lebert's intransigence in
microscope science was most attractive, but his yes-manship in politics
may have alienated Broca and his group.

Into this magnifying device Broca seems to have poured all the
revolutionary exuberance that had been frustrated by the political
fiasco of 1848. Here, indeed, was another great embattled cause. To
make it appear less unreasonable, he presented his preoccupation as a
money-making project; he decided to give a course.

"Nothing came of this project,"[11] he wrote. But by the end of the
same year (1849) another outlet for the microscopist's drive came into
view: "Last week I heard by chance that two years ago the Académie
de Médecine had opened a competition on the question of cancer.
The memoirs must be handed in by February 29, 1850. I was very sorry
not to have been informed of this before. In any case, I never fancied
sayings like 'Little will hold who too much will embrace.' It is just a
matter of holding on more tightly, I think. It will be rough to convert
that Upper House of Medicine, the Académie, to the new doctrine."[12]

The final product came from an assembly line of the sort reportedly used by Alexandre Dumas in the ceaseless manufacture of
historical fiction.[13]

"That memoir has eaten two months out of my life, but that
memoir has been deposited. At what price, though, Good Lord! No
sleep for four nights, copyists highly paid for their night work, friends
willing to give me their most precious possession — their time — and
artists whom I had do some fine plates for me. All this has successfully
given birth to a memoir of 600 pages in grand folio with 25 drawings
and five plates. . . . "[14]

Nearly nine months later: "In a secret committee meeting today,
the Académie has taken a decision about the prize in morbid anatomy.
The name of the winning author is not known yet, but the number of
the crowned memoir is. It's mine."[15]

The twenty-five-year-old prosector had won the Prix Portal of
1850 in a display of efficiency that puts many a 20th-century effort to
shame. This solid monograph, occupying 364 pages in the 1853 volume of the *Mémoires de l'Académie de Médecine*, shows no sign of its
fevered production. Verbose by our standards yet lively, it is in essence
a well-organized account of Lebert's teachings. In addition, it contains
the results of Broca's own work as a pathologist and microscopist and a

discovery that secures the author a long-overdue place among the great names in cancer research: his detailed description of malignant neoplasms spreading by venous channels, probably done for the first time.

The "artifices of style"[12] that the young author uses to present these new ideas and impress the jury consist of telling them that he shares the caution and maturity of their judgment. "The actual findings are not always in accord with generally accepted ideas. *It is the duty of serious men to accept innovations only with the greatest reserve*, as this is the only available barrier against the invasion of such things as magnetism, hydropathy, homeopathy, with which our era is teeming.

"The Académie wishes to see new ideas. We reject both the exclusive use of the microscope and the blind proscription of this precious instrument—we employ every available method, including the clinical."[16]

Like Lebert, he stresses this clinical approach, the need for keeping detailed, accurate case notes on admissions and re-admissions to the hospital, including the patients' addresses for follow-up visits at their homes, and, finally, for post-mortem examinations, work, he writes, "not for a genius, perhaps, but for an ordinary, conscientious observer, such as we take ourselves to be."[17]

Classically, cancer comes in a hard form, scirrhus, and a soft one, encephaloid; it may be colloid, melanotic, or one of a thousand undefinable and controversial variants. But essentially, "*cancer is characterized by the presence of an element without analogy in the body economy; this deserves to be termed the cancerous element.*"[18] Actually cancer can be diagnosed with the naked eye, as a rule merely from finding its juice [Cruveilhier, 1827].[4] Present in all cancers, this may rarely occur in some non-cancerous tumors. Cancer juice consists of a "serous fluid, cells, and nuclei."[19] This, and this only, unstained, was used for study, after squeezing the tumor and wiping the juice off with a blunt blade, avoiding pressure at this step. The material was pressed lightly between glass slides. The lens objective No. 7, by Nachez, ("the best, by the way") yielded magnification up to 460 diameters.[20]

In a short historical and somewhat condescending account, he gives "a few words on the cellular theory." In 1849 or 1850 this was still recent history, something Broca had just grown up with, a consequence of the improvements in the construction of the microscopes made during the 1830's. Aside from the nucleolus, discovered in 1836 by Gabriel Valentin,[21] nothing was known of the finer structure of the nucleus, nothing of chromosomes, or mitosis, and hardly anything of cell division. Virchow is credited with the first utterances about cell division in 1852, and by inference he decreed his famous *omnis cellula a cellula* in 1855, following an idea of Goodsir's in 1845 and of Remak's in 1852, not to mention Raspail's original formulation of 1826. Raspail is quoted on July 21, 1826: "I hope I shall be forgiven for saying that the date of these words will remain important; I believe that the time is not far away when this scientific challenge will no longer sound fantastic nor over-confident: *Give me a cell within which other cells can be formed—and I shall hand you the organized world: every cell comes from a cell*; omnis cellula a cellula." But science had to wait some thirty years for the patterns and mechanics of nuclear division to be formulated—the *omnis nucleus e nucleo*, by Flemming.[22]

"The elements of organized beings start with myriads of little microscopic bodies called nucleated cells,"[24] writes Broca, keeping a cool and open mind as to some conflicting theories, e.g., whether nuclei are solid or vesicular. Naturally, he also mentions the primordial amorphous, slimy *blastema*. This powerful myth of the spontaneous generation of cells in the body was dying hard, sticking even to the clearest minds. Broca does not quite share Lebert's complete conviction regarding this blastema. He does declare that all regular tissues must be the successors of embryonic cells, that the new growth of benign tumors is analogous to the normal tissues from which they originate. But malignant, "heteromorphous," destructive growth remains "without analogy in the economy."[25] Cancer elements looked and were different; hence, they might well have a different origin. (Tubercles, incidentally, shared this distinction of heteromorphism.) But in his actual description of cancer cells, based on several hundred of his own observations, Broca is, with Lebert, in agreement with most modern criteria: atypism, then called heteromorphism; pleomorphism, called variability in content, shape, and size (for which the precise measurements and range are given); the presence of multinucleated, giant or "mother cells"; the large nuclei. "Free nuclei" are numerous.[26] (No doubt these refer to cells with minimal cytoplasm, described by Max Schultze in 1861.) Protoplasm is not mentioned. The word had been coined in 1839 by Purkyně, but for "undifferentiated fetal tissue"; it was not used in the modern sense before Schultze in 1863.

Broca's description of cancer cells is complete except for cell division and mitosis. But they are not quite absent either, for we read: "Once only, it is true, but so clearly that no doubt remains, have we seen an arrangement, hitherto noted only in plants: a division, or fission (*fissiparité*) of one large cell into two secondary cells, attached to one another by a tiny process. The large primary cell was 0.12 by 0.04 mm.[27]

"In cancer, and in cancer only, are we able to find all the various kinds of elementary vesicles that exist in the series of organized beings. All imaginable types, every possible mode of production — multiplication, such as isolated development, endogenous generation, *fissiparité* — exist together or separate in this pathological tissue: such is its power of increase and reproduction. If it is true that monsters often are degraded organisms which in some of their parts repeat the features and dispositions of types belonging to a lower rung of the ladder, one may say without exaggeration that cancer is a pathological monstrosity."[28]

There was — as there still is — uncertainty as to the origin of cancer. "Is there in the stricken organ or in the whole organism something at work which precedes its appearance? Anatomy has found nothing so far, and it even seems probable to me that anatomy will always be silent on this point."[29]

Many pages are filled with the gross morbid anatomy descriptive of the local proliferation, the ulceration, and the lymphatic spread of cancer. We pass to more fundamental questions.

There are many ancient anecdotes of contagion by cancer, Broca said. He dismissed as "poetry" the idea of Klencke's that a healthy body might be infected from the outside by independent cancer cells that, like parasites, might send colonies into other organs: "Some subtle minds in Germany have taken this seriously."[30] On the other hand, he gave credence to Langenbeck's so-far unique and surprisingly succesful experiment of producing cancer in the lung of a dog by injecting "encephaloid" tissue suspended in lukewarm water into the animal's veins.[31] Peyrilhe ("Cancer is as hard to understand as it is to cure") had tried this earlier, but his housekeeper had put the noisy animal out of its misery by drowning it before fruition of the experiment.[32] This kind of cancerogenesis in any case must be exceptional, he argued. The "old dogma of transformation of healthy into diseased tissue — *degeneration*" — was categorically and high-handedly rejected. "*Never does a completely formed tissue change into another tissue* . . . [33] A homeomorphous tumor has no more chance to become cancerous than any part of the individual who harbors it."[34] Cancer might remain stationary, but whether it ever could completely disappear was extremely doubtful. "The few examples in the literature are a good deal less than conclusive."

"Without sharing the blunder of some Germans who literally animalize the cells, one may concede to cells some sort of a separate existence. It is by no means unphysiological to suppose that, once alive, they should be capable of development, of undergoing various alterations, to break up or dissolve later. Figuratively speaking, the cells would go through youth, adult life, old age, and die. But such a supposition need not hold true. I do not contest their growth; it seems probable. In fresh cancer production one finds many free nuclei and some small cells: larger cells are found in older tumors. Hence, it is natural to suppose that cells grow by absorbing, through endosmosis, the serum by which they are surrounded. . . . [35] How did new elements arise? Here the cell theory was applied with all its exaggerations. According to this hypothesis new cells developed in the interior of the old ones, which broke up. This had to be exceptional. Increase of cancer was due to the same cause as its first appearance."[36] In all this, Broca conformed with the blastema theory.

As to the propagation or spread of the disease, he rightly rejected Vogel's theory of fibrous or connective tissue as the main source of germination for all tissues,[37] a theory still shared by Virchow with regard to the origin of cancer.[38] (It was reminiscent of Lamarck, the evolutionist whose "cellular tissue" of 1796 and 1809 as the general matrix of cell organization referred not to cells as we understand them, but to "membranes," i.e., connective tissue. Lamarck's was, thus, not an early "cell theory.")[39]

After treating the invasion by cancer of neighboring tissue and of lymphatic channels, Broca came to the role blood vessels played in the malignant growth. They proliferated, he said, and nourished the tumor, but against prevalent opinion he insisted that cancer was not created in them, that they were always passive channels.[40]

With the eye of the engineer, he evaluates the relative forces and resistances at work. "Arteries, when invaded, tend to rupture and cause hemorrhage owing to inter-arterial pressure. The thin venous walls are disorganized by cancer with the greatest ease. The interior pressure of veins is always less than that of even the softest surrounding tumors. . . ."

With loving detail he described—in what he apologetically called "a somewhat lengthy discussion"—"one of the most remarkable events. In the struggle between the distending force of the venous blood and the pressure exerted by the growing cancerous mass, the latter prevails . . . and the encephaloid substance breaks into the blood stream. . . . The first observation of this we owe to a communication by M. Velpeau to the Académie in 1824 . . . where he described the destruction of the vena cava and the extension of an encephaloid cancer into the interior of this vein.

"M. Velpeau supposed that the intra-venous cancerous matter had originated in the interior of the vena cava. But several persons who were shown the specimen—among them Breschet and M.

Chomel and Andral—saw that . . . this cancerous plug was a sort of vegetation from the external encephaloid mass.

"Analogous facts have been observed by M. P. Bérard . . . and by M. Cruveilhier. . . . Not all these authors have interpreted the existence of cancerous matter in the venous lumen in the same way. The honor of having demonstrated its actual origin is due to M. Bérard."

Broca added six pertinent observations of his own, microscopically verified, and called the phenomenon the first degree of cancerous invasion of veins. In the second stage, blood still continued to flow but the destruction of the venous wall was complete.

"In the third stage, flow is entirely arrested. . . . Once obliterated, the vein is taken up by a more or less firm clot . . . soon to be infiltrated by cancer elements. At an even later stage, it is often difficult to tell precisely, with the naked eye, where the cancer ends and the clot begins. Microscopic examination soon relieves these doubts. . . . At the cardiac end . . . the plug . . . forms a bulge which is exposed to the onslaught of the blood column; under the shocks of the pulsating blood, this bulge disintegrates and is carried off by the centripetal stream."

Here Broca entered entirely new territory. He discovered the venous spread of cancer and was afraid nobody would believe what he had seen or agree with this interpretation.

"I repeat that on simple inspection of the specimens, it seemed evident that fragments of the plug must have been broken off by the blood stream. But it might be said that this is a hypothesis. In order to be positive . . . one would have to find such fragments floating in the venous tree between the tumor and the heart . . . at least sometimes. This, too, I have seen to happen. . . . My third observation dispels any doubt. The left iliac vein and the inferior vena cava contained irregular, friable masses, of mixed white and dark red color: these were shreds of encephaloid matter surrounded by blood clot. . . .

"Once detached, these fragments . . . can travel up to the heart, pass across the right cavities and reach the ramifications of the pulmonary artery."

Every possible objection was considered and refuted. Always, for instance, he observed primary and secondary cancer in the same, never in opposite, femoral veins nor in any vein outside the area of drainage nor in the presence of a healthy venous wall at the primary site.

"Finally, and above all, the fact has significance only when submitted to a microscopic check. Simple clots, discolored and softened, may deceptively resemble encephaloid material."[41]

He sensed both the importance of his "doctrine" and its precariousness in the eyes of his readers. A "positive truth"? No, simply "data," "inductive conclusions," "reasoning," though by no means "supposition" or "imagination." More observations were needed, however, and, above all, "injecting cancer cells and nuclei into the blood stream . . . has hitherto not been fruitful. It would be surprising if Langenbeck had indeed succeeded in producing multiple cancers, for his experiments were badly done. In putting a question to nature through an experiment one must, so far as possible, set up conditions similar to the natural condition. Once and once only, a certain amount of cancer material was introduced into the blood of dogs. A few animals died promptly, in a few hours or at the most after a few days. These deaths must not be attributed to the cancer, but to the sudden irruption into the blood stream of a too-large quantity of foreign matter. Other animals recovered and showed no cancer. But was this a true imitation of phenomena as they occur in nature? Does the infective substance unite with the blood stream suddenly and as a single dose? Here is what ought to be done: Inject specific elements in very small doses and repeat this daily for a variable period; do not leave the economy [organism] time to get rid of the noxious material; keep on adding the infectious agent. . . . Inject (1) cells and nuclei forced from cancer serum by several washings with lukewarm water and several filtrations; (2) serum freed from cells and nuclei; (3) juice, composed of both serum and microscopic elements; (4) small fragments of solid cancer substance. . . ."[42]

Broca refused to go beyond his observation of venous spread. Strangely, some organs tended to produce primary cancer, such as the breast, stomach, intestine, thyroid; whereas others harbored mainly secondaries, such as bone, liver, and brain.

The term *metastatic*, in the contemporary sense of cancer breeding in the blood, he thought "outdated . . . except in the restricted sense in which it also denotes the multiple abscesses following phlebitis." Circulating fragments may indeed be responsible, he supposed, for setting up secondary deposits, originating from a primary which may be said to have started the "infection." "I have fought, with decisive arguments," he says, "the hypothesis of Carswell according to which the substance of every cancer originates in the blood and is subsequently deposited in the various organs."[42]

His microscopic observation of cancer particles carried by the venous blood from a local origin to a distant site gave striking support to the tentative concept of blood-borne metastases. The spread via lymph channels was fairly well accepted. Few were as bold as Watson in his widely used textbook of 1843, where he taught, "*blood*" is the main channel." Of this Watson had "scarcely a doubt"[44] but no evidence, and it was an overstatement. Broca had supplied that evidence. Yet he kept the doubt, even sixteen years later when he finally published his *Traité des Tumeurs*; the doubt also never left Virchow's mind. The reason? There are metastases for which to this day no itinerary through vascular channels has been satisfactorily charted, and factors of general and local "predisposition" cannot be entirely eliminated. In 1866 Broca's scepticism was all the more justified, for knowledge, as he pointed out, was "neither more nor less advanced on this point than on the cause of secondary lesions in syphilis . . . glanders . . . typhoid and cholera. . . . "[45]

Thus, the blastema theory remained the credo of French biologists for a few more decades. It was strongly adhered to, for instance, in an interesting M.D. thesis, *De la Génération des Eléments Anatomiques*, reprinted in 1867.[46] The author, one of Robin's pupils, ignored—or did not take the trouble to refute, as Broca had done—the work produced in Germany. This young dissertator was to achieve far greater fame in the world than almost any of the figures in this book—in politics, not in science. But Georges Clemenceau, the "Tiger" of World War I, did have an M.D. degree.

Academic secretaries and professors congratulated Broca. "This morning I met M. Ricord. He was with a friend, a personage all decorations and no hair . . . a member of the Académie, as I soon learned. I doffed my hat and was ready to pass when Ricord called me, 'I would kiss you if we were not in the street,' he said. And turning to his friend: 'I sound affected, but he is one of my pupils; meet M. Broca, your laureate.' 'This is a compliment for both pupil and teacher,' uttered the gentleman, all decorations and no hair. (He doffed his hat, too, so I could see he had no hair.) Maybe you will enjoy all these puerile details."[47]

His students gave their suddenly famous instructor "the most *gracieux* present for a surgeon" in the days when house calls were still taking care of most surgical emergencies: a magnificent set of instruments for doing amputations, of an entirely new design [four knives; four large saws; curved, rotatory, and with two blades; a chain saw; a small straight-backed saw; an osteotome; needles of several kinds and a pincushion for them; a tourniquet; three kinds of forceps; a tenaculum (retractor), etc.] Some of the tools could be demounted so as to fit into a charming inlaid mahogany box, resembling "an elegant case for a flute." This set, designed by one of his students, was immediately copied and for sale at Charrière's, the fashionable instrument shop.[48]

Four years later, long after the Académie had made up its mind to publish Broca's memoir, the academicians could not be expected to have come around to its revolutionary teachings.

"When the School and the hospitals began to open their doors to these innovators ...," the surgeon Horteloup recalled thirty years later,[49] "a showdown was due in the Académie.... A case report about an 'encephaloid' of the testicle in a child aged three ... and the patient's cure. What was 'cured' in this case, M. Robert, another microscopist, asked, the surgical incision or the disease? The cure of cancer was so exceptional ... that even the diagnosis in this case ought not to be accepted without reservation.... A most remarkable discussion ensued. It would be hard to say who won.... The balance seemed to favor the Young School.... By his articles in *Moniteur des Hôpitaux*, M. Broca became one of the keenest participants; they were a resounding success."

Horteloup also quotes from a letter Paul wrote to his parents in March, 1855,[50] about "an expected congratulation for my articles on the discussion of cancer ... can you guess from whom? Not the late Emperor Nicolas, but almost. For aside from his Holiness the Pope of the Universal Church, I know of nobody more important in the eyes of the true believers. It simply is Monseigneur le Duc de Bordeaux [the Bourbon pretender, uncrowned "Henry V"]. From his castle retreat of Frohsdorff, this King of France and Navarre continues to protect the arts and sciences like his ancestor Louis XIV. His physician lives on a sort of familiar footing with him and has a subscription to the *Moniteur des Hôpitaux:* His Majesty does not disdain to cast a glance at our columns from time to time. Poor idle prince! Having nothing better to do, he is a champion of the cause of the microscope. Those who are *out* are always a little rebellious. And so he said to Doctor Carrière, his physician: 'When you write to Paris to renew your subscription I insist that you let M. le docteur Broca know that the King of France and Navarre has his eyes fastened on him, that he appreciates his talent and independence, and that he sees with pleasure a pen as able as his in the service of science and progress.' Is it not a joy to see this poor devil taking himself seriously?"

Unquoted by Horteloup, the letter goes on: "Every medal has its reverse. After telling me a hundred times directly and through others that I am the only honest micrographer, my friend Velpeau has just honored me by publishing a pamphlet principally directed against my person, with little nasty insinuations regarding my 'weakness.' He accuses me of having altered his speech so as to refute it more effectively. But Baillière, the publisher of the Bulletins of the Académie, has informed me about these tactics. Velpeau waited until all my articles were published; then he edited his speech to make the contested passages disappear, and six weeks after the debate was over . . . he began to cry foul. I had to prove that the foul play was his. . . ."

The argument was essentially about the peculiarity of what we call "basal cell" or skin carcinoma — "epithelial" or "cancroid" then, and also about fibroma against sarcoma. Velpeau, the leading surgeon in Paris, furiously denied that there was any difference between the basal cell cancer of the skin and the other kinds, such as cancer of the breast and the internal organs. Lebert and his school, however, found no "cancer cells" in "cancroid" and no metastases at a distance.

"M. Broca, who in 1850 conceded the recurrence of cancroid in lymph nodes only as an *infinitely* rare exception, who supported the view that pseudo-cancer does not multiply, or only locally and if not removed in its entirety, is he still of the same opinion?" Velpeau asked.

He, Velpeau, knew cancer when he saw it: "Certain cancers one cannot mistake, and I believe I can diagnose them with complete assurance. I have under my eyes a tumor of the breast. . . . And I should not be able to say that such a tumor is scirrhus — not unless I have submitted it to microscopic study? . . . In cases that are less clear-cut, if I am in doubt, I say so, and I consult the microscope. If the microscope confirms my supposition, I am a little strengthened thereby; if it is opposed, my doubt increases; but knowing that the cell can be absent in true cancer and be present in a benign tumor, the microscope can never completely make up my mind for me. . . ."

Some cancers are curable, but it is not for the blundering microscopist to say which. "I am appealing to the lights of clinical diagnosis in direct opposition to microscopical diagnosis. . . . it should assist but not try to lead us."[51]

Not being a member yet, Broca could not confront Velpeau on the floor of the Académie. *"Is Microscopy of any use in Pathology?"* was one in a series he wrote for *Moniteur des Hôpitaux*.[52] "The motive that turns so many eminent men against a thing so obvious as the microscope must be a very powerful one. . . .

"Let us get down to earth and to morbid anatomy. It started over three hundred years ago . . . had its period of fairy tales and anecdotes . . . and for the first two hundred years did not deserve to be called a science. Generalizations having been formulated by now . . . no one was shocked; consequently morbid anatomy enjoyed general acclaim.

"One day — about a century ago — the vast genius of Morgagni undertook a methodical cleaning up. . . . Morbid anatomy . . . would throw light on every disease. . . . No longer was he concerned with the mere discovery of lesions but with making precise statements about the nature of the various diseases in relation to their sites and causes—*de sedibus et causis morborum*. You might think the progress made that day was eagerly welcomed. Undeceive yourselves. As soon as Morgagni started to breathe life into his nascent theories, the very people who had been favorably disposed to morbid anatomy before it had turned into a science suddenly because its adversaries.... People who believe they know something find it embarrassing to unlearn and be sent back to the schoolbench....

"A strange objection was made against the modern trend in morbid anatomy. 'What you find,' Morgagni quoted his critics, 'are only gross lesions; the elementary ones escape your senses because they reside in invisible particles.... (*Quippe in occultis invisibilium particularum conformationibus posita.*)' Thus, the Young School of Padua was taken to task for not studying elementary particles—those very same ones, that is, which the microscope has revealed to modern eyes. How times have changed! Precisely the opposite reproach is being made to the Young School of Paris....

"From our beginnings ... over and over again we were told—especially those of us interested in surgery—that in order to understand disease, we must first study the lesions ... use all available means! We obeyed ... but this is what happened.

"For a long time the cabinets of the curious have contained an instrument called the microscope.... Without the microscope, we were told, what would we know of the anatomy, physiology, and embryology of plants... of infusoria, of the composition of blood, chyle, sperm, the nature of the cerebral pulp, or the structure of glands...? We believed it... and started without hesitation on what seemed an open road....

"The circumstances were most favorable. A resounding cry of admiration had gone up throughout European science. Cellular theory had just made its appearance. Raspail had said, like Archimedes, 'Give me a cell, and I shall build you an organism!' The Germans, always in search of unity, seized upon the idea.... Everything owed its existence to modifications and transformations of elementary cells. Things looked better still on the day when Müller investigated pathological tissues and found cells in them, too, or tissues of cellular origin. Unity, that will-o'-the-wisp pursued for so long, seemed on the verge of being caught ... thanks to the microscope!

"Among us, cellular theory has shone only with a passing light. But Germany, where it was born, is still under its spell. This, by the way, is the main point of disagreement between the German and the

72

French micrographers. Blinded by their unitarian theories, our neighbors across the Rhine will not admit the specificity of various cells. . . .

"Nevertheless, just because it was so all-embracing, cellular theory made no frontal attack on any of the current doctrines . . . But when clinicians turned micrographers, when they compared the natural history of the illness with that of the tumor, they clashed with current doctrine. . . .

"At first there were some who tried to prove that the microscope was a source of illusion and error. . . . Next, they tried to make the micrographers contradict each other. . . . It was considered a good joke to send them bits of tumors without the benefit of the slightest information or even with deliberate misinformation. This new campaign had only limited success. . . .

"At present the debate is in a new phase. Not the precision but the usefulness . . . of applying the microscope to the diagnosis of certain tumors is being contested. . . . Microscopy is given its due for information about the mite causing scabies, the echinococcus, the parasite of ringworm, and thrush . . . about pus and other pathological sediments in the urine. More, it is considered excellent for differentiating between true cancer and hypertrophic tumors (or adenoids) of the breast. . . .

"Let us state that M. Velpeau, the most redoubtable adversary of modern theories, has never taken part in the petty crusade against this new means of investigation. . . . His conclusion was, not that the microscope will always be useless, as some have had him say, but that it has been useless so far. . . . This at least will reserve us a future should we succumb in the present struggle. . . .

"The history of the two or three cases which M. Velpeau adduced are, we cannot deny it, quite embarrassing for our tenets. Thus a cancroid in the *left* lower lip with a recurrence deep in the superior maxilla on the right is difficult to explain if on both occasions the pathological product was indeed confirmed as epithelial in nature.

"We have no reason to doubt this, although M. Velpeau has not given us any detail. Again, the recurrence of an epithelial cancroid in the form of a tumor with cancer cells, if confirmed by other observations, might cause us much embarrassment. But wait: a fact may be modified or altered by so many different circumstances! One such, for example, is that several tumors reach the same micrographer on the same day. He examines them all but mixes them up or confuses the order in his reports. . . . Again, we might get only a tiny bit of tumor tissue, and the most scrupulous examination reveals no cancer elements; our report that the tumor is not cancerous is given without reflection that cancer might be contained in the remaining tumor which we have not seen. . . . Actually, one should not give an opinion on the structure of a pathological product unless one has the whole of it under one's eyes. Let us add that micrographers may be mistaken. . . .

"M. Velpeau says himself (*Traité des maladies du sein*, Preface, p. xiii: '. . . I do not mind to affirm that, at the bedside, the micrographers have never seen me mistake any tumor of this kind for the other kind.' He could say nothing to please us more. It is conceded, then, that the external signs of the cancroid are so different from cancer that M. Velpeau never makes a mistake! The conditions that can be diagnosed with such certainty, both during life and anatomically, *by the naked eye as well as the microscope*, are not identical conditions. . . .

"The other difference to spread a gulf between these two affections is the event of general infection. The cachexia which ordinarily terminates the life of a patient with cancer is constantly absent in cases of cancroid. There is not a single well-documented case in the literature of epithelial tumors found in the viscera of a patient with cancroid. . . .

"M. Velpeau insists on the possiblity and the frequency of local recurrence in cancroids. . . . He knows well that we deny neither. . . ."

"Certainly, we did and still do maintain that recurrence in cancroid is much less frequent that it is in cancer. M. Velpeau does not agree. We are unfortunate in finding ourselves here in opposition to such a great and masterly expert. Some consolation, however, we may at least derive from our ideas; not only do they conform with what we have seen ourselves but also with the opinions expressed by most classical authors."[52]

By and by, the clinicians became convinced. This was the door, opened by Lebert, through which Broca and his friends led French pathology into the laboratory. No matter how wrong the "Young School" was regarding cancerogenesis, its claims for separating "epithelial" tumors from ordinary cancer were defendable, and their influence on the practice of surgery is undeniable. "Cancroid" or skin cancer is still considered a relatively benign lesion and hardly ever produces widespread metastases. The "fibroplastic" tumors, i.e., meningiomas, and sarcomas, etc., have turned out to range through every degree of malignancy, but even the most malignant forms will take the arterial and not the lymphatic route of dissemination. In time, few surgeons anywhere would dare to get by without someone doing the microscopy and passing judgment on the relative malignity of the biopsy specimen.

Yet, to this day not all animosity is gone between laboratory and clinic. Ostensibly shaking hands in public, they still do not always see eye to eye and behave just like those two subtly contrived allegorical ladies — La Théorie et la Pratique — that adorn the frieze high up in the courtyard of the old École de Médecine.

Aside from the sixteen articles in Moniteur des Hôpitaux, Broca wrote forty-six papers on tumors, not including his contributions to Costello's Cyclopedia of Practical Surgery[52] on various subjects, translated into English. Finally there was, unfinished, the Traité des Tumeurs in two volumes.[54] Odontoma and a study of dental cysts were first descriptions. Here he also showed up Virchow's inconsistencies on cancer origin, in which the blastema was replaced not by primitive cells but "inter-cellular tissue." Broca further pointed out that Virchow's or Raspail's "omnis cellula e cellula" still sounded more like an order than an observation: at best it was a possibility. It failed to fit the contemporary classifications of tumors, "just as the theories of Lamarck and Darwin . . . fail to fit the classification of animals."[55] He resisted generalization before all the facts were in. To him the differences between various tissues were fundamental; they could not be the result of differentiation of one primitive entity; he considered it unlikely that cancer might be the result of dedifferentiation of mature cells. If anything, his belief in the "blastema" had hardened. Spontaneous generation, i.e., the origin of an organized living structure from an amorphous substance seemed a necessity in his non-vitalist order of things. For Broca this basic assumption was not contradicted by the development of the animal from the ovum, its many cells from the one. Cancer cells simply could not be following this circular line of derivation. Cancer cells, to Broca as well as to Virchow — and to us — are largely recognizable as such, no matter from which organ they take their origin. It seemed absurd to believe that from all the various parent tissues, well differentiated as they are, there should spring another tissue that does not resemble them, yet does carry some inner consistency and must follow some dreadful law of growth all its own. The evidence for dedifferentiation was not at hand when his second volume on tumors appeared. But even with this evidence, the steps from healthy to cancerous tissue and from there to death remain rather mysterious. Soon, however, other interests, other campaigns crowded out the microscope for Broca.

But no chapter on cancer is complete without its quack. Broca's appeared on the scene in the spring of 1855 in the shape of a Doctor

Landolfi from Naples, "brandishing a well-known caustic. With this he cauterizes every breast he comes across," Broca told his parents. "The august Princess Mathilde is infatuated with him, and our august Emperor has given orders to set up the illustrious foreigner as the head of a hospital service. Great excitement at the Administration des Hôpitaux; they hate to be bothered . . ." No doubt, "the vile charlatan, as ignorant as a captain of the dragoons,"[56] was given a tough time by Broca heading a commission charged by the Administration to investigate the man's merits. They found Landolfi had simply dressed up with bromine chloride the current caustic of Dr. Canquoin: chloride of zinc and antimony. The bromine gave the paste an interesting color and insufferable odor, produced intolerable pain, was useless, disastrous,[57] just "another illusion in the history of cancer."[56] And as in the doggerel by one of Velpeau's internes on another "black doctor,"

"The whip of science
scored a hit.
The cure for quacks is
Make them quit."[58]

ᘓVIᘔ
Trifles and Tribulations

 "Just a few lines to tranquilize *you. What a word! It would make the Académie Française wince . . ."* (February, 1851)

*W*hat I have to inform you," says the discursive author of *Tristram Shandy*, "comes, I own, a little out of its due course; it should have been told a hundred and fifty pages ago, but I foresaw then 'twould come in pat hereafter . . . "[1] Some left-overs, then:

If at the end of 1848 all hopes of major social change were dashed, business was good even for the recent prosector. Pupils were not lacking despite the Republic: "I have a group of Americans whom I teach operative surgery worth 120 francs at the end of a month. Another group is waiting . . . Some Egyptians . . . want to dissect in my cabinet for 150 francs each. I am not decided . . . I prefer French or American students. . . ."[2] Broca's new-found affluence and his main sphere of action, the École Pratique, made him move from the "agreeable and well laid lodgings" in Rue d'Arcole to a small apartment, Rue Jacob, 19. "Less grandiose . . . but with a very bright cabinet for my microscope . . . a lovely little terrace lined with boxes full of soil for seeding with creepers to make a charming bower . . . the view enormous, wonderfully kept gardens . . . plenty of air and light, a splendid vaulted entrance hall . . . respectable inhabitants . . . 75 francs more . . . ."[3] Unable to find an apartment with hardwood floors in the *quartier*, he provided himself with an extravagant rug: "I do not care for living on cold tiles. . . . For reasons of economy and necessity I also must buy a book case."[4]

Shelves, books, and cases full of notes, "innumerable slips on every item of interest,"[5] were always a serious problem as were the charges of prodigality pouring in from Sainte Foy.[6]

His last year as an interne had regretably come to an end. His mark in the last examination (all in public) was only "very satisfactory": "I defended the view against M. Chomel that there is no disease without a lesion, as everyone must do who knows his anatomy and physiology . . . But M. Chomel was adamant: 'These surgical gentlemen,' he said 'pretend to know more about medicine than internists do.'"[7]

"I am a doctor, you will have my thesis [*On the spread of inflammation: Some Statements on tumours called cancerous.*] with the next mail. It was graded 'extremely satisfactory'." But the event was one of the least exciting in his career; another had stirred up his feelings.

"I am writing this in the room of a dying man who to me was a teacher, benefactor, and friend. . . . I have been staying part of the days at his bedside and have not left him last night. . . ."[8]

Five days later: "My dear old chief died in our arms the day before yesterday. . . . It nearly always happens that success spoils the heart; in public life, in the excited rush of their existence most of these men forget what they once were; family ties are nothing to them, friendships only springboards, honesty a sham and a means to advancement. If ever there was a man showered with favor of fortune, it certainly was Blandin. Yet how different was he from all those people with a dried-up heart. One had to see the way he lived with his family, like a simple, naive, and affectionate little man from a provincial town. . . . He often told me, 'Take heart, my friend, go on working, I had to start just like you. I promise that you will arrive.' He always kept his promise. To recommendations for unworthy candidates no matter from which quarter, he gave an evasive reply and his decisive vote often to someone he knew least.

"My heart is shattered, I cried like a child. While he was alive I did not know that I loved him so much. No doubt, I have lost a powerful protector, but this notion did not torment me for an instant. Besides, what he had already done for me was much more than what he might have done later. He supported my first steps; now I am able to get on by myself . . . I was unable to write; there was a host of things to do, announcements, the funeral. . . . His wife is inconsolable.

"She said: 'Stop this clock, I shall not want to see it move again.' As I was doing her strange bidding I noticed that it was thirty minutes past noon. I managed to jump into a carriage and arrive at the Faculté just in time for my thesis and the sad honor of announcing to the professors of the School the death of their colleague."[9]

Death was in the Paris air for yet another reason. Cholera, claiming 10,000 victims in Paris,[10] had once again made its way from the

Ganges to the Seine; India's infested waters and poverty were mirrored in the West. Paul minimized its dangers to the fairly well-to-do and resisted his parents' urging to come home. He was not going to be "a traitor both to science and to humanity."[11] In May he came down with jaundice, but after a few days he was "feeling wonderfully well . . . headache and lassitude gone . . . waiting for a cutlet which I shall wash down with some excellent Bordeaux. . . . Not going out yet . . . yellow as a Mongol . . . but having a lot of company. We amuse ourselves watching the intensity of my skin color and of my icteric urine decrease. . . . Going back to the country. . . . Château de Villeron, a large park, guns, hounds, and horses — everything for getting a lot of exercise and doing nothing . . . had to promise them I would return."[11]

He now writes daily. "When I am alone I work a little. . . . Perhaps I should not tell you this, but I am reading that wild sort of literature: novels by Dumas, the *Musketeers*, for example. I shall soon have devoured about thirty or forty volumes; as you know you finish one of them in two hours."[12]

Never had he been or would he be so relaxed. "I ventured out to expose myself to the eyes of the good Parisians and bravely sat down in the Jardin du Luxembourg. A friend had come along; we rambled on about a host of things, read the newspapers, watched the little boys play ball. I felt so well in the open air, so pleased to loaf and have the good conscience that I had nothing to do. . . . We amused ourselves by studying the impression my beard of three twelfths of an inch and my Russian hide were making on male and female passers-by. . . . Under my temporary mask, I do, in fact, look no more like a Frenchman than the President of the Republic does. Except that I (and here I remain well within the limits of the most angelic humility) quite frankly do not look quite as stupid. . . ."[13]

Broca saw in Bonaparte an evil far greater than the cholera. The intense hatred that this man aroused is easy to understand. A word taken from modern American usage perhaps best describes the monarch and the epoch that bore his stamp: phony. How could one take seriously a man whose name seemed to usurp the unique glory of the First Napoleon, claiming dynastic legitimacy while both uncle and nephew were self-made upstarts? There was a ridiculous touch in his somber, dandified, blasé, heavy-lidded countenance, his beard of "a soldier on half-pay during the 1st Empire," and his mutually incompatible actions. These things irritated and exasperated many who did not directly suffer from his regime. In order to arrive, Louis Napoléon tried on every ideological costume, like repetitive disguises put on by the crafty comedy characters of the period. He had written a socialist pamphlet but created a new plutocracy; he had no heart for war but led France into many such enterprises; he favored, and in his youth had personally fought for, the cause of Italian independence but soon began to support the Pope against a free Italy; his democratic principles resulted in a police state and suppression of free speech. Brought up as an exile in German-speaking countries, he had a funny-sounding German accent. Few rulers have presented an easier target for cartoonists. Yet the country almost forced the Emperorship upon him, and there is no denying that many prospered under his regime.[14] "We have a democratic government, with a legendary Emperor at the top; the principles of '89 [1789, the first French Revolution] below, a cult of idolatry for the fellow, and the Church kissing Caesar's boots. Stupid and repulsive," runs an entry in the diary of the brothers Goncourt.[15]

History is well acquainted with this type of cunning dilettante who seizes power because among better equipped men there is none who dares deny it to him. Add a mass of deluded voters who in a plebiscite will sweep a mountebank into imperial or dictatorial power—after he has flouted every principle of the constitution that had already given him the presidency. The Parisians, more sophisticated and proletarian than the rest of France (after a small insurrection quickly and brutally put down), gave him only 133,000 out of their 300,000 ballots. After the famous coup d'état of December 2, 1851, the country as a whole counted nearly seven and a half million votes for, and only a little more than half a million against him. But by the end of 1849 all liberties gained in February, 1848, already had been suppressed.[16]

Broca's reaction, six days after the Prince-President had seized dictatorial power, was this: "I have nothing to say. Nothing! Silence is sometimes more eloquent than words. What mine signifies will not escape you; let me rather talk about my case of books. . . ."[17]

Only three short sentences. Unusual for this correspondent, the clipped reticence may be interpreted as a precaution in case mail should be intercepted in days of creeping terror. But the cry of silence is not uncommon when *unspeakable* has become a poignantly meaningful term. In his last letter of 1851 he adds:

"Things are a little calmer now; missives may circulate more freely. It may still be a little hazardous to talk about public affairs, but I think I can tell you about my own. Your fears on my behalf were justified, but nothing materialized. The fact that there had been an insurrection was made use of to arrest men supposed to be capable of exerting some influence on the elections. Thus one of my colleagues, a very popular man with the students [presumably Deville] was deprived of his freedom until this morning. All those who have not belonged to any [political] society and have not taken part in the insurrection are now being released. Hence, one may be sure by now of not being arrested. But at the time when my letter arrived I never went out without an overcoat, a few gold coins, a portable ink-pot, and white paper, everything appropriate, that is, for making my sojourn in prison tolerable. I was quite certain that I had stayed away from any political movement. I was even in a position to prove that I had not left the Hôtel-Dieu since the first day. But arrests are sometimes made at random these days. A resemblance or a report by a secret agent whom one has the misfortune to displease may suffice for getting food and board at the expense of the government. Your second advice was quite unnecessary. I do not need to cool my hot head; I am reformed of my political preoccupations. . . . What remains of France? A handful of intelligent men, who are neither lawyers nor bankers, who have no-thing to gain or to lose from a change of government, who have gathered around the new democratic principle without self-interest and who wish to support the oppressed classes, men who accept being treated as demagogues by you frightened conservatives. . . .

"The people! They rise up in certain départements at the news of the coup d'état; they vote for the fellow who made it unanimously next day. The Paris worker! He lines his garret with the portraits of Victor Hugo or Michel de Bourges; one day he learns Michel is in prison and Hugo in exile: delighted, he shows his full approval by his vote. By no means do I want to make excuses for turn-coats. But I begin to understand why so many who owe position and fame to a justified popularity may become the most ruthless enemies of the people. I understand how others have come to despise humanity, be-cause I have come to pity it for its foolishness. I cannot take it seri-ously. Indifferent myself, I can condone others who are egoists. God forbid that I go farther in this deplorable direction. . . ."[18]

During that first and worst year of the dictatorship, his letters were destroyed by the family for fear that their home might be searched and in terror of the notorious *commissions mixtes*. These were secret tribunals set up in every department of the country, em-powered to keep under house arrest, exile, imprison, or deport to a penal colony anyone, without trial and without so much as a record kept. The number of those affected came close to 20,000. Among them was an intimate friend, another prosector, Amédée Deville. A few years Broca's senior, he had embarked on a promising academic career. Almost certainly none of his own activities could have made him suspect. But his father was a *montagnard*, a deputy of the extreme left and in prison since 1849. On December 13, 1851, Deville, Jr., about to start his lecture, was arrested. Released, rearrested, he was shunted through the various prisons; his name was added to the list of deportees. The professors of the Faculté intervened in vain. Luckily a storm delayed his deportation to Cayenne, one of France's worst penal colonies. The ship returned to Brest; the delay and more interventions commuted his sentence to exile; for a short time he was back in Paris.

> Broca to Deville, 12 April 1852:
> My dear Deville,
> Dr. Colson, a member on the Board of the Royal College of Surgeons of Great Britain and one of the most important men in the medical profession in England, has just been spending a few days in Paris, and I had an opportunity to meet him. I spoke to him about you. Your youth, your work, and the persecution to which you are being subjected have highly aroused his interest and good will. He very much wishes to see you and would be happy to do something so as to lessen some of the bitterness of your stay abroad. Through his influential position he may be very useful to you, but above all you may congratulate yourself for being able to get in touch with a man of such tact and generous feelings. Courage and au revoir! Affectionately, your devoted comrade
>
> P. Broca[20]

Velpeau also had some advice for the young French surgeon, his pupil, forced to go to England. He gave Deville an introduction to Lawrence, whom he considered a good English surgeon. Nevertheless: "Be careful. Their surgery seems backward to me; they feel it, and they do not wish us to look too closely. On the other hand, do not sacrifice our surgery to theirs by being too obliging."[21] Was this what got Deville into trouble with his hosts? Was it national pride too jealously asserted—and by which side more? In January, 1854, an article, *The Museum of Guy's Hospital,* appeared in *Moniteur des Hôpitaux,* by Paul Broca, then one of its main contributors, protesting that Deville had been refused admission to the Museum of Guy's Hospital where he had gone to work.

Deville, unable to "live for science" in London, had to seek an "easy fortune in private practice"; in a few years his savings amounted to 12,500 francs. "But he was a broken man," Broca said. "Shadowed by French police agents in London, he saw them everywhere. . . . He would not even trust a letter box. . . . Acute mania broke out in 1861. . . . After several months his family put him into the asylum at

Ivry. . . ." There Deville died seventeen years later, "one of the most deplorable victims of the coup d'état. . . ."[19]

Of course, life was not all grudges and drudgery. Inviting his father to visit him in Paris was a recurring theme with every promise of spring,[22] but for another three years the invitation was resisted.

Loving care bestowed on other members of the family included the treating of Aunt Jourdit's shingles by a sixth-year medic in the 1840's:

"So you have been ill, my poor aunt? Fortunately nothing serious, one of those disorders belonging to the great category of *bobos* in which almighty medical science can display its shining triumphs. Your half-girdle of blisters will by now have begun to make you suffer less; however, if they open up so as to become painful in contact with your clothing, I would urge you to rub them lightly with olive oil, to cover them with a thin layer of very fine powdered starch and to stay at home for a day or two, with food and drink as usual. If you should have occasion to use this method, a little crust will form, which comes off after a few days. This is the most efficacious treatment in cases where the pain persists for a long time, which is due to the opening of the blisters."[23]

Consultations among friends, too:

"Jules Cadars had a head cold, refused to look after it, and his mother wanted to give him an herb tea. Hence interminable discussions. . . . In order to spare both the goat and the cabbage I prescribed a flannel waistcoat. Jules agreed because . . . he had sworn he would not take anything by mouth. His mother was satisfied because it was treatment. The flannel waist coat has been crowned with the most brilliant success. How wonderful is the physician's role, how noble his mission on earth."[24]

The shingles and a head cold were not only proper subjects for a surgeon's scorn: the academic fashion in internal medicine was skepticism. Before the rise of the biological sciences, surgery was no doubt the leading discipline in both theory and practice.

How, for instance, did a gentleman order his shirts in Paris, rather than at Sainte Foy courtesy of a grateful aunt?

"An artist will subject you to a single inspection, two minutes to give him the three or four principal dimensions of your person. The rest is deduced by means of geometry and arithmetic. The artist maps out your carcass in his own shop; this will guide him in the construction of your envelopes. One fine day, by appointment, he arrives at your home, shirts in one hand, bill in the other. He is careful to catch you as you are about to be getting up. You choose a shirt from his parcel at random; you try it on. If it fits, you keep it on all day. If it does not—but it always does. . . ."[25]

He expertly chooses a three-seated cabriolet, second hand, as a gift for his parents.[26] Help also had to be given to friends; in the struggle for success their mutual assistance was as keen as their rivalry.

"One of those feverish weeks. . . . Jarjavay was so absorbed by family matters of extreme urgency during the first week of writing his thesis that eight days before the deadline he had not put down a single word. He was on the point of giving up and asked me for advice. I disapproved. . . . No man must ever give up in any *concours* he has started. There was only one week left, and I agreed to take over the first half of his thesis. A wild drive ensued. . . . I was up for three consecutive nights as in the days of my cancer memoir."[27]

An anatomist trained in the surgery of the day, Broca had to win a position as *Chirurgien des hôpitaux*—also called *Chirurgien du Bureau Central*—before a permanent position to head a service became vacant. The first time around, in May, 1850, proved to be Broca's first defeat. One of the examiners was a recent convert to the Orfila clique, and Broca was dropped in the preliminaries, as was Deville, his most serious competitor, then still at liberty but compromised by his father's political record.[28]

A prodigious memory and unfailing prowess in delivery were the prerequisites for this sort of competitive self-exhibition. For the young lecturer, too, public speaking still presented some problems, mainly a towering stage fright.

"I had two misgivings: Would I have any students? And would I be up to this kind of lecturing? You see, I am known as an anatomist and a teacher of operative technique, but surgical theory, at my tender age [of twenty-six] and as a man unknown in this field? Would they believe me capable? I was afraid of being stodgy, dogmatic, talking about patients in the clipped statements that describe a muscle or the proper use of the scalpel. Today, after my fourth lecture, I am rid of this anxiety. I am not used to being modest with you. Modesty between people who love each other as we do is really a weakness, a lack of understanding of one's own worth, or just hypocrisy trying to hide the obvious. My amphitheater [300 seats] has in fact been constantly full, and not just full but overflowing. Over fifty students have to stand around my table and out into the corridor. . . . Above all, I have noticed that *le discours, la phrase, le speech*—call it what you will—comes to my tongue with as much ease, or better, than the severe and frigid statements of anatomy. . . . They rewarded me with warm applause. . . ."[29] As *professeur libre*, he was an exponent of the "free-lance" and extramural teaching, encouraged as an old tradition by the Faculté but frowned upon by the police and abolished with the reconstruction of the École Pratique in 1878.[30]

Accounts of what his students thought of Broca as a lecturer date from a decade or two later: "Dr. Broca was giving no didactic lectures," according to an analysis by Maurice Reclus, one of his internes, "only occasionally would he take a subject from its origin and follow it rigorously into all its developments. Usually a digression slipped in; the main topic seemed somehow forgotten, but reentered soon, and suddenly you could see the whole question singularly illuminated. . . . His presentation was not rich; his thoughts did not spring as fully garbed from his brain as they are in the periods of some orators. He often searched for a word, and the effort betrayed itself in a forceful forward movement of his head and arms; yet once found, that word burst forth, impetuous, strong, and magnificently precise. You felt that there was a struggle; this and the final triumph tremendously enlivened and strengthened his talks. They were truly great and as if cast in bronze."[31]

Others were more critical. Horteloup, for instance, agreed with Reclus; he, too, missed in Broca's delivery the breadth of the periods that characterize Broca's writings. But he found the speaker's strained effort hardly enjoyable, especially when coupled with a habit of "switching from a low to a high pitch without obvious reason."[32] Paul's family and friends used to tease him about this.[33] Yet another student was rather charmed by his master's tenor voice, its "brilliance vibrating with a trace of the southern accent" and with "the lively eye, the strong and ample gestures." The peculiar impediment in the flow of Broca's speech and manner—rocks and boulders heightening the drama of the rapids—expressed rather well his keyed-up perfectionism, the conflict between the vigor and the inhibitions of his nature.

Towards the end of 1851 Broca founded, with Verneuil and Follin, the other two members of the "Young School," a private teaching partnership which he described to his parents as a project "gigantic and without parallel in the past." As *professeurs libres* the three prosectors were to lecture in rotation, twice a week, on "descriptive, general, microscopic, surgical, regional, and philosophical" anatomy. A course in surgery and one for competitors in the *concours* of the Bureau Central soon brought Broca's lecture schedule to seven hours a week. "If this does not enable me to do well in my own *concours*, I really must be good for nothing. . . ."[35]

During the spring of 1853 he had occasion to attempt this *concours* for a third time. At the same time he tackled the *concours de l'agrégation,* the most important and exciting of them all. (A single *concours* now gives access to both titles: *Chirurgien des hôpitaux* [or *du Bureau Central*] and *Chirurgien agrégé,* conferred respectively by the Assistance Publique and the Faculté.) Naturally, several odds were stacked against the high-keyed candidate. In order to protect an obstetric surgeon (one of the five competitors), all questions about the "structure" of organs must be eliminated as they might unduly favor the three microscopists: Broca, Verneuil, and Follin, who now entered the ring as rivals. Next, he might not get a large audience for one of his star performances. This was important. In that big public show the acclaim by the professional crowd influenced the examiners. As Orfila had just died ("let him go to paradise if he can"), the Faculté was closed for two days of official mourning, and the public was confused about the reopening. To make things worse, he had to perform in a minor hall, the main amphitheater being occupied by a lecture. And to top it all, the tables for the examiners had been arranged in such a way that Broca was forced to turn his back to the connoisseur audience! "I remonstrated, and . . . the tables were turned around . . . already something. Besides, the audience was larger than I had expected. Students going to a lecture, others coming from an examination or from the library, dropped in and the hall was crowded. . . ." It was a toss-up between Follin, Verneuil, and Broca, "the inseparable triumvirate as we are called. There is an enormous distance between us and the others."

Broca had Gerdy, Malgaigne, and Cloquet in his favor. But Follin "has friends, all his chiefs are alive. He is not going to give an inch. . . ." The obstetrician might be second; the fifth candidate was a professor's son and might do unexpectedly well.

"For four months nearly, and some weeks daily from four to six, these performances were taking place at the Faculté. The concours for the Bureau Central of the Assistance Publique was sitting three times a week at the same hours, splitting up my favorable judges. . . . In the hospital *concours* most of the candidates have the advantage of being older men. But the administration seems very favorably disposed toward Follin and me. Last year . . . it was on the side of the insurgents. . . . Yesterday the General Secretary accosted me: 'Well, three positions. I hope this time you will go through like a letter in the mail!' 'Who is going to put me in the slot?' 'You can jump well enough to get there all by yourself. Anyway, if I may tell you so, this year there is neither a professor's son nor a politician among you. . . .'

Defense of Agrégé Thesis. (Note the expensive agrégé hats or toques.)
(Courtesy Bibliothèque Nationale, Paris.)

"Professor Monod . . . came over to me the other day. . . . 'What,' he said, 'you are not yet in the Bureau Central? That's very bad.' 'I have done everything, sir.' 'Oh, I did not mean you,' Monod said, 'I meant your examiners!' "

His chances were not bad; after all, he thought, comparing odds and fine points: "Need I to tell you that my two friends were a little below my expectations? Follin was erudite, if perhaps a little heavy, and his outline not entirely satisfactory. Verneuil was full of grace and wit, but his lecture a little empty; he also had a very difficult question and was not too familiar with the numerous operative procedures . . . The obstetrician was talking some incredible poppycock with considerable nerve. . . ."

Richard, the fifth candidate, "came before me and consequently I was unable to hear him because during this time I was locked up and under guard [according to examination protocol]. But all agreed . . . that he . . . was evidently the best so far. Hence conditions were rather unfavorable for me when I got in. . . . I added a historical chapter on this region [the mandible], from Hippocratic times to the eighteenth century. My material was better organized than his, my evaluations considered more thoughtful; in short, I am first in the oral test, as I have been in the written one. . . .

"The outcome in the struggle of the Bureau Central is more doubtful. . . . The written question seemed made for me: *What are the occasions in which a surgeon should practice intervention in cases of cancer, and those where he should refrain?* 'What? Cancer, and you complain?' Yes, I do, because on these things I have some thoughts that are unlike most other people's; yet I owe it to my conscience to say so, and at every turn this shocks the holders of the ruling doctrines. . . .

"These are the remaining tests:

"(1) Agrégation. A lecture with 24 hours preparation; a clinical lecture of 45 minutes on two patients, and a thesis for which you get twelve days. The defending of the thesis . . . will take from May 15 until the first of June.

"(2) Bureau Central. A lecture of fifteen minutes on a patient. After this only ten candidates can go on; the others are eliminated.

"Then begins a second series of tests consisting of a lecture of half an hour on two patients, and two operations on the cadaver.

"I trust papa will arrange everything so that he can come the day after I shall have deposited my thesis. . . .[36]

"Do you know what I am doing in these days of torment? . . . Wasting my time. Here and there I go to the theater; I have reread some of the classics. And these last two days I have taken up Italian." Two years earlier he had taken up German on a similar basis. "Language instructors make you waste your time. . . ."[37]

Summer was nearly here, and, "a joke's a very serious thing," the moment for a bit of revealing whimsy had arrived: "What, not a moment's rest? . . . . Is there no pity in your hearts? After my trials you want to plunge me into the tribulations of marriage, from the Scylla to the Charybdis, from the *concours* to the wedding ceremony? I surely would love to get married but, please, let me first catch my breath! . . .

"You need not worry at the moment. The sea is calm, and no Parisian girl on the horizon. I am not exactly a romantic. My heart is not made of tinder. . . . Some brazen hussy, then?" No, he was fondling his agrégé hat, so ardently desired, so shapely, and so ruinous, setting him back 871 frs. 95!

"I would have to lie if I were to hide my self-satisfaction. But do you know what makes me even happier? The almost naive happiness of my father. . . . I still see him in the courtyard of the École de Médecine, at the moment when the results of the concours were announced. He expected it, he even knew I was going to be first. But when he saw me, surrounded and embraced by so many friends and cheered by the crowds, he nearly cried. He too had to embrace somebody and, running into some other successful candidate whom he did not know in person, threw himself into his arms and kissed him with effusion. I warn you that I am going to keep father here as long as I can. . . . For thirty-seven years this man has not had a vacation. You might as well let him have a little rest. You see, one does not have an *agrégé* for a son every day. . . ."

⁓VII⁓
Rickets to Rotifers

"The least questioned assumptions are often the most questionable."

$\mathcal{L}$earned societies were a way of life. To meet, several afternoons a week the men who shared your interests, if not necessarily your standing, to watch, perhaps to influence, the movement of learned stock and personal stature was vital for knowing and being known, for publications and publicity. Men founded clubs and societies to further a cause, to shine within a group, to feel secure in its bosom. The nineteenth century explosion of worthy causes exceeded even that of the population. A movement of movements was afoot, manifestos aplenty, and the gushing energy of progress formed multiple whorls of men bent on their burning tasks. Our present-day scientific meetings are sporadic, desultory, and lifeless in comparison.

From the seventeenth century on, the bulk of scientific progress was transacted in independent, at times secret and persecuted societies. Protection was not infrequently needed for frail new causes — and for their protectors as well. The Universities and Academies themselves, though endowed in Europe by the state, have enjoyed variable degrees of independence in professing opinion unpalatable to the ruling power. Unlike learned societies, they usually form part of the Establishment.[1]

The great French Revolution had abolished all institutions of higher learning as hotbeds of reaction and drains on a shrunken treasury. A savant was a suspect. But given the nationwide needs of the sick, the previously separate medical and surgical schools were soon resurrected. They also were unified as "Écoles de Santé." "Health" was to replace the outdated separate notions of Medicine and Surgery. The term "Santé" was discarded again, but not the unification. In 1821, an

École de Médicine and a unified, eventually Royal, Académie de Médicine came into being. It is, unlike the Académie des Sciences, not one of the four Academies that form the more august Institut de France or Académie Française.

As non-official societies blossomed, each published its Bulletin, Revue, Mémoires, etc., according to function, frequency, and subjects. Only a little later a privately owned medical press appeared on the scene (on the model of the British *Lancet*, founded in 1823), designed to furnish medical information for the non-affiliated professional reader. By 1801 nine clinical and eight non-clinical medical journals were in existence in Paris—too many for the founder and editor of the government-sponsored, all-embracing, *Journal Génerál de Médecine, de Chirurgie et de Pharmacie*. M. Sédillot felt badly about other people's "mania of publishing medical journals . . . spreading to France from abroad. . . . Every great European nation produces as many as fifteen to eighteen journals and 200 to 300 volumes concerned with Medicine. . . ." With Life short, he mused, and Art long—what would Hippocrates say if he were to witness this everwidening discrepancy?[2] Before 1860 not more than a dozen or so medical and biological societies existed in France; there were 85 of them by 1902,[3] and so it went on, by "spontaneous generation," fusion, or "fissiparité"—the split that may create a rival. Lebert, for one, found that all original work was channeled through these societies rather than through the Faculté and the Académie.[4]

Just before the turn of the century (1797), the desire for professional progress and for independence from the Establishment had made two young surgeons, Bichat and Dupuytren, found a Société Médicale d'Émulation. (Pinel was another founding member.) After Bichat's death, aides and prosectors of the École Pratique gathered in a Société Anatomique, which was finally constituted by Cruveilhier in 1826, with twelve titular members.[5] "It will perhaps please you," Broca, Aide in Anatomy and barely 23, told his parents in the spring of 1847, "that I am a member of the Société Anatomique. . . . I had to pay twelve francs for my diploma—just another piece of parchment."[6] The Society then consisted of not quite two dozen titular members and a few more dozen associates; an interne named Charcot was one of those. They met every Friday between 4 and 5 p.m., with the venerable Cruveilhier in the chair. A mere glance at the journal's index shows that Broca almost immediately became the Society's most prolific contributor and remained so for the next six or seven years. Two months after joining, he was on the editorial committee. "I had 31 out of the 33 votes; please note that I was delicate enough not to vote for myself."[7] Proudly he saw his name appear on the opening page of each issue. By 1849 he was a titular member. Aside from cancer, his first presentations showed his interest in musculoskeletal disorders: rickets, osteoarthritis, and muscular dystrophy. They all benefited from micropathological investigations.

Rickets is no longer a common scourge of childhood that leaves its mark on the adult frame. But before it became a mere matter of food additives, pathologists and clinicians could do no better than describe the visible changes in the bone and try to correct the crippling results of a mystery.

After Portal's confusing work, Rufz in the 1830's had referred to the spongy epiphysis of the growing bone, called *spongoid* by Guérin (now "osteoid"), erroneously attributed to extravasated blood and to secondary demineralization of normal bone.[8] This was the background Broca finally gave in 1852. The rest of his 78 pages shows that he was the first to point out the essential change in the tissues, findings generally credited to Virchow,[9] whose 99 pages on the subject appeared in the following year.[10] Starting from work done on the normal growth of bone (by Howship, by Miescher, and by Robin), Broca grasped that rickets was an interference with ossification, due to a primary disorder of nutrition. The work received a 500 francs' prize from the Académie des Sciences, thus recognizing in it the brilliant reduction of a complex problem to the single factor of faulty development.

Secondary demineralization, on the other hand, was operative at a distance from a tuberculous focus, a "white tumor," and analogous, Broca thought, to the softened bones in an immobilized limb.[11] The question of blood supply was not raised.

Osteoarthritis, *arthrite chronique sèche*, a related subject, Broca tackled in collaboration with his friend, Deville. In numerous presentations the two authors assembled all the pathological features that separate this condition from others affecting the joints, conditions that hitherto had mistakenly been ascribed to gout and acute rheumatism, or made into special entities, such as "ankylosis," "eburnation," and so on. They recognized that arthritis began at the synovial membrane, and they listed all the now well-known changes in blood vessels and connective tissue.

Broca, and Redfern in Edinburgh, independently but simultaneously, reversed the old Hippocratic idea that cartilage was as dead as hair and nails. To speak of diseased cartilage had theretofore made no sense, not even to Cruveilhier, until Broca originated the idea that cartilage (like teeth, cornea, and the crystalline lens of the eye), was alive through "imbibition" (diffusion) of a nutrient fluid derived from distant blood vessels. He described in detail the results of a chronic process, accepted and ill-understood to this day under the name *degeneration*. Modern textbooks to the contrary, all this was exciting news then.[12]

Members of learned societies naturally did not draw all their excitement from the scientific transactions alone. As Secretary for 1850, Broca was called upon to write the annual report. "It had been the custom," he told his parents, "to name, over and over, and not without a few shakes of the censer, the various members who had presented specimens or made communications. . . . The only purpose that I could see in this was to flatter each individual member and get his vote for being elected to the vice-presidency in the next session. . . . I planned to do differently and mention only real discoveries. . . . To cause such a shock meant to risk making enemies and compromising one's election. . . . The board meeting last Friday . . . was stormy. . . . The great majority of the committee are former secretaries. They moved to insert into the minutes a word of censure of my autocratic action. . . . The censure was tabled. The story made the rounds. . . . People wanted to hear this proscribed report. . . . Monday the great hall of the Faculté was overflowing . . . I was covered with applause. . . . In the evening, at Véfours [at the Palais-Royal, more than ever an elegant supper place] there was an unusually big crowd . . . the dean of the Faculté, four *médecins* or *chirurgiens des hôpitaux*, several *agrégés*, present and past members of the Faculté, many of them for the first time after a long absence. . . . My friends—you don't have warm friends unless you know how to make hot enemies—well . . . eighty out of the ninety members composing the Society attended in order to vote. . . . The committee left the room, beaten. . . . My election as Vice-President was unanimous. . . ."[13]

Next to bones and joints were muscles. Feet and their muscles have had a lot to do with the march of neurology. A series of Broca's contributions, beginning with 1847, were made apropos "club-foot," a burning subject. It is under this heading that they went into his bibliography and oblivion, because most club-feet have causes other than primary muscle disease. According to a modern standard text on that subject, "the conception of a group of primary dystrophic disease of muscle . . . was only fully developed by the work of Wilhelm Erb published in 1891. . . . The French neurologist Duchenne in 1855 . . . considered the disease to be a juvenile from of progressive muscular

93

atrophy. . . . Méryon . . . first established in 1864 an idiopathic disease of muscles. . . . In 1865 Duchenne concluded that the disease was primarily one of the interstitial muscle tissue. In 1865 Griesinger was the first to confirm the presence of abundant adipose tissue in the large muscles. . . . In 1866 . . . Eulenburg and Cohnheim . . . remarked on the absence of any changes in the central nervous system. . . ."[14]

Thus the development of the myopathic concept is traced from 1864 through 1891. Yet even Duchenne, rightly credited with much of the pioneer work, considered the condition dependent on spinal cord damage in 1855 and adhered to this view for another ten years.

Broca's *Description of the muscles in a case of club-foot* dates from 1851:

"All the muscles of this limb with fatty change still show muscle fibers that are well recognizable but more or less wasted. The fatty change is far from evenly distributed. The distribution is bizarre. . . . It seems proven that the fatty condition of the muscles has preceded and determined the formation of the club-foot. . . .

"It would seem natural to attribute the change to a lesion of the central nervous system. Such a lesion did not exist in the spinal cord which I examined with the greatest care. I do not know if any existed in the brain as this had been removed at the hospital. . . .

"If . . . due to a nervous lesion . . . the muscles would have to be affected according to the distribution of nerves. This is not the case. . . .

"Several muscles are adipose in the center, and healthy at the extremities, in others the fatty changes are at the two ends only. . . .

"To what are we to attribute this morbid condition? . . . I leave to others the answer, and only state the fact. . . .

"To sum up . . . (1) An idiopathic alteration of muscles is the primary cause. (2) This results in atrophy and finally disappearance of muscle fibers. . . . These muscle changes which I have extensively described in our bulletins of August, 1849, . . . and in February, 1850, seem of the same nature as those of which M. Aran has traced the history in the *Archives de Médecine* last September. . . ."[15]

He was too modest. Aran was linked with the tradition that confused a muscle disease with a central nervous system affection, as Duchenne had done during the 1850's. The young Broca was the first to observe, understand, and explain the essential pathology of muscular dystrophy. He may have been stimulated by Cruveilhier. In the following year the venerable pathologist told the members of the Académie de Médecine that since 1832 he had been demonstrating to his students the absence of sensory changes clinically and absence of changes in brain and spinal cord at autopsy in patients with chronic muscle wasting. But this "primary or idiopathic muscular atrophy" he ascribed to disease of the anterior spinal nerve roots, and he made no reference to Broca's brilliantly reasoned case for a primary disease of the muscle tissue itself; it was briefly mentioned by one of the discussants.[16]

A further point in the twenty examples of club-foot that Broca kept showing since 1847 was a refutation of "fibrous transformation," an idea by Jules Guérin, whom Broca had refuted on the pathology of rickets. It was fashionable to believe that in every club-foot the calf muscle with its Achilles tendon was the primary villain of the piece. A "convulsive" disorder, a "contracture" and "fibrous transformation" of this muscle, were to blame. Broca showed that the gastrocnemius was shortened secondarily, owing to the weakness of the antagonist muscles.

Not all deformed feet were the result of disease, and two or three eighteenth-century authors had drawn attention to the injuriousness of shoes.[17] In point of tightness, the ladies' footwear of Broca's time possibly outstripped the worst examples in history. "Shoes notoriously present anterior extremities far narrower than the digital portion of the feet. . . . Under heavy pressure these mobile appendices ride one on top of the other and distribute themselves in two layers, so to speak; one dorsal, the other plantar. . . . Other, paralytic, conditions, as in club-foot, may produce similar deformities. . . . Nevertheless in most cases shoes are to blame. . . ."[18] Bunions—*oignons* in French— were the natural sequel to this subject. In another study he exposed their relationship to bursae, nerves, nerve tumors, and chronic pressure in an anticipation of Morton's metatarsalgia.[19]

Broca also was fascinated by the man whose only means for earning a living was to thread needles in peep shows by using his big toe, helped by its three smaller fellows, his lips, and his tongue. James Ledgewood, he reported, was born of perfectly healthy Scottish stock, intelligent and handsome. But nature had given him no hands and no forearms, and no leg below the left knee; on the right foot one toe was missing. Through training the tactile sensibility of his right big toe and the medial surface of the second toe had become "excessive." "To evaluate the degree of this tactile sensibility I used the well-known experiment [Ernst Heinrich Weber's of 1834[20]] where the two points of a divider are slightly separated and applied to the skin simultaneously, so that one can see whether the subject experiences the sensation of one single prick, or of two distinct ones. . . . Repeated experiments on myself and a number of other persons showed that the pulp of the fingers gives a double sensation if the points are two millimeters apart; however, you need a distance of nine to ten millimeters to get the same result on the pulp of the toes.

"Well, . . . Ledgewood's first two toes show, in certain parts, a tactile sensibility as exquisite as that of the fingers of the hand. . . ."

As to the cause of congenital amputations, he expressed a thoroughly modern view. He thought it certain that "in this case at least, Montgomery's theory of intrauterine strangulation of limbs by bands does not apply. . . . Malformation or rather nonformation has taken place."[20]

He strongly believed congenital deformations were developmental rather than mechanical in origin. Thus when a case of fusion of two cervical vertebrae was shown as an accidental finding at the Société anatomique, Broca remarked that "the even appearance suggested a primary fusion of vertebrae analogous to that normally presented by the sacrum. M. Depaul believes the fusion to be due to some disease . . . that all congenital malfunctions are due to intrauterine disease.

"M. Broca believes in primary deformities, i.e., in aberrations in the germ, and not in accidents arising in the course of development; he calls these deformities malformations."[21]

Was this sort of thinking in line with Calvinistic predetermination? In any case, his reluctance to accept facts on superficial evidence, his tendency to look for a cause one step back, showed itself in the demonstration of a ruptured aorta caused by cancer that had eroded its wall. Broca remarked that practically all such ruptures are due to some pre-existing pathologic process, rather than to trauma.[22] On another occasion he pointed out that the so-called intra-uterine fractures of the fetal skeleton were practically always associated with other malformations, especially with the absence of other parts.[23] Yet this kind of judicious generalization was not allowed to go too far. Among the congenital dislocations of the hip, for instance, some certainly were due to acquired disease and not to malformation.[24] Broca also first described, in 1857, those bizarre, benign, usually symmetrical tumors of the long bones that have received a number of names, among which *diaphysial aclasia* is the most colorful. His own term, "exostosis of growth," makes a faulty growth process responsible for this variety of osteochondroma. The tumor is found on the diaphysis; with the lengthening of the shaft it has grown away from its origin, the epiphysial cartilage.[25] This work first appeared in the *Cyclopedia of Practical Surgery* by Costello, an English publication for which he wrote several chapters.

More work on the foot included the conservative treatment of dislocations of the astragalus (talus), against the prevailing operative mortality of 25 percent, and the description of subtaloid dislocation.[26]

The inventory of his 250 odd contributions to normal and morbid anatomy in the 1850's include a third pair of suspensory muscles at the back of the tongue, which he christened amygdalo-glossus;[27] the proof that the splenic pulp or "mud" (*boue* in French) is composed of organized material, nucleated cells in fact;[28] some new and correct opinions on the structure of the liver;[29] the arcades of arteries supplying the gums.[30] They include dye experiments to show "compression or obliteration of the cortical veins in the nephritic kidney and their . . . noncommunication with the general circulation."[31]

Another minor discovery was *Broca's pouch* so-termed in current medical dictionaries, defined in Gray's *Anatomy* only as the "tissue resembling the dartos tunic of the scrotum" and in a gynecology text as a "well-defined sac with an inner opening toward the inguinal region."[32] "M. Broca," the Bulletin of the Société Anatomique reported in 1851, " . . . suggests for it the name *sac dartoïque de la femme*. . . . The pouch accounts for inguinal hernias in the female, . . . for the shape of tumors in this region, and the formation of abscesses. . . ."[33]

Nearly all these products of a tremendous industry and acuity possess more than ephemeral merit; hardly any are without originality; some belong to the forgotten classics of the period. But Broca still owed the world a major work. For the time being, most of his contributions to descriptive anatomy found a place in a fine atlas that bears his name. At the age of twenty-five Broca took over this publication in installments; the third and fourth volumes of the bound work, published in 1866, dealing with the viscera, were entirely his own. He had in fact saved the enterprise from the brink of extinction, to which Bonamy, its originator, had taken it by his laziness. For the first two years, 1800 subscribers had been attracted partly by Beau, the excellent artist of the plates. When subscriptions were falling off, the publisher, Masson, offered Broca a fee of 200 francs for each new installment. The final contract included the author's freedom to interrupt production during *concours* or vacations and the right to authorize another edition. Cautiously, Broca did not bind himself in writing. As usual, he justifies the effort — thirty or more loose leaf installments — as "an asset for my ultimate *concours*," with a possible yearly profit of about 10,000 francs for three years, and a reduced need for taking on private students.[34] He did not get around to the nervous system, which was added to the second edition by Ludovic Hirschfeld and Leveillé.[35]

Excellence in anatomy and pathology meant excellence in surgery. After five years of Fridays at the Société Anatomique he began to add Tuesday afternoons at the Société de Chirurgie. On November 11, 1852, he was invited to Rue d'Anjou-Dauphine, formerly the home of Cuvier's, Geoffry Saint-Hilaire's, Jussieu's Société Philomatique, occupied of late by the Surgeons' Society,[36] to read as a preliminary to membership his paper on dislocation of the astragalus.[37] A committee composed of three men—none of them a particular friend of Broca's—reported on this and on his "footwear" memoir.[38] Larrey fils, a military surgeon, regretted that "the author had not consulted the military surgeons on these deformities. . . ." Seven weeks later Broca was a titular member, joining his friends Lebert, Follin, and Jarjavay, with Verneuil soon to follow. In 1858 Broca became General Secretary for five years and President in 1865; Follin, his closest friend and rival, was president two years later.

When Broca joined, the Société de Chirurgie had existed less than a decade. "Truth in science, honesty in art," was its lofty motto.[39] Several members of the Académie de Médecine had preferred to discuss surgical matters outside that circle of longwinded elders. By 1852 the Société had everybody with a name in surgery on its roster, had received an official "encouragement" in the form of 500 francs, and was soon honored by the government with the stamp of *utilité publique.* Soon also it moved to its own premises, the Renaissance palace of the former abbots of St.-Germain-des-Prés, just off that square, Rue de l'Abbaye. In 1935 it inflated its name from Société to Académie de Chirurgie.

As Broca's teachers in the science and the art, the truth and the honesty of surgery, there had been Blandin, an example of kindness; Gerdy, of intransigence; and Malgaigne, impressive not only with the scalpel but with the pen of the polemicist and the critical touch of the historian. As a young man Malgaigne had fought infectious disease and tyranny in Poland; later he made and demolished several reputations. Broca had followed Malgaigne's thought in the matter of strangulated hernias—complications due to inflammation—in his agrégé thesis.[40] But he refused Malgaigne's offer to take over the owner-and editorship of his *Revue Médico-Chirurgicale.*[41]

As he was reviewing the medical scene in the professional press, Broca exposed himself to some retributory criticism, which he wittily or sharply countered. Acrimonious or not, these exchanges covered a good many of the recent advances.[43] Thus, his article on chloroform anesthesia in *Gazette Hebdomadaire*[45] was a full review, including the history of its discovery in Boston, seven years earlier. "The news of this event was received with a mixture of astonishment, fear and admiration. . . . Admiration alone remained. The American discovery, more fortunate than so many others, was promptly accepted by the whole civilized world."

The concept of anesthesia and analgesia of course occupied most minds. Among the chemicals considered possibly useful was also carbon dioxide, at least as a local anesthetic. Follin had experimented with it, and Broca claimed success from injecting it into the bladder for relieving pain, relaxing the bladder wall, and eventually curing chronic infection.[46] In the 1960's treatment of the bladder and stomach linings—with carbon dioxide snow (dry ice)—was again being hotly discussed.[47]

In a more obscure corner of therapeutics, surgery was attempting to cure, not pain, but "vicious habits" with psychosurgery. Broca's case, in 1864, was one of "inveterate nymphomania treated by infibulation."[48] "A little girl aged five, very intelligent before the onset of her disastrous habit, had for quite some time indulged in masturbation. Her mother's surveillance, a chastity girdle constructed by Charrière, nothing would help. Section of the nerves to the clitoris I thought unreliable and leading to recurrence. Amputation of the clitoris meant irreparable destruction of the organ of voluptuousness and an excessive measure in a little girl who may recover. . . . During the operation this unfortunate child addressed words of tenderness and compassion to her genital organs, which struck us as revealing her mental condition and her ideas concentrated on a single aim. . . . Infibulation, much used in the Orient to enforce chastity, may have never before been used against nymphomania."

To the modern mind the participants in this macabre discussion on the treatment of masturbation were lacking in charity, not to say sanity. Broca was later "forced" to undo the infibulation and perform a clitoridectomy after all, likewise without success. He felt obliged to add a follow-up note in his annotated bibliography of 1868.[49]

Pain, infection, and blood loss were the three main factors that marred the operative results of those admirable surgeons. It is probably true that in many other technical respects, they would have had only a few things to learn from our contemporary art.

These three factors made necessary the endless preparatory work in the dissecting room, the years of practicing and standardizing operative procedures on the cadaver so that surgeons could find, practically in their sleep, the anatomical structures and landmarks and to proceed with lightning speed. It also explains why surgeons had a reputation of being rough and intolerant of their assistants. It probably was, at least in part, the strain of having to work so fast, for the patient's as well as for their own sake, that has produced some of those highly strung prima donnas of the healing art. Dr. Robert, talking about general anesthesia in 1863, still found it necessary to refute the criticism that anesthetics do not benefit the surgeon because, as some surgeons say, "they can no longer talk and give orders to their patients." But "those screams ... used to deprive us of the freedom to think and of the sureness in the use of our hands. . . ."[50]

No wonder, also, that many surgeons were far from knife-happy and that the time they actually spent in the operating room was far less than in this century. More time was used for other pursuits. Broca was a reluctant surgeon. "I have a private patient, a real one! He was on the point of getting acquainted with my scalpel for his fistula," he wisely said in 1854, "when, very luckily for me, on the day before the operation, he was seized with a terrible fever due to the pain which put him within two fingerbreadths of the grave. It has forced me to visit him regularly twice a day during the past three weeks."[51]

Loss of blood, too, often made nonsense of bold and even faultless surgical technique. To replace this loss became the subject of renewed scrutiny. After Harvey's laws of the blood circulation, after Sir Christopher Wren's first intravenous injection and Richard Lower's first dog-to-dog blood transfusion,[52] injection of lamb's blood had by 1668 become so popular in France, Broca told the Society, that it had to be forbidden except in cases specially sanctioned by a Regent of the Faculté de Paris. For a while, "transfusions" were given for everything, including "tired blood," with animal blood probably used exclusively. Dangerous as this obviously was, a madman receiving this treatment was reported "to have lost his confusion and stopped beating his wife."

The idea was revived in 1818 by James Blundell, an English obstetrician, who used small defibrinated amounts of human blood in half a dozen of cases and experimented with animals, but he and a few followers in the ensuing decades failed to do any convincing good. Professor Oré, one of Broca's Bordeaux friends, was among the first to tackle the problem on a larger scale. During the 1850's Broca collected 79 cases of transfusion for various indications. He rightly considered the procedure justified only for replacing blood lost. The method merited much attention, he felt. Thirty-eight out of 46 (80 percent) of Oré's cases of puerperal bleeding had recovered, and 5 out of 10 traumatic cases had also done well. The criticisms leveled at his stimulating report were mainly of skepticism; had this "operation" really been necessary?[53]

While blood-letting was on the way out and transfusions on the way in, taking samples of blood for testing was still far from the horizon. The spirochaete, the Wasserman, and other serological tests all belong to the twentieth century. As a student of Ricord, who had cleared up John Hunter's confusion between syphilis and gonorrhea, Broca had some interesting thoughts of his own on what we call "latent syphilis."

The discussion was on the demerits of "syphilization" (and note the spelling, please). This was a vicious but originally well-meant therapeutic outgrowth of Ricord's diagnostic method, which consisted of inoculating the secretion from a supposedly venereal lesion into the same patient's skin. If the ensuing lesion of the skin had a syphilitic appearance, that diagnosis could be made with confidence.[54]

Pocks (syphilis) was linguistically associated with *smallpox* — *la vérole* with *la petite vérole* — and the manner in which Ricord achieved his diagnosis resembled Jenner's vaccination. Consequently, if smallpox virus afforded protection against that disease, perhaps the "virus" of the syphilitic pocks might protect against this one? Indeed, there were doctors, *horribile dictu*, who in the 1840's set out to "immunize" healthy people against syphilis in this way. Fortunately, such benefactors were few and did not long persist. But in 1853 an Italian professor still advocated "syphilization" as superior to mercury. Cullerier, an old syphilologist, tore his book to pieces in the Société de Chirurgie—politely, as the Italian colleague was a corresponding member. The point Broca made in the discussion was characteristic of his searching outlook. "I deplore the error of syphilization as much as our rapporteur does," he said, "and I rise against those vast tatooings, those experiments which are always useless and often harmful. . . . But after the harm has been done, let us try to derive from it what benefit we may. . . . The problem of viruses is one of the most important and controversial in pathology. . . . The question is whether the syphilis virus can always be successfully inoculated" [i.e., is the effect of inoculation always certain; is there, in twentieth century jargon, 100 percent take?] "There seemed to be cases where on the contrary, an immunity did get established if only for a short duration, and the same perhaps could be deduced from a study of the census and health checks of prostitutes, subject as they are to frequent reinfection." Cullerier replied that he did not know and did not care to know. Follin supported his friend by saying that such a theoretical interest was justified.

Justified it certainly was, regarding our unsolved problem of "latent syphilis" and of partial or transient immunity to the disease. The

101

discussion was one of those where the speaker who raises a general problem meets the deaf ears of those who see only the practical side of the question. Broca wound up by saying, "As long as they are true, facts may be worthwhile without being useful. . . . If the syphilitic virus cannot be successfully inoculated, inoculation remains no longer an absolute diagnostic touchstone for the disease. Yet the differentiation of venereal diseases and the classification of the signs and symptoms have mostly been based on the result of inoculation.

"As a former pupil of M. Ricord's I have made his teachings my own because in most cases clinical observation seems to confirm them. But there is no denying that the syphilitic virus cannot always be successfully inoculated."[55]

The exchange of information about diseases and their remedies, national jealousies notwithstanding, had for centuries known no boundaries. By the mid-nineteenth century the reactions of one world capital to the learned goings-on in another were fairly swift, thanks to steam engine trains, telegraphy, the medical press, visitors, or corresponding members of learned societies. In the fall of 1859, a flurry of excitement, on both sides of the English Channel, followed reports on the use of a certain poison. On its spelling no agreement had yet been reached: in England it was called *woorara* or *wourali*: Alexander von Humboldt had earlier transcribed it as *uiaraery*. Some hundred years before, the South American Indians' arrow poison had been brought to Europe, and its power to paralyze muscle studied ever since.[56] There was a number of descriptions, by Orfila and others; work was being done in Paris, mainly by Claude Bernard and Brown-Séquard. It seems to have been the idea of a pupil of Bernard's, a Dr. Vella in Turin, to use what the French called *curare* for breaking the fatal spasms, especially of the diaphragm, in those frequent cases of tetanus that followed both accidental and surgical wounds. Dr. Vella was at the time in close contact with the French army, stationed in Italy to help the Italians win their freedom from Austria.[57]

"Desultory, for nearly 100 years" is what trials with curare before 1932 are called in a modern standard textbook of pharmacology,[58] and a monograph on tetanus of 1963 presents curarization as a "recent" therapeutic method, with credit to publications of 1947 and 1950.[59]

Dr. Vella saved a soldier by using curare. The news from Turin reached Paris rather quickly, and on October 5, 1859, Chassaignac in the Société de Chirurgie was able to report a second successful case.[57] This report was followed by, among others, a comprehensive one by Broca.[60] It mentions the priority of Sir Benjamin Brodie and Dr. Sewell, who as early as 1811 had made some abortive trials on horses.

Regardless of the mode of administration, Broca said, "curare acts the same everywhere, provided the doses given are in keeping with the particular ability of absorption via the various routes . . . these will determine its spread." Thus subcataneous injection or local compresses to the wound would be effective, depending on their doses, he felt, but the best and safest control could be obtained by mouth: diluting an accidental overdose by giving food or eliminating it by induced emesis.

Everyone agreed that effectiveness would best be checked by some standardized purified extract such as the curarine on which Claude Bernard was working. When Follin reported a failure in a patient he had treated by injections using a Pravaz syringe—each drop containing about 0.03 gram—Broca felt that probably not enough had been given.

In London skepticism prevailed. The *Lancet* issue of December 17, 1859, published a letter by a Monsieur Jules Broca, giving his address as "Brunswick Hotel, Jermyn Street" and the date as December 10, 1859. This M. Broca criticized a Dr. Harley for stating that woorara was not absorbed by the stomach. He quoted several French authorities to the contrary, among them a M. Martin and a M. Magron. Dr. Harley, in his rebuttal to the letter "said to be from the pen of 'M. Jules Broca,'" doubted very much if there existed such a person; the writer's assertions also were "palpably absurd," his authorities misquoted, and his ignorance such as to split Martin-Magron in two.

The author of a modern monograph on curare was taken in by the letter writer's identity: McIntyre (1947, p. 7) quoted the *Lancet* correspondence of 1859 and commented that "Broca (meaning Paul) came off second best."[56] Samuel Pozzi fell into the same trap in putting together Broca's bibliography. Somewhat cryptically, he listed among Broca's publications of 1859 an item called "*Suite de la discussion sur le curare (moeurs anglaises)*": *on the treatment of tetanus by woorara (The Lancet, 1859, December)* [in English]. Amused, no doubt, by the "English oddity," Broca had kept the item among his papers.[61] He was in Paris at that time.

The excitement regarding curare hardly over, Broca—his mind, as we shall see, full of more far-reaching projects—addressed the Société de Chirurgie December 7 and 14, 1859, on:

"*Surgical anesthesia produced by hypnotism.*

"The facts to which I wish to call your attention are strange, and so close to topics hitherto banished from serious scientific discourse that I first of all wish to plead for the Society's indulgence. . . . But the practical consequences are so important that I felt it my duty to set aside all other considerations. Any new method would deserve to be criticized . . . if a completely inoffensive anesthetic agent were available, if circumspection could safely hold in check those accidents. . . .

"In 1843 M. James Braid published a work called *Neurypnology or the Rationale of Nervous Sleep, considered in Relation with Animal Magnetism.* . . . [The facts had hitherto been mentioned only in the *Dictionnaire de Médecine*, etc. by Littré and Robin.] I had no knowledge of them when a few days ago my friend Azam, Assistant Professor of the Surgical Clinic in the School of Medicine of Bordeaux, brought them to my attention. He probably is the first in France to repeat M. Braid's experiments. In these two years his results have been remarkable. As he and I were discussing the nature of the cerebral phenomena constituting hypnotism, it occurred to me that I ought to find out whether hypnotized individuals might not become insensitive to the pain of operations, the way certain cataleptics probably do and, in a few instances, persons subjected to magnetism, notably the lady who a long time ago had been operated on by M. Cloquet. M. Azam agreed, and, to encourage me in following up my idea, he stated that several times he had pinched the skin of hypnotized individuals without producing any pain.

"Shall I admit it? The fear of appearing gullible made me first try the experiment surreptitiously and without a witness. A lady of forty, somewhat hysterical and bedfast for a slight indisposition, seemed perfectly suited for this trial . . . Taking from her mantelpiece a little flask of gilded crystal, I asked her to look sharply at this object which I placed at about 15 cm. in front and a little above the root of her nose. After three minutes her eyes were a little red, her face immobile, her responses slow and difficult. I took her hand and placed it above her head . . . I gave her fingers the most bizarre attitudes; she kept them thus until the end of the experiment. Finally I pinched her skin in several places using a certain amount of force, and she did not seem to notice it. . . . I applied slight friction to her eyes, followed by an insufflation of cold air onto her face. The lady immediately came to; and although during the experiment her responses had been perfectly sensible, she seemed to remember neither what she had said nor what I had done to her.

"In view of this result I thought that by pushing the hypnotic state far enough I might obtain sufficient insensibility for performing certain operations safely. . . ."

Together with Follin, they chose the next Sunday afternoon, Broca continued, and in the presence of the ward sister at the Hôpital Necker, he achieved a cataleptic state within two minutes in a convalescent girl who for the next seven minutes kept "various postures that an athlete would find hard to maintain. . . ."

"A second girl, more lively and intelligent than the first," was not a success.

"Despite this failure . . . we proceeded to operate . . . on a twenty-four-year-old woman . . . with vast burns and a voluminous and extremely painful abscess on the edge of the anus. Exhausted by pain, and very faint-hearted, she was in extreme fear of the operation, which she understood was necessary. . . ."

In the presence of the hospital administrator, Broca told her he was going to put her to sleep, using a lorgnette, and although after about seven minutes the woman continued to express fear, Follin made a large opening into the abscess. There was "a slight crying out, lasting less than one second. . . . She did not pull away and did not contract the muscles of the face and limbs. . . ." When awakened after fifteen minutes and able to lie on her burnt back, she remembered nothing, was cataleptic and insensitive to pricks for another twelve minutes. Next day Velpeau reported the event in the Académie des Sciences.

After Broca had again seen Azam he realized that Braid, in an appendix, had already advocated the method as an anesthetic.[62] His own merit, Broca said, would be only in rehabilitating a forgotten method, if indeed it was going to have any place in surgery. The hypnotic method, he added, was used by the sculptors of antiquity to make their models hold still, by the "omphalopsychic" monks of Mount Athos staring at their navel, by Indian fakirs converging their eyes on the tip of their nose, by students in Strasbourg and performers at fairs in southern France immobilizing chickens or roosters, and by North American Indians subduing young bisons. There also was Dr. Esdaile's *Natural and Mesmeric Clairvoyance with the Practical Application of Mesmerism in Surgery and Medicine*, London, 1852. Broca also drew the analogy to religious mass ecstasy and to the famous magnetic *baquet* [tub] of Mesmer himself. But there must be enormous individual differences, he thought, which probably would make hypnosis impractical for surgery, not to mention the attendant fuss. Most serious of all was the objection that in England, where the method had been started with some success in 1842, it had already fallen into desuetude.

For the time being, however, the wave of interest was running high. Follin reported three hypnotized patients, none completely anesthetic. Verneuil had achieved anesthesia on one second trial in one subject; then, on himself, only eye fatigue, double vision, a heavy head, but "no discomfort"; M. Mathieu, the instrument maker, very soon got tired and asked to be let off; and Dr. Auzias, a fourth subject, just felt dizzy. When Depaul doubted that Broca's patient had been anesthetized because she had cried out, both Broca and Verneuil protested that even patients under chloroform will scream. The important thing was that she could not remember anything on coming to.

Old Professor Cloquet, absent at the previous meeting, now gave his account of how a Dr. Chapelain thirty years ago had repeatedly "magnetized" a very nervous, sixty-year-old lady for pain due to an ulcerated cancer of the breast and again when Cloquet dissected the tumor and axiliary lymph nodes. Apparently insensitive during the procedure she broke out in laughter as he was cleaning the wound at the end. "These facts raised quite a storm when I communicated them to the Académie . . ." M. Cloquet added, "but I am prepared to repeat what I answered then, to wit, that . . . you may accept the fact without having a ready explanation."

Verneuil reported some successful experiments with a hypnotizing apparatus hurriedly constructed by Mathieu. Richet immediately applied to six patients what he had just learned but had to use chloroform.[63] A committee was appointed to study the question.

Too fussy and unreliable, as Broca had characterized it, hypnotism for surgical anesthesia died quickly, and periodic resurrections have been short-lived. In keeping with Broca's recommendation, its study as a psychological and therapeutic phenomenon mushroomed a few decades later to invade the clinic as well as the parlor. Dr. Azam, the Bordeaux surgeon, cautiously kept the flame burning, while Liébault and Charcot reaped fame as its high priests: the practice was only pushed aside by the method of Freud after he, too, with hundreds of others had come to France to study hypnotism.[64]

In the late 1850's most French doctors, if asked about Broca, would have identified him with his treatise *On Aneurysms and their Treatment*.[65] Three years of labor[66] and the critical analysis of 1100 records had gone into this "definitive" work of 931 pages, published in 1856. Probably everything worth reading that had ever been said about, or done for, aneurysms, including the nineteen known methods of treatment, was assembled here, critically, historically, theoretically, practically, from the pathological and prognostic points of view. It set the old and confused record of a puzzling, frightening, and very often killing condition and represented a great moment of medical history then and a greater one now. Broca was well aware that he had recorded not only history but surgery in the making "in the firm belief that real science is only dawning, and that the least questioned assertions are often the most questionable ones." His model had been Malgaigne's monograph on fractures and dislocations. "Like Malgaigne I have made it my point, to confront the classical descriptions with the actual observations . . . so as to clear the subject from both the erudite sterility of those who concern themselves with the past and the comfortable ignorance of those who concern themselves only with the present." Overcoming the "erudite sterility" of the previous centuries was the acknowledged success of nineteenth-century medicine. That it began to suffer from overshooting this aim and that Broca diagnosed the spread of "comfortable ignorance" long before it reached the extent of our time are more unexpected. *Aneurysms and their Treatment* was one of the last books in the classical manner as well as one of the first modern monographs on a relatively limited subject. (Its thorough index is still something rather unusual in French texts.) It not only developed an understanding of current ideas out of the succession of past lines of thought, but also marks the threshold for vascular surgery, which came into being in the second half of the nineteenth century.[67]

Broca added a novel concept about the mechanics of blood clotting, the basis of rational treatment: "Broca's active and passive clot," according to Matas, a later innovator and comprehensive writer on aneurysms.[68] Broca recalled that spontaneous thrombosis in the arterial sac, due to diminished flow, had in one form or another occurred to Jean Petit (early eighteenth century), Hodgson (1819), and Bellingham (1847). Oriented towards physiopathology and engineering, Broca saw the safest means of rendering aneurysms harmless as enhancing the natural tendency of clot formation in the sac: this was his *active,* i.e., good, hard, fibrous, organized thrombus. The "bad" kind, which he called *passive,* was the soft product of mere clotting that may be seen in the test tube. Only active clot could lead to the ultimate obliteration of most of the aneurysm (pp. 105 – 125).

This physiological consideration and the failure, so obvious, of most of the methods in use made Broca hail the new technique by O'Bryan Bellingham: indirect compression, safe from infection and bloodless but also incomplete. This meant a mechanical contraption, fitted around the affected limb and left in position, with only minor adjustments, for days, weeks, and even months, bearing down on the feeding artery through the intact tissues. What appealed to Broca was the production of "active clot," through a decreased and slowed-down rather than an interrupted blood flow to the lesion. Statistically "compression is superior to ligature," Broca concludes (p. 875). But only statistically for, he confesses, "I am mistaken. There is one factor in favor of ligature, that is, if science ever ought to make allowance for the self-indulgence of lazy surgeons. Ligature is a striking and swift procedure, apt to fill the spectators with admiration. Once he has properly tied the vessel . . . the surgeon's conscience is calm. . . . How far more delicate is one's position if one applies indirect compression! No laurels to be gathered here; instead of a dramatic curtain fall, there comes the sequel of those slow, careful, unspectacular adjustments, so tiresome in their minute detail. A thousand complications may arise . . . and the fear of failure, the awareness that most accidents during compression may be laid at your door, the insecurity that takes hold of the mind, to the point of wanting to give up, because the compression may be ineffective and because you begin to wonder if you had altogether been justified in avoiding the risks of ligation. . . .

"Circumscribed swellings in the course of arteries, usually pulsating, filled with liquid or solidified blood, often giving rise to a bruit, very apt to increase in size . . . their various characteristics due to communication with the arterial blood flow" (p. 3), i.e., aneurysms, were much more common in Broca's day than ours, especially the traumatic variety of the limbs, resulting from knives and low velocity bullets — according to statistics, particularly common among the English and Irish. Bloodletting, too, was a frequent cause. Hematomas in communication with an artery, but lacking a membrane around them, or sac, should be called "diffuse," not "false."

"There is nothing false about them," (Broca quotes Gerdy) "except that expression — due to confused thinking" (p.4). Social, systemic, as well as traumatic causes were recognized. Besides hemorrhage, aneurysms may cause pressure in their surroundings; embarrassment of the heart was not known. The communications between arteries and neighboring veins — a great variety of them — were classified into *aneurysmal varix* and *varicose aneurysm* in English. This distinction of Broca's — the second type may lead to serious circulatory disturbances (p. 24 ff.) but not the first — is of considerable practical importance. In such patients he described changes in temperature, blood pressure, bone growth, and skin appearance that result from venous and capillary congestion, the whole series of curious findings one associates with twentieth-century observers.[69] By 1861, Broca had engaged the services of Marey, the physiologist, who came over to the Bicêtre to study some of Broca's patients by his new method of recording the blood pressure. (Taking blood pressures as a routine began only some thirty years later; we still use a small modification of Riva-Rocci's sphygmomanometer of 1896. And only during the last few decades have the plastic tube and the blood vessel graft, together with a host of other safeguards, decisively changed our outlook and made the excision of aneurysms practical. This was literally murder before then.)

Ligature of the feeding artery is still being done, but only for aneurysms of the brain. On these Broca's book gives only an English post-mortem statistic (p. 44 ff.), showing a 0.8 percent incidence; they were not diagnosed then in the living. On the other hand, hemiplegia, transient or permanent, resulting from carotid ligature done for other conditions, was known since Ashley Cooper's first attempt in 1805 (pp. 467, 504, 599). In 1867 Broca was proud to avoid this complication by tying the common carotid of a patient whose internal carotid had ruptured "into the tympanic cavity."[70]

For the modern reader, the enjoyment of the book lies in the delicate precision with which it disentangles the developmental threads of invention, discovery, skillful application, and claim to priority. The latter often involves posterity and national pride. If history is bunk, modern historians love and live to debunk it. Broca is at his best as a detector and protector of the rightful claim; even these historical endeavors show his appetite for novelty.

Tying the artery, not close to the aneurysm, as Dominique Anel had done, but at some distance from it, was an ingenious method usually ascribed to John Hunter. Hunter was the first great English rival of French excellence in eighteenth-century surgery; Pierre Joseph Desault was his French counterpart. Broca quotes all the arguments in favor of the Englishman and is able to refute them. The year 1785 was the same for either man's original ligation but with a head start of six months for Desault. There possibly was a go-between, another surgeon travelling from Paris to London (p. 449 ff.). Broca has traced the whereabouts and the backgrounds of several illustrious eighteenth-century surgeons and their assistants. Moreover, "I think I can show that Desault acted in the full knowledge of the [physiological] cause. He discovered the real principle underlying Anel's method; Hunter was guided by an entirely erroneous theory. Science is on Desault's side, empiricism possibly on John Hunter's." Not only ligature but indirect compression also finds the two men pitted against each other (p. 676). "It is generally believed that indirect compression was the child of the so-called Hunterian method: an error because, both in France and England, Desault and Hunter compressed the artery before they ligated it." The year was again 1785; again Desault preceded Hunter by about seven months.

Another example of rehabilitation through detection concerned the forgotten Roman originator of all vascular surgery. Broca was the first medical historian to get hold of the writings of Antyllus (third century A.D.) preserved by a Byzantine compiler (Oribasius) who lived about one hundred years later. This transcription was also lost until 1831, when a Cardinal discovered it in the Vatican. A librarian in Paris acquainted Broca with this forgotten item.

Until Broca showed that this was the first man to tackle the frightening problem of incising an aneurysm between ligatures, the name of Antyllus was known only from a brief and garbled Arabic account, and his method had been credited, in a distorted form, to two authors. One of them was Paul of Aegina, a compiler of the seventh century. That man, Broca indignantly pointed out, had not only plagiarized Antyllus, but also made nonsense of his meaning; the other, a sixth-century compiler, Aëtius, had described a rather different method (p. 201 ff.).

On Aneurysms and their Treatment did not exhaust Broca's interest in the history of medicine. Several years later he seconded Verneuil in a series of lectures at the Faculté. "Lucid and scholarly," according to Garrison,[71] is Broca's charming account of Celsus, the famous Roman "surgeon." Celsus' books, Broca could easily convince his audience, were not written by a practitioner for practitioners. Celsus, unlike those first-century A.D. paid professionals, was a gentleman. His surgical treatise, part of an encyclopedia, was written by an amateur who may have practiced the art as a hobby for the benefit of family and servants.[72]

Such debunking extended to recent history and contemporary institutions and touched some very sensitive spots. Soon Broca was known not only as the author on aneurysms but also as the obituarist of Gerdy. Like several others that Broca wrote, this was an obituary with teeth in it about an extraordinary personality.

When Professor Gerdy died in 1856, the Société de Chirurgie's choice of a eulogist for one of its most eminent members fell on their youngest colleague. The honor was unusual but warranted by the fact that Broca, though only thirty-two and Gerdy's junior by twenty-seven years, had been his only confidant. Had the old lonely man befriended Broca just because he was so young and untarnished? They had a good deal in common, and Gerdy had been Broca's mentor and model ever since that young man's abortive internship at the Charité ten years earlier. Now he was going to expose rather than "inter with their bones the evil"; Brutus and Marc Antony in one, he would exhibit "the general wrong of Rome."

At every turn of his arduous yet brilliant career, Gerdy had to suffer from the corrupt practices of the academic system. Lack of protectors—the greatest of Gerdy's handicaps—was due to his contempt for seeking them. There were others, natural ones. Broca's

Éloge Historique[73] told the story of a tall, strong, but lazy farmer's boy, suddenly galvanized into tireless industry when his indigent father made him take up medicine in 1813 to shield him from the even more dangerous and bloody metier of soldiering under Napoleon I. But not only did Gerdy suffer from malnutrition, a tuberculous knee, recurrent chest trouble, smallpox, and a nearly fatal case of cholera while treating the victims of the great epidemic of 1832, he was also handicapped by acute anxiety. At oral examinations only a bag of ice applied to his heart was effective against those palpitations.

At the age of twenty-two he had published some fundamental papers on the structure of the heart muscle and the physiology of peripheral blood vessels. This was followed by his classical account of the structure of the tongue.

In the *concours* for the prosectorship Gerdy was up against a conspiracy that linked Bogros, who could dissect but hardly spell, to Breschet, the professor who could hardly dissect. Gerdy uncovered the plot by which Bogros obtained his written composition from Breschet by frequently leaving the examing hall. Bogros remained *préparateur*; Gerdy got an official appreciation. "Gerdy had told me the story many times, even shortly before his death. . . . It was not so much the men involved, but the act in itself: intrigue triumphant, fraud rewarded, justice violated, and the *concours* turned into a parody. . . ."

In 1833 Gerdy won the professorship in "external pathology" over Blandin; in 1837, aged forty, he was a member of the Académie de Médecine.

Now the stammering and speechless former examinee displayed his gifts of blistering and stern oratory, especially against the man he perhaps hated most, because he suspected him of underhanded dealings: almighty dean Orfila. Orfila had prevented Gerdy from winning a professorship in physiology. This was the first occasion for an open break.

Gerdy died at the age of fifty-nine. "In science, his great name remains; in history, his beautiful character. He is both one of the most original authors of our time and one of the most prolific. . . .

"His fault was to despise people; he wanted everybody to be like himself, without blemish. He did not care to remember that a person may lapse one day yet rise the next. This is why he made few friends. . . . He had two great passions: ambition and hatred. But his ambition was noble and his hatred without pettiness. . . . When his enemies were down he would not pursue them. . . ."

This "scabrous and dangerous piece" immediately appeared in serial form and with a comment in *Moniteur des Hôpitaux*. The

Société de Chirurgie printed it in its Mémoires only seven safe years later. Old Professor Cloquet was quoted as asking Broca if he thought he had told the truth. Broca (taking this as a reproach for some incorrectness): "I think so." And Cloquet: "You told hardly one tenth of it!"[74]

Truth and merit, denied by the perfidious establishment, had to be championed, not only to rehabilitate the dead but to help the living. Added to the couple of learned societies where he was a member and the Académie where he was not, there soon was another forum, and the man who received Broca's support was Brown-Séquard.

It had been Follin's idea to found a Société de Biologie. Biology, still a rather new word, was in Paris for a time almost synonymous with that Society. Biology and the nineteenth century started in the same year; the authorship of the term was German (Treviranus) and—independently or not—French (Lamarck). In August Comte's taxonomy of the sciences Biology became number five, followed by a baby sister he called Sociology. Charles Robin was a disciple of Comte and cofounded the Société de Biologie together with Follin in the summer of 1848. Under the life-long presidency of Prof. Pierre Rayer, they were joined by Claude Bernard, Brown-Séquard, Lebert, and a few others; somewhat later by Charcot, Velpeau, Verneuil, and Broca. Every Saturday at 3 p.m. they met in the loft of the École Pratique; there were no vacations; titular members signed an attendance sheet and were liable to a fine of one franc per meeting unless properly excused.[75]

The most prolific early contributor to the Society's Comptes Rendus was a somewhat eccentric and exotic figure: Charles Édouard Brown-Séquard was born on French Mauritius to an American father; his mother's name gave that distinctive hyphenated touch. Struggling for acceptance of his controversial work on the transmission of sensation in the spinal cord, he needed a helping hand. He eventually replaced Claude Bernard at the Collège de France and became known as one of the foremost neurologists and physiologists in two hemispheres, but in 1852 it was through Broca that he obtained a lectureship at the Philadelphia Medical School and later a professorship at the Medical College of Virginia. One of Broca's letters of recommendation, to Dr. Roy Wood (1797 – 1879) of the University of Pennsylvania, reads in part:

"For years Brown-Séquard has exhausted his resources and imposed upon himself incredible sacrifices in order to carry out extensive researches in experimental physiology. Today he has nothing left save an honorable character, profound erudition, and scientific articles which everyone can appreciate. . . ." Two years later, Broca wrote again about his friend, this time to the College of Virginia: "He is not a Frenchman, although educated in Paris and speaking the language like one of us; although acknowledged to be possessed of eminent talent, he has nevertheless been unable to attain an official position, only because he is a foreigner."[76]

The letters indicate that, barely in his thirties and Brown-Séquard's junior by seven years, Broca was the best qualified—or most willing—person in Paris to recommend to America this "American" friend who, incidentally, could speak hardly any English. Returned from this successsful trip, one of many, to the United States and England, Brown-Séquard resumed his prominent role in the Société de Biologie in 1855.

On July 21 of that year, Broca, as the rapporteur of a committee that included Claude Bernard and Vulpian among its six members, read a report to the Society on *Properties and Functions of the Spinal Cord*, evaluating the experiments of their eminent colleague, Brown-Séquard.[77]

Members submitting their observations, discoveries, or refutations of accepted theory were not only providing information but asking for a verdict regarding their claims. Whenever, owing to its scope, the subject matter warranted a more thorough examination, a committee was appointed. Where experimentation was involved, an author could substantiate his claims only by demonstrating them in a laboratory. The members of the committee might watch or repeat and check his experiments and spare neither time nor effort to obtain "evidence." The resulting report was often instrumental in establishing a reputation: the Society's stamp of approval acted almost like a patent. This document itself often had considerable individual merit as an amplification, commentary, or digest.

Olmstead, Brown-Séquard's biographer, seems to find it quite natural that neither Claude Bernard, a physiologist, nor Vulpian, a neurologist, headed this committee, but Broca. He considers him to have had at that time the requisite reputation as a specialist in neurological matters. But Broca's work on the brain was then still ahead. Broca, it seems, knew Brown, as they usually called him, through that generous man with a flair for promising talent: Martin-Magron, in whose laboratory Brown had made his apprenticeship. It may be of some relevance, too, that Brown was an ardent fellow-republican.[78]

"The report," Broca wrote,[79] "had produced quite a commotion in the scientific world; the *ancients* have not reacted to it yet—and, mind you, not for lacking the desire to do so. This revolution ought to have taken place five years ago, but Brown was then a poor devil of a poor republican, unknown, awkward in his speaking and writing, and with the only merit of simply being the foremost physiologist of our time. He was too big, yet not big enough. A conspiracy of silence was organized around him, and the unfortunate fellow, without bread or support, was forced to leave France and find a living in America. Two months ago he returned with some savings. I found this nonsense had gone too far and that it was time to stop it. When Brown came back to the Société de Biologie to speak about his experiments, I started a vigorous campaign for him, which has occupied the Society during several meetings. The president, although also an *ancient,* had to make up his mind and pursue the matter by appointing a committee. And so I made my report — not for the physiologists who would have liked to shelve it — but for the general medical public, who is indifferent to scientific information only when such is not available. Public opinion has spoken in favor of Brown. All of a sudden he is as important as he deserves to be; it is even being said that the *Institut* will have to give him the *grand prix* for physiology. This is how one gets the *ancients* on the move, and I do not regret having abandoned my surgical work for a few days in order to concern myself with this important physiological question."

Broca's standing up for Brown, shown also in an open letter of support,[80] against Bouillaud who had called Brown's discovery of the endocrine function of the adrenal gland "amusing," may also have been one of the reasons for the apparent coolness between Claude Bernard and Broca. Bernard and Brown were rivals.

Broca's report[77] said that the spinal cord was just a bigger sort of mixed nerve, until Charles Bell (Broca does not mention Magendie) demonstrated that it gives issue to separate motor and sensory nerve roots. But Sir Charles hated doing experiments, and so he concluded that the cord as a whole was likewise — and lengthwise — divided into a posterior half cylinder, which was sensory, and an anterior one, which was motor. "It would be difficult to find a point in the history of science at which contradictions had arisen as numerous and as odd. . . . Longet, finally, criticized all intervening experiments as artifacts . . . took a spinal cord, cut it across, stimulated the anterior and posterior segments at the head and tail end, and arrived at a slight modification of Bell's original theory. This became universally accepted, especially in France. . . .

"But it is only one more deception added to the many others preceding it — so much debris cluttering up the grounds of history. M.

Brown-Séquard's beautiful experiments have just torn down this well-cemented edifice, foundation by Charles Bell, capstone by M. Longet, and all. . . ."

There followed Broca's comments and description of the crucial experiments, some of which he had repeated himself. Vivisection without anesthesia was not an empty word: hemorrhage and shock required periods of recovery after each operative step. The dividing of the posterior columns of the cord (leaving the rest intact) done by Brown-Séquard was accompanied by much momentary expression of pain, the animal still being able to walk. Pinching of the hind limbs was not accompanied by increased pain, no matter how often the experiment was repeated by the members of the committee. (On one occasion they were joined by Dr. Marshall Hall from England, whose theory of reflexes had made history.) Stimulating with a steel pin the tail end of the posterior column cut produced pain much more severe and prolonged than when this stimulus was applied at the head end of the cut, a most surprising effect that suggested to the committee a pathway descending first, then ascending to the brain.

"Before sacrificing the animal, M. Brown-Séquard invites me to explore the grey matter. To this end I stick a needle straight in between the two lips of the previous section; it successively transfixes the grey matter, the white commissure, and penetrates into the corresponding inter-vertebral disc, i.e., it passes through the whole cord except for the posterior columns, which had been cut at this level before. The animal does not even notice this maneuver. . . .

"To terminate the suffering of the victim I open the carotid artery. . . . Before death ensues we observe that the hyperesthesia of the lower limbs increases as the animal weakens. . . . Now the slightest touch produces convulsive twitches."

The post-mortem showed Brown-Séquard's "staggering precision . . . not one fiber too few, not one molecule too many" of the posterior columns he had divided.

Nine experiments are reported, conducted to show that: (1) motor and sensory functions persist after the dura mater has been opened, (2) cutting of the posterior, so called sensory, columns does not abolish sensation, (3) on the contrary, it induces hyperesthesia below the section, (4) the caudal end is more sensitive than the rostral, which reverses ideas about nervous currents and their direction, and (5) the gray matter itself is insensitive.

Some of these experiments also showed that, with the posterior columns intact, sections including the grey commissure abolished sensation, and that the same section abolished motility. A midline longitudinal cut also abolished sensation. Section of the restiform bodies (inferior cerebral peduncles) remained without alteration of painful sensation, as did section of the posterior columns at the calamus scriptorius. Yet "their sensibility was abolished" as Broca put it. (By "sensibility" he most likely meant something we would call "conductivity.")

In vain do we look for a lateral hemisection of the cord in this series of experiments. Yet Brown-Séquard's fame rests chiefly on having shown that pain fibers in the spinal cord cross over from one side to the other; in this report this fact receives only brief mention.

No doubt a certain confusion accompanied Broca's admiration for Brown-Séquard's still somewhat confused work. The bewilderment is evident in Broca's concluding words: "We know that he is bravely working on a reconstruction to follow his work of demolition. We wish him every success. But even if he should fail in his difficult undertaking, his part would still have been great; for to have overthrown error is as glorious as to have found the truth."

Almost at once Broca championed yet another great scientific cause. It was germane to one of his recurring ideas about organic matter: some forms of it, seemingly dead, are in fact not. Cartilage, he had observed, though like the cornea of the eye naturally deprived of blood supply, was alive, capable of absorbing nutritious fluid, and subject to pathological processes, hypertrophy for instance. Active clot also did not seem to be dead. This makes it a little less surprising to find Broca as the rapporteur of yet another investigating committee. In March, 1860, he delivered that "masterly report, of a value undiminished by the passage of years, *On the revival of dessicated (dehydrated) organisms.*"[75] (The words appear thirty-nine years later in the speech commemorating the fiftieth anniversary of the Société de Biologie.) It is significant that one member of this committee, which included Robin and Brown-Séquard, was the chemist Marcelin Berthelot (1827-1907), a man of great fame for having synthesized alcohol and other organic compounds and thus refuted the generally accepted belief that the formation of organic substances required the intervention of "vital" activity. The subject, Broca said,[81] was of the greatest possible importance; it had been agitating the press and the academies for the past year, reanimating a debate that already had divided the savants of the previous century.

The animals in question, discovered by Leeuwenhoek in 1701, had been called *resuscitant* by Spallanzani, owing to their ability of coming to life, after prolonged desiccation, when again brought in contact with water. There were three such kinds: some belonged to

116

the *rotifers;* the others, called *tardigrades* or water bears, are a form of arthropods; the third group, *anguillulae* or eel-worms and wheat worms, are a subdivision of the nematode group of parasitic worms. All three varieties are barely visible to the naked eye. The controversy, on which the Society had been honored to pass judgment by the two contestants, was between Professor Doyère of Rouen and Professor Pouchet of Paris. Doyère was in agreement with Spallanzani and in favor of "revival," i.e., that these animals, once dead, did regain life. Pouchet sided with Leeuwenhoek in favor of "survival": that in this world there was no life after death; the "death" of these animals was only apparent. In 1745 Needham had struck a compromise by introducing the term "vitality," as something almost like life but not quite life itself.

To modern readers acquainted with the historical background of Pasteur's discoveries, Spallanzani's victory over Needham, the champion of "spontaneous generation," is well known, also that their contest was re-enacted in the 1860's, with the defeat of Pouchet (in the role of Needham) and his "heterogenesis" at the hands of Pasteur. A sort of vitalism was re-confirmed by the story of micro-organisms, but the idea of life created from non-life survived. In the eighteenth century this had been attributed to divine intervention and was, in fact, an article of faith. It was refuted by nineteenth-century science in the particular instance of bacterial contamination and infection. Paradoxically, spontaneous generation remained an article of faith in reverse and for materialistic science.[82] Some present-day biologists see in "anabiosis" or "cryptobiosis," as[83] Doyère's "resurrectionism" is called, a way life may have originated on earth.

In 1860 the metaphysical implications were even more obvious. The modern reader may shrug them off as a "semantic" or "pseudo-problem" and demand a definition of terms: "What do you mean by life, and what by death?" This attitude is as controversial as the subject itself. Broca felt that "latent" life, a current version of Needham's compromise, was an empty word, lending itself to any kind of interpretation. "Latent" was a concept borrowed from thermodynamics and not based on any biological fact. "Those who seek the truth must avoid all amphibology," all double talk. There was an honest decision to make between resurrectionism and anti-resurrectionism. Either an animal was in fact dead and could be resurrected by water, or it was alive and merely passing from a passive to an active stage. The point was to find by suitable experiments to show whether (1) there were appreciable and demonstrable signs of life in such creatures after they had been desiccated, and (2) whether the ability to return to life was "preserved under conditions *absolutely incompatible with any sort of life.*" The first point had not really been contested; as to the second, the anti-resurrectionists would invoke states like syncope, lethargy, hibernation, the state of the chrysalis, etc.: life reduced to a minimum, but still life. As it recently had been shown that protein coagulates at about 65 degrees centigrade, even the anti-resurrectionists agreed that subjecting the animalcules to 100 degrees centigrade would set up an effectively lethal environment and hence be a fair test. Never mind, Broca commented, that no one had so far been able to prove whether these tiny animals did in fact contain protein. The temperature of 100 degrees was a mere convention, he said, in accord with the experiment made with infusions containing "germs," as used in the argument against spontaneous generation. He did not express himself on that subject; Pasteur had not yet entered the fray.

During the early summer of 1859, there arrived for the committee in Prof. Gavarret's physics laboratory at the École de Médecine boxes sent by M. Doyère, filled with bits of moss taken from old roofs at the battlements of Toulon and other cities, all harboring the precious yet really quite common little things. In the late summer and fall of the same year, M. Pouchet, too, brought his leaf mold, collected on the cathedral of Rouen. Pre-dried animals on hourglasses were also delivered into the hands of the committee by the contesting scientists. An ink spot would mark the place on the hourglass where a desiccated tardigrade could be located under the microscope. Alive and wet, it had been left there three days ago; it had since dried out and showed no sign of life. At 3:20 p.m., a few drops of water were added to the "body." "At 3:38 p.m.," says the report, "the animal moves one paw." "At 3:45, it is entirely revived and begins to walk." And so on. By and by, more rigorous tests were devised. The dry periods were lengthened up to eleven weeks, under a dry vacuum, frozen, heated up to 140 degrees centigrade, with varying speeds in the temperature increase. In November the members of the commission began to devise some experiments of their own, introducing complications and controls and counts, until March of the following year. Moreover, one could quote well-authenticated reports from the literature of some rotifers surviving, dry, for eleven years; some wheat worms had even made it up to at least twenty years.

There were great individual and species differences, but "rotifers," Broca said in his conclusion, "may revive after a stay of eighty-two days, in a dry vacuum immediately followed by exposure to 100 degrees centigrade for thirty minutes." To him it was most important that the experiments gave no support and were in fact in contradiction to the vitalist point of view. They could be interpreted only in the light of certain physical changes taking place in the chemical properties of the albuminoid substances which compose the animal body.

To us these experiments have another significance, practical rather than philosophical. Transposed to a neighboring field, as yet untouched at the time of that report, i.e. to bacteriology, the study of survival (or revival) is germane to the corollary practical question of how to *kill* micro-organisms most effectively, especially their drought-resistant forms, Pasteur's spores. The committee's experiments might have shown the way to steam sterilization, but in the 1880's and 1890's the inventors of that technique had a more empirical approach.[84] Nevertheless, the resuscitating animals clearly demonstrated that even the creatures that die the hardest—or are the hardiest revivers—cannot stand high temperatures associated with humidity. The experiments also showed that fractionating the attack, i.e. reheating the organism after re-exposure to a moist atmosphere, will kill as certainly as will temperatures much above the boiling point of water.

These two reports were not the only nor the most important pieces Broca communicated to the Société de Biologie. A more personal scientific concern was to divert him from the medical field and to alienate him from the Société de Biologie. His flair and eagerness for novelty had driven Broca in so many directions that they might seem to be just so many distractions. Yet the productivity of that decade almost approached that of a lifetime in its magnitude.

⟊VIII⟊
Founding, Fathering, Feuding

⟿ | *"My heart is not made of tinder . . ."*

*B*y the end of 1853 every battle to establish an academic career was won. Broca had become a name well known by the profession in Paris and not unknown abroad. Yet entering his thirties, he was still without his own hospital service, without any private practice to speak of, and single.

Two or three years earlier he had called private practice and marriage "the two extinguishers of science."[1] But since then he had moved to 20, Rue de Grenelle, in the fashionable Faubourg Saint-Germain, just outside the Quartier Latin, taken a servant, and changed his mind somewhat.

One steady patient was the man with the fistula who had escaped his scalpel. As promised, Broca "pampered and doted on him," twice daily, in fact. *"Mon client et mon déjeuner"* —the phrase keeps recurring—were attended between 9:30 and 10:30 a.m., and again at 8 or 9:30 p.m., except Saturday. As for the rest of his weekly schedule, three times, for three afternoon hours, he saw the patients passing through the Bureau Central to be admitted to a hospital, a screening job he found tiresome. The other three afternoons were partly taken up with examining candidates for the externat. On four afternoons he attended learned societies; the fifth was reserved for giving "the last touches to the new issue of the Journal." He gave two lecture courses in surgery: one private; the other, for Gerdy, who was ill. One afternoon a week he worked with Beau on his atlas of anatomy; evenings and nights were spent preparing lectures and case presentations and writing. And Monday through Saturday every day from 11:30 a.m. to 12:30, he attended to his extremely modest private consultation. "Unfortunately I am not through with it all on Saturday night. . . ."[2]

The journals were *Moniteur des Hôpitaux* and *Gazette Hebdomadaire de Médecine et de Chirurgie*, founded that year by the remarkable, non-practicing Doctor Amédée Dechambre, later editor of the *Dictionnaire Encyclopédique des Sciences Médicales*, that treasure-trove of medical knowledge. Other co-editors at one time or another were Verneuil, Vulpian, Charcot.[3] But Broca quit the *Gazette* when on July 7, 1854, its title head bore the amplification: "Published under the Auspices of the Ministry of Education."[4]

He foresaw that Dechambre would have to play the game and always save the face of the authorities — "what fun!"[5] Underneath that fun, the "Young School of Paris," Broca and his microscopist friends, were earnestly trying to reform the standards of academic decency as well as surgical pathology. They encouraged the timid, but challenged and checked the profiteers of the frivolity and nepotism currently corrupting society and the profession.

"Fun," too, in an irritating way, was the return of Roman Catholic influence, especially through the Empress. But Church dogma could no longer be accepted whole-heartedly, not even by government officials, no matter how ample their lip service. The pressure was, nevertheless, sufficient for the Minister of Public Education to take a lively interest in what the teachers of the medical profession were writing and saying. Doctors were not infrequently received in audience, not necessarily to discuss the health of the nation or of His Excellency. Verneuil, for instance, had lectured on the nervous system. "He had made himself guilty of a crime," wrote Broca, "when he stuck to his subject and said nothing about the soul. . . . He also went astray to the point of mentioning that the union of the sexes was the law of nature. . . . The Reverend Father Veuillot who uses so much moderation as the editor of *L'Univers* wrote a leading article which said, in essence, Verneuil had employed his talent for showing that chastity was an anti-physiological virtue, that the soul died with the body. . . . The Minister of Education asked Verneuil to write to Veuillot a letter containing 'a forceful protestation in favor of the soul.' Verneuil refused, the Minister called for him, received him rather well, told him the most piquant things about the Ultramontanes, but added that one must humor these people, etc. After a long conversation, Verneuil indicated that he had nothing to add to his letter, whereupon Fortoul [the Minister] thought it better not to publish it.

"I tell you this government is stupid. On its side it has power, money, victory abroad, terror within, the Bank, a school for scoundrels, and the inexhaustible class of imbeciles. It has arrogated to itself the right to suppress every spoken or written criticism; it is Voltarian like the devil, and believes in nothing but homeopathy and the turning tables. But it will let itself be harassed by this creeping Ultramontane sect.... It bows in their face, but sneers behind their backs, and sends for the philosophers in order to tell them: 'See this drivelling, vile, filthy Veuillot? Take a good look and kiss his arse!' Amen."[10]

Meanwhile Broca returned to the Hôtel-Dieu, where he had been a nobody first, an interne later, now two months in charge "of the first surgical service in Paris—a good way of getting some practice in clinical teaching." It was vacation time. But those of the students who remain "I shall again teach how to take the road to the surgical wards which ... has been trodden very little since the death of Dupuytren."[6]

It was at this time that Broca, having been called to the country to perform a hernia operation (a house call!), missed the train back and had a strange experience for a lecturer: "I arrived in Paris at 4:30 p.m. ... changed clothes, was at five o'clock to dine with the Commandant and left him at five minutes to seven for my lecture. About half way through my talk, sleep caught up with me—having been up all night, battered by the ride from Les Ormes in an open cart, tired also from the emotions associated with the operation, which had been long, desperate, and full of unforseen incidents (clearly, they would not have called me for a simple case), and on top of it all that hurried, copious meal with the white wine from Bergerac.... I even had a dream in which I was talking to Alexandre Dumas. I woke up only a few minutes before the end [of my lecture], just in time to notice that I was through with the fractures of the spine. I was not a little worried. Had I said or done anything silly? The students would not have failed to laugh, but they did not. I asked my preparateur, but he said the lecture had gone as usual. He showed me his notes, and indeed I had given a very reasonable talk ... I pass this on as food for your psychological meditations...."

In 1854 the unheard of had happened: four consultations on four consecutive days, with greater earnings in one week than in all his previous practice.[7]

Meanwhile, history had not been standing still. At his coronation in 1852 Napoleon III had pacified his subjects—"Empire means peace" were his words—but from the spring of 1854 to that of 1856, France, allied to Great Britain (and a rather passive Austria), was involved in war: not so much to cure or comfort Turkey, that chronically "sick man," but to prevent the rising fourth great power, Russia, from conquering Constantinople and gaining a foothold on the Mediterranean. All concerned were crusading against infidels of one sort or another and preserving Holy Sites in Palestine. France must also defend her Catholic interests in the Middle East together with the rights of small nations: The Emperor that is, must please the liberals at home as well as the church.

The objectives and conduct of this war were as involved and confused as the action of Verdi's *Trovatore*, first performed the year before.[14]

From our Paris correspondent: "There is much talk about the cholera in the Army of the East. Private medical letters say that already by August 10, 6000 soldiers were dead of cholera, i.e., one in twelve. The English are much less affected. Our troops are demoralized beyond description. . . ."[8]

Naturally, the enemies of the regime were looking for any sign indicating its imminent fall. Broca did not share these illusions: "As to the event that will determine my marriage [i.e., the fall of Napoleon and the legalization of divorce], M. Thiers says it is much closer than the turning tables predict. He goes to Perrotin, his publisher, to hand over a volume of his *Du Consulat et de l'Empire* and to cash in 50,000 francs. 'You are going to have us arrested,' he says to Thiers. 'Never mind, just go ahead with the printing. This whole establishment will be cracking up by the time we shall be reading the proofs.' Orleanist illusions. . . ."[9]

On the academic front Broca felt strongly with the students who made life difficult for Nisard, a historian at the Sorbonne. Nisard propagated a way of thinking that became rather widespread in the following decades and is usually associated with Nietzsche; it has done much mischief. "He professed that there were two kinds of moral standards," Broca explained to his parents, "an ordinary kind that forbids stealing, begging, killing, committing perjury, etc., and another kind: the morality of great men and rulers who need not conform to these minutiae. Nisard had said this in connection with Tiberius, but the allusion to Bonaparte was clear. . . . For three consecutive days the students at the Sorbonne repeated the scenes in which I had taken part while I was young. Whistling at Nisard, drubbing the police sergeants until the military had to be called in. . . . This is not all. A few days ago . . . at the funeral of David d'Angers, the sculptor, several thousand students carried Béranger, the old writer of popular songs, in triumph on their shoulders, again shouting: *Vive la liberté!* . . . On the preceding day there had been posters at the

École Pratique: 'Patriotic students are invited to attend the funeral of David d'Angers to honor the ashes of a great and pure republican . . . !

"In government circles there is consternation over this unanimity in all the schools. One does not know what to do with all the arrested men. How deal with a thousand voices shouting in unison at Nisard's lectures 'Tell us about the morality of the Second December!' The École Normale in open opposition . . . the students of the École Polytechnique at the parade, refusing to shout *Vive l'Empereur!* and their school liable to be closed for this. In five years, when these young men will be at the head of the country, the government will fall."[10] The wishful thinking of the Royalists had finally invaded this liberal head, too.

But, as a bridge over the Seine and a boulevard testify, there were ultimate victories: on the river Alma and with the fall of Sebastopol. Boulevard Sébastopol then extended to the Left Bank: the present Boulevard St. Michel. It is fittingly ungainly. "This is Philadelphia or St. Petersburg, but no longer Paris," Théophile Gautier said.[11] By April, 1856, the Treaty of Paris was signed, more or less confirming a polite status quo, but a great boost to the regime.

Naturally Broca had to listen, year after year, to the chorus of friends and family, persuading, helping, pushing him to get married. By now he was quite willing, if not eager. Romantic love did not come into it. The future bride had to fulfill certain qualifications; he was choosing her as he would for a close friend or relative. He seemed to adopt a paternal attitude, that of his parents, in fact, raising thereby an issue of conflict: religion. To find a wife for himself might be easy enough, to find a daughter-in-law for his mother more difficult. Clearly of two minds, he would comply with the wishes of his family but resent them.

"All my life has been a long act of obeisance. You ordered me to be a *pion* and I was a *pion*; to study medicine and I did; to work and I have; to get married, and I am ready. . . ."

But it was not easy. They would not let him marry a Catholic girl, while pious Protestants would not give him their daughters on account of his undisguised lack in religious fervor.

Fortunately France is a big country and Paris a big city with many potential brides, some even Huguenots; some of these will even consider a prospective husband whose devotions do not include the cause of Protestantism. The tragi-comic predicament of falling between two stools, was to have a happy solution (the pun is inevitable), Lugol's solution.

The liquid that bears this name is a well-known mixture of iodine and potassium iodide, one that later became a standard staining technique in bacteriology and a treatment for hyperthyroidism. Dr. Jean Guillaume Auguste Lugol had been a prominent and prosperous physician since 1812 and an authority, based on many a pertinent publication, regarding the treatment of scrofulous (tuberculous) lymph-nodes with iodine. This he had introduced into medical practice in the 1830's, in various forms and vehicles of application — internal, external, topical, and general, even as iodine baths. Despite his excellent reputation he had no higher academic title to his credit. "Every day," a critical medical directory commented at the time, "the Institut gives rewards to discoveries of infinitely lesser importance. The Académie de Médecine would have lost none of its lustre had it opened its doors to M. Lugol, and more than one of its members might have reason to envy the fruitful career of this man!"[12]

Perhaps not insignificantly, we find Broca publishing a paper in the 1858 *Moniteur des Hôpitaux* with the title: *On a vast abscess, due to congestion of the iliac fossa, groin and buttock, cured by a single iodized injection.*[13] But by then, Lugol was no longer alive, having died in 1851 a widower, at the age of sixty-five, leaving behind a boy and a girl.

Adèle Augustine Lugol had been brought up by an aunt. A somewhat severe beauty, we gather, she no doubt fulfilled all the Brocas' criteria of nubility. And so we come to this entry in the Marriage Register of the Protestant Parish in Paris, No. 307, p. 159. "Monday, July, 1800 fifty seven [sic] upon Deposit of a certificate of civil marriage contracted the same Day in the Mairie of the 1st *arrondisst* of the City....They received the nuptial benediction by the minister Athanase Coquerel, minister of the Holy Gospel, one of the Pastors of the Reformed Church of Paris." Signed P. Broca — and nearly a score of others, including Jean Benjamin and Annette Broca, come from Sainte Foy for the occasion, cousin Élie and his family, Augustine's brother and their mother's family, with Pastor A. Coquerel winding up the procession.

"Marriage," the 1929 or 14th edition of the *Britannica* cooly informs us, "marriage as an ideal is the end of a romance; it is also the beginning of a sterner task...." It would be a distortion, albeit of a legitimate view, says the article, to deny out of hand that marriage is in some way "the operation of the sexual instinct and the sentiments connected with those instincts, such as ... the manifestations of romantic love," a distortion also to affirm that it has "its foundation in

125

Mme. Augustine Broca (1835-1914). (Oil portrait owned by a member of the family. Artist unknown.)

economic relations." Marital sex is given in the *Britannica* its due for being, like economics, only a means to an end: the offspring.

These austere reflections are added here for the reader who regrets, as the author does, the lack of information about how Paul courted Augustine. Mme. Broca chose not to suppress her late husband's earlier, vexed if sober self-revelations in this matter;[14] had she also permitted us to read his account of the ultimate courtship she may possibly have made him appear less cold-blooded. But as she chose not to, we are left to speculate and to argue about romance, as opposed to the realistic appraisal of a partner's suitability: physical, intellectual, social, and economic. Was such an appraisal all Broca had in mind, at least vis-à-vis his parents? Despite his mother's opinion, which "found

126

him wanting in matters of amorous dreaming,"[15] was it only his supreme endeavor to be rational?

As to the "means to an end" given in the above definition, by June 7, 1858, i.e., within a year, Broca was able to write to Amédée Deville in London: "Although I have no time to spare, I do not want you to see my wife's delivery announced to you in a strange handwriting. I am the father of a little girl who came quite fast and without giving her mother any trouble. It was all over in four hours, and things could not be better. I am happy and must tell you about it because I know it will please you./Yours ever,/P. Broca"[16]

The baby girl was christened Pauline; in the next year Auguste was born; André was last in 1863. From 1857 until after Broca's death they all lived at 1 Rue des Saints-Pères in the corner house facing the Louvre across the river. It was a fairly new building, very comfortable for the period, and only a few steps from the Académie de Médecine.

The family establishment on the bank of the Seine reinforced the ties with Sainte Foy. Augustine took more than her share in the correspondence and became very close to her new parents; the children soon eclipsed the Faculté as news worth reporting. If anything cast a shadow on this union, it can only have been Paul's foreseeable passion for work and Augustine's worry for his health. His habits and attitudes changed little; she had married one of the busiest husbands, in Victorian days at that. "Today, Sunday, we had a conjugal outing," Augustine wrote after one and a half years of marriage, "and spent two hours at the Louvre. I said to Paul that once a week he might well constrain himself to go out with his wife. As a matter of fact, this does not displease him too much; he is particularly fond of taking Mlle Pauline along."[17]

In 1864 another member of the family came to join their household: old Dr. Benjamin. Mother Broca had died.

Shortly afterwards Broca fought one of the few lost battles of his life, on slippery ground and against a well-entrenched foe: the Presbyterial Council of the Reformed Church of Paris. The subject of contention seemed innocent enough: his registration as a voter on the Council's electoral list. As there was no separation of Church and State, the Reformed Church, like that of any other denomination, was subject to rulings issued by the Ministère de la Justice et des Cultes. But these rulings were vague enough so as not to curb all exercise of freedom—or the abuse of it by those holding power within the religious organization. Broca maintained the law was on his side when he demanded to be registered as a voter by simply mailing in the documents that identified him as a Protestant. That he did not attend the service he thought irrelevant and a matter of his own conscience. Had he not always paid his dues faithfully? A law required voters' registration lists to be open to inspection the year round. The Protestant Council, however, made these lists available only between Christmas and New Year and insisted on the personal attendance of each applicant. The reason for this policy was, no doubt, to lecture and humble whomever the Council regarded as a black sheep, but especially, it seems, to reduce the number of new and potentially liberal voters who might upset its conservative composition.

In a printed pamphlet of well over 6,000 words,[18] directed as an open letter to the Minister of Justice and Religious Affairs, Broca regretfully felt obliged to expose the underhand dealings of his Church in what the Council called the "affaire Broca."

A hundred odd years later Broca's insistence may appear quixotic, in poor taste, almost paranoid. But he had to bring up a family in a certain faith, and the composition of the purveyors of this faith was not irrelevant. He must have felt that time and energy spent on this matter were justified, if democratic process and liberal ideas were ever to gain a hold—at least in his own Church, no matter how little attracted he himself was by the cult or even the tenets of his religion.

Feuding and founding continued. To found a family had been expected of him as the outlet and target of normal virility. Had he or anyone else expected that this would not satisfy his excess energy, that he also would have to become the founder of a learned society? Was he influenced in this step by the fact that Follin, closest friend and perpetual rival, had founded one such, the Société de Biologie, a decade earlier? Historical facts seem obvious and inevitable, yet the details bear the hallmark of chance and unforeseen struggle.

At the fiftieth anniversary of the Société de Biologie in 1899, Professor Gley, its president, made some remarks that must have sounded naive, if not, on the contrary, disingenuous to those who could still remember the whole story. Gley was wondering why some of the important work of that early period, germane to the Society's purpose, had not been transacted in its bosom. He gave Broca's discoveries as an instance of this strange omission. Perhaps, he surmised, the anatomical nature of Broca's work had masked its high physiological import. "It is a fact that, after founding his beloved Société d'Anthropologie, he left the older neighboring Society and devoted himself entirely to his own." Gley also admitted that the Société de Biologie had then kept away from such subjects as transformism or Darwinism. Again he wondered why. Had this been due to Robin, who as a disciple of Comte was out of sympathy with evolutionism?[19] In preparing his speech, he may have been looking exclusively through his own

Society's proceedings, and, of course, the answer to his query was not there. What he found and gave prominence to was Broca's report on Brown-Séquard[20] and on the "resuscitant animals."[21] The first had taken place in 1855, the second in 1859, *after* Broca had founded his own Society; both were published in the *Comptes rendus* of the Société de Biologie. In vain would one look in these pages for a memoir that Broca read *between* these dates, i.e., in 1858. Yet he had read it, then and there, at least in part. The subject of it soon grew to a four-part essay and found a home in a new periodical, just founded by Brown-Séquard: the *Journal de Physiologie.*[22] It was reprinted as a 238-page monograph; part four was again published six years later under the title, *On the Phenomena of Hybridity in Genus Homo,* in an English translation commissioned by the brand-new Anthropological Society of London, as one of the basic books for its library. It shows that the question of species is the origin of anthropology. Why the omission of this important work from the publications of the Société de Biologie?

The story starts in a rustic setting: "On a trip to Montauban in October 1857," Broca had written, "my friend M. Léonce Bergis, who is a distinguished agronomist, took me to his country house and showed me three crossbred animals which he had brought from Angoulême as a gift from M. Roux."

They were, as Broca said in his memoir, a cross between a female rabbit (*lepus cuniculus*) and a male hare (*lepus timidus*) — two different species. Buffon had already tried to cross them, and a certain Carlo Amoretti had in 1774 been invited by the Abbé Domenico Gagliari to dine on such an excellent hybrid animal.

M. Bergis in Montauban was the possessor, Broca goes on to say, of two female hybrids of the first generation (½ hare, ½ rabbit) and a male animal of the second generation (¾ hare, ¼ rabbit). Each female had already had a litter of five that were ½ hare on the maternal and ¾ hare on the paternal side, i.e., themselves ⅝ hare and ⅜ rabbit. "M. Bergis was kind enough to let me have one of these. I demonstrated it at the Société de Biologie a few days after my return to Paris. The animal is being taken care of at the Jardin des Plantes by my colleague, M. Vulpian. Although kept in a narrow cage, it has developed into a finer fellow than any ordinary rabbit. With the existence of leporids well established [this is what Broca called them], more complete information about their fertility was needed. I next went to Angoulême. My colleague Macquet introduced me to M. Roux who showed me his establishment with the most charming eagerness. This was October, 1857; the six or seven generations of leporids then already in existence represented a rather lucrative business. During that year M. Roux had

129

sold more than one thousand on the Angoulême market. There still were many left, of every age and generation. Within a few moments I was able to recognize at a glance the various degrees of crossing.

" . . . A second trip to Angoulême reassured me of the continuing prosperity of M. Roux's establishment, the leporids now being in their fourth generation.

" . . . It is necessary to give M. Roux's experiment a determined physiological direction, but it will take me five to six years to obtain decisive results. . . . What in addition now must be established is whether the direct crossing is fertile in the direct line." M. Roux had taken three years to get the two species to reproduce, we learn. Copulation would take place only at night and only when the young, rather timid, hare did not sense any human around. The wild hare was much more gentle and played much longer with the female rabbit than a wild rabbit male would before copulation. The litters of five to eight were also smaller than the twelve or so produced by domestic rabbits. But wild hares among themselves rarely had more than four or even fewer offspring. The first generation ½ × ½ leporid looked very much like a rabbit.

What conclusions did this observation in animal husbandry suggest? "From now on one would either have to fuse in one species, hares, rabbits, and leporids — which is absurd — or admit . . . that the classical doctrine of the permanence of species is entirely mistaken.

"We have shown *a priori* that this theory rests on a pure hypothesis and on false reasoning; *a posteriori* it is impossible to attribute the enormous variety of races in the family of domestic dogs to climate and accident; a conclusion which also holds for the races of man. . . . Hybridity cannot serve as a touchstone for [distinguishing] species."

Clearly, this conceptual result of the mating process was as exhilarating to some as it appeared almost obscene to others. It was not so much the bare fact as its implications that were so scandalous. On a minor scale, the storm was akin to that unleashed by *The Origin of Species* published a year later: a controversy about the definition, and the finitude, of species.

The members of the Société de Biologie were no old fogies; they prided themselves on their eagerness to accept new and audacious views. But there were limits. It was a topic that questioned the story of Genesis; it might shock outsiders and jeopardize the Society's standing with the authorities.

Professor Rayer, first and lifelong president of the Society, "full of prudence and diplomacy . . . was embarrassed almost to the point of malaise."[23] He begged Broca to desist from further propounding these embarrassing theories. Broca complied; at the same time he insisted that a forum must be made available for his or anybody else's unorthodox views. He was willing to give in, not to give up. To have Brown-Séquard return a service and publish the work in his journal was not enough. He was not alone in feeling that something else must be done to offset this frightened departure from the professed aim of the Society: the free interpretation of facts. Even fifty years later, the memorial speaker may have wished to cover up with a few words of surprise the discreditable incident.

Broca's permanent allies rallied around him. Follin, Verneuil, Robin, Brown-Séquard, and another physician were ready to form the nucleus of a nascent society.[24]

As "biology" had been chosen to serve to denote a number of disciplines concerned with the manifestations of life, "anthropology" was to integrate a somewhat related group of subjects centered on man. "To found" not only means to establish a base, but also to melt or mix. To create something novel from the association of existing parts, as in the *Gesamt-Kunstwerk* of Richard Wagner's operatic experiment, was typical for the grandiose and synthetic nineteenth-century mentality. Anthropology, as Broca and his friends understood the term, also grew directly out of his present work on hybridity, for it showed man subject to the same laws as the animal world. If *anthropologos* was used by Aristotle to characterize people who talk too much about themselves or their acquaintances, it began to do double duty in the sixteenth century as a term describing the physical and the mental frame of man. It thus covered the quirks of personality and for some hundred years was synonymous with what we call psychology. The crossroads at which anthropology—and the concept of man— continued to stand in Western thought is clearly indicated in a dictionary published in 1693. For according to the *O.E.D.*, Bartholin (Thomas Bartholinus?) divided "*Anthropologia* . . into two parts; viz. *Anatomy*, which treats of the Body, and *Psycology* [sic], which treats of the Soul." In the nineteenth century, anthropology chose to go its own way, so did psychology, equally split into an experimental and an introspective branch.

The systematic exploits of eighteenth-century explorers and world travellers set man up as a subject no longer exclusively for the moralist. Physicians, lawyers, and statesmen began to share the topic with geographers, ethnographers, and naturalists who began to see man in the context of natural history. Human specimens from the four corners of the world, in all stages of cultural development, were now frequently confronted with each other; they aroused an ardent curiosity and the need for comparison and classification.[25] Moral questions, economic considerations, and social trouble aroused a good deal of feeling. The problem of slavery, fiercely discussed everywhere, was just about to start a civil war in the Western Hemisphere. In France, as elsewhere, societies purporting to study such questions — too controversial for the universities and academies — had been in existence for some time. In Paris, a Société des Observateurs de l'Homme, uniting naturalists, physicians, archeologists, historians, and philosophers, had been founded in 1799, soon after the great revolution. Its projects had been the drafting of an "anthropological topography of France" and an "anthropography of the various regions of the world." But its practical aims of instructing world travellers, collecting of museum specimens, and setting of prizes more and more turned the proceedings toward historicism and psychological speculation. In an atmosphere of Napoleonic wars, continental blockade, political enthusiasm, and philanthropism its members ended up by concentrating on the independence of Greece — and by being merged with the Société Philanthropique.

A similar fate awaited a more active group of scientists who called themselves Société Éthnologique de Paris. In 1839, it, too, had started out with the firm purpose of studying the physical as well as the cultural properties of the human species. But it was drawn more and more into the controversy about slavery. When in 1848 this was officially abolished in France, the Société Éthnologique found it had lost its raison d'être and quietly stopped meeting. But it had been a model for the Ethnological Society of New York, founded in 1842, and for its London counterpart of 1843.

In Paris, anthropology, under this title, had had an official chair for three years. Armand de Quatrefages de Bréau had given this name to the subject he taught in his position as Professeur d'Anatomie et d'Histoire Naturelle de l'Homme. Coined in 1838 by Quatrefages' predecessor Serres, who is also responsible for the term "paleontology," the title was a significant amplification of "Human Anatomy." The department was housed in an old royal institution, the famous Muséum d'Histoire Naturelle, in the Jardin des Plantes, formerly Jardin du Roi, made world famous by the great Buffon. Buffon's *Histoire Naturelle de l'Homme* was published in 1749, with clear indications that the author considered his own genus of *Homo sapiens* a worthy subject for the zoologist or at least as something to be studied by the same method as the rest of nature.[23] The trend of studying man as an object in nature also coincided with the slowly developing principle of conferring human rights to every member of that species.

According to Balzac, it was high time for promoting anthropology in France. In a lesser known short novel from his *Scenes of Provincial Life,* called *The Old Maid,* published in the 1830's, Balzac had understood only the psychological and historical side of the term, as a science of "myths, pressing on us from all sides, good for everything, explaining everything," good even perhaps to prevent revolutions. He pleaded "the need for this new discipline" and appealed to the enlightened solicitude of our ministers of public education to create chairs of anthropology, a science in which "we have fallen back behind Germany,[26] the Germany of Kant and especially Blumenbach, father of racial science."[27]

Around the river Dordogne, where Paul Broca had grown up, there existed a natural storehouse of prehistoric material. Here he had come to grips with fossil bones — and with Cuvier — at a time when he still had hopes of becoming an engineer; then, as an aide in anatomy, he had been selected by Alexandre Thierry to sort out and describe the skeletal remains in a recently dug up ecclesiastical cemetery.[28] In the eleven years since, filled though they had been with innumerable medical matters, Broca had kept reading not only history but almost everything published about paleontology. He was thoroughly familar with Buffon's and Lamarck's ideas regarding the transformation of species as well as with the more recent views on the pre-biblical, the awful, the unmentionable antiquity of man.

There were two obstacles to the founding of a society where all these matters might be openly discussed: finding members and getting permission from the government. The would-be founder's burning need for such a venture was at first not widely shared. Likely candidates were the former members of the dissolved Société Éthnologique. But they were a tired lot and refused to join. It took six months to add another thirteen names to a nucleus of six: Béclard, professor of surgery, and de Fleury, another agrégé; three members from the staff of the Muséum d'Histoire Naturelle: Isidore Geoffroy Sainte-Hilaire, Lemercier, Gratiolet; more physicians: Delasiauve, Rambaud, Antelme, Bertillon, Dareste, and Martin-Magron, the professeur libre of the École Pratique who had coached Broca and his friends for the internat. Finally there were two not strictly medical men besides Geoffroy Sainte-Hilaire: de Castelnau, editor of the *Moniteur des Hôpitaux,* and Grimaud de Caux, an elderly hygienist. Most of the men were in their thirties.

With these eighteen signatures, some given half-heartedly and only as a favor, Broca once again went to the Minister of Public Education. Rouland found the matter potentially embarrassing, perhaps outright dangerous. Worse than ethnology, which smacked only of anti-slavery, anthropology suggested subversion and the spirit of 1848; something vaguely degrading to man's immortal soul, possibly in conflict with the teachings of the Church and the interests of the Empire, perhaps even a threat to the precarious security of His Majesty. Why should an Imperial Minister whose position was not too secure take such risks?

Rouland decided he would not let himself be pushed into a decision. It never was good policy to say "no" outright. With impeccable logic the Minister argued that, after all, the case was outside of his competency. There was a question of security involved. The right of assembly was something to be granted by the Prefect of Police; Rouland forwarded the application to him.

But the art of dodging was not confined to the cautious man who was the Minister of Public Education in 1858. The Prefect of Police likewise did not wish to dirty his fingers by permitting on the one hand, or by outright forbidding, on the other, a score or so of ideologists to meet twice a month for a couple of hours in order to discuss obscure topics. Instead of throwing the file into the waste basket, as probably had been the hope of the sender, he politely addressed it back to the Minister of Public Education. Both these experienced officials expected, no doubt, that the signataries, especially the initiator, would get tired of running to and fro asking for audiences.

They had not reckoned with the determination of M. Broca. He decided that his old tactic of going straight to the top was not always the best approach to getting things done. A division chief of the Prefecture proved to be a much more yielding target.

Broca also could not have chosen any better spokesman for this project than Ambroise Auguste Tardieu, professor agrégé in legal medicine since 1844, a pupil and successor of Orfila, a helpful colleague at the Hôtel-Dieu, soon to be a full professor and dean of the Faculté de Médecine. As to popularity with the police, Tardieu was unsurpassed. Only recently he had published his report on the 156 victims of the Orsini bomb plot that had nearly killed the Emperor on his way to the Opera. Abortion, infanticide, strangulation, suffocation, poisoning—Tardieu knew all the answers. A brilliant casuist, experienced in the ways of the legal mind, he also knew how to put the case for anthropology in such a fashion as to make it acceptable to a division chief of police. And that man knew that licenses for all sorts of enterprises were given according to the number of people involved.[29] Gatherings of less than 20 people were not forbidden. The division chief ruled that those 19 savants were harmless enough and might be suffered to meet. There were only two provisions: First, they must never talk politics or religion, i.e., not discuss society, church, or government. Second, in order to implement the first proviso, a plainclothes officer of the Imperial Police must be present at each session and make a report to headquarters.

After two years of this, police participation in anthropology was withdrawn; the scholars had lived up to their promise. It also was benevolently overlooked that the membership had swelled to one hundred by the end of the first year. Minute scrutiny of the members' moral and political character apparently did not turn up anything grossly reprehensible. After two years the Society was officially approved by Rouland; within five years it acquired full status as a "public utility."

On May 19, 1859, a few days after the French had again gone to war (for the freedom of Italy from Austrian rule), the first permanent Society in the world that called itself anthropological was holding its first meeting in a little room of the École Pratique, with the Dean's permission. Having several members in common with the Société de Chirurgie, it soon, and for the next seventeen years, enjoyed the hospitality of that group, in that stern reddish Renaissance structure at 2, Rue de l'Abbaye, the former palace of the abbot, round the corner of St. Germain de Prés. Broca remained Secretary—later General Secretary—until his death and in charge of publications. Not being in the President's chair made it easier for him to moderate the discussion without seeming to dominate it. Martin-Magron became its first President.

It was clear to everyone that besides ethnology Broca's project would include many biological aspects, especially the skull and its contents. The group of naturalists and physicians was almost immediately joined by a member of the Académie de Médecine, old Baillarger, the alienist and brain anatomist, who nearly twenty years before had discovered the layers of the cerebral cortex.[30]

Along with the founding of the Society, Broca obtained a room in the École Pratique to be used by him and the titular members as a private laboratory. This was not just a debating society. At the same time, the work here would be as far removed from his daily surgical practice as he could wish, another outlet for his multiple pursuits, with scope for leadership. The centrifugal forces in him that had threatened disruption were channelled in a definite direction. He had unmistakably established himself as the head of French anthropology.

IX
The Human Group

 "One may ask how a discussion about such a simple subject can go on for so long . . ."

*H*ad Broca not launched anthropology on its permanent course, our universities might never have devoted departments to that subject. This is not an overstatement. It borders on the miraculous how a strong tradition has kept as a single discipline the diversity of physical, cultural, and social anthropology; in other words, paleontology, archeology, ethnology, comparative anatomy, vital statistics, medical geography, psychology, linguistics, and whatnot. It needed a *tour de force* to weld together this multiplicity of only moderately germane subjects in one definition—and in one learned society, a body of men with only moderately common interests. As to Broca's definition, anthropology was to be, simply but grandly, "the study of the human group, considered as a whole, in its details, and in relation to the rest of nature."[1] "Group" was humble, non-committal, and sweeping; "considered as a whole," a homage to the eighteenth-century concept of idealized man, including the "noble savage," while "in its details" incorporated the new emphasis on the varieties, the group specimens, races, or nations. The "relation to the rest of nature" was what we call man's ecology; as "general anthropology" it might take in pathology and even the anatomy of the brain.

This new study of Man, anthropology, presents the nineteenth-century version of humanism or at least its legitimate extension. It aimed at origins rather than tradition, facts rather than conjectures. Nothing was to be taken for granted: living creation must no longer remain anthropocentric, just as the universe had ceased to be geocentric three hundred years earlier. The animal kingdom, meanwhile, had expanded to include man, whereas the divine right of kings had shrunk to almost nothing. Before Broca, anthropology was a science both restricted and obscure. So was his Society in its beginning: "tiny and pitiful to the point of seeming unable to survive," as he recalled twenty years later.[2]

In the first year of its existence, the Société d'Anthropologie indulged in discussions of the "perfectibility" and the decline of races: the fate of the savage. But the very first paper was duly on the ethnology of France, duly presented by the Society's originator.

To Broca the French were a mixed "race." This, he pointed out, in no way affected their fertility, vigor, or intelligence. The assertion had better be strong. He rejected the current view that only pure races were able to last and prosper, and he did not subscribe to the belief that primitive man was everywhere extinct.[3]

In his work on hybridity Broca had shown that inability to crossbreed was a poor criterion for the definition of species. And if, as the existence of the leporid had shown, crossbreeding was possible, fixity of species could by no means be absolute. It was a matter of degree, of four degrees, as he suggested: *agenetic* are those mongrels that remain infertile; *dysgenetic,* those that achieve occasional success in propagation; *paragenetic,* those with limited success; and *eugenetic,* those that show unlimited facility in producing offspring, no matter what the proportion between the parent and the new species. The same four possibilities of interbreeding applied to the human races. The proposition that no mixed race can endure he found "frightening."[4] But whether "race" was an equivalent to species, subspecies or variety, he left open. Blumenbach's five-pronged division into white, yellow, black, red and brown (Malayo-Polynesian), Broca found more practical than Cuvier's three types or P. Bérard's fifteen. But "race" or "type" with limited meaning was a scientific concept: it was non-committal and fictitious, a construct, an ideal, like the Apollo of Belvedere. "A ceaseless tendency of the human mind invites us to personify abstractions"—here he was echoing what Gerdy had said about disease entities. "Ideal types should never be allowed out of the mind and into the domain of facts."[5] Admirable words, often repeated by Gerdy's and Broca's successors, often in vain, usually unquoted.

On the other hand, we must not forget that racism began to look like an anachronism only in the twentieth century. We must not expect a Broca, a Lincoln,[6] indeed any enlightened minds, to have believed in racial equality. The attitude was humanitarian, at best. Plain common sense, and even the most careful observation by the means then available, clearly showed that other races were unable to meet white standards measured by white values, in science, technical achievement, or art. Only through anthropology could the inquiry deepen and cause the "leukocentric" attitude of white scientists slowly to crumble.

Purity of race as a bona fide argument untainted by political intentions—racism, that is, pristine, abstract, and elegant—was a French product. Comte de Gobineau, man of the world, diplomat, prolific writer of fact mixed with fiction, had regretted the dying of aristocracy. His learned work of 1853, *On the Inequality of the Human Races,* was a piece of romantic nostalgia for "purity" lost. Purity, hence superiority of race, was embodied in the "Aryans," or what in the melting pot of time was left of them to dwell high above the— alas—mixed crowd of Frenchmen and other whites. Germanic tribes, having entered history latest, were only the least sullied of the Aryans, but de Gobineau was not guilty of equating them with his contemporaries across the Rhine. His Aryan race was deduced from the recently discovered affinity of languages spoken in a geographic area that stretched from the Indian to the Atlantic Ocean.

The problem of race as it applied to nationalism was preceded by the problem of slavery. In keeping with its multiracial composition, the United States had its early flourishing school of scientific segregationists. Nott and Gliddon, mentioned by Broca in his paper on the French, wrote from the 1830's on, when slavery was abolished by the British. At the time the world's most extensive collection of skulls was in Philadelphia, gathered by Dr. S. G. Morton; his *Crania Americana* was a standard work. Nott, a pupil of Morton, was a physician in Mobile, Alabama; Gliddon, an Egyptologist; the circle was rounded out by Meigs and the Swiss-born Agassiz.

Whatever their individual opinions, their common demoninator was "polygenism." Polygenists postulated separate origins for the human races. Bound up with this tenet in the American school was the everlasting inferiority of Negroes and other non-whites. For this very natural reason, the authors of the Bible had ignored those inferior races. When races mix, this school claimed with Gobineau, the product was inferior, or the mixing finally resulted in the absorption of the inferior by the superior race, which would undergo an eventual repurification. Gliddon, a scholar with an evangelist's ardor, did not admit to any political bias; Nott was an outspoken anti-abolitionist.

Racial theory was deeply divided: besides "polygenism" there was "monogenism," which postulated a common human ancestry. But like polygenism, monogenism, too, had its advocates of slavery, and abolitionism could be found in either camp.

Monogenism, in its orthodox variety, derived all men from Adam, and some monogenists felt that the text of Genesis did not preclude the existence of subhuman varieties destined to be slaves. The victory of Darwinism finally perpetuated a monogenism that espoused, rejected, or disregarded Scripture. Today you will find polygenism generally discredited among the followers of Scripture and of the *Descent of Man*. Or so it was until fairly recently. One gathers from the theory of C. S. Coon that a sort of polygenism may be making a comeback. According to Coon, separate races, akin to those existing today, antedate *homo sapiens*. [7]

Broca, perhaps contrary to expectation, was a polygenist. He opposed the one-ancestor doctrine with its implication that mixture meant decay and slavery. His Voltairian upbringing (Voltaire himself had been a polygenist) and presumably his aversion to all monolithic systems made him espouse polygenism as the view that allowed latitude and tolerance. Monogenism, in his opinion, was a forcing of facts into a straight-jacket of theory. He made monogenism responsible for the fallacy of "the pure race." To polygenists, he maintained, this abstraction was a sin against logic. In order to explain the existing diversity, monogenists had to establish primary and secondary (or derivative) races, but nothing, in his opinion, could have changed white into black, black into yellow.

And while he admitted differences in intelligence, aesthetic appeal, or military power, he found the argument of a physical or moral degradation, used in order to maintain slavery, repulsive. Monogenism allowed slavery "to retain a shadow of legitimacy in the eyes of a few theorists"; in the polygenists' view, "manifest violence stands condemned by all except its profiteers. . . ."[8]

What did he have to say about the origins of his own nation? Caesar's Gauls, Gaels, or Celts had been short and dark. In their majority, he said, they had occupied the center and north-west of the country. In the Auvergne and in Brittany they had remained relatively unmixed, as shown by the clusters of particularly short recruits in these areas, drawn and plotted by him from a study of conscription lists, a novelty in anthropological method.

On the other hand, the Kimris, Cymris, or Cimbers—Caesar's Belgae—had been tall and blond. With their long dolichocephalic heads they also differed from the round-headed brachycephalic Celts. The Kimris, moreover, had high foreheads against the wide brows of the Celts; their noses were long and curved downward, against the Celtic small nose; they had long faces, a protruding chin, and less body hair than the Celts, with their rounded faces and hairy bodies.

(In other words, the Kimris had all the features of what—later—was called "Nordic.") Their country was in the north-east of France between the Seine and the Rhine.

While Celts and Kimris did on the whole not remain separated, *Aquitani* had remained remarkably unmixed. Confined to the area around the Pyrenees, they were the ancestors of the present-day Basques. To the south-east, in the valley of the Rhone and along the Mediterranean, a fourth group had settled; it was Latin. When later—with the fall of the Roman Empire—Francs, Burgundians, Visigoths, and Normans overran the country, the Celts and Kimris kept their genetic hold on the population. This was generally true, although modified to some extent: the Celts became a little taller, mainly by mixing with the Latins, and the Kimris decreased their size by incorporating the small-statured Germanic tribes. Broca supplied a map showing the average statures by departments. At that time he dismissed potential causes for size, such as food, climate, economic status, hygiene, and crowding for they were contradicted by what he considered the facts; he claimed the differences, such as they were, to be solely of a genetic nature.[9]

Broca's first ethnological paper is a clear refutation of the "Celtic myth" and the cult of the pure race. His attitude never changed. Neither here nor anywhere in his writings can we find him making the slightest claim for French superiority or correlating it with the configuration of the head. Such an idea is in open contradiction to anything he ever said or did. Nobody who has as much as glanced at his work will suspect it. Yet even a writer such as Ruth Benedict in order to strengthen her cause in the fight against racism has grouped Broca with the earlier racists.

Parallel with the Celtic myth ran a larger one: the Aryan. It assumed that a genetic bond must exist between people when languages have common roots. Paradoxically, the German originators of philology, or linguistics, were humanists, but it was this very science that gave Aryanism, anti-humanism, its support. The humanist tradition, as we know, did not altogether prevail in Germany and for that matter, not without a struggle in France either. From the latter two-thirds of the nineteenth centruy, the racists were at work against each other within the European community.

Among the upholders in the Société d'Anthropologie of a certain brand of Aryanism was a brilliant Bavarian-born physician, like Gall and Lebert a German expatriate. Dr. Franz Ignaz Pruner (or Brunner) had spent a great deal of his life as the personal physician to the Egyptian Viceroy, hence the aristocratic title of Bey, affixed to his name. Widely travelled in the Mediterranean and in Asia, he had studied contagious disease, anatomy including craniometry), linguistics, and history, and settled in Paris and the Société d'Anthropologie. The Franco-German war of 1870 drove this German Francophile to Italy where he outlived Broca, who had been his junior by sixteen years. [10] Pruner-Bey's lasting contributions were a classification of races by the cross-section of their hair[11] and his keen opposition to Broca, which added much sport to the anthropological sessions. He was not one of those whose "modesty equalled their erudition."

We must not assume that Pruner-Bey was anything like the vulgar chauvinists and racists of his or a later day. Thus, he said, a previous speaker had "very much exaggerated the physical differences between Semites and Aryans . . ."; as he switched to linguistics: ". . . since Wilhelm von Humboldt all savants have been in accord on the absolute distinction between Semitic and Aryan languages. . . . But does it follow that they have no affinity? . . . Wilhelm von Humboldt . . . did also say that the two systems might have had a single source. . . . We know that populations have changed their language. Turanians have become Semites; Semites, Turanians. . . . Most philologists . . . are of the opinion — unproven — that for languages there must have been several centers of creation. . . . It would therefore be more than difficult to locate such centers. Moreover, they would be in entire disagreement with the facts of natural history."[12]

Broca rejected monogenism even in linguistics and just as much the leading role which linguistics claimed for itself in anthropology. [13] In a sarcastic talk he exposed the fundamental and die-hard error of seeing in language a natural, rather than an artificial and cultural criterion of classifying man, an early sign of the cleavage between physical and cultural trends in anthropology.

He objected to unnecessary neologisms whenever the traditional terms, if arbitrary, were at least not misleading. Why "Turanian," for Mongolian? Pruner's source for this term was Professor Max Müller of Oxford, who had gone so far as to postulate an ancestor called TUR, "a venerable personage," Broca said, "forgotten by Moses but not introduced to sit among the sons of Noah. . . ." Of course, he did not wish to belittle — on the contrary, he was an admirer of — the linguists' discoveries, and he was not denying that language nearly always represented the oldest available monument of a people. But you were on much safer ground if you determined characteristic analogies and discrepancies from the physical organization. He also was not talking here about that integral part of man, the faculty of articulate speech, but about language, the manifestation of that faculty. He had to disagree with the view that language was something innate and that, therefore, all languages must have a common origin. There were several theories about this origin: "Let us by all means have each our own way of looking at questions of primary origin. . . . But let us also be careful not to confound teleological aspirations with the demonstrable facts available in the neighboring science. . . . Maybe you are right. How can I tell? Maybe you are not."

Difference in language—as between say, the Chinese and the French—may be greater than the respective physical differences. On the other hand, Syrio-Arabs, Basques, Berbers, and Indo-Europeans, all very close in their physical characteristics, spoke vastly different languages. Physical characteristics were much less subject to modifications in the course of time. A conquering nation, though small in number, may impose its language on the conquered, whereas the physical type of the resulting mixture depended on the relative numbers of the two. "Of course, anthropology cannot do without linguistics, whereas linguists seem to be doing very well without anthropology. . . ." Take Baron von Bunsen: "Too versed in the study of linguistics to claim that all languages are derived from Hebrew, von Bunsen decided he would at least show that all language families could have issued from the lost tongue spoken by the first human couple . . . and so protect the monogenism of the Bible from the objecting linguists. But at what price! He had to suppress about half the Bible. In order to reconcile the divergence of Sanscrit, Hebrew, Coptic, and Chinese that has existed from time immemorial, he had to presume, first that Noah's deluge had taken place ten thousand years before our era, next, that this deluge had not been universal, and finally, that another ten thousand years had passed between Adam and Noah."

Languages changed extremely slowly; it might take a hundred thousand years to make von Bunsen's hypothesis likely. "The idea of such antiquity does not frighten me. No doubt, those human beings who saw Europe covered by glaciers, who at a time incomparably more remote still fought the rhinoceros and the mammoth with stone weapons did speak a human language. But this is so long ago, whereas the five or six thousand years of our history are only a moment in the life of mankind. . . .

"I cannot help using an analogy here," Broca went on, and for the first time in these discussions (the year is 1862), unexpected in this context, the curtain goes up before one of the most dramatic events in the history of science. "For the past few years a work, remarkable, unusual, and spellbinding, has caused a readers' furor in England. It will soon come out in French; its title is: *On the Origin of Species by*

Natural Selection." He went into an exposition of this new theory, concluding that "M. Darwin is asking only for time. . . . We may trace our genealogy back to the trilobites of the Silurian era. Well now, is M. Darwin right or wrong? I do not know, I do not even care to know. I find sufficient food for my curiosity in things that are accessible to science. When M. Darwin tells me about my trilobite ancestors I do not feel humiliated, I only say to him: How can you tell? You have not been there. And those who refute him know no more than he does. . . .

"In conclusion, I have only looked . . . for the way *facts* are being replaced by *conjectures* . . . and I tried to show the difference between a linguistic and an anthropological fact.

". . . To anthropology, consequently, linguistics contributes information, but no laws. It ought to take part in our debate as one of the witnesses but not as the judge."[13]

After this far-reaching direction had been given to an important aspect of anthropology, Pruner-Bey took up the defense of linguistics in a whirl of lyricisms. "Philologists have united what naturalists had frittered away; they have separated what the others had awkwardly pieced together: power and glory to them! . . ."[14]

Naturally these discussions covered a range of topics by no means exclusively European or Celtic. They show Broca's salutary rejection, not only of facile conclusions in matters of fact, but also of a certain parochial complacency in some members of the Society.

The Smithsonian Institution had sent its publication, *Archeology of the United States or Sketches Historical and Biographical of the Progress of Information and Opinion Respecting Vestiges of Antiquity in the United States*, by Samuel Haven, July 1856, and another work on Mexico. The Red Indians naturally were a subject of great interest, both popular and scientific.[15] Several meetings in the summer of 1862 were devoted to them and to their natural historians, especially those with first-hand experience in the New World. The American aborigines had at first been thought of as descended from Canaanites (Hebrews) and their lost tribes. Later the old Platonic, or Egyptian, story of Atlantis was applied to the New World; according to contemporary views, other well-known races, white or yellow, were to have invaded the western continent.

The controversy naturally centered on the physical attributes of that new-found race. De Gobineau had already pointed out that every color of skin ("from Congo black to an Englishman's pinkish white") and every possible feature was to be found among the Indians; consequently innumerable branches must exist. According to Morton, it

143

was an old adage with travellers that if you have seen one Indian tribe, you have seen them all. In America, the indigenous people were regarded as a uniform race, different from all others, except for the Eskimos, who were allegedly Mongols with an Indian language.

After Dally had reviewed the American school of polygenists, Broca remarked that Morton and those after him had evidently exaggerated the uniformity of the American races. They were in fact more varied than the Caucasian, the color of their skins being just as multiple as de Gobineau had stated—Broca did not re-mention his name but quoted a number of other reports—except that no Red Indian had been seen who was quite as black as the Negroes of the Congo.[15]

All colors of skin, Pruner-Bey agreed, were encountered except the famous but non-existing bronze, assiduously copied from one author by the next. Nor was there anything Mongolian about the Eskimo, and Pruner-Bey spoke scathingly of that science from across the Atlantic and of its motivation, which was only too obvious. Plurality of human species, multicentric creation, and persistence of type, as well as the very great antiquity of man, were all doctrines originally French. And, said Herr Franz Brunner *aus Pfreim in der Oberpfalz,* was there anything in the American method to show that certain cachet of ingenious initiative, thoughtful analysis, and, above all, that exquisite precision, which had at all times been the inalienable appanage of the French mind? "All these lucubrations by the American authors are in my opinion a scaffolding constructed on ill-coordinated borrowings. . . ."

Two weeks later Broca, still irked by the Gallic chauvinism of the German doctor responded: "I leave the defense of the American scientists, so severely and summarily judged by M. Pruner-Bey . . . in the care of M. Dally. I wish to limit myself to one thing: If Germany has had her Blumenbach, England her Prichard, America has had her Morton; French anthropology so far can boast no name of equal rank."

Closer to home, the vexed question of those Celts kept coming up again and again, still unsettled, a foggy concept to this day. *Who and what are the Celts?* Broca asked with some exasperation.[17]

"All Caesar said was that the inhabitants of the Celtic part of Gaul differed from the rest by their customs and their language. Other authors added . . . that they were of a height a little below the average, and had dark eyes and hair. These are the *Celts of History.*

"The Celtic Country appears as some unknown portion of Central and Western Europe situated North of the Pyrenees, on the sources of the Danube, near the river Po, or by the North Sea. These Celts had taken their arms to Iberia, Italy, Greece, and Asia

144

Minor. . . . Pausanias said that the Galates who plundered Delphi were first called Celts, then Gauls; Strabo, that this confusion was due to the greater fame of the Celts; according to the learned Pelloutier, the Celts had occupied all of Europe: Germans, Danes, Getes, Scythes were all Celts to him. These are the *Traditional Celts:* more or less everywhere and not anywhere in particular.

"According to linguistics, on the other hand, the Gauls of the Celtic and the Belgian countries had not been speaking the same language, for this would contradict all historical accounts, but languages allied to one another and to those spoken in the British Isles—a natural group emanating from the Indo-European languages. These were called *Celtic languages,* even before their Asiatic origin was known. The language of the Celts living in Gaul is that of which we know the least, i.e., only a few isolated words and proper names. The term was chosen, anyway, not for a linguistic reason but because among all these peoples the Celts have played the greatest part in history. Once the name for these languages had become common usage, all the people who had spoken them were called Celts. If one is not in the habit of distinguishing between language and race it is easy to maintain that before Roman and Germanic times all the peoples of Gaul and Britain were of the same, i.e., the Celtic race. And so everybody was called a Celt whether he was dark or fair, tall, or small. . . .

"There are, thirdly, the *Celts of Archeology* and, fourthly, the *Celts of Craniology.*

"As to the Celts of Archeology, there are two kinds: those of today and those of twenty years ago.

"Twenty years ago every monument in Western Europe antedating the Roman era was Celtic. Dolmens, tumuli, mehirs, cromlechs, every utensil, whether of earthenware, bone, stone or metal, was Celtic. . . . Why Celts? Because they were more famous than anyone else.

"But thanks to the remarkable and rapid strides modern archeology has made, we are on the most perfect scientific grounds when we state that the monuments alleged to be Celtic twenty years ago are of two different periods; the stone age on one hand, and the bronze age on the other. Yet others, even more recent, contain some iron objects. Comparative studies . . . have shown that the primary inhabitants of Europe belonged to the stone age, while the use of bronze was introduced by more civilized man, probably of Asiatic origin. . . . The Celtic period begins with the bronze age; the stone age period is pre-Celtic.

"Although there are analogies between them ... the Celts of Linguistics are confined to Western Europe, whereas those of Archeology have been followed to places much closer to Asia.

"We are left with the *Celts of Craniology*. On the basis of the archeological record and of comparisons between the stone age and bronze age skulls, the famous Retzius found the former to be brachycephalic (in the Baltic area), the latter dolichocephalic. From this interesting discovery he generalized that pre-Celtic populations were without exception brachycephalic, whereas dolichocephaly came to Europe with the Indo-European conquerors, and they, he thought, should be called Celts on the basis of linguistics and archeology. He attributed a Celtic origin to every dolichocephalic skull, whether from Northern, Central, or Western Europe—at least any one antedating the Teutonic and Germanic races. But M. Thurnam, also on archeological grounds, found that the bronze age monuments in Great Britain were erected by a brachycephalic population. M. Retzius' Celts are therefore dolichocephalic, M. Thurnam's brachycephalic. . . .

"In summary: The Celts of History are a confederation of peoples in Central Gaul. The Celts of Linguistics are the people who have spoken and are still speaking the so-called Celtic languages. The Celts of Archeology are the people who inaugurated the bronze age in Europe. The Celts of Craniology finally, are the people who brought dolichocephaly to the native brachycephalic European population, according to Retzius; whereas according to Thurnam they are, on the contrary, the people who brought brachycephaly to the native dolichocephalic British population."

As he had predicted, nobody has been able to settle this problem, stated here with such a judicious blend of wit, clarity, erudition, and open-ended finality, in a manner more provocative than hardly anyone before had dared in these circles. Confused, simplified, and reconfused, the subject seems to keep haunting modern presentations. Their authors might do worse than base their analysis on the just quoted model.[18]

Almost month after month in 1864[19] and then year after year, Broca continued the attack on the Celtic, the Aryan, and the linguistic myths, hammering into his listeners the concept of the multiple origin of races and nations and the need for admitting ignorance in the absence of evidence. Every factor must be considered: wars, for instance, had not always been like modern war. The extinction of a race, if not of the whole human race, had become a possibility only in Broca's time.

"What may have happened then one must not judge from what sometimes happens today. Europeans, with their formidable civilizations, their irresistible means of destruction, their floating cities driven around the world by steam, will descend upon an island situated at the antipodes, inhabited by a few roaming savages, stupid, naked, unarmed, and leaderless. Suddenly the two extremes of the human series confront each other, and if the foreigners, their numbers ceaselessly mounting with the arrival of new colonists, decide that it is in their interest to destroy the natives, they easily crush them with their immense material superiority. This is why there are no Tasmanians left in Tasmania. But there would be if those unfortunate people had been fit to provide some useful service to the English settlers or had been gifted with that degree of additional intelligence which enables African Negroes to be slaves; there still would be some left if their island had been a spacious continent allowing them to retreat from their aggressors, as the Redskins did in America, or if they had found a refuge in nearly inaccessible mountains as the bears do in the Pyrenees. In a region not coveted by the civilized man's greed, they would have been left in peace. Attacks by a stronger and more intelligent race are not enough to cause the extermination of another. The disproportion must be excessive. . . . Even so the anthropologically pure type of the invader will not prevail. The conquering warrior does not take pride in abstemiousness. What he likes doing is to kill the men; what he likes even better is to keep the women for pleasure. Blood mixtures are almost inevitable. The character of the victorious race is thus modified, unless the difference in color is so striking that the offspring is recognized at first glance and thus condemned to form an ever distinct caste. . . .

"The 'Celts,' as some wish to call the Asiatic conquerors . . . one nation. . . . But no one can say where in Asia this great Celtic nation was to be found, ready to vomit its million warriors over Europe. . . . Originally, as I see it, there was a simple emigration, a people of herdsmen and warriors moving over the Caucasus and perhaps across the Hellespont and settling with their cattle in a small corner of Europe, subjugating the natives, then mixing with them, imposing their language and nationality on them, inoculating them with their skills and customs.

"From this focus stepwise emigrations and invasions were issuing . . . less and less "Celtic" in blood . . . but under the name Celt. . . . The name appears at a relatively late period and only in central and Western Europe.

"The populations whom we bundle together under the collective name of Celts were peoples distinct by their nationalities and their dialects. . . . Let me add that they were often at war against each other, that they notably differed in their customs, clothes, social organization, and, finally in their physical character—hence the interminable discussion about fair and dark Celts. As a matter of fact, the color of their eyes and hair varied according to that of the indigenous races. . . . The original color of those who had crossed the Caucasus could not be identified after so many successive dilutions.

". . .What has spread over the whole of Europe was not a race but a civilization.

"In summary: where do the European languages come from: From Asia. And the European races? From Europe."[19]

It was in lower Brittany, the ancient Armorica, that most of the genuine Celts had apparently been best preserved; in 1866 Broca once more attempted to trace the Celts of France and disentangle them from the non-Celts. He drew up a map, based on his own method of using military exemptions due to undersize (below 1.56 m. or 5 ft. 2-2/5in.) and found the frontier between tall and small almost exactly where Caesar had drawn his between Belgae and Celtae. Of course, these were not pure races, for already some two thousand years B.C. they had been assailed by another tall, blond race, coming from the Baltic and speaking an Indo-European idiom. These may have invaded the British Isles; in France they stopped short of the most southwestern corner. France was called the "Celtic" country before it became "Gaul." A second bellicose and racially similar invasion from across the Rhine occurred one thousand years later. By now the Celts had been better organized, and they put up a fight, the outcome of which is unknown. Practically nothing was known about the real Celtic language; had it, after all, been close to Cymric or Gaelic? Caesar—not a linguist himself—was silent about any differences in the idiom or the need for interpreters between the two main native groups in Gaul.

Of the so-called "Celtic" languages, which must have been numerous, only six were preserved, falling into two groups: Cymric (or Brythonic) and Gaelic (or Goidelic). The Cymric group consisted of Cymraeg, spoken in Wales; Cornish in Cornwall (extinct since the eighteenth century); and Breysad or Armorican, in lower Brittany. The three Gaelic dialects were those still spoken in Scotland, Ireland, and the Isle of Man, respectively. But Galli had little specific meaning; they might be Gauls, Galates, Gallots, or Wallons, found as far afield as Galicia, Portugal, Wales, or wherever the name "Celts" had penetrated—and even where it had not. Thus no one had been able to prove that a people with the original name of Celts had ever invaded Scandinavia or the British Isles. The Walloons of modern Belgium, racially related to the Cymri, speak a neo-Latin dialect. But the early inhabitants of the Celtic part of Gaul, surviving in lower Brittany to

Broca's day, spoke a Cymric not a Gaelic idiom, imported by Britons. In the fifth century these Britons, no longer protected by the Romans from Anglo-Saxon and other attackers, had taken refuge in Brittany. People from Wales and people from lower Brittany, separated for centuries, still had a few mutually intelligible words in common because both their dialects were Cymric. But a man from Wales was lost among the Irish: their language was Gaelic.[20] This is the position, still or again, taken by modern scholars.

Running as a parallel and corollary to the Celtic was the Basque controversy. The subject here was not language and history but skulls, longheadedness (or dolichocephaly), and having a low cranial index, a subject charged with powerful emotions. The cranial, or cephalic, index is the ratio of breadth to length, of the transverse to the longitudinal diameters of the skull. Expressed as a percentage, the index is high in broad, short heads (brachycephaly) and low in narrow, long ones (dolichocephaly). This fundamental formula of craniometry had been devised and named by the older Retzius of Sweden. In Scandinavia collecting and measuring crania had started almost with the beginning of the century as the efflorescence of romantic feelings for the past, of the national democratic and scientific urges. In general, the drive behind the dolichocephalic myth was for social and national prestige, to be backed at all cost by hard scientific fact. The worship of the old aristocracy, suffering a progressive eclipse, had been based on verified family trees. To keep up with the princes, the bourgeoisie of each nation fancied itself a noble family and felt the urge for a fine ancestry of its own, the finest possible. Hierarchical valuation still pervaded every analysis of fact, and snobbery, both individual and collective, was one of the most powerful driving forces of the nineteenth century. The most appealing physical criterion of national excellence was the long skull. Perhaps the belief in its superiority has even deeper roots, as the practice of deforming the newborn head in many old cultures suggests. At any rate, Aryans, it was said, were "favored" by a long skull, a low cranial index. Had these noble dolichocephalic warriors and pioneers not overcome the less civilized—also less gallant and less destructive—native breeds? Must those, therefore, not have been brachycephalic? Brachycephaly, a high cranial index, was also considered a trait of the lowly pre-Aryan Basques. To Broca this assumption was utterly repugnant. Was it really supported by the facts?

During the 1860's as he had done on his honeymoon, he vacationed in the Pyrenees, now with his growing family. After passing through Sainte Foy, he stayed at Sainte-Jean-de-Luz. There he combined his personal family interests with those of his larger family, gathered at 3 Rue de l'Abbaye, every other Thursday, except in September and October.

As a result, in the fall of 1862, sixty Basque skulls arrived at that address, a gift to the Society by M. Broca and M. Gonzales Velasco, associate member in Madrid. They were random samples from a graveyard in a small remote community on the Gulf of Biscay. Broca himself had "extracted" them with the help of Señor Velasco, but he asked that the details of the skull-snatching not be included in the proceedings. Even the full place name, Zaraus, was as a rule discreetly referred to as "Z..." or "the cemetery of the province of Guipuzcoa."[22]

Some much cherished anthropological beliefs were shattered by these skulls. It was an unexpectedly complete vindication of an idea he had been entertaining for some time, Broca said, for Basques were hitherto thought to be brachycephalic "because of Retzius' study of two skulls in Stockholm and some valid historical and ethnological considerations. In Denmark, Sweden, and Great Britain, with a current dolichocephalic population, deep layers of soil have yielded brachycephalic skulls. The same is true of skulls found under tumuli supposed to antedate the Celtic period. Thus, the notion arose that autochthonous brachycephalic races had inhabited Europe before the Indo-European races came from Central Asia. . . . In their mountain residences the Basques have from the beginning of history preserved their nationality, as well as their language, which has absolutely nothing in common with the Indo-European or any other living or dead language known. All this makes it quite certain that they are the last survivors of a race antedating the arrival of the Celts, supposedly the conquerors of western Europe.

"Last August, M. Velasco gave me a perfectly authentic Basque skull from a cemetery in the province of Guipuzcoa. . . . Now Nr. 60 in our collection," he pointed out, with some affection for that stimulating first specimen, "it is rather dolicho- than brachycephalic. It aroused in me the first doubt about Retzius' theory . . . Of the remaining fifty-nine only seven were not frankly dolichocephalic, only two frankly brachycephalic, and even these not excessively so (cranial indices of 83.24 and 82.73, respectively).

"Retzius gave no precise figures; in any case I believe that such have only relative value."

Hence, Broca compared them with his old collection of Parisian skulls. In these the average cephalic (the modern American usage is "cranial") index was 79.45, as against the Basque average of 77.67, a difference that made Parisian skulls more brachycephalic by 1.78, and even more so against a group of medieval Paris aristocrats (relatively dolichocephalic at 79.18 average but with a very wide scatter). "I may remind you of a previous paper[23] in which I called *pure dolichocephaly* indices below 75; *sub-dolichocephaly*: between 75 and 77.77, or 6/8 to 7/9; *mesaticephaly*: between 77.77 and 80, or 7/9 to 8/10; *sub-brachycephaly*: between 80 and 85; and finally *pure brachycephaly*: over 85. According to this classification, none of the Basque skulls is truly brachycephalic."

Cranial capacity, too, was on the average high in the Basque series (1.485.88 cc.) against that of the oldest Parisian skulls (116 specimens at 1.427.56 cc.) or those taken from modern private graves (90 specimens at 1.484.234 cc.) or from modern pauper graves (1.403.14 cc.). Only a recent series from the Paris morgue (suicides mostly) showed a higher average (17 specimens at 1.517.29 cc.)

Growth of the brain, he now thought, was coincident with progress in civilization, material ease, and the educational standard within any given "race."

Cranial capacity was a significant natural characteristic. Yet he was far from drawing the conclusion, he said, that Basques were more intelligent than Parisians. "Intelligence . . . depends on the relative development of the parts of the brain. . . ." Measuring the various regions separately, he found that the anterior skull of the Basque, "speaking absolutely," was smaller than the Parisian. "What makes the Basque skull so large is the considerable development of the occipital region."[24]

Señor Velasco sent another eighteen from the Spanish side, and in 1867 Broca collected fifty-eight skulls of French Basques dating back to 1532 from a cemetery at Saint-Jean-de-Luz.[25] Of the latter only ten were dolichocephalic, but they came from a locale closer to France, where the population was not purely Basque.

Link by scattered link, some of the immensely long chain of prehistoric humanity was being pieced together. The double connotation of the word "history" expresses a cross-fertilization of ideas. In the term "natural history," as in classical Greek, history simply means "inquiry" or "knowledge." The Science of History, in its conventional meaning, changed its character during the nineteenth century. From being a tradition it became an adventure: from being merely the recognition it became the analysis of the past. The result was both an estrangement and a yearning. Historians emulated explorers and natural scientists. The sacred myths and concepts underwent treatment by profane methods. But the converse was equally important: the historical concept penetrated biology and geology. Increasingly, animate and inanimate forms were explained by their past. In embryology and in theories of evolution, natural history became a history of nature. This fusion produced an aggressive, an offensive line of research: prehistory, the combination of archeology and paleontology.

Within the first few months of its existence, Broca's society paid homage to the man who, twenty years earlier had begun to subvert the Judeo-Christian world's ideas about how long man, the artisan, had been this earth's inhabitant. In 1839, Boucher Crèvecoeur de Perthes, the customs officer with a passion for the past, had found his first flint axes in the gravel quarries of Abbeville in the Somme (in northern France), in a layer then still called "Diluvium" or "Drift." This term, originally identified with the Great Flood or the last of a series of such cataclysms, became identified with the later or Upper Tertiary. (According to the O.E.D., "diluvium" was an eighteenth-century word for the third geological period; Quaternary, for the fourth, does not appear before 1843.) Boucher de Perthes dated his findings to a period before the earth's crust had finally settled in this region — much earlier, that is, than the beginning of those five or six thousand years which, in the eyes of the Bible-confident, had marked man's presence on earth.

Animal fossils and the occasional flint implement had kept turning up since the Middle Ages and sporadically an inspired heretic had declared them to antedate Adam and Eve. At the beginning of the nineteenth century, Cuvier's compromise between dogma and the fossil record had been that a number of cataclysms and re-creations must have occurred; the single and rather recent creation recounted by Scripture may have only been the last of a series. This took care of fossils, large reptile bones, and such. But man was still too sacred for being pushed back tens or hundreds of thousands of years. Only a crank would claim to have found tools of an Adam living before Genesis. Cranks being numerous and true discoverers extremely rare, it was always safe to assume that a person claiming a startling discovery was a crank. Incredulity was allied to fierce beliefs. Heated or icy, the hostility discoverers were shown by most fellow scientists then makes our own academic climate appear truly post-glacial. But in 1859 an on-site inspection by some advanced visitors from across the Channel, among them the revolutionary geologist Lyell,[26] vindicated Boucher de Perthes, the "amiable fanatic," as Lady Prestwich called him, whose "countrymen from the Institute left him in the gutter."[27] His heirs withdrew his books from the market and prevented the story of his "martyrdom" from reaching the public until the end of the century.[28]

The exhibit of 1859 at the Société d'Anthropologie showed to many thrilled viewers for the first time those flint axes that have formed since, row on row, the rather dry fare offered to visitors by museums small and large.

In the letter accompanying the exhibit, Boucher de Perthes spoke of his original surmise in 1838, "that if fossil man—or the products of his industry instead of his bones—were to be found some day, it would have to be . . . in diluvial deposits, where flint lies in the company of skeletons belonging to the great mammals. The daily press repeated this kind of prediction; my numerous later researches have proved it to be correct." A prediction quite damaging to its prophet; suspicion added to disbelief: was he not himself a man with an axe to grind? Disbelief, if not suspicion, was expressed even by some members of the Société d'Anthropologie. Those haphazard, rough-looking shapes— were they really tools, deliberate artifacts of human beings, rather than the work of some stream that had polished some pebbles? Axes? Why, some did not even have a hole in them to attach a handle to; at best they might have been wedges. (Some of them were indeed spurious.)

Broca warmly defended the authenticity of these objects. He explained the differences between early rough and later polished stone and brought the consecutive use of bronze and iron in relation to the variously developed skulls that already had been found here and there—proof that the ancestors of our ancestors had been so primitive physically so as to produce such primitive tools. (Sir John Lubbock's respective terms "paleolithic" and "neolithic," date only from 1865.[30])

Nomads had used stone to cut wood; people no longer nomadic were able to mine metals with which to work the stone. A modern Robinson Crusoe might not do any better. He was rebuked for underestimating the intelligence of his own race; anyone with a little intelligence would fast produce better implements than these diluvial axes.[31] But as the clash of opinion died down, it was only another instance of rough common sense having to give in to the polished evidence.

What sort of basis did Broca have for his remarks? It was solid only in theory, vindicated later by finds still unknown to him. But it was shaky in fact, and some of the early claims regarding prehistoric human skeletons are no longer accepted. Broca knew of the Cannstadt discovery of 1700, the Lahr find of 1823, Schmerling's Belgian preadolescent skull of 1828, and Schaaffhausen's Neanderthal specimen of 1856. He was also familiar with some other work going back to the 1830's or just being published by Édouard Lartet, whose vision equalled Lyell's and Boucher's.[32] The Stone, Bronze, and Iron Ages had been established in the 1830's by C. I. Thomsen of Denmark.[33] In addition to these men, we must in many instances give credit to the blasting and digging of the ugly railroad for waking up the sleeping beauty of

153

prehistory. Thus, in 1868, was Cro-Magnon man unearthed—and the belief buried by Broca that paleolithic people had a broad head and a small brain. It also was the largest and most complete find to link Quaternary animals, man, and their tools to their well-defined geologic environment.

Only about forty miles east of Sainte-Foy-la-Grande, the Dordogne, meandering down the green and blue countryside of the Périgord, is joined by a tributary, the Vézère. Cliffs of a chalky, ghostly gray, "bizarre shapes of rocky wall suddenly narrow the invigorating valley. . . ." A closer view of them reveals "a multitude of caves, some natural, some assiduously cut out, some still used as annexes to their rustic dwellings by the men of our time. Romans, Normans, and Britons have one after the other occupied this *Petra* of the Périgord.

"But the oldest and strangest cave dwellers who took shelter in the rocks of Tayac were indubitably those hunters of . . . a host of animals either extinct or gone from our climate. Such stations are numerous around the Vézère. These natural grottos, patiently explored by M. Ed. Lartet and Mr. Christy, have finally revealed the secret of their inhabitants, their primitive industry, and their savage existence. . . ."

The speaker at the Société d'Anthropologie is Louis, son of Édouard, Lartet; the date May 21, 1868. His manuscript is entitled: *A Burial Site of Troglodytes in the Périgord (Skulls of Les Eyzies).*[34] *Une vive curiosité,* he calls the tremendous excitement that seized these specialists at the news that skeletons, presumably of great antiquity, had been unearthed by the railroad workers.

Some distance away from the little railroad station of the borough Les Eyzies, there is a spot called Cro-Magnon. Probably no cave would ever have been suspected there had it not been necessary to widen the tracks. To do this, they had to take off a pile of "talus"—debris some 12 to 18 feet thick, a gigantic block of about 8400 cubic feet, and a rock shelf. When the workmen entered what was revealed as a cave, they saw human skulls. Thanks to the understanding managers, construction was interrupted until the archeologists had completed their own work, "after overcoming a few unexpected difficulties with the help and the kindness of the Prefect, the Mayor, and the Curé." (Lartet did not specify the difficulties—perhaps a superstitious and hostile local population.)

The floor of the cave was covered with three or four fairly distinct layers of ashes, broken and calcined bones, worked flint, and bone implements, interrupted by layers of gravel. Passing a mammoth's tusk firmly embedded in the debris, Lartet, Jr. proceeded to the back of the grotto, where he discerned a group of human bones lying within a space of about 5 feet in diameter. Scattered among these human remains were some 300 sea shells, all perforated, presumably necklaces, bracelets and other personal ornaments, even an amulet made of ivory, and similar small objects.

The various layers suggested that the Cro-Magnon shelter had first served as a meeting place for the hunters coming here to share their prey. When the cave floor rose with "kitchen refuse" and clean-up gravel leaving only about 4 feet overhead, the place proved uninhabitable. Before they finally abandoned it, they seemed to have returned once more to hide their dead.

Broca's account of the skeletal remains followed.[35] The mammoth remains pointed to an antiquity even greater than that of the previous reindeer findings at Les Eyzies, by Lartet Sr. and Christy (Christy, Lartet Sr.'s collaborator, had been a British banker like Sir John Lubbock, the creator of the terms "neo-" and "paleolithic." They belonged, with the German barber Schliemann, who excavated Troy, to a class of top amateur experts now almost extinct.[30]) It also seemed that the same troglodyte people had been living through this gradual change of climate and fauna.

What had previously been found of Quaternary man suggested a small breed, with skulls of rather small volume and a more or less prognathous face. Negroid or Mongoloid and not taller than today's Laplanders—those were the guesses variously made of this paleolithic population. While this might be true, the underlying theory was probably a prejudice "which I have been fighting for a long time, namely that there was only a single race of man extant in Quaternary Europe. . . . The facts here contradict—as they nearly always do—our preconceived ideas. In shape and volume of the head as well as in the dimensions of the long bones . . . the Quaternary race of Les Eyzies differs from that of the Belgian caves at least as much as the most dissimilar races do." He gave the detailed reasons for the presumable age and sex of the three most complete skeletons: two male, one female. One of the older man's thighbones showed a healed fracture. The skull of the female, about thirty-five years old, had a hole in the left frontal bone, 33 by 12 millimeters. In all probability it was due to a blow with a flint axe. She must have survived her injury, for around the hole, on the inside of the skull, there were signs of increased vascularization and the formation of delicately porous new bone, possibly developed in less than two or three weeks. Judging from the injuries, these must have been violent people, but while the old man may merely have had a hunting accident, the woman was evidently slain by a murderous hand. The third skeleton he designated as that of an adult male without facial bones.

The long bones having lost their epiphysial ends, their full length could only be estimated. In the case of the old man, the shaft was at least 439 mm. long; according to the medico-legal standards of Broca's day, this suggested a corresponding body height of 1 m. 80 (6 ft.) The other skeletons were not far behind in size—estimates which Broca considered very exceptional for the races of his day. (Von Bonin's revised estimate is 5 ft. 6 in. or 168.4 cm.[44]) The thigh bones were consistently thick, with an unusually broad *linea aspera,* this line giving insertion, no doubt, to powerful thigh muscles—quite different from that in apes. Similar shinbones had been found in dolmens and by M. Eugène Bertrand, just out of college, in the Montmartre diggings for the new Boulevard Clichy. In contrast to Retzius' assumptions about prehistoric skulls, these were very dolichocephalic.

The facial skeleton was also striking. Such wide cheek bones had never before been seen in dolichocephalic heads nor even in brachcycephalic ones. It was mainly due to very wide, but not high, rectangular orbits. Though fairly straight from the forehead down to the chin, the face did have a slightly prognathous feature in the forward direction of the upper alveolar ridge beneath the upper lip.

In the woman's face all the old man's features appeared attenuated; the orbits and cheek bones, less wide; the lower jaw, less imposing.

What kind of people were these troglodytes, so human with a few simian features? They were intelligent and perfectible, Broca emphasized. To find the time for being idle, to cultivate the arts, "rare at all times but truly extraordinary then,..." was the manifestation of a "fine cerebral organization, attested by the morphology of the skulls owned by the race of Les Eyzies. . . . Did this race, as a forerunner will, succumb to an inclement environment into which it tried to introduce a premature progress? Or did it . . . escape extermination, but fall back into universal barbarism?" All that could be said, he concluded, was that the race of Les Eyzies had been different from all others, ancient or modern, known until then.

"Cro-Magnon man" has remained, not only the first, but the best described prototype of *Homo sapiens,* and Broca's listeners had witnessed the making of history in prehistory by the time they adjourned at 5:30 p.m. (Technically, "Cro-Magnon man" refers to his skeletal characteristics, "Aurignacian" to his contemporary implements and the animal bones found at near-by Aurignac; together with the Solutrean and Magdalenian they are part of the "old stone" or Paleolithic cultures.) Geologically speaking, they belong to the Quaternary or fourth period, starting with the Pleistocene ("most recent") about a

156

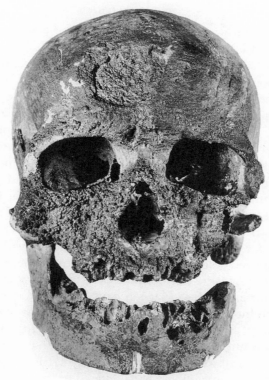

Skull of Cro-Magnon man.
(Courtesy Musée de l'Homme, Paris.)

million years ago, while modern or Cro-Magnon man made his appearance with the Holocene ("all recent") some 350,000 to 100,000
years ago. Cro-Magnon man is supposed to have flourished between
the last two of six glacial periods; Neanderthal or Mousterian man
seems to have lived in the preceding interglacial period or the "Middle," as opposed to the "Upper" Paleolithic of Cro-Magnon man. Little
was known about the glacial periods at the time of the discoveries at
Les Eyzies. Naturally, Broca's interpretation was the immediate object
of Pruner-Bey's violent criticism, who maintained these skulls were
Mongolian, not mongoloid, or rather Esthonian, the long bones showing signs of rickets, to suit the theories of Retzius and Virchow. Broca,
both earnest and caustic, seems to have prevailed.[36]

Some human skulls dating from prehistoric or historic times may
present strange shapes, others have rather carefully made defects. The
perforated kind first came to light in the Western Hemisphere through
Ephraim George Squier, United States Commissioner to Peru, foremost archeologist in American Indian matters, according to Broca.
Leaving Peru in 1865, he took with him a gift from his gracious

hostess: a skull with an intriguing hole. In the following year, Dr. Gardner showed it to a somewhat incredulous New York Academy of Medicine as a "supposed case of trephining of the calvarium of one of the tribes of South America." In 1839 a similar hole had been depicted in *Crania Americana* by Morton, who thought of it as "inflicted by some blunt instrument, probably the back of a war axe."[37] In due course, Squier took his Peruvian relic to Paris to get a second opinion. Broca presented the skull to his Society and to the Académie de Médecine in 1867.[38] It became the subject of much comment before coming to rest at the New York Museum of National History, first in a long line spanning the globe from prehistoric to present times.[39]

Broca speedily replaced "supposition" by assertion. The hole was clearly due to trephination, not accident. The patient had survived the operation for seven or eight days (Nélaton, the well-known surgeon, gave him two weeks) because the margins of the opening were still sharp, yet there were signs of postoperative inflammation, just as in the woman from the Cro-Magnon cave tens of thousands of years earlier. But the Inca had not been injured, in battle or otherwise, but operated on with surgical skill; the hole was quite regular. The four straight incision lines had been made with some sharp instrument to allow the removal of a square of bone, 15 by 17 mm. Early surgical technique in the Americas must have differed from its Greek counterpart; the Greeks had used a circular and serrated iron trephine.[38]

Few believed him. Savages, Indians, and such, may have made pottery, but surely they could not have aspired to making trephine holes.

The subject rested for a while, until something even more peculiar was excavated from under a neolithic dolmen in the Département Lozère in Central France: skulls showing bone defects two and three inches wide, not square but with scalloped edges and with bone discs inside these skulls. The discs were the work of human hands, polished and, as could be ascertained from their different thickness, *taken from another skull.* A number of such bone discs could also be picked up at random from the floor of this and other graves. An occasional one of the discs had an artificial perforation bored through, no doubt for being suspended on a string and worn as a charm.

These neolithic findings by Prunières occurred seven years after Broca had shown the more or less contemporary Peruvian skull.[40] Next, another member of the Society picked up a note from the *Gazette Hebdomadaire,* entitled "Strange Therapy" and referring to the surgical practice by some South Sea Islanders of making a T-shaped scalp incision and scraping the underlying bone with a piece of broken

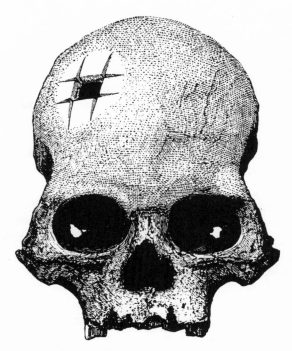

Trephined Peruvian Indian skull from Squier's collection in the American Museum of Natural History. (In E. G. Squier: *Peru: Incidents of travel and exploration in the land of the Incas*, New York: Harper & Bros., 1877, p 457.)

glass down to the dura mater, ostensibly for the treatment of head-aches, dizzy spells, and such.[41]

The "indications" for these procedures were naturally as puzzling to the surgeon who pondered them in his own practice as they were to the anthropologist. By 1874 M. Prunières had much increased his collection of trephined skulls and amulets, and Broca had found some, too. None of these bits and holes, Broca and Prunières agreed,[42] were accidental, pathological, or traumatic. Some, no doubt, had been chiselled out after death, this practice probably having a religious significance: the manufacture of amulets. Other skulls, however, had obviously not been scraped posthumously. Their margins showed the effect of a scar-formation that must have taken at least six months; in some cases the state of repair suggested an interval of years between operations and burial. The defects appeared on skulls of all ages; one in particular had been worked on in early life and again post mortem; as if those who survived the operation had an aura of sanctity about them.

Broca said he had at first doubted the therapeutic aim of neolithic surgery or that neolithic people might have regarded the brain as the seat of disease. Desperate for an answer, he had thought of the practice

159

as a ritual. But the report about these operations being performed by uncivilized present-day populations and the numerous analogies between the modern savage and prehistorc man made it appear quite likely that those neolithic ancestors did have a therapeutic effect in mind. Effect on what? Disease of the head, of course. There were no signs of skull fracture on any of these skulls, hence surgery for traumatic conditions—as practiced much later by the Greeks and after—could not have been intended here. The indications must have been medical ones: epilepsy, idiocy, insanity, and so on. These afflictions had at all times been attributed to supernatural causes. Ceremonies for the exorcism of demons were still being practiced by the Church. Perhaps the treatment of the "sacred disease" by trephination, almost abandoned today except in cases of depressed fracture of the skull, Broca said, was originally based on the idea of letting the demon escape through such an opening, especially in children. Operation at an early age was suggested by the well-healed bone edges, the elliptic shape, and the sloping edge from the outer to the inner table of the skull, presumably done as a removal in layers by scraping with flint chisels, easy only in children's skulls. (Scraping with a piece of glass, he himself had done the operation in four minutes on the skull of a two-year-old, but had taken fifty minutes in an excessively thick adult skull, "counting the periods of rest due to fatigue of the hand.")

The presence of bone amulets inside the trephined skull was probably caused by a funeral rite to compensate the deceased for his former loss and to ready him for the after-life.

Broca thus admitted both the ritualistic and therapeutic significance. Since then research has turned up more agreement on the basic issue, i.e., the deliberate performance of trephination to cure a man from suffering, no matter whether of a demon or a blood clot, or whether primitive humans associated mind and brain the way we do.[43] A neurosurgeon and a historian in Lima, in an extensive monograph on the question, favor headache as the most likely indication, in preference to epilepsy and insanity. Present-day Algerian Kabyles, too, the Peruvian authors say, seem to practice trephination mostly for headache. They consider it a minor intervention and charge less for this service than for setting a fracture.[39]

Neolithic trephination and amulet-cutting formed the subject of Broca's closely reasoned address at the Internatioal Congress at Budapest in 1876. No doubt, epileptic children, recovered in later life as they often do naturally, formed the basis for that practice both on children and on cadavers. Neolithic mysticism may be traced down to modern times, in the Andes and elsewhere. Jehan Taxil, in his *Traité de l'épilepsie, maladie vulgairement appelée au pays de Provence la goutette aux petits enfants,* published in 1603 in Lyon, had referred to the therapeutic practice of scraping the skull through, or at least the outer table, as being then something "ordinary," together with advocating powders and ashes from skull bones as local plasters for the head or to be taken in potions, pills, and even carried in knots and bags around the neck, like amulets, "according to Sylvius." Especially the skull bones of Egyptian mummies were considered effective. No eighteenth-century pharmacy was without a jar inscribed *Ossa Wormiana* ("sutural bones," separate pieces of skull bone that sometimes result from aberrant suture formation) — the supreme remedy for epilepsy. Some of them resemble neolithic amulets.[43]

Ancient superstitions had motivated other peculiar practices. Ambitious parents tried to shape their children's destinies by deforming their heads. The demonstration in Budapest of such a skull, from a grave found in an Hungarian river bank, gave Broca an opportunity to unroll the broad canvas of Cymbrian wanderings, according to where in several European countries this custom had turned up. Hippocrates had called the artificially lengthened heads *macrocephalic* — considering them an "acquired heredity" (sic) — to be found at the shores of the Black Sea. After the Caucasus, after Tiflis, the "Crimea" must have been the land of the "Cymri" until, according to Herodotus, the Scythes chased them away around 671 B.C. They must have spilled and scattered along the Danube and other major rivers as far south as Switzerland and Northern Italy, as far north as the so-called "Cymbrian" peninsula, which is Jutland. Finally they settled in Belgium and Northern France, with colonies in the west (Départment Deux Sèvres) and between Toulouse and Narbonne in the south. In all these regions the *déformation Toulousaine* could be found; in some localities, heads of the living today show one or both of two deformities: a minor "annular" one produces a sort of saddle on top of the head; the other appears as the famous backward and upward slant of the flattened forehead (known to us from Mayan art). In France, mainly around Toulouse, until Broca's day, the asylums contained a far greater number of these deformities than did the general population in the area. The deplorable practice seemed to give rise to cerebral damage with attendant insanity, imbecility, and epilepsy. Broca referred to this practice as a Germanic habit; German scholars prefer to ascribe the deformity to the Huns and Tartars. But the deformed skulls show no mongoloid features; the historical, geographic and physical evidence seems to favor Broca's hypothesis.[45]

At the same meeting in Budapest, Broca read a paper by an absent colleague on the origin of the Gypsies. It culminated in a plea, especially directed to the Hungarian hosts, to collect in a museum all possible objects pertaining to this fascinating and ancient Aryan race, which probably had introduced bronze and copper to the European northwest. One of the Hungarian savants brushed off this proposal by characterizing the Hungarian Gypsies as so uncivilized, half-naked, and dirty that they would not be let inside France. But another Hungarian anthropologist said he had seen them in Paris, and the Gypsy detractor quickly ate his words when Broca stated: "I had the honor of being their physician."[46]

His almost systematic questioning of generally made assertions included "inferior" groups; logically it had to be extended to the anthropological position of the African. Not only was Broca keen to prove that the blond Kabyles of North Africa were indigenous and not descended from Vandals, i.e., invaders from Europe,[47] but he also tested and found wanting the hypothesis that the Negro's lowly position was in keeping with some anatomical feature indicative of that lowliness. Was it true, for example, that Negroes have longer forearms than whites, and did this feature spell inferiority?[48] Most monogenists believed this; for them it was a sort of degeneracy from the white standard. A few, like James C. Prichard, had opined that intellectual and social progress, together with a change in the environment, had on the contrary caused the rise of some races over others, leaving the Negro on a scale somewhere between animals and Europeans.

With nine male and six female Negro skeletons at his disposal, Broca measured the humerus and the radius of each, expressed the length of one bone as a percentage of the other, established the maximum, minimum, and average proportions, and found that the alleged difference was indeed considerable.

But what did this really mean? Why should a long radius be taken as a sign of inferiority? Measuring the upper limb bones of an Eskimo, an Australian aborigine, and the famous Hottentot Venus—all having "a social development far inferior" to the African Negro who is "barbaric perhaps but not savage"—he found these assorted exotic forearm bones relatively shorter than the shortest European ones. "If one can draw any conclusions from so small a number of facts" it is that "it would be hard to persist in calling a long forearm a sign of inferiority."

This was in 1862. Returning to the same subject in 1867, he pointed out another fallacy. Paradoxically, Negro and European arms are not really comparable. To be fair, you have to express the upper limb as a percentage of the lower limb. The latter being, on the average, also longer in the Negro than in the white man, the proportion between arm and leg yields a greater figure in the white man than in the Negro race. On this basis, in other words, the Negro has, in fact, the relatively shorter arm. He is therefore farther removed from the simian proportions, Broca delighted in pointing out, than the white man![49]

Another alleged "stigma" of the Negro was the position of the foramen magnum in relation to the longitudinal diameter of the base of the skull. In 1764 Daubenton had first applied geometry to craniology; Camper had soon followed, measuring the facial angle. About a century later, Owen and Richard claimed that the anterior border of the foramen magnum in whites is always situated forward, i.e., halfway on the longitudinal diameter of the skull base. As you descend the accepted hierarchy of the human races and from there on further down to the primates and other mammals, the Negro's foramen magnum on an average ranges nearly an inch behind the white man's. True, Broca conceded, but only if you fail to correct your measurements for the Negro's prognathism, which puts him at a disadvantage as to the length of the base of the skull. If the extreme protrusion of the Negro's maxillary bone is taken into account, his foramen magnum actually lies nearly two inches farther forward on the corrected diameter, ahead of the position hitherto given.[50] Broca's reasoning here may not be acceptable to all, but his desire for justice in racial matters is unmistakable, given the contemporary idea that physical characteristics spell out racial excellence.

Physical anthropology was not a science until it became based on such measurements and such criticism. Hence, methods had to be worked out, measuring devices that play such a large part in physical anthropology. The commanding position Broca occupied among his anthropological contemporaries was owed as much to his technical inventiveness as to his ability as an organizer and contributor of novel, challenging, but sound opinions. Here is the list which Fletcher compiled from Broca's eighty-odd papers on craniometric and osteometric apparatus:[53] craniograph, goniometer (new), stereograph, cadre a maxima, micro-metric compass, occipital goniometer, cranioscope, porte-empreinte endocraner (molder) endograph, millimetric roulette, endometer, sphenoidal crochet, optic sound, pachymeter, acoustic sounds, craniostat, facial demi-goniometer, auricular goniometer, goniometer, orthogon, flexible goniometer, goniometer of inclination, tropometer (twist of humerus). A year before he died he compiled a "ready-reckoner," or manual, for anthropologists on the methods and fallacies in measuring skulls and other bones.[51] A first edition of this had appeared in 1865. It contains the instructions for workers in the field, for instance, the scales for identifying the colors of eyes, skin, and hair in fifty-four numbered shadings, printed with a new technical process so as to resist damage by water and sunlight.[52]

One of the main problems in craniometry was to determine the standard plane in which to place the skull for study. "Broca's plane" is the horizontal line drawn from the alveolar ridge, at its midpoint, to the occipital condyles. It became a subject of much international controversy. The chief disadvantage to its use is that the facial bones in many skulls are poorly preserved. Eventually most countries accepted the so-called "Frankfort plane" as the basic position; this corresponds to a line drawn through the infra-orbital ridge and the openings of the ear canal. Both planes have their objectors; most modern textbooks give both.[54]

Obviously, Broca was supplying a widely felt need. While many of these instruments are no longer in use, some have been re-invented, and Broca's goniometer, osteometer, osteometric board, dynamometer, sliding and spreading calipers have undergone only minor changes; his skin and eye color standards have been revised and reprinted by various successors (e.g., Hrdlička, 1904), and he may well have inspired several of the numerous instruments devised by his pupils. Their acceptance in Germany is suggested by Emil Schmidt's *Anthropologische Methoden* of 1888. Of the forty instruments illustrated there, nineteen are Broca's. Dr. Hoyme calls him the major contributor to anthropometry during the two decades he lived as an anthropologist, and this period has yielded a greater number and variety of instruments than any period since. She presumes that leadership in instrument design shifted from France to Germany because of the widely accepted revisions in standard measurements adopted by the German Anthropological Congress, held in Frankfurt-am-Main two years after Broca's death.[54] In 1870 Thomas Huxley had declared craniometry to be of subsidiary importance. Today we cannot help feeling that Broca, his school, and the contemporaries in other countries have squeezed the subject dry. In driving the method to the utmost, he showed what it could and what it could not do. Although he admitted its limitations, he exhibited no impatience and voiced no disappointment, but he increasingly turned to studying the brain. It is not Broca's figures nor his apparatus, but his part in the birth of a science, his teaching, and attitude that continue to be inspiring.

"What do you think of Broca?" I naively asked an anthropologist at the Musée de l'Homme in Paris. "Broca? Without him, we wouldn't be here!"

⇒X⇐

A Manner of Not Speaking

⇒⁝⃗ | "*I have given it the name aphemia.*"

*L*anguage and languages, their origin and mutual affinities, began to interest the historically minded in the latter part of the eighteenth century. In Broca's Society, linguistics was discussed with some passion as an aspect of racial and national origins. Eventually speech as a natural function of the brain became a major topic.

Disease has always spurred physiological inquiry; malfunction of speech has led to its study as a biological phenomenon. A man may lose his speech in various and peculiar ways—certain aspects of it, in fact, while others remain intact—as the occasional result of "apoplexy, coma, or other similar great afflictions of the head . . . because the faculty of memory is extinct."[1] The statement goes back to the Renaissance. But what are facts without a theory? And what is a theory without a series of judiciously selected facts? Speech, the vehicle, and brain, the vessel of human thought, must be related. But how? And why find out? And how?

Before the nineteenth century so little was known about the cortex of the brain that hardly anybody gave it much thought. To say this is not to reverse cause and effect. Knowledge is the source as much as the result of inquiry; each propels the other. Almost totally unexplored as to their functions, the cerebral convolutions were not even considered mysterious. By Broca's time, this grotesquely shaped, fast-decaying and unmanageable organ had attracted only a few investigators.

165

Broca's own interest in the brain was stimulated early by his teachers Leuret and Gerdy; it became the dominant concern for half of his productive life. In his omnivorous readings and his close contact with Leuret at the Bicêtre Asylum, he could not help becoming familiar with his chief's book, *On the Comparative Anatomy of the Nervous System as Seen in its Relations to Intelligence.*[2] It was the first large work to base a description of the cerebral convolutions on the certitude that their "number, shape, arrangement, and relationships are not haphazard." The contrary opinion, Leuret maintained, could be held only by a person who had not examined a sufficient number of animal brains. Each family in the animal kingdom had a convolutional pattern generally characteristic of its kind. You only had to look at the brain of a bear, for instance, to be impressed by the regularity of its folds. Indeed, mere deductive reasoning ought to have convinced everyone that this most important organ of the intellect, no less than of instinct and passion, must altogether be organized on lines that were at least as fixed as those of any other bodily part. The overall degree of intelligence, however, could not be deduced from the complexity of the gyri, Leuret thought, except when such comparisons were made within a single family.

A unique source for several generations, Leuret's book also paid homage to Luigi Rolando of Turin, for having ten years earlier expressed the new concept of regular cerebral folds and for having first described, in the human brain, the main vertical fissure that separates the anterior half of the hemisphere from the posterior. *Rolando's fissure,* as Leuret called this most important landmark, had, however, not been mentioned by the Italian author at all. Rolando had pointed to the two parallel vertical convolutions that border the fissure; in so doing he had given credit to Vicq-d'Azyr—or rather to the Frenchman and illustrator who had depicted them. Leuret had used a posthumous edition of Vicq-d'Azyr's, so adulterated by its editor that the crucial plate was omitted. *"Sottement"* (stupidly), Broca commented many years later, adding, "Rolando's name was given by chance to the fissure that separates those two convolutions. But this time chance was not unfair. As to the convolutions, Rolando's work is much superior to Vicq-d'Azyr's. Rolando was the first anatomist who conceived the convolutions as fixed *in general* and who tried to subject them to methodical analysis. Among all the predecessors of Leuret and Gratiolet, it is he who deserves the greatest praise. It is, therefore, correct that this eminent man's name be indelibly recorded in the history of the cerebral convolutions."[3] By the time Broca wrote this, Leuret-Rolando's convolutions had been shown to represent the main motor and sensory functions of the body.

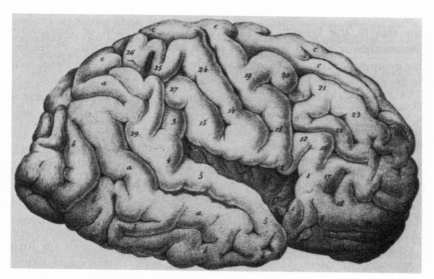

Rolando's illustration of the human brain, right hemisphere, lateral surface. With insignificant modifications, acceptable as a modern representation of the human brain.

1, 8, 9, 12, 16, 17, 18, "3rd or inferior frontal gyrus or convolution (1 is approximately Broca's area *(in the left hemisphere)*; 21, 22, 23, "2nd" or middle frontal gyrus; c, c, c, "1st" or superior frontal gyrus; 13, 19, precentral gyrus; 14, 24, postcentral gyrus (central sulcus — of Rolando — between them); 15, 27, supramarginal gyrus; 29, angular gyrus; 6-7, Sylvian fissure; 4, 5, (superior); a, (middle) temporal gyrus; b, (inferior); and occipital gyri. (Luigi Rolando: "Della struttura degli emisferi cerebrali," *Mem. R. Accad. Sci.* Torino, Vol. XXV, 1830, pp. 103-145.)

Leuret's psychiatric practice, illness, and finally death prevented him from writing the second volume of his *Comparative Anatomy*. This was done by Pierre Gratiolet, deputy head of anatomy at the Museum. Discovered while still an interne at the Salpêtrière, brilliant but lacking protectors, Gratiolet had to wait nineteen years for his professorship; two years later he died at the age of forty-nine. All this time he had been troubled by *res angusta domi*, Juvenal's phrase, used by Broca in the obituary speech for his colleague:[4]

> "How can they hope to arrive, with their talents choked off
> In the domestic squeeze . . ."

There was much to separate Broca from Gratiolet, but they also had much in common: their birthplace, for one thing. Broca's senior by nine years, the son of a local physician, Pierre had left Sainte-Foy-la-Grande when he was ten years old. Catholic, Royalist, and married to a titled lady, Dr. Gratiolet, Sr.'s failure and departure were presuma-

167

bly due to the boycott of the wealthy, republican, or Bonapartist Protestants at Sainte Foy. After seven years in Bordeaux, Pierre lost his ever unsuccessful father and an only sister. He moved to Paris, soon to be followed by his mother—and by more poverty.

Gratiolet, not a practicing physician but unsurpassed in his day as a neuroanatomist, was an elegant stylist and a debater of gently aristocratic manners, while his physical appearance, according to the beardy portrait we have of him, must have rather suggested a backwoodsman. In the interval between the two volumes of his common venture with Leuret and before he joined Broca's Society, he published a magnificent monograph of his own, with atlas, *Cerebral Folds of Man and the Primates.* [5]

In 1854 this was the situation Gratiolet found in brain folds: "Vesalius, Th. Bartholinus, or Galen, for that matter, attach little importance to them. Thus Th. Bartholinus says: '. . .the convolutions have the appearance of intestines; they are not made for the intellect as Erasistratus holds—asses have them too—nor for any purpose or use as others think; but in order to . . . protect the cerebral vessels against the danger of rupture from violent movement, *especially during full moon* when the brain swells in the skull' (*Anatomia reformata* p. 139; 1656). [This notion of Bartholin, italicized by Gratiolet, is perhaps not quite as absurd as it sounds. It may well be that a woman's brain does periodically swell a little before and during the menstrual period.]

"But one of the greatest anatomists of modern times returns to the idea of Erasistratus, for Willis says (*Cerebri Anatome*, cap. X, 3, p. 294, *Opera Me lica et Physica*, Lugd. 1676), '. . .The manifold tendencies of the animal spirits require multiple cerebral folds and convolutions for the storage of sensory impressions, as if in various cellars or warehouses, and so enable these impressions to be evoked for any given occasion. . . . The gyri are few in quadrupeds, yet in some, such as the cat, they are found in a certain pattern; wherefore these animals can meditate and reminisce, though hardly anything except what the instincts and needs of nature . . . suggest.' [Translation by this author from the original Latin of Willis, which Gratiolet quotes.]

"Despite the importance attached to them since the seventeenth century," Gratiolet continues, "no anatomist up to the end of the last century has tried to discover the law of their arrangement in man. . . ."

Had the advent of phrenology with Gall and his disciples been of help? "Gall no doubt might have given greater precision to this part of the cerebral anatomy had he not been preoccupied with his vain system. But with him, it was not a matter of discovering these, but to furnish proof for his own hypothesis. It is a sort of paradox, and at first hard to explain, that the study of the convolutions was actually neglected by the adherents of Gall, while it was most advanced by the most outspoken opponents of phrenology."[5]

This was a perceptive statement, if not quite fair to Franz Joseph Gall (1757–1828), originally Gallo, the internationally famous expatriate from Vienna—branded as a materialist by his Emperor—with whom all accounts of cortical localization begin. True, Gall was not much of a convolutionist; on the other hand, most of the devastating criticism leveled against him failed to advance this aspect of the matter. Without Gall's deserved reputation as an anatomist of the brain on one hand and his wrong-headedness as a phrenologist on the other, medical men might not have been shocked into studying the cerebral cortex then and there: in Italy, France, and Germany during the first quarter of the century. The criticism heaped by sober intelligences on this imaginative if wayward mind—libertine, scholar, naturalist—was based on the risible psychological entities for which he claimed that compartments existed in the brain. This was not all, for Gall also pretended that he could guess which of these entities prevailed in a given person by looking at, or passing his fingers over, the relative prominences on the skull overlying those compartments.[6] Nevertheless, Gall has played a great role in deterministic thought about the functions of brain and mind—a long line stretching from the eighteenth century to this day, traveled by physicians and philosophers alike.[7] (Gall's impact in the early nineteenth century is paralleled only by that made in the twentieth by another Viennese doctor who first shocked, then shaped, contemporary thought about mental mechanisms and was placed in the most exclusive section of the thinkers' pantheon: Freud.) Auguste Comte, for instance, about to reform the calendar (thirteen months) named the last four weeks of the year after the greatest men in modern science: Galileo, Newton, Lavoisier—and Gall. Scientific psychology, a twentieth-century psychologist wrote, was "born of phrenology, out of wedlock with science."[8] But to Gratiolet, Gall was guilty of "the most ridiculous analysis ever made about the faculties of human understanding."[9]

In Gratiolet's cerebral anatomy the white matter of the corona radiata is related to the cortex as cutaneous nerves are to the skin. Without the benefit of a neuron theory, he nevertheless concludes that the folds are somehow in contact with the spinal cord fibers. The idea had first been emitted by Gall; Gratiolet is undecided whether each fold is connected with every part of the body or whether it has "its own special connections with the main centers of the organism that give rise to distinct excitations." He appeals to experimentation.[9]

But Gratiolet no longer envisages the cerebral cortex as being in its entirety an organ of the intellect, as Foville, for instance,[10] had done. Some areas—called "projection areas" since Meynert's studies of the 1870's[11]—may be given over to "lower" functions of a physical nature. Where more cortex is available, as in higher animals and men, its excess—Meynert's subsequent "association areas"—will be serving the intellect. Yet the position which a given brain's owner occupies in the hierarchy of nature remains the paramount principle in Gratiolet's thought—and not only his of course. The idea of higher and lower functions, the admixture of moral and cultural values in the study of cerebral structures and mechanisms, has never quite ceased to bedevil students. How could it have failed to occupy the minds of mid-nineteenth-century anatomists? Gratiolet, in particular, was a man of the older order. Reluctantly he had come to terms with the fact—a fact that he more than anyone since Aristotle was just establishing in detail—that in all these brains from man down to marmoset, there was this strange analogy of shape. Primarily concerned with their shape, number, and order, Gratiolet showed and named the essential parts which man and primates have in common and their same general disposition, except for the greater complexity in man. Where they are not similar, they are at least homologous.[12]

The main part of the work is thus concerned with sober descriptions and accurate comparisons. Still, about a quarter of the text is given over to comment and speculation. The minor differences within the order of the primates must also apply to the human races; the higher and lower forms of cerebral development justify the assumption that human races are different species of the genus *Homo*. Such a statement, Gratiolet says, "is by no means contrary to the text of Genesis."[13]

Gratiolet's contribution deserves particular mention, for this was the drift of opinion when he joined the Société d'Anthropologie as one of its founders. It included an early refutation of ontogenesis repeating phylogenesis, even before this theory had been effectively formulated. With much bright sunshine on brain morphology, with a good deal of overcast on the question of race, the attitude was as benevolent as it was prejudiced.

Broca was faced with a great number of such problems that could not be avoided, for they were relevant to science, yet must be handled with extreme care because they touched on metaphysics, politics, and religion. As secretary he recorded what was being said (from memory), but he also moderated the discussion; this did not prevent him from taking part and taking sides.[14] By 1869 the Society was sufficiently affluent for the treasurer to suggest the hiring of a stenographer. "This would introduce a profound change in our customs," Broca demurred and was seconded by de Quatrefages, who found it would affect "all our conditions of existence." "A lot of fuss, waste of space and money, under the pretext of exactitude and to the detriment of science and our funds," a third member remarked.[15]

There is an axiom—not entirely tenable, but accepted by many today as it was then by the followers of Gall—which says that the most human, valuable, and intellectual parts of the brain are the frontal lobes, because their complexity is greatest in man.

Consequently, the frontal lobes were a platform on which the upholders of order and class in all things, including the cerebral convolutions, could meet the few surviving partisans of Gall. The first group, with Gratiolet, based their argument for the superior excellence of this part of the brain on comparative anatomy; although progressive in the method of detailed observation, their interpretation remained as conservative as were their politics. The second group, late adherents of Gall, rather out of date as accurate anatomists, were, on the contrary, advanced both in their clinico-pathological views of the brain and in their political radicalism. Both groups influenced Broca. In the Société d'Anthropologie the spokesman of the second group, the localizers, was Dr. Auburtin. The only mark this man has left on recorded history is that of having been the mouthpiece for his father-in-law, Bouillaud.

Professor Jean Baptiste Bouillaud, the "red dean" of 1848, reportedly prided himself on being the model for Balzac's ever-recurring kind Dr. Horace Bianchon.[16] But the resemblance between this fictional character and the real Bouillaud consists of little more than a birthplace (Angoulême), of an apprenticeship with Dupuytren (Balzac's Desplein), a doubtlessly intended likeness of poverty and integrity, perhaps also of mildly leftist tendencies.

A portrait of the real man attributes to Bouillaud "dignity in bearing, a facile diction, high associative sagacity (note Gall's term), a habitual tendency to generalize, and independent character—but also too much awareness of his own merit, so that he takes risks that sometimes end in failure . . . He likes to pose as a misunderstood man, gets angry at the slightest show of opposition, and is found in an eternal state of discontent and excitement. He believes posterity is waiting for him. . . ."[17]

An important innovator himself, Bouillaud was always ready to ridicule others, such as Sée for his introduction into France of salicylates in the treatment of acute rheumatism, Pasteur, and even, when it was presented at a meeting of the Académie de Médecine, the miraculous phonograph that seriously or not, he suspected to be a ventriloquist's trick.[16] Impulsive but tough, he outlived Broca, reaching the age of eighty-three.

Broca, of course, knew Bouillaud well. As an interne, he had admired, supported, and slightly criticized him in 1848, been invited to his house, and at one time had toyed with the idea of studying internal medicine with him. Bouillaud was a pupil of Broussais, hence an ardent bloodletter. He also had elaborated a germinal idea of Broussais' that rheumatic fever was the cause of endocarditis. And with Broussais he had fallen under the spell of Gall.[16] When he was twenty-nine, he challenged an unbelieving and hostile Académie Royale de Médecine to accept his *Clinical studies— showing that loss of speech corresponds to a lesion of the anterior lobes of the brain— a confirmation of M. Gall's view regarding the seat of the organ of articulate speech.* Gall's view, soon generally discredited, had been that speech was localized in that part of the brain that rests on the roof of the orbit. The firmer the resistance to this view, the more convinced Bouillaud became of its truth. In 1825, in 1839, and again in 1848 he mounted his attacks against indifference and ridicule, but with such skill and conviction and from such a position of high repute as a formidable opponent and a great teacher, that no matter how skeptical, his audience gave him a hearing each time. He was still and again fighting for the cause when it got a grand airing in the 1865 sessions of the Académie. His target, Pierre Flourens, politically conservative and the principal demolisher of Gall's scientific reputation, was the period's prime authority on the physiology of the brain.

"No physician who is in the least familiar with clinical studies," Bouillaud had said in 1825, "has failed to observe many defects in locomotor functions produced by an illness of the brain. The inflammation causes spasmodic movements, cerebral compression, more or less widespread paralysis. It is therefore not without a good deal of astonishment that we read in the work of M. Flourens, on *The Properties of the Nervous System,* that the brain exerts no immediate and direct influence on muscular phenomena. . . .

"But it is not enough to know, in a general way, that the brain is indispensible for the production of several muscular movements; we must in addition determine whether or not each one of the various parts that compose the brain initiates a particular movement and find out in particular whether there are not several nervous centers involved in muscular movements. . . .

"It would be wrong to believe that the limbs are the only moving parts for which there are particular *centers* in the brain. The same holds for all the organs charged with muscular activity under the reign of the mind: such among others are the tongue and eye, those two admirable instruments which play such an important role in the mechanism of mental functions. . . . To adduce the proper evidence, it is necessary to establish by observation that the tongue and its congeneric organs can be separately paralyzed in the act of speaking, that is to say, without other parts being affected at the same time; on the other hand that they can retain the control of their movements while other parts—the limbs, for instance—are deprived of their own use. This is what I am going to prove first. Next I shall attempt to determine the site of the nervous center which rules over the mechanism of the speech organs. . . .

"The three case histories I have just given prove that paralysis of the speech organs can exist independently of any other paralysis. . . .

"Speech is a kind of articulated gesture. . . .

"Note that it is absolutely necessary to distinguish two different phenomena in the act of speech. There is the ability to produce words as signs of ideas while preserving their memory—and the ability to articulate these same words. There exists, as it were, an internal and an external speech; the latter is only the expression of the former. The nerve system which governs the formation of signs is not the same as that which produces the movements of the speech organs, for it is not rare to see speech suspended, either because only the tongue and its congeneric organs refuse to pronounce the words, or because the memory of these words fail us. Perhaps the grey matter of the lobules is the organ of the intellectual part of speech, whereas the white matter is the organ which executes and coordinates the muscular movements for the production of words. . . ."[18]

Here was a whole program of cerebral localization—cerebral in general, frontal for speech—but in the depth rather than the cortex and without reference to convolutions. In 1839 Bouillaud offered experimental evidence: there had been Cullerier's patient who had shot himself in the head with a pistol and presented a large gash over the frontal lobes: "Curious to know what effect it would have on speech if the brain were compressed, we applied to the exposed part a large spatula pressing from above downwards and a little from front to back. With moderate pressure, speech seemed to die on his lips; pressing harder and more sharply, speech not only failed but a few words were cut off suddenly."[19]

In the stormy February and March days of 1848 Bouillaud defended Gall once more, stressing the coordinating influence of the anterior lobes on speech, adducing many examples, some indeed so poorly documented that they failed to carry conviction. One of the critics, a M. Rochoux, quoted numerous authors against Bouillaud: Cruveilhier, Foville, Piorry, Bérard, Velpeau, Lallemand, etc. Bouillaud became more and more emphatic: "At this very moment there is a patient at Bicêtre who has all the freedom of his intelligence and his movements . . . but he cannot speak. [This is one of several such cases, no doubt, possibly Leborgne himself, admitted in 1840, the patient Broca described thirteen years later.] Very well, then, I am not afraid to affirm that this man carries a deep lesion in the anterior lobules of the brain; if he did not, my doctrine would be false and I would not hesitate to say so, for I am no less disposed to confess an error than to proclaim a new truth. . . .

"In closing, I propose to M. Rochoux that we both offer a prize of 500 francs.

"Herewith I offer 500 francs to anyone who will provide me with an example of a deep lesion of the anterior lobules of the brain without a lesion of speech."[20]

And there the matter rested for another thirteen years: Bouillaud's boiling indignation with so much lack of understanding, his rash wager, and the impassive sarcasm of his adversaries. There also rested M. Rochoux's "holistic" and rather modern view of brain functions, together with Baillarger's reasoning about the impossible unilateral lesion affecting speech.

In the Société d'Anthropologie, the first mention of "loss of memory for words" was occasioned by the application for membership by Dr. Dally on March 7, 1861. The year before, Dally had described such a case, a man who could repeat spoken words and copy written ones, but do neither spontaneously. It was a case "not altogether rare in science," de Castelnau commented, but also an example of what "a subtle analysis of the intellect disease was apt to perform." And he scorned those *psychologues d'inspiration* (speculative analysts): "positive psychology must be based on strict observation of cerebral function, normal and abnormal physiology!"[21]

It was in the following month that "loss of memory for words" reappeared as a subject. Since February the Society, well along in its second year, was in the middle of a discussion on *les grosses têtes*, "the big heads,"[22] or the importance of cerebral volume in relation to form. In its course the initiator, Gratiolet, also did not escape reprimands for talking about the soul and dealing in metaphysics and mysticism.[23]

Broca did not go into the metaphysics of the argument. He quoted Gratiolet to the effect that the cerebral volume of individual races was of almost no significance: shape, not mass of the brain, ought to be correlated with intelligence. Furthermore, Gratiolet had declared that as the function of thinking was indivisible, so was the brain as the organ of thinking; science had no positive data. The very principle of cerebral localization, Gratiolet had concluded, was wrong.

Broca countered these speculations with some measurements, in part his own. The sexes differed in that the male "average maximum" brain weight was 1410 grams, the female, 1133, with variations slightly greater in the male. Body height, too, seemed to have less influence on brain size in females. (Mere averages were misleading, Broca argued, but the plotting of curves on a system of coordinates was not yet adopted. Hence, he used the terms "average maximum and minimum" to allow a more accurate and meaningful breakdown.) Further it seemed established that intelligence "disappeared" if the brain weight dropped below 1133 grams in the male, below 970 grams in the female. There also was the record of the excessively large brains of great men, such as Pascal's, Byron's, Cuvier's, Schiller's. The racial correlations also seemed to favor the idea that superiority was vested in the larger skulls. Thus, setting the Australian aborigine at 100, the African Negro was comparable at 111.6; the German, at 124: "the figures expressing rather accurately the racial hierarchy." While the correlation between intelligence and cranial capacity was "remarkable — *all other things being equal*," it was not absolute. "An enlightened person cannot think of measuring intelligence by measuring the brain."[24] Still, it was remarkable.

With the problem of drawing conclusions from skull to brain size, the difficulty of measuring the capacity of the former was increasingly realized. Controversies about specimens depicted in books, criticisms of method in gauging and of the figures published, began to be the order of the day. In the case of Cuvier, Gratiolet had secured the great naturalist's battered old hat for measurement. True, the relic was a large size with diameters of 21.8 by 16 centimeters, but M. Puriau, the fashionable Paris hatter, informed Gratiolet that equally large ones were sold to ordinary customers, thirty percent of them, in fact![25]

The debate had steadily gathered momentum from the start when, among the skulls converging on Paris from the four corners of the world, Gratiolet had selected one of a Totonac, an Indian tribe from the Gulf of Mexico. Surprisingly to some, it was larger than the average "Caucasian" skull. But as only the complexity was decisive, especially that of the frontal convolutions, a large skull *per se* was of no great consequence.[26] When Auburtin objected that the volume of the frontal lobes indeed was significant, he needed to take only one step to expound his father-in-law's work on speech and another to wind up saying that both anterior lobes were never found intact completely or even relatively (whatever that meant) as shown by the autopsies of individuals who had lost the faculty of speech but not the rest of their intelligence. The complete destruction of both frontal lobes in a person still speaking would alone invalidate that theory.[27]

Interrupted by other subjects, the discussion continued into June. It now involved both problems: the correlation between brain volume with intelligence and the possibility of localizing mental functions in distinct parts of the brain. With great conviction and skill, Gratiolet fought an almost united opposition, until he regretted having brought up "the little spark causing a philosophical explosion."[28]

Broca began to discuss localization on March 21.[29] It was, he said, "the natural consequence to the philosophical movements of the eighteenth century. Times for saying without hesitation that in the name of metaphysics the brain, anatomy notwithstanding, was indivisible, like the soul, were past. The relationship between mind and matter was being questioned; in the midst of all the uncertainties surrounding this great problem, anatomy and physiology, hitherto reduced to silence, at last had to speak up.

"The initiator of this kind of scientific reform was Gall. His incontestable merit was to proclaim the great principle of cerebral localization; indeed, one may say that this was the starting point for every discovery in cerebral physiology in our century." Broca believed "in the principle" but naturally had his doubts as to the feasibility of "constructing a detailed system of localization" à la Gall, of performing "a dissection of the intellect" and of "ever establishing sufficiently clear-cut and unassailable" divisions.

He also had great respect for Gratiolet. Quite opposed to him on grounds of religion, politics, and philosophy, Broca gives the impression that beyond the admiration for the talent of the older man, he felt something like affection for the sincerity of Gratiolet's conviction and the charm of his manner, aside from the sympathy with his struggles.[30] Gratiolet seems to have reciprocated these feelings, and there was a certain happy satisfaction, rather than mere politeness, when he found certain areas of agreement with the permanent leader of their group.[31]

To Broca, the view of convolutions as distinct organs seemed to be supported not only by physiology and pathology suggesting their distinct functions, but by anatomy showing their different structure. Baillarger had taught him his method of viewing thin slices of cortex pressed between glass slides: gently, by using little balls of wax as buffers to cushion the pressure between the slides. Broca granted that there was a *fundamental* sameness of the cortex. But in addition to Gennari-Vicq-d'Azyr-Baillarger's "white line," which characteristically splits the gray matter of the visual cortex, there existed differences in the pattern of the cortical layers according to their respective sites in the brain.

These characteristics were less marked than the white line, and he had not studied them sufficiently to dare describe them as yet. He did not wish to build what he called "a system," but only to establish "a principle."[32] In modern terms, he foreshadowed cytoarchitectonics, i.e., Meynert's idea, published seven years later,[33] and Brodman's, at the beginning of this century.[34] One might indeed say it has remained a principle, tending to degenerate into a system.

This was May, 1861; during the previous month, on April 4, Auburtin first introduced the medical aspect, i.e., disturbances of speech. In the April 18 meeting, Broca, with some urgency, inserted into the debate a recent and pertinent observation of his own.[35]

"Apropos the reading of the minutes," the record says, "M. Broca presented the brain of a fifty-one-year-old man who had died [on the previous day] in his service at the hospital Bicêtre. For the last twenty-one years this man had lost the use of his speech. As it is planned to deposit the specimen at the Musée Dupuytren and to publish the complete records in the *Bulletin de la Société Anatomique*, only a short resumé will be given; the case is quite similar to some of those about which M. Auburtin has talked at the last meeting." After reading the case history and demonstrating the brain, Broca relinquished the floor for Gratiolet to continue his part of the discussion concerning volume and form.

This matter of loss of speech was sufficiently important to justify the brief interruption and to take the observation to a medically more representative society. Localization seemed at last confirmed. For the first time in six years, Broca thought he again had a major topic to bring before the Société Anatomique. There, in August, he began by describing the opinions and circumstances confronting him before he had come to deal with the present case.[36] "The value of facts is not determined by the circumstances under which one observes them," he said, "and yet the impression they make on us depends to a large extent on those circumstances. When a few days after I had been listening to the argument of M. Auburtin, I found one morning on my service a dying patient who twenty-one years ago had lost the faculty of articulate speech, I gathered his case history with the greatest care because it seemed to serve as a touchstone for the theory of my colleague."

He gave credit to Bouillaud, saying that in modifying the phrenologists' system he had saved it from shipwreck. "In individuals who are neither paralyzed nor idiots, the abolition of speech is a symptom of sufficient importance" he said, "that it seems useful to designate it by a special name. I have given it the name aphemia (aphémie) (alpha privative; phemi, I speak, I declare). For what is missing in these patients is only the faculty to articulate words. . . ." (*Langage articulé* is what Broca called this special faculty. In English, as in French, "language" means any form of symbolic expression, but in English the word also means the individual vocabularies and grammars used by different nations—called *langues* in French, "tongues" in English. "Language" has many aspects, of which speech, the making of articulate sounds, is only one. The natural and precise English term for the method of expressing things by articulate sounds is "speech," not "language." Hence, "speech" has been chosen here to render the restricted meaning of the French word *langage*. Some translators, e.g., von Bonin, whose translation I follow in part, have used "articulate language" for the French term *langage* and reserved "speech" for the French *parole*, as in *perte de la parole*, i.e., "loss of speech." These English translators probably have done so in order to avoid "articulate speech" as redundant. I felt neither the adjective "articulate" should be sacrificed, for it characterizes the act of coordination, nor "speech," the short precise English term for sonorous verbal communication. "Articulate" and "articulated" are interchangeable forms.)

Here Broca opened—or reopened—a long line of argument as to what the people so affected have lost. The corrolary—what they have left in the way of speech—is often nothing but one or a few meaningless syllables, an occasional swear-word. But they do remember words, for they understand them. Bouillaud had considered this defect as the faculty to coordinate the movements for articulate speech. "Was it then a locomotor ataxia, limited to the articulation of sounds?" Broca wondered. In that case they might have lost a mechanical and not an intellectual faculty. The alternative might be "the loss of a special kind of memory, the memory of the procedure which one has to follow in order to articulate words," i.e., the memories which a child has to acquire as it learns to speak. In this case aphemia might be an intellectual disturbance. He favored the second view. But for the moment he was not too concerned with that side of the problem, he said. The thing which he felt "could no more be doubted was the existence of a special faculty of articulate speech as I have defined it."

"There are," Broca said, paraphrasing and amplifying Bouillaud, "indeed several kinds of language. Every system of signs which permits us to express ideas more or less intelligibly, completely and rapidly, is a language in the widest sense of the word. Talking, mimicking, using finger signs, symbolic or phonetic writing, etc., are thus so many kinds of language. There is a general faculty of language which governs all these expressions of thought; this may be defined as the faculty of establishing a constant relationship between an idea and a sign, whether the sign be a sound, a gesture, a figure, or any kind of tracing. Moreover, every kind of language requires the play of certain organs of *emission* and *reception* . . . ear . . . eye . . . touch . . . larynx or tongue, palate, face, arms, etc. . . .; intactness of muscles and that part of the central nervous system whence those nerves arise . . . of the sensory apparatus, nerve, and that part of the central nervous system whither it goes . . . finally, that part of the brain on which depends the general faculty of language as defined above."

All these three may be intact, he thought, and yet articulate speech may be impossible.

He stressed this point of isolation, for in adults he had seen this faculty perish independently of all others; it must therefore be special. Hereby hangs the whole point of the demonstration: "If all cerebral faculties were as distinct and clearly circumscribed as this one, we would at least have a definite starting point from which to tackle the controversial question of cerebral localization. Unfortunately, this is not the case. The greatest hindrance to progress in this area of physiology lies in an insufficient and uncertain analysis of functions, an indispensable preliminary to investigating any organ.

"Regarding this issue, science is so little advanced that it has not even found its base. For what is being contested today is not this or that phrenological system, it is the principle of localization itself. In other words, the question we must answer first is this: are the parts of the brain concerned with thinking all identical, or do they all have different attributes?"

This base has not yet been found more than one hundred years later. The principle of localization, or representation, of intellectual functions, was not allowed to settle and has not been settled. What precisely are individual intellectual functions? How are they delimited? Is "articulate speech" one of them, or is it only something like one of Gall's ludicrous entities?

He had used much caution, Broca said. "Although I believe in the principle of localization, I have been and still am asking myself, within what limits may this principle apply?" One thing, however, he thought was well established by the science of his day, namely, "that the most elevated cerebral faculties such as judgment and reflection, the faculties of comparison and abstraction, have their seat in the frontal convolutions, while convolutions of the temporal, parietal,

179

and occipital lobes are affected by sentiments, predilections, and passions." Although Gallists and anti-Gallists were then pretty well agreed on this point, it is the most dated of their concepts, and it came to be so less than twenty years later, thanks, in part, to Broca's own researches.

At that moment, however, the idea was compelling that the convolutions were anatomical entities. "There are in the human mind a group of faculties and, in the brain, groups of convolutions, and the facts assembled by science so far allow us to state . . . that the great regions of the mind correspond to the great regions of the brain. ["Great regions" is an expression that appears in Louis Foville's work on the anatomy of the brain.[37]] It is in this sense that the principle of localization appears to be, if not rigorously demonstrated, at least probable." Everybody was agreed that all faculties called intellectual have their seat "in this part of the brain" — i.e., in the convolutions. (Broca does not use the words "cortex" or "gray matter.") It seemed, therefore, very probable that articulate speech was an intellectual function rather than a mere coordinating mechanism. And "if it were demonstrated that the lesions which abolish speech constantly occupy the same convolution" — rather than affecting indifferently any convolution or lobe — "then one could hardly help admitting that this convolution is the seat of articulate speech." He envisaged an intermediate third possibility, one lying between strict localization in a single convolution and no localization at all. "Let us assume that the lesions of aphemia always occupy the same lobe, but in this lobe not always the same convolutions . . . it would consequently have its seat in a certain region, a group of convolutions. It then would become very probable that the cerebral (mental) faculties are localized by regions and not by convolutions."

It is unlikely that any other single preserved human brain has aroused more attention than the one Broca was describing. It formed the focal point in the convergence of the ideas traced here, and it was the starting point for thousands of similar specimens bottled in preserving fluids or as plaster casts — and for floods of ideas and ink. It has been revered and belittled. The manner of its preservation has been criticized and so has its temporary unavailability: the first because Broca failed to cut it. "I have refrained from studying the deeper parts," he said, "in order not to destroy the specimen which I thought should be deposited in the [Dupuytren] Museum." He sensed its historical role. Destroying the specimen by cutting would not have advanced the problem of localization, for nature's own gross destruction had made clear enough what was gone. Against this well-motivated omission

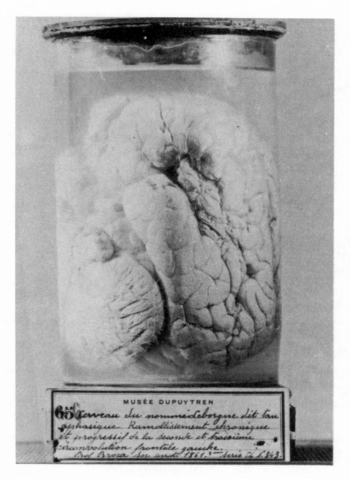

MUSÉE DUPUYTREN

Brain of Leborgne, alias *Tan*, from the Musée Dupuytren. Note bottling in erect position. (Courtesy Dr. Juster, Institut de Parasitologie, École Pratique, Paris, 1962.)

only minds running in grooves can lay the charge of something amounting to pathologist's "malpractice."

Unavailability is a fate that not infrequently befalls collections such as that of the Musée Dupuytren, where this brain was deposited. It seems to exist, for with the help of friendly attendants and a flashlight I have been allowed to take a specimen so labelled up into the light of day from its dusty shelf in the basement of the École de Médicine in Paris where it had rested since 1940. The loose wooden block on which the jar stands bears the inscription: "65. [with a '6' or 'b' pencilled next to the printed number and the printed '6' crossed out]. Brain of a man Leborgne called Tan aphasic. Chronic and progressive softening of the second and third left frontal convolution.

(Prof. Broca Soc. anat. 1861, 2nd series V. 6 P. 343).”[36] Still, an ever so slight doubt is attached to its identity. For note the number 65: according to Broca, it was deposited as number 55, a. This is indeed confusing. And finally, Pierre Marie gives 56 as its number.[38]

"The patient died on April 17 [1861] at 11 o'clock a.m." Broca's report continued. "The autopsy was performed as soon as possible, that is to say after twenty-four hours. The temperature was hardly elevated and the cadaver showed no sign of putrefaction. The brain was shown a few hours later in the Société d'Anthropologie, then immediately put in alcohol. This organ was so altered [by disease] that one had to be very careful in preserving it. Only after two months and after several changes of the fixation fluid, did the specimen begin to harden. Today it is in perfect condition . . . ."

After a hundred years had elapsed, at least two authors felt, independently, that Leborgne, i.e., the patient, deserved the publication of an *In Memoriam*.[39] After all, even one of Pavlov's dogs was given a monument.

Leborgne's history has often been told but his basic disease has never been satisfactorily diagnosed. Broca had no qualms when he spoke of a "chronic and progressive softening" of the third convolution of the left frontal lobe. Neither the history nor the appearance and description of the specimen allow a confident clinical and pathological interpretation in modern terms. Epileptic since his youth, aphasic at the age of thirty, progressively weakening on the right side at the age of forty—first in the arm, finally hemiplegic and bedridden for seven years, he gradually lost his intelligence, also his vision, and died at the age of fifty-one of cellulitis with gangrene of the paralyzed right leg. Mainly the early history of epilepsy arouses the suspicion that successive thrombotic infarcts may not have been the correct diagnosis but some more smoothly advancing disease.

Broca's acquaintance with this hopeless patient lasted barely a week. "Since M. Auburtin had declared a few days ago that he would renounce it [Bouillaud's doctrine] if we could show him a single case of a well-characterized aphemia without a lesion in the frontal lobes [we see how Auburtin was Bouillaud's man to the point of uttering such devastating threats!],[27] I invited him to see my patient, above all in order to know what his diagnosis might be and if he would accept the outcome of this observation as conclusive. Despite the complications that had supervened in the last eleven years, my friend found the present condition and the antecedents sufficiently clear for stating without any hesitation that the lesion must have started in one of the anterior lobes."

But before asking Auburtin, Broca first made sure of his own ground. His skill in examining what now would be called "a neurological case" was well up to the task; he hardly missed a trick. In the unending quest for new "test batteries" that have been worked out in the following decades of organized neurology, few methods have been devised to give us a more complete, accurate, and convincing picture than Broca's clinical examination. Nor would it be easy to find fault with his post-mortem findings. His description of Ledgewood, the "phocomelic" congenital amputee, his association with Brown-Séquard, his discovery of the pathology of muscular dystrophy suffice to convince us of his calibre as a "neurologist" before he gave proof of his insight in the case of Leborgne. ("Neurology" was originally a mere anatomical term suggested by Thomas Willis for peripheral nerves, like "osteology" or "mycology." Only toward the close of the 19th century did it acquire meaning as a clinical specialty.) The history was taken with the thoroughness he had brought to any other of his pursuits, always, it seems, with the idea in mind that he was on the threshold of a major discovery.

Despite the epilepsy of his early adult life, Leborgne had been able to take up the trade of a last-maker. "His attendants, his ward-mates, and those of his relatives who came to visit him were asked in turn . . . but we could not find out whether the loss of speech had started slowly or rapidly or if any other symptom had accompanied the onset. . . ." Although already quite speechless for two or three months before his admission to the surgical ward, he seemed quite normal in every other respect. Normal, except that "his only answer to any question was '*tan, tan*' to which he added a great variety of gestures quite successful in rendering most of his thoughts." His anger at not being understood—"the catastrophic reaction" of modern authors—increased his vocabulary by the same swear-word that Dr. Auburtin had reported of his patient, i.e., "*Sacré nom de Dieu*" (God damn).

"*Tan* was reputedly selfish, vindictive, and mean; his ward-mates loathed him and even accused him of stealing. To a large extent," Broca explains, "these defects may have been due to the cerebral lesion; in any case they were not so marked as to be considered pathological, and although this was Bicêtre, nobody ever thought of committing the patient to the insanity ward. Later he became too disabled to do any harm, and he received little attention, except through teasing and making him angry.

"There was even less information available about the last seven years of his life, for by then he had lost that little celebrity he owed to his singular malady. He never soiled his bed, and as the sheets were changed only once a week, the orderlies had failed to notice the diffuse cellulitis for which, on April 11, 1861, he was transferred from the chronic wards (of the Hospice) to the Infirmary. By then it had gained the entire right lower limb.

"This unfortunate man, unable to speak or to write with his paralyzed right hand was quite a difficult subject to study. His general condition was furthermore so poor that it would have been cruel to torment him with over-long investigations.

"However, I noticed . . . that the right side of his body was less sensitive than the left—which had no doubt made the cellulitis less painful . . . except to palpation, and the few incisions I had to make caused him to squirm and scream."

From the sensory examination, Broca passed on to the motor; next he mentions the intact function of the sphincters. "But," he continues, "swallowing was done with some difficulty." We are in the cranial nerves; mastication—intact—is followed by: "No deviation of the face; however, when blowing, the left cheek seems a little more puffed up than the right, indicating that the muscles on this side were slightly weakened."

(This statement has been criticized as an error, which it is not. Leborgne's normal left cheek was puffed up because his lip closure was air tight on the unaffected left side. "*Ce côté*—this side" correctly refers to the weakened right corner of the mouth where air was escaping).

There follows a detailed account of Leborgne's normal tongue; the difficulty in swallowing was due to "beginning paralysis of the pharynx"—no side given. "Only the third state of deglutition was labored." Larynx, timbre of voice, the vowel sounds, were all clear.

Tan could hear a watch tick, but his eyesight was diminished: "When he wanted to see the time he had to take his watch into his own left hand and hold it in a peculiar position, about 20 centimeters from the right eye, which seemed better than the left." This was not the finding of the right-sided homonymous hemianopia, which, incidentally, would have meant little at the time. Broca also did not use an ophthalmoscope—although his friend Follin had introduced Helmholtz's invention of 1851 in France—nor did he check any reflexes, a routine not established before the last quarter of the century, but neither of those would have yielded additional information.

More crucial was this: "The state of his intelligence could not be exactly determined." Broca was "certain, however, that *Tan* understood almost all that was said to him, but he had only gesticulations of his left hand available for issuing information. "Numerical answers were his best; he gave them by opening or closing his fingers. I asked him several times how long he had been ill, and his reply was either five or six days." *Tan* correctly indicated the number of years spent at Bicêtre (21) by opening his hand four times and holding up one additional finger. His relatively intact intelligence and memory for old routines were also shown by his ability to tell time consistently from Broca's watch, on which the sweep hand was not working so that the patient was confronted with three hands standing all relatively still. He also understood such rather complicated questions as those referring to the sequence of his paralyses. "He first made a little horizontal gesture with his left index finger as if to say, 'I get it.' He then in succession pointed to his tongue, to his right arm, and to his right leg.

"And yet, some questions which a man of average intelligence could have answered even by the gestures of one hand remained without reply. It seemed to annoy him greatly when at other times we were unable to understand his answer. At times, finally, his answers were clear but wrong; thus, he falsely pretended to have children. Hence his intelligence was no doubt profoundly affected, either by the damaged brain or by his raging fever, but he evidently was more intelligent than one needs to be for talking."

Broca described the post-mortem findings in the greatest possible detail. "In summary, these were the organs destroyed: the small inferior marginal convolution of the temporal lobe (superior temporal); the small convolutions of the insula, and the corpus striatum; finally, in the frontal lobe, the inferior portion of the transverse (precentral) convolution and the posterior half . . . of the second and third frontal convolutions. . . . Three quarters of the cavity at least was carved out of the frontal lobe. . . .

"The other parts of the hemisphere were less firm than normal . . . and all were notably atrophied . . . but normal as to shape and continuity. . . . As to the deep parts . . . I could half-way examine the ·inner surface of the anterior horn of the lateral ventricle when I dissected off the pia mater and inadvertently enlarged the existing open communication between that ventricle and the cavity. There I saw that the whole corpus striatum was more or less softened, whereas the thalamus had its normal color, volume, and consistency."

Weighing only 987 grams, the brain was by about 400 grams, i.e., nearly one pound, short of the average weight for fifty-year-old *males* (Broca's italics). "The destruction of organs around the left Sylvian fissure no doubt contributes much to the diminished brain weight, but . . . removing the same amount from a healthy brain I found that this weighed only 50 grams. . . . A generalized atrophy of the hemisphere is therefore extremely probable, and this becomes a certainty when one considers the remarkable thickening—up to five and six millimeters—of the meninges and the false arachnoid membrane."

The vast elongated crater dug out by the disease from the surroundings of the Sylvian fissure was filled with fluid before Broca aspirated it and "had a capacity equivalent to the volume of a hen's egg. . . . It stretched backward to the Rolandic fissure . . . was entirely in front of it, and the parietal lobe was healthy, or at least relatively so, for no part of the hemisphere was preserved in its absolute integrity."

Faced with this extensive site of destruction, how did Broca pick out, from the many convolutions affected, that single one, i.e., the "third frontal," (inferior frontal gyrus) for the seat of aphemia?

Throughout this account he repeatedly stressed two facts; one, that this was a slowly progressive lesion "taking twenty years to destroy a relatively limited portion of the cerebral mass"; the other, that the process must have started in the center of the defect, in the area that was destroyed in the greatest width and depth; this was the third frontal convolution. More distant parts, such as the superior temporal gyrus, were softened but not totally annihilated. As aphemia was the first and, for a long time, the only gross shortcoming of Leborgne, Broca reasoned that this primary clinical symptom coincided with that primary anatomical lesion in the frontal lobe. So much for the first ten years of his illness. In the following period of eleven years, up to the patient's death, Broca distinguished two further stages. In the first, the man's right arm and leg had become paralyzed; to this corresponded the softening in the corpus striatum, then undisputed as the motor organ for the contralateral limbs. "Everybody knows that the cerebral convolutions are no motor organs," Broca said, in the traditional belief that the gyri were destined for higher things, things of the mind. At most he would concede that they were coordinators of movements. It took more than the demonstration, nine years later, that electrical stimulation of certain cortical areas invariably produced movement,[40] to dispel this belief, and Broca lived to correct his views on this matter.

Finally, the lowered intelligence of *Tan's* later years was accounted for by the presumably late "spread" of the softening process to the rest of the frontal convolutions and to the generalized cortical atrophy. This represented the second stage of the second period. "That the patient did preserve any intelligence at all is hard to understand; with a brain like this it seems unlikely that one can live for any length of time."

He thus confirmed M. Bouillaud's opinion, he said. But there had been so far too few precise anatomical descriptions to prove the localization of any particular faculty in any particular lobe, although this was extremely likely. Far more difficult to answer, he said, was the question as to whether articulate speech depended on the whole lobe or one of its convolutions in particular; whether localization was arranged by a single faculty being related to a single convolution; or whether (functional) groups of the one went with groups of the other. Only further observation would tell, and he pleaded that observation be made accurately and with the help of the new nomenclature.

No discussion of this paper is on record, either in the Anatomical or in the Anthropological Society. But Broca, and probably those around him, sensed its importance, and from then on he was hot on the trail of this disorder.

It so happened that his next case[41]—an old man named Lelong—was not only clinically of a similar and apparently equally clear-cut variety; it also showed a less extensive, in fact a "perfectly circumscribed" lesion. In the first case there had remained "some uncertainty" about where the lesion had started. The localization of Tan's aphemia was based on a "reasoned analysis of the anatomical facts." But it had given Broca the idea "that if ever there were to be a phrenological science, it would be the phrenology of convolutions, not bumps. . . . I will not deny my surprise bordering on stupefaction when I found that in my second patient the lesion was *rigorously* occupying the same site as in my first; not only were the same convolutions affected but they were so at the same point, i.e., immediately behind that middle third, opposite the insula, and *precisely on the same side (left)*." The year was 1861; the day of cerebral dominance had not officially dawned. Broca marveled more at the fact that in both cases the primary focus corresponded (italics are now his) "*to the same point on the cranial wall*—I realize how partisans of phrenology will seize here upon the argument in favor of their system. . . . These facts are perfectly compatible with the hypothesis of localization by convolution . . . or even, if you wish, by compartments corresponding to invariable points on the cranial box." And yet: "I am inclined to attribute to pure coincidence the absolute identity in the sites of the two lesions."

There were some clinical differences, though, as well as some in the etiology as Broca saw it. To start with, Lelong, unlike Leborgne, was eighty-three when he suddenly collapsed. Recovered within a few days, he gave his daughter the impression that his tongue was paralyzed. The speech impediment was, in fact, his only real trouble, and it turned out not to be due to a paralyzed tongue, but to an extremely defective vocabulary, with difficult enunciation to boot. On October 27, 1861, eighteen months after his first stroke, the old man fell again and fractured the left femoral neck. Thus he became a surgical patient.

He was well enough in every other respect, but had only five words at his disposal: *Lelo* (for his own name), *oui, non, tois* (for *trois*), and *toujours*. "Do you know how to write?" Broca asked him. Lelong: "*Oui.*" "Can you?" "*Non.*" "Try!" "He tried," Broca says, "but he was unable to direct the pen. His usage of the word *trois* (three) was sufficiently curious to be described in a little more detail. He always accompanied this word by making a sign with his fingers because he knew that his tongue was being false to his thoughts, and so he would correct his unintentional mistakes by this gesture. Owing to his age, he had been an inmate of the Hospice of Bicêtre for the past eight years, and so he would lift eight fingers, while saying *trois* (three) in answering a question to this effect. Or, for example: 'Do you have children?' '*Oui*' 'How many?' *Trois!*' And he would lift four fingers. 'How many girls?' Again he lifted two. . . . He had some very expressive gestures. . . . 'What did you do before you entered Bicêtre?' '*Toujours,*' and with his two hands he grabbed an imaginary spade, stuck it into the ground, lifted it out again, and threw out a spade full of earth. 'So you are a digger?' '*Oui,*' and he nodded. Indeed he had been a digger, as I later learned. . . ."

Lelong died twelve days after his fall, enfeebled and with sacral decubitus. Broca was anticipating the post-mortem with some anxiety, not daring to predict the findings. Would the lesion be similar to Leborgne's? Lelong's slightly greater vocabulary impressed Broca as a differential feature, also the differences in the course the disease had taken in these two patients. But, his belief in localization by convolution was strengthened, for this time the lesion "was clearly confined to the second and third frontal convolutions, with the latter more affected than the former, and in a portion of their posterior third." The difference in the nature of the aphemia which, in his anxiety perhaps, he had exaggerated, he interpreted as being due to the nature, as opposed to the site, of the lesion, for the latter was identical with Leborgne's. Such an interpretation was in any case a regrettable deviation from a fundamental principle of modern neurology, i.e., the very principle of localization, which says that the site of the lesion determines the clinical sign, the very principle Broca was trying to uphold. "The special nature of aphemia as a symptom was not dependent on

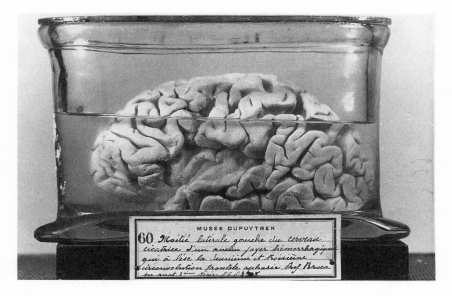

Presumably Lelong's brain. Musée Dupuytren. The inscription reads in literal translation: "60. Left lateral half of the brain (.) scar of a hemorrhagic focus having damaged the second and third frontal convolution (.) aphasia. Prof. Broca Soc. Anat. 2nd series, Vol. 6, p. 398" (probably Vol. 36). (Courtesy Dr. Juster, Institut de Parasitologie, École Pratique, Paris, 1962.)

the nature of the underlying disease," he himself had said in the Leborgne paper, "but only on its site, for the lesion was sometimes a softening, sometimes an apoplexy, sometimes an abscess or a tumor, and to complete his demonstration, M. Auburtin quoted another group of cases with traumatic lesions of the anterior lobes, etc."

Leborgne had suffered from "chronic-progressive softening of the brain"; Lelong from "apoplexy," i.e., cerebral hemorrhage: "M. Pied-vach, my interne on the case, has shown microscopically that hematin crystals were present to account for the small orange-yellow colored patches in the wall of the lesion."

"Softening," as opposed to "apoplexy," was not seen by Broca as the result of a vascular lesion. In this matter, too, he was under the spell of Bouillaud, who considered softening as an inflammatory or "encephalitic" process, the then current view. Only gradually, under the influence of Virchow's work on cerebral thrombosis (1846–1856), did infarction and softening of the brain become identified.[42] What Pierre Marie nearly half a century later considered to have been Broca's failure, he ascribed to Broca's natural period-bound lack of understanding of cerebro-vascular pathology.[43]

The interest aroused by those two communications was at first purely local and professional. The Paris press, maliciously resounding with the catcalls heard at the premiere of Wagner's *Tannhäuser*, took no notice. Newspapers were barely beginning to carry articles about sensational scientific "breakthroughs." But professional excitement was slowly mounting. What had merely been a quixotic hobby-horse of Bouillaud's suddenly became an entity, well-defined both clinically and anatomically, by a man known at least as much for his cool thoroughness as for his pioneering drive.

Eager and critical clinicians were looking for cases of aphemia, and they called on Broca to verify the findings: each brain of man or woman bereft of speech became a wobbly touchstone lifted from its bony casing. As might have been expected (a treacherous fortune smiles on the first stage of most discoveries), the first few cases did confirm his views. Others, less favorable, followed.

After two years, Broca spoke again in the Société Anatomique, consolidating and defending his views against some facts that seemed to invalidate them.[44] First, there had been Charcot's patient with undeniable aphemia but "complete disorganization of the inferior or external parietal convoluton which forms the upper border of the Sylvian fissure" (gyrus supramarginalis). No frontal lobe lesion. "Instead of being exclusively localized in the posterior portion of the third frontal convolution," Broca said, "might the seat of articulate speech not extend to the inferior parietal convolution which is directly continuous with it? Several anatomists are known to consider the two convolutions as one, calling them the convolution around the Sylvian fissure (*circonvolution d'enceinte*—Foville, Rolando). If this were the right way of looking at the matter, one might conceive of a lesion affecting the posterior portion of the convolution around the Sylvian fissure to produce aphemia even though its anterior portion, as part of the frontal lobe, be approximately intact." Was this, after all, the final truth? Not really; he took it back: "But all this is too hypothetical; we must await further facts. Indeed, let us not forget that in those other fifteen observations of aphemia, the lesion has constantly occupied the same site in the third frontal convolution. One negative fact does not destroy this series of positive ones; in pathology and especially in cerebral pathology, there is no rule without some exception. . . ."

Broca's reference to Foville's *circonvolution d'enceinte* strikes us as most important, buried through it is in his massive insistence on the frontal convolution. A. Louis Foville, rather neglected by Gratiolet and a little off-handedly drawn into this discussion by Broca, had not been interested in the confining concept of cerebral lobes. He had a much more sweeping notion of the convolutional pattern. Between

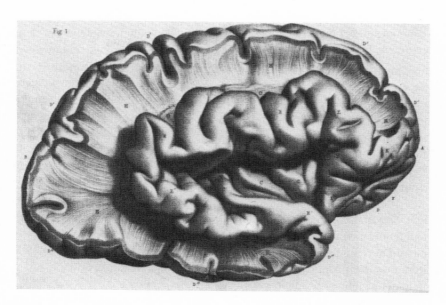

Foville's illustration of the human brain, right hemisphere. *Circonvolution d'enceinte* comprising, in our terms, inferior ("third") frontal, supramarginal, angular, and superior temporal gyrus, here dissected as a wall or enclosure around the Sylvian fissure (middle cerebral artery). (A. Louis Foville: *Traité complet de l'anatomie . . . du système nerveux*, Paris: Fortin, 1844. Drawing by E. Beau.)

Gall's and Gratiolet's publications Foville had written of the "great regions of the brain"; he saw the cerebral hemispheres structured on the framework of three generous loops. The first of these, honored by Foville as being the only one of the "first order," was at the inner and under surface of the hemisphere; he called it "convolution of the hem" (*ourlet*). It was the forerunner of Broca's "great limbic lobe." The "second order" had as its first loop a single span that encircled the whole superior border of the brain's convexity. But our concern is with the "second loop of the second order": the *circonvolution d'enceinte*. (The rest of the convolutions were all third and fourth order.) Like the wall of a fortress, the *circonvolution d'enceinte* forms a ring or belt around the Sylvian fissure, encompassing the third (inferior) frontal gyrus, the gyrus supramarginalis of the parietal lobe, and the superior temporal gyrus.[37] Anathema to anatomical purists, as it is not a single gyrus, this nevertheless is practically the speech area as most of us see it today, the "Sylvian region."

Foville's professional background resembled Leuret's, and as a psychiatrist, he never returned to any public discussion of the cortex. He scoffed at any attempts to ascribe any particular function to any particular convolution.

191

While Charcot's case had been the first exception in a series of fifteen cases so far, another exception, even more remarkable and significant, was held against Broca. A frontal lobe lesion had failed to produce aphemia. This time, however the *right* hemisphere was affected. "The most striking thing is," Broca continued, to everyone's surprise unperturbed, "that in all cases the lesion was on the *left* side of the brain, even in that one exception — the case of M. Charcot. . . . In twenty-five further aphemics . . . who are still living and were seen by myself and others . . . the accompanying hemiplegia is on the right side, hence the lesion in the *left* cerebral hemisphere.

"From the physiological point of view this is a most serious matter. The question of distinct seats for various functions . . . is no doubt extremely important. But if it were shown that one particular and perfectly well determined faculty . . . can be affected only by a lesion in the left hemisphere, it would necessarily follow that the two halves of the brain do not have the same attributes — quite a revolution in the physiology of nervous centers. I must say that I could not easily resign myself to accept such a subversive consequence. In a recent publication[64] I felt obligated, therefore, to express my reservation; I was asked for a counter-proof. . . . We must have case histories followed by autopsies to prove that lesions of the posterior third of the third frontal convolution on the *right* side do not affect the faculty of articulate speech."[45]

The case just shown was this counter-proof needed for the "subversive consequence," i.e., left hemisphere "dominance" as it came to be called. Here was the answer to the suggestion of single lobe lesions, ridiculed by Rochoux in 1848, "as though the loss of one eye would cause blindness!"[20]

But, for another reason, we must now pay attention to the date given above in Broca's reference to his own "recent publication." It was an annotated bibliography (*Exposé des Titres et Travaux*), which he had compiled for his candidacy (then unsuccessful) in the Académie de Médecine. This date was April, 1862.[46]

It was eleven months after this date, on March 24, 1863, when a Dr. Gustave Dax deposited the posthumous memoir of his father Marc, with the Académie de Médecine.[47] This interval would prove Broca's absolutely good faith in the matter. For it has been alleged, and it is in fact quite possible, that through some "leak" he may have obtained knowledge of this memoir, although it was not published until two years later. Moreover, it must be admitted that the "alibi" of 1862 is a printing error and should read April, *1863*. (A. Souques, author of a very interesting paper in 1928, serves as devil's advocate.[48])

Dr. Marc Dax had been practicing medicine at Sommières, about 20 miles north of Montpellier, until his death in 1837. In the last year of his life he achieved his crowning success, perhaps unwittingly, when he read a paper to a Congress of Physicians of Southern France at Montpellier. Though relatively short, the paper was the fruit of some 25 years of compiling cases of patients who had "forgotten the signs of thought." In every one of these patients, the brain was damaged on the left side. There were some forty records of his own, to which his son in a companion paper had added 140, partly his, but mostly gleaned from the literature.

All of the original forty-odd cases were poorly documented and without post-mortem confirmation yet still allowed this astute man—Dax, Sr.—to state "that not every affection of the left hemisphere will necessarily lead to a change in the memory for words; but if this memory is altered by any disease of the brain, one must look for the cause in the left hemisphere, and look for it there even if both hemispheres are affected."[49] In most of his cases this diagnosis was based on the co-existing hemiplegia, i.e., on the law of crossed pathways between brain and limbs—the law of decussation.

The subject of loss of speech is in several ways tied to Montpellier, where Lallemand had been interested in it and where Lordat had given in 1820 a classical account of the mechanism and psychology of speech and its clinical disorders, not attempting localization by any means. Later Lordat himself lost (and regained) his speech as the result of a stroke and stated that his memory had been disturbed for words only. His term for the disorder was "alalia," and he distinguished "verbal asynergia," the defect of coordination of speech movements, from "verbal amnesia," the memory defect.[50] If he was among those listening in 1836 when Dax may have given his paper, he certainly kept as silent as everyone else about that small-town doctor's remarkable observation. The memoir had not been published and perhaps not even presented at that meeting. But some twenty-seven years later a hand-written copy of it was found among the papers of a former dean at Montpellier and handed to Marc Dax' son Gustave, who took it to Paris. With this account and his own added collection, Dr. Dax, Jr., deposited his father's memoir on March 24, 1863, as recorded in the bulletin of the Académie. On the same day a committee, consisting of Bouillaud, Béclard, and Lélut, was charged with examining this work.[47]

Obviously, if by April, 1862, in the previous year, Broca had thought of making public any ideas of his own on the "predilection" (as he later called it) of speech for the left hemisphere, he would have used this as an argument in June, 1862. That June a case had been shown in the Société Anatomique of a right-sided lesion in the third frontal convolution that seemed to contradict his thesis: the patient had spoken normally. Broca then had excluded this case and explained that the lesion was much more forwardly placed than Leborgne's and Lelong's had been; there was not a word about the affected side of the brain.[51]

On the other hand, it so happened that his application as a candidate for the Académie was published in the same issue of the Académie's *Bulletins* on the same page, and in the same correspondence column, that announced the deposition of the Dax memoir. This date was March 24, 1863.[47] The annotated bibliography of Broca's work (*Titres et Travaux*),[46] which contains his tentative views on the left versus the right hemisphere, accompanied this application. It must have been given to the printers some time ahead. Almost certainly, therefore, Broca's account was written before anyone, except Gustave Dax and perhaps his close friends, had known of the work of Marc Dax. It is thus not correct to say[48] that on April 2, 1863, Broca *wrote* for the first time that the statistical evidence favored the left side of the brain for speech. March 24, 1863 was the date on which he submitted for the published record what he must have written quite a while before. Broca also referred to a remark about left-brainedness he had made at the Société de Biologie as early as January, 1863, but that Society hardly ever published any discussions, and so one cannot be surprised at not finding it recorded in its *Comptes rendus*.

While the old academicians were dragging their feet and perhaps not keeping their lips too tightly sealed, the Dax memoir was not made public through 1863 and, in fact, not until December, 1864. But by April 2, 1863, ten days after its deposition, Broca, who up to that time had collected eight cases of aphemia, had spoken about the disturbing coincidence in the Société d'Anthropologie. "Remarkable," he said, "how in all these patients the lesion was on the left side. I do not dare to draw any conclusion from this and am waiting for new data."[44] He kept repeating, both the coincidence and his reluctance to regard it as more than that. On March 3, 1864,[52] he reported that he had collected twenty such observations "for almost two years," i.e., since 1862.

According to the strict rules of the Académie, no one except the members of the study committee must know the contents of a memoir before the reporting member has made it public. Yet the name of Dax, with its implication, was inadvertently dropped in public several months before that.

In August, 1864, at a meeting of the Société de Biologie, a Dr. Bouchard presented a case of aphemia without a lesion at Broca's site, although the detailed autopsy report speaks of "capillary hemorrhages in the left third frontal convolution: among others." In conclusion, Bouchard said, "This observation does not confirm Broca's theory . . . and it neither helps, nor detracts from the theory of Dax, because both hemispheres are affected." Broca, as well as Charcot, was present at the autopsy of this case. [53]

No doubt, the cat was out of the bag. If Dr. Bouchard and, one must assume, at least some in his audience were aware of it in 1864, there is no reason why Broca should have been ignorant of Dax' work—even in 1863, even ten days after it had reached the Académie. We may remember his comments on the laxity with which that body had guarded the secrecy of his own cancer memoir thirteen years earlier. [54] Dax, Jr., for one, may very well have leaked to friends his father's findings supposedly locked in the files of the Académie, accessible only to three committee members. Secondly, we cannot ignore Broca's ties, direct or via Dr. Auburtin, with Bouillaud, who was on that three-man study committee.

It would be naive, on the other hand, to reproach Broca for having been disingenuous. Suppose he had been informed. How could he have divulged his information without compromising Bouillaud, who was entrusted with keeping secret the contents of the Dax memoir? And if Broca did know what was in it—which is far from certain—he was not going to be rushed into accepting it as proved, certainly not before his own material had confirmed it. But the more cases he himself collected, the more inescapable became the asymmetry of the brain with regard to speech. Anyone as keen to assemble a large and convincing series may have been forced to the same conclusion that Dax, but not Bouillaud, had drawn. Broca almost certainly had noticed the coincidence regarding left hemispheres after seeing eight instances of it at the time when he wrote his annotated bibliography, before he could have heard of Dax.

It is never easy, nor is it in good taste to set this sort of record straight; the effort smells of the police inspector. And it is hardly worthwhile; parallel discoveries are so commonplace. But insinuators must be fought on their own ground; here it is one of oblique logic. "Broca," they seem to say, "had not noticed cerebral dominance but pretended that he had, yet did not believe in it when it was obvious!" In fact, he was only combining a keen eye with caution, as well as with discretion. But he had to come to his own defense when his contemporaries, too, were hinting that at the time of his first publication on aphemia in 1861 he must have overlooked or even suppressed the work of Dax.

"I do not like discussions of priority," he said in 1865, "and would have refrained from pointing out that the discovery of Dax, Senior, as it had not been published, was null and void as far as history is concerned. . . . But several people gave me to understand that I should have quoted Dax, Senior's opinion. . . . I do not wish anyone to believe that I have sinned by ignorance or voluntary omission. Before his son mentioned it, the existence of the memoir by Dax, Senior, was as unknown in Montpellier as it was in Paris. Having looked in vain for any trace in every periodical of 1836, I asked Dr. Gordon, librarian of the Faculty of Montpellier, to be so kind as to inquire a little into this matter. M. Gordon has not been luckier than I. The Congrès Méridional held its third session in Montpellier from July 1 to 10, 1836. No work was published, and no trace of its proceedings remains . . . The *Revue de Montpellier* (1836, v. 51 and 53) summarized the subjects of medical philosophy that were discussed. The question of speech is not mentioned. M. Gordon has personally interviewed twenty physicians who were at Montpellier at the time. They had no knowledge that the memoir in question was read at the Congress or published anywhere. This is the information I have been able to gather. I am not going to contest the authenticity of this memoir; it is not impossible that it was prepared for the Congress but not read. What I wish to state is that I really could not have guessed at the existence of a manuscript which was not exhumed until two years after my brief publication on aphemia."[55] (A friend of Gustave Dax at Montpellier found a manuscript among the papers of his own deceased father, a copy of Marc Dax' memoir. It was in the handwriting of Gustave. The friend published the fact as proof—apparently still needed in 1879—that the memoir had circulated among the friends and family of Dax, Senior.)

Even if this were not so, neither the pioneer work done by Dax nor that of his teacher Lordat, of Lallemand, nor even that of Bouillaud in any way detracts from Broca's new emphasis on the anatomy of the brain as related to its functions. It is sometimes said that Auburtin was the prime mover of Broca's interest. After all, Broca was a surgeon, Souques says,[48] and have surgeons ever been known for their interest in the brain? (This in 1928, when Cushing had already done his best work in neurological surgery!) Can anyone believe Broca was boning up on the brain or on how to examine such cases, in the period between April 11, 1861, when he first set eyes on *Tan,* and a week later, on April 18, when he presented his case to the anthropologists, or on May 19, in the anatomists' meeting where he gave what is probably the most important single paper on aphasia? If so, he must give Broca even greater credit.

The case of Broca and Auburtin is one of confusing the bullet with the trigger. Broca, the neurologist, and Broca, the anthropologist, can be understood only from this anatomical background. For him the localization of function by cerebral convolutions was an exercise undertaken for the greater glory of anatomy.

Of the three committee members, it was Lélut who had been charged by the Académie to report on the Dax memoir. This was not done before December, 1864, no doubt because Lélut considered the whole thing as so much nonsense in the wake of Gall and his pseudo-science. He was not present himself; Béclard read the report. It began by misquoting the title, regretted the "honor" of this task, admitted that its author (i.e., Lélut himself) was prejudiced and recalled the case of an epileptic, speaking right up to his death, with a left hemisphere turned into a mash. With a compliment to the late Dr. Dax, Lélut's proxy regained his *fauteuil* within two or three minutes.[56]

Surely, this attitude was no longer fair or appropriate in such a day and age. Whatever one's views, the matter could no longer be regarded as phrenology! Bouillaud felt the spur and opened the discussion.[57] It was April, 1865. The delay was caused by a series of talks, including one on the ravages to health by smoking tobacco. But once started, the debate kept going, with a baker's dozen of speakers for 11 consecutive Tuesday afternoons, i.e., until well into June. Bouillaud spoke nearly three whole sessions, calling Gall, "the Copernicus, Kepler, and Newton of physiology"; Broca, "the St. Paul of the new doctrine who had undergone a brilliant and fruitful conversion, to which I am happy to say M. le docteur Auburtin, my intimate ally in respect of doctrine and family, is not completely alien." But he felt Broca's doctrine was still very far from sufficiently proved. About Dax he had not much to say, but found him vague and shockingly misinformed about his, Bouillaud's, work. (Dax had indeed not only misquoted Bouillaud's title, but, far worse, reversed Bouillaud's thesis by making him "attribute the cause to a paralysis of the tongue!") Still Dax served well as a stick to beat Lélut with. There was nothing funny, strange, or contemptible, Bouillaud said, about the predominance of one side of a paired organ over another. There are, for instance, a number of acts that are being ordinarily and even exclusively performed by our right limbs; one might speak of right-handed people being left-brained.

Thus Bouillaud seems to have given here the first hint at hand-brain-dominance in April, 1865. Two months later, i.e., two months too late to claim priority, Broca in his own Society expounded his views on right-and-left-handers and left cerebral dominance.[55] Gratiolet had observed that the convolutions of the left hemisphere started to develop earlier than those on the right; hence, the more developed left hemisphere would be the first to learn to speak, and would remain dominant.

How about left-handers? In the previous year at the Salpêtrière, Broca had seen the brain of a woman with complete absence of the left *circonvolution d'enceinte,* i.e., Foville's gyrus surrounding the Sylvian fissure — probably due, he said, to the observed congenital absence of the Sylvian artery. It was the first time he had seen the "convolution of speech" absent in its entirety in a "non-aphemic" person. With her right limbs atrophied and sensibility impaired, her right hand had been totally useless, her gait hemiplegic, but her speech preserved. Naturally, this woman had to be and was left-handed.[55]

He and his students had studied her brain shortly after the woman's death on November 3, 1864, and he told them of his ideas — still unpublished. For some time, he had observed, too, that there was no direct correlation between the extent of the lesion and that of the speech defect. And he had come to the conclusion that the two hemispheres might supplement each other in some measure, a fact that did not negate specific localization. An amputee learns to use his other hand because his intelligence is intact, but that of the aphemic, he conceded, does suffer to a certain degree. Hence, he can regain only very little speech with the help of his right hemisphere. Even this statement must not be taken as absolutely valid, he said.

Here Broca put forth ideas we associate with a much later stage of aphasiology, ideas about *Gestalt,* plasticity of the child's brain, and speech therapy for the aphasic. "Has anyone attempted to re-educate him? Has he been taught every day, every hour, every moment, the way a child eventually learns to talk? Personally, I am convinced that, although one cannot restore the intelligence which an aphemic has lost together with a part of his brain, one might obtain considerable results by using sufficient perseverance, by treating him with the untiring persistence of a mother. . . . When I was at Bicêtre I kept an aphemic patient on my ward for several months. Frequently, while making rounds, I devoted several moments to him and ended up by extending his vocabulary a good deal. But what good is such a short lesson? You must not believe that in this matter the education of an adult is easier than that of a child; on the contrary. . . . This is not only a question of muscular skill. It is likely that to arrive at his goal the adult uses a different method from the child. . . ."

The patient who was given speech therapy by the surgeon at Bicêtre was also unable to read. Broca retaught him the alphabet first, syllables next, but utterly failed in trying to make the man combine syllables to form words. "I did not give up, though. . . . I showed him the polysyllabic words whole and got him to know quite a few this way. . . . But he was recognizing them only by their general shape, their length and some difference . . . when we substituted, say, an *m* for an *n*, an *e* for an *s*, a *p* for a *q*, or an *l* for a *t*. That is to say, he recognized words only as one recognizes a face or a landscape without ever having analyzed its details. Clearly, then, this aphemic was learning to read by a procedure essentially different from the one he had used as a child.

"This failure, however . . . does not prove that the healthy hemisphere cannot substitute for the affected one. I am convinced that a lesion of the left third frontal convolution, apt to produce lasting aphemia in an adult, will not prevent a small child from learning to talk . . . as the example of the epileptic woman at the Salpêtrière had shown. . . ."[55]

As to the ongoing discussion at the Académie, there is a little confusion in its *Bulletins* regarding the order of speakers in the sessions of May 16 and May 23. On May 23, in any case, a jocular mood seems to have seized the assembled professors. It either was a reaction to the tedium spread by the pedantic Piorry or triggered by his monstrous term *amnémonomie*. But it is likely that the trap sprung for Bouillaud was well prepared. Velpeau suddenly claimed the "Bouillaud Prize," the 500 francs offered in 1848 for having observed the case of a patient with destroyed frontal lobes not having suffered from loss of speech. After a long and heated discussion, Bouillaud had to pay.

In the previous session the most formidable protagonist had entered the arena, a cool mind whose *Clinique Médicale de l'Hôtel-Dieu* is an outstanding document of the contemporary level of internal medicine. A peak, really; its wisdom, drama, and elegance make it still worth reading. If Professor Armand Trousseau had been interested in loss of speech before Broca, he did not make his interest public until 1862. Whether or not he had had ideas on the subject he immediately was keen enough to test the blossoming doctrine of the young surgeon whose reputation so far had rested on other and more solid grounds. In Trousseau's series—135 cases by 1865—125 had left hemisphere lesions. As to the "32 cases of mine, that are known also to M. Broca, 14 conform to his doctrine and 18 do not. . . . Of those 18 unfavorable ones, 11 have been verified by autopsy, 7 have not. . . . It thus may be said that M. Broca's contention is less generally true than that of M. Dax, and especially that of M. Bouillaud." But even Bouillaud does not pass muster.[59]

"Diverse regions of the brain contribute to the formation of speech. . .," Trousseau concluded, taking something from everybody, giving credit to no one, his view balanced, his contribution sterile and eclectic. The intellect of the aphasic was not intact; "his mind limps," he graphically said elsewhere.[60]

"Aphasic," but we have so far not heard the word *aphasia*, Trousseau's word. We have referred to Broca's aphemia as a "blossoming doctrine," but Trousseau took good care to make the term, at least, wilt fast by substituting "aphasia" for "aphemia."

The word a person has introduced into the language is something he may hope to be remembered by or at least something that will live if and when he is forgotten. Now, in her malicious way of being just, tradition has sentenced both "aphemia" and Trousseau to relative oblivion, while keeping alive the bastard term "Broca's aphasia." Trousseau's greater weight stood behind the newer word; perhaps its sound, too, was more elegant or had a more familiar ring. This, of course, was not the reason given when it was launched upon the contemporaries who had barely been made aware of its bulkier and grimmer-sounding predecessor. The petty substitution was all couched in pedantic propriety, which Trousseau exhibited in a footnote to his published lecture *On Aphasia.*[60]

Although the discussion on aphasia at the Académie involved Broca as much as any of the actual participants—just as the one on cancer had done eleven years earlier—he could do nothing but bottle up his excitement or take it for airing to his own Society. "I did not yet have the honor of being a member. Perhaps the chair might not have turned down a request for my being heard, but I was unable even to ask for this favor because my state of health forced me to take a trip to the South. Arrived at Montpellier, I was reading some medical journals, and it was through them that I learned of the priority claim of M. Dax, Junior, in favor of his late father. . . . Finding myself in that very city I was very naturally curious to obtain the text of this work. . . ."[62] The search led only to negative results.[55]

The year of this statement, Broca's last on aphasia, was 1877; after a long interval, at the height of his fame, a member of the Académie de Médecine for over a decade, he had the satisfaction of seeing Bouillaud join world opinion. "I am happy to hear M. Broca's explanation, which to my mind gives a definitive answer to the question of priority. Indeed," the mellowed octogenarian finally conceded, "it is to him that belongs all the honor of having made the important discovery about the seat of the faculty of speech."[62]

This view prevailed for one hundred years until, in the 1960's, a few writers felt it ought to be challenged on various and sometimes contradictory grounds. Their critical claims included such fancies as Broca's failure to grasp the significance of a discovery which was Bouillaud's anyway (Stookey[63]), or that his showmanship was the decisive factor in its acceptance (Boring[64]), or that Auburtin (rather than Bouillaud), Broca, Ange Duval (a surgeon in Brest who published two cases of traumatic aphasia as late as 1867), and Dax, father and son, all own equal shares in the "controversial" discovery (Critchley[65]). The foregoing account of the events shows that Broca's circumscribed localization in a convolution went far beyond Dax' mere lateralization and Bouillaud's vague frontal lobes and makes redundant a detailed discussion of those claims, supported as they are by a confusion of facts and/or dates.

But what was Broca's illness that made him leave Paris for the south of France in the spring of 1865? Presumably, coronary artery disease. Augustine never ceased to worry over her husband's health, and Uncle Pierre diagnoses it from Sainte Foy as "overwork" in a letter to his brother Benjamin. (After Mme. Broca's death in the previous year, Benjamin had moved to Paris to live with Paul and his family.) For good measure the devout uncle threw in "pride," a sin as well as an agent of disease, and the latter the chastisement for the former. By June, Paul was better and "back to run his service at St. Antoine." But Uncle Pierre still had misgivings about his nephew's "lack of sleep despite the use of opium," about "noble pride . . . and the running after so many hares of so many colors without catching a single one."[66]

Meanwhile Broca's concept continued to struggle for recognition—on the whole successfully. Criticism concerned definitions of the various types of speech disorder. What precisely was meant by "memory for words," "faculty of expression," and "locomotor ability necessary for articulating sounds?" And was "mental effort" now a new factor, Dally asked in May, 1866, apropos a patient with a writing defect. Such a priori definitions, Broca retorted, have always been leading us astray: "The analysis for which you are asking will slowly emerge from the pathological facts. . . . It seems probable to me that these patients (with aphemia) have lost a particular kind of memory, but I cannot concede by any means that this is the memory for words."[67]

Commendable caution, but the pressures for making crisp definitive statements are apt to prevent over-candid evasion. Another two years and many cases, autopsies, and meetings later, Broca's views took their final shape. After that he practically ceased to study this thorny and slippery subject. This was his conclusion:

"Loss of speech is not a particular disease, nor is it a single symptom always to be covered by the same term. The symptoms may belong to any one of four essentially distinct groups. . . .

"In the first group are those patients who fail to speak because they have no ideas to express. . . . They are deprived of their intelligence in its highest form, expressed by the Greek word *logos*. I suggest that in these cases the loss of speech be designated by 'alogia.'

"In the second group I place those patients where the conventional link between ideas and words has dropped out. In various ways the patients still manage to understand the signs which they are offered and show their understanding; they can even pronounce confused words that often have no connection with the ideas they intend to express. They have forgotten the meaning of the words they utter, and they have no better understanding for those being uttered around them. Sometimes, though, they are able to show that they are not devoid of all memory: they recognize objects, faces, and places. . . . The memory they have lost is only a special one for words: in most instances written as well as spoken ones. To characterize this condition I would use the expression 'verbal amnesia,' already employed by M. Lordat.

"For the third group I have proposed the name 'aphemia.' The aphemic patient has ideas, expresses them by gestures, even by a few words; their pronunciation . . . and meaning are more or less well-defined. The vocabulary of the aphemic is in some cases non-existent, in others reduced to a few monosyllables or a few swear-words, or a few strange words belonging to no language whatever. In other cases, finally, the vocabulary is somewhat greater, and one might ask . . . whether there is not a certain degree of verbal amnesia present. But the clear distinction from the previous group lies in the patient's understanding of what is said to him. . . . Clinically there may be cases that are doubtful . . . in the way the diagnosis between a cyst and a lipoma may be doubtful. . . .

"In the fourth group there are the cases where the mechanical agents of articulation have lost their function as a result of changes in muscles, nerves of those parts of the brain on which these nerves depend . . . such as in an even incomplete hemiplegia of the tongue. . . . The word 'aphonia' will not do as it is reserved for the abolition of voice. . . . Another word is 'alalia' . . . which I suggest for this group . . . and I would add the epithet 'mechanical' for being more precise."

202

What about the site of the corresponding cerebral lesion? Though essentially different, aphemia and amnesia are rather likely, he thinks, to have their lesions situated very closely together.

"There are good reasons to suppose that the memory for words must have a close relationship to that portion of the brain which governs the pronunciation of words."[68]

But he will not, here or elsewhere, affirm, deny, or even mention the possibility that definite areas may be concerned with loss of speech other than the posterior end of the left third frontal convolution; he does not come back to Foville's *circonvolution d'enceinte*. The asymmetry of brain function, incidentally, is not mentioned here.

Broca was invited to read this paper before the Congress of the British Association for the Advancement of Science held August 19 to 25, 1868, in Norwich.

British medical opinion was awakened to the question of aphasia by reports of the protracted, spectacular, and at times farcical discussion of 1865 in the Paris Académie de Médecine. Using the *Lancet* as our weather-vane, we find in that year what must be one of the first English articles on the subject,[69] by Frederic Bateman, physician to the Norfolk and Norwich Hospital, who invited Broca to participate in the discussion there.[70]

In his paper Bateman concluded that "the majority of cases recorded tend to favour the doctrine of localization in the *left* hemisphere, further investigations, however, being required to substantiate M. Broca's statement that the lesion is limited to the posterior part of the third frontal convolution. . . . The question remains . . . one of the *questiones vexatae* of the day. . . . English observers should place on record any cases that may fall under their observation. . . ."[69]

Lancet heralds the first international bout on aphemia in its August 15, 1868 issue:

"M. Broca at Norwich

"A very interesting discussion on Aphasia is likely to take place at the British Association meeting at Norwich. M. Broca, whose anatomical researches in connexion with aphasia have done so much to clear up this difficult subject, will be present . . . in the discussion on Dr. Hughling Jackson's paper on the same topic. It will be no small attraction to the meeting that visitors will thus have the opportunity of immediately comparing the best English and the best French views on the pathology of this remarkable disease."[71]

Lancet also reported the meeting of "the medical philosophers" as culminating in the papers by Jackson, Broca, and Mr. R. Dunn . . ."

adding that Dr. Bateman had collected 75 observations of aphasia, with 27 autopsies, 18 of which failed to confirm Broca's localization. "It must be stated," *Lancet* concludes, "Professor Broca, in reply, combatted with great ability the objections to his theory and explained away the cases referred to by Dr. Bateman. The subject is still open to further discussion."[72]

Little they knew, perhaps, what an understatement the last sentence turned out to be. But was Bateman the only serious opponent? What had Dr. Jackson to say? On September 19, 1868, an editorial in *Lancet* (p. 385) tells us something about that, with appropriate critical detachment, and an introduction full of *mots justes* applicable today, about the "singularly tangled controversy" involving "those confusions which depend upon mere differences in words"; about "a man with a brain that could think, and a tongue that could wag quite well, but without any power to make the thinking and the tongue-wagging coincide. . . . It is certain that there was at first a great disposition to settle this matter . . . by a rude application of a bastard phrenology." But, and here *Lancet* takes us to Jackson, "if there be one writer more than another to whom medicine is indebted for having first drawn attention to the insufficiency of this kind of view, it is Dr. Hughlings Jackson. He it was who . . . insisted, first, that language was a very much more complicated faculty than had been assumed; and secondly, that if a very large number . . . showed lesions about the neighborhood of the third frontal convolution, that was as much as to say that a large proportion of those cases had lesions in the immediate surroundings of the corpora striata, i.e., in the most important centre and meeting-place of the various fibres of the brain. . . ."[73]

Two years later the exalted position held for two hundred years by the corpus striatum was usurped by the precentral convolution.[40] But aside from this upheaval, the argument remains valid and worth pursuing: "Dr. Jackson has added most important observations on the different degrees with which the intellectual and emotional kinds of speech are affected. He has shown that the man, who cannot by any possibility find the right phrase for a merely indifferent object, will *swear* with the utmost precision as well as vigour."[73]

Jackson also was careful to add in a footnote to this observation that the aphasic's relative facility for automatic utterances "was in principle long ago formulated by M. Baillarger. . . . I ought to have reproduced this quotation in the first installment of this article. . . . I do not remember from what book I took the quotation."[74] He may have taken it from Baillarger's speech, which finally lent some wisdon to the 1865 discussion at the Paris Académie de Médecine.[75]

The *Lancet* editorial adds that Jackson "has shown, too, that aphasia is by no means so rigorously separated off from other varieties of cerebral disease, affecting the intellect on one side, and muscular movements on the other, as had been carelessly supposed by some."[73]

"I used to suppose there was a part for words," Jackson said at Norwich, "and besides a distinct coordinating apparatus for the movement of words, and that Broca's convolution was a sort of cerebellum for articulation. It is quite true that the defects I have recently mentioned ('ataxy' of articulation and mistakes in words) are very different (i.e., one from the other), but then they are not altogether different. . . ." For some time he had been pointing out, he said, that "the ataxy of articulation was a quasi-mental defect—an inability to combine muscular movements in a particular mental act. . . . It was hard to say where obviously motor symptoms ended, and mental ones began . . . not only hard, but impossible, even using the words 'motor' and 'mental' in the popular sense. I now think that the only differences . . . are differences of 'compound degree.'"

On an earlier occasion, in 1866, Jackson had written: "I must say here that I believe less in some of the views propounded by Broca than I did, although I think the scientific world is under vast obligation to him for giving precision to an important inquiry. Yet I cannot but think that my disagreement with M. Broca, as well as the differences of opinion on this subject, are to a great extent due to different ways of putting the same thing. . . . Indeed, I think the evidence I have collected goes to confirm many of his statements as to facts, but I have for some time ceased to go with him in a few of his inferences. I think, then, that the so-called 'faculty' of language has no existence and that disease near the corpus striatum produces defect of expression (by words, writing, signs, etc.) to a great extent, because this is the way out from the hemisphere to organs which the will can set in motion. Hence, as I believe, disease of the convolutions near the corpus striatum is the cause of chorea, which, as regards to limbs, is not so much a disorder of mere motion as disorder of those movements which are voluntary and educated, or at least co-ordinated."[77]

The corpus striatum need no longer arrest our attention, except for the modern reversal of defective function—aphasia and chorea—the former ascribed to convolutions, the latter to the basal ganglia, and give the aphasia prize to "Broca's convolution" as Jackson terms it here, perhaps for the first time. But Jackson's fairness, one might almost say humility, and his minimizing the controversy by lifting it to a semantic level are wholly admirable. Still, is the statement that "ataxy and mistakes in words are very different, but then they are not altogether different," not altogether confused or just a touching way of stating the unresolved confusion inherent in the subject, a frank admission of defeat? If "the so-called 'faculty' of language has no existence," what are we trying to localize? And why do we never see much wrong with "it," when parts of the brain are damaged that do not enclose the left Sylvian fissure?

Scientists have been divided by Charles Darwin into "lumpers" and "splitters." Alalia, aphemia, verbal amnesia, alogia—especially the two middle ones that make up aphasia—were, to the clean-cutting, surgical, and French mind of Broca, categories, without which an intelligent approach to any subject was impossible. There was, in fact, very little that divided the French view from the English. Broca was well aware of the intricacies, the pitfalls, the cases that failed to conform, but he left the matter the only way that seemed compatible with his unalterable tenet of the supremacy of the frontal lobe. It was a closed subject. For Jackson's compromising and psychologizing attitude, the long line of clinical psychologists following him, have, in the words of the late Lord Brain (1961), "done little to advance our knowledge of the fundamental problem of the relationship between the mind and the brain in the sphere of speech."[78] Nor has the subject gained much from the innumerable subsequent ways to cut and redecorate the cake of aphasia.

The drive to localize function steadily gained momentum following Broca's discovery, with many efforts to map first the convolutions, then the smaller areas of the cortex according to their microscopic characteristics. Within a decade, the spark of "Broca's convolution" fired the experiments by Fritsch and Hitzig, who discovered the function of the precentral gyrus; its electrical stimulation yielded movements of the limbs and face and also of the tongue, throat, and lips: the anterior half of the cerebral hemisphere, motor; the posterior, sensory. If so, Broca's frontal area might take care of articulating; the parietotemporal "sensory" area might serve for remembering and understanding speech. As an ever more detailed analysis of the various aspects of speech and allied disorders was attempted, deFleury (1865–66) pointed out that the loss of remembering and understanding words might be a sensory, or rather acoustic, defect. Later Bastian coined the term "word deafness"; Ogle named it "agraphia." From there it was only one step to draw a diagram, showing how either the "incoming" impressions from the eye (reading) or from the ear (listening) might be blocked for words or the "outgoing" blocked for motor acts; between them there must be a nodal point somewhere for pure ideation—a point of view ridiculed by Gratiolet before it was even made—and early fought by Jackson. The "a priori" definitions were beginning to hold sway and to lead astray, as Broca had warned. Several "speech centers" were in fact "required."[79] The first such diagram was sketched by Adolf Baginski, a general practitioner and pediatrician, then of Nordhausen in Saxony. His examples of speech disorders were two cases of uremia, without any gross cerebral pathology.[80] This was in 1871; aphasia, like Alsace-Lorraine, was firmly in German hands.

Three years later—thirteen after *Tan*-Leborgne had come to post-mortem—a small book, only 74 pages, was published in Breslau.[81] It resulted in establishing the second best-known name in the history of aphasia. "Wernicke's aphasia" fell into place with the current idea that a sensory complement to Broca's motor aphasia was in order. Carl Wernicke was a pupil of Meynert, most eminent representative of that German school of psychiatrists who considered "the diseases of the mind as the diseases of the brain."[82] Meynert and Wernicke had become convinced that, as the latter puts it, all sensory nerves "indisputably" end in the occipito-temporal lobe, meaning by "all" not only the optic nerve, but the olfactory nerve, the gustatory nerve, and the posterior column of the spinal cord conducting sensation of touch and position as well. This was stretching things a bit far, especially without mentioning the parietal lobe. In his little book called *Der Aphasische Symptomen-Komplex,* Wernicke said that the acoustic nerve's connections, although not yet proven, could not be doubted on physiological grounds. Yet we must not localize, he said, "the phrenologists' psychic functions, arbitrarily delimited by popular usage, but only the most elementary functions. . . . Broca . . . had refrained from considering extensive areas of the brain surface and had the courage to postulate an anatomically well-circumscribed speech center. . . . There is no doubt about Broca's aphasia. . . ." Wernicke stated "that there is a continuity between the third frontal and the first temporal convolutions"; the latter will be assigned to "acoustic word images." (We again meet Rolando-Foville-Broca's "convolutions around the Sylvian fissure.") And he proceeded to draw diagrams.

Ten cases were described, only four of them with autopsies. They were disappointingly inconclusive. There was nowhere a clear-cut analysis and correlation between symptoms, signs, and sites of destruction; the postulate of the introduction was left unconfirmed.

After the somewhat dogmatic simplicity of Broca's concept and the noncommital attitude of Jackson there came the remodellers, subdividers, embellishers, and railroad fans. On paper, they criss-crossed the cerebral territory with more and better lines. The more inscrutable and messy the brain specimens looked, the more free-wheeling finesse went into the interpretation of symptoms postulating brain centers and connections between them, cortical, subcortical, and trans- cortical. No one even half-interested in the nervous system could escape the fascination. Only an occasional independent mind became fed up and dared to question this unrealistic trend while not discarding localization altogether. Sigmund Freud was one of the questioners. After Wernicke, in 1883, he became another one in a long line of assistants in Meynert's Clinic in Vienna and worked there for five months. To Freud, Meynert was "the greatest brain anatomist of his time"; Freud knew Baginski, too, for he abstracted neurological litera- ture for the *Archiv fur Kinderheilkunde*, edited by Baginski, the first diagram-maker, and he visited him in Berlin. Freud at one time con- sidered a job in a pediatric clinic. At the age of 35, Freud was lecturing on aphasia; in 1891 he published a book on the subject[83] — a flop as to sales but considered the best thing he had done in neurology by the author himself. "Impertinent," he called it, for it brought some fresh air into the over-involved and stuffy atmosphere around the prob- lems.[84]

But what looked like the decisive blow to unwarranted localizing was struck at the beginning of this century, when debunking had become a fine art. It was delivered by Pierre Marie, a man who was not only a famous successor of Charcot, who like almost everyone else had more or less accepted Broca's aphasia and, also like everyone else, had elaborated a diagram of speech disorders, but a man who also could boast: "I shall at least have the satisfaction that as a former interne of Broca's, and most proud of it, I may show that my chief has been mistaken, his mistake being highly excusable, and even inevitable, given the state of knowledge and the prevailing conditions of the period."[85]

Such was the general interest, by then, in both aphasia and debunking, that Pierre Marie published his findings in *Presse Médicale* and in *Revue de Philosophie*. His historical account was grist to the mill of a famous anti-scientific philosopher of the early twentieth century: Henri Bergson.

"At that time," Bergson told his Boswell, "they were accepting without question this enormous construction entirely based on a small and poorly observed fact: a pseudo-fact which had been swallowed without a check because it confirmed Bouillaud's thesis then in fashion [sic]."[86]

Pierre Marie, in order to overthrow "the complex apparatus of the fanciful schemas" that in fact had overgrown Broca's work, had to topple "the monument" down to its base. His three articles, entitled *Revision of the aphasia question,* appeared in 1906, the first with the devastating subtitle: "The third frontal convolution plays no particular role in the function of speech."

Marie first reviews a number of cases of his own, studied for ten years at the very same Bicêtre. (Aphasia, in Paris, remains tied to the place. Where else would a fashionable novelist like Georges Simenon have his aphasic hero hospitalized in *The Bells of Bicêtre,* 1962?) On the clinical side, he takes an extreme position of what had been Baillarger's, Jackson's, and Trousseau's views, namely that aphasics have a mental disorder that defies classification: "Aphasia is one", he says, as Gratiolet had done, "one and indivisible," and this, he thinks, might go under the name of "Wernicke's aphasia." Some patients have an additional defect, that of articulation: this combination is what Broca saw and might be called "Broca's aphasia." The defect in articulation may occur by itself, without aphasia—this Marie calls "anarthria" to distinguish it from "dysarthria" caused by brainstem-cerebellar lesions; Broca had come to call it "alalia." In other words, Marie, like so many of his predecessors, slices the cake his own way but uses a bigger knife. On examining the brains of these patients, he finds that the lesions responsible for aphasia pure and simple are found in Wernicke's area, i.e., the convolution surrounding the hind end of the Sylvian fissure.

As to "anarthria"—here he mapped out a subcortical *quadrilateral,* fighting shy of Broca's convolution that overlies it—Marie drew an area essentially taking in the insula with the subjacent ganglia and internal capsule down to the lateral ventricle. The destruction of the third frontal convolution in Broca's first case and all subsequent ones was held accidental and without bearing on the speech defect. In too many cases with Broca's aphasia, his convolution was found spared. According to Marie, Leborgne's aphasia was due to the destroyed supramarginal gyrus—not included by Broca in his description—as well as the superior temporal gyrus, which Broca had included.

But when I look at Leborgne's brain I doubt whether the supramarginal gyrus is in fact destroyed, and in Lelong's case the third frontal convolution is almost certainly not intact. That Lelong, moreover, was senile, not aphasic is another unwarranted assumption of Marie's. Hence, the statements by Marie and his pupil Moutier, on other cases and brains that support the statistics against Broca's area, are not entirely convincing.

A missing portion of the convolutional mass will always remain hard to identify with any precision. Our insecurity becomes even greater when we are asked to take the word of someone with an axe to grind who has done the identifying. And who without such an aim would bother to check?

Marie, far more authoritarian than Broca had ever been, already in his early fifties and at the height of deserved fame, became the leader of a revolutionary avant-garde. It was a time when Broca's case, once the symbol of bold innovation, had become bound up with subsequent—and by now antiquated—pedantry. Another series of vehement discussions took place, this time in the Société de Neurologie. The fight, mainly between Marie and Dejerine, who defended Broca, ended in a draw.[87]

Still, Marie opened the third period of aphasiology, if we count Broca's as the second and that of his forerunners as the first. But Marie was not able to eradicate "diagram-making" entirely, nor was he successful in his "iconoclasm" of the father-image of Broca, his former chief. (Both terms in quotation marks are from Henry Head's beautiful English classic of the 1920's.)[88] Moutier, Marie's standard-bearer, who in his monumental thesis, L'Aphasie de Broca, assembled the greatest possible amount of damaging material against his chief's former chief, felt obliged to conclude: "Broca was first to apply vigor and method to the treatment of the disturbances of speech. He made the confused science of speech take a colossal step forward, and his clarity of vision, loyalty to method, prudence and modesty in conclusions deserve an admiration which no one will ever deny him. Broca's aphasia has come to stay, and this is supremely right."[89]

Broca's aphasia had not only come to stay through innumerable publications of this third period, but it was vindicated in the fourth, which began around or even before 1940, when neurosurgical procedures had become sufficiently safe and humane to allow "vivisection" on humans. Excisions of Broca's area are done when it is diseased. Many of these patients are aphemic before operation; otherwise the area is understandably out-of-bounds for surgeons. Two factors mainly militate against a clear-cut appraisal: congenital pathology and surgical excision. Neither brings about as much dysfunction as acquired diseases do, such as strokes and tumors. Usually, however, excisions of Broca's area are followed by aphasia, although this may last for only a few days. But the same is true of the other speech areas that lie on Foville's circonvolution d'enceinte—the gyrus around the Sylvian fissure.

Of even greater interest were Penfield's experiments of stimulating electrically various parts of the cerebral cortex, both those commonly associated with the "faculty of speech" and occasionally others that are not. This procedure is apt to suppress the patients' ability to speak. But it is most apt to do so when the stimulating electrode is applied either to Broca's or to Wernicke's area, perhaps even more so in the former. With minor exceptions, no interference is seen when the stimulus is removed far enough from these critical zones.[90]

The question of handedness and cerebral dominance has been much advanced in the last two or three decades, and it seems that even in left-handed people, the left hemisphere "has its say."[91] Also small lesions affecting Broca's area may produce only transient aphasia.[92]

Thus speech, a function hard to define, is localized in an area equally hard to delimit. Aphasia is not "indivisible," but it also cannot be cut up like a pie. It cannot be strictly confined to any particular lobe of the brain, to any single one of the convolutions, or even, strictly, to any one of their combinations. Nor can it be tied to any histologically circumscribed cortical area. Yet loss of speech does result from partial, by no means ubiquitous lesions of the brain. And no matter how reluctant we must be to talk about a "seat of language" in the brain, it would be wrong to deny all validity to the concept of a special speech faculty, to a principle of localization, or to Broca's method of nailing down the problem. His was one of those over-simplifications that grow into bewildering complexities — like Euclid's or Newton's — the way sprouting seeds are oversimplifications, necessary for the growth and the understanding of trees. We may argue about psycho-physiological theory; in practice we cannot abandon "Broca's area."

~XI~

Portraits and Projects

"Some men are specialists . . . others have a more restless turn of mind . . ."

*I*nseparable, like the brothers Goncourt of the literary salons, the Brocas, father and son, were a common sight in medical circles.

Benjamin was compensated by the professor for having taught him the rudiments of medicine on their rounds through the countryside of Sainte Foy. This happy perpetuation of a father-son relationship, strange yet natural, was a wonderful way for the sprightly country doctor to spend his retirement. A widower in 1864, he had moved in with the young Brocas. Far from retiring, Benjamin supposedly "assisted" his son in his private practice; he even became a titular member of the Société d'Anthropologie. On surgical rounds, "the merry, talkative, little old man" may at times have stolen the show, holding forth with his comments on the case.[1]

No matter how immersed in anthropology, Broca, we must not forget, spent the greater part of his day on ward rounds, lectures, operating schedules, *concours*, faculty committees, meetings of the Société de Chirurgie, and the Académie de Médecine, where he became a member in 1866. In the following year he was full Professor of External Pathology; in the next, of Clinical Surgery.[2]

The morning began at the hospital at 8:30 sharp. On his way to the ward (Reclus of Sainte Foy, his interne recalled), the master would hastily don the apron held ready for him by an orderly and rush to the first bed, without a word or so much as a glance at his internes. A discreet whistle might pass his lips as he removed a dressing. The least unusual finding would arouse his curiosity, make him embark on a full-scale clinical discussion, and forget himself for so long at that one

212

bedside that he compromised the remainder of his rounds. Departing only towards noon or later, he would often leave his internes in a state close to exhaustion.[3]

Not surprisingly, this multifarious, unending drive, these widely separated mental operations, tended to create the impression of absent-mindedness. "At times," according to Pozzi, another one of his closest pupils, "his mobile face would assume the dreamy, distracted look so well-known to his friends."[4] Another portraitist speaks of the contrast between the studied calm of the high and balding forehead and "the collision of thoughts going on underneath."[5] The men around Broca seem to have felt as though in the presence of a temporarily becalmed volcano. Yet the existing portraits convey a placid and pastoral assurance, an almost Olympian serenity: "the ample brow that has become legendary" above eyes, "dark brown, velvety, somewhat heavy-lidded, caressing, infinitely attractive."[3] Good nature also speaks from the lips, which in the portraits appear full, sensuous, and benign. Quite often, though, they would turn "a little ironical and very imperious"; they were in fact "almost always pursed in a skeptical smile," the smile on "the lips of the professor who has never ceased to be a student."[5] And yet on the whole, "one might ask what his countenance reflected more faithfully: his intellect or his heart."[3]

So far we have been practically looking at a still life. "You did not know Broca," Pozzi says, "unless you heard and *saw* him speak, especially when the conversation turned to one of his favorite subjects. He would throw back his head, his face would become astonishingly animated, his body tense. . . . This lent his conversation, which at times rose to veritable eloquence, a particular charm and bite. . . . Esthetic or literary topics were no more foreign to him than questions of history and politics. Interested in everything, he had his personal and well-reasoned opinion about everything; this he expressed with as much fire as he would put into the search and demonstration of any truth, major or minor."[4]

To Reclus he seemed "infectiously cheerful. I cannot recall anything more pleasant than the hours spent with friends at his table, when he would give himself over to that broad and strong gaiety so characteristic of people in robust health. The most enjoyable stories welled up from his tireless memory. . . .

"In this harmonious and charming home, the hours seemed shorter. . . . There was an atmosphere of perfect calm — a promise of lasting happiness. . . . Some minds are productive only under extreme tension; they are obsessed by an idea, long before they can find the

Broca in his fifties.
(Courtesy National Library of Medicine, Bethesda, Md.)

form in which to express it; 'they labour in pain.' M. Broca would start or resume his task with ease; he was always ready and so marvellously organized that his mental activity never sagged. . . .

"We might be reproached with deliberately obscuring one of the most prominent traits of M. Broca's character did we not mention here the ardent passion with which he always and everywhere asserted what he thought to be the truth. He did not listen well to opponents, he would not stop to consider their objections; he marched forward without wasting his time on obstacles, or on the susceptibilities he might stir up; wholly dominated by his idea he would proceed like a force gathering momentum."[3]

"This ceaseless mental tension would occasionally cause him to be blunt and irritable, but soon his kindness would get the upper hand and make him try to cover up the other man's mistake. Often, though, his great moral superiority caused him to be severe. He hated charlatanism and saw it everywhere, sometimes even where it did not exist; his tone was often mocking and supercilious, and together with his critical acumen he kept too much of the ardent young polemist.

"We must never forget the role which this noble man played in science and society. Nothing you might say about his moral qualities would be an exaggeration. At a time when young men were indulging in the noisy pleasures fostered by a despotic regime . . . when the Medical School seemed nothing but a hotbed of favoritism and intrigue, Broca and his friends . . . were our hope, a hope never disappointed. . . ."[6]

How difficult it is to balance the features, to reconcile the paradoxes! A fatherly fanatic, an unbending anti-dogmatist!

Like Gerdy, the introvert, like Lallemand, the extrovert (another congenial mind for whom he wrote an aggressive obituary)[7], Broca was made a "knight" twice (the files of the Legion of Honor left much to be desired), not counting the episode that nearly got him the cross in 1848, when, so as not to embarrass the Director of the Assistance Publique, he refused it.[8] He never wore it, either. Contempt for the regime, a certain austerity in his Calvinist background, and the tedium of the social climb prevented Broca from having ambitions of this sort.

Ambitious, though, was the program for his clinical teaching of surgery at the Pitié. In 1868 Gazette des Hôpitaux, taking nearly two full columns to announce his course, found the new professor at forty-eight rather young for the venerable chair, yet incontestably qualified by "vast and varied knowledge in every branch of biology."

"Clinical medicine," Broca was quoted as saying in his first lecture, is "pathology in action." His intention was to go beyond the teaching routine of most of his illustrious predecessors, who were generally satisfied with discussing a patient's diagnosis, prognosis, and treatment. In addition to these obvious and time-honored matters he would dwell on etiology, pathogenesis, anatomical structure, normal and abnormal mechanisms underlying symptoms. To bring basic science to the bedside, to illuminate the inventory of signs by projecting them on a background of recent discoveries — preferably one's own — was considered revolutionary then; it has become the hallmark of good teaching.

What was Broca like as a surgeon? Lacking the benefit of a sufficiently advanced physiology and bacteriology, patients were on the whole well advised to shun surgeons — and vice versa; hospitals, too, were best avoided.

In surgical matters, the public tends to place emphasis on technical skill. Both the adoration of digital virtuosity and the contempt for the mindless butcher obscure the fact that, especially in the nineteenth century, a vast number of contributions to biological thinking about the human body were owed to surgeons.[9] Professors of surgery who, like Bichat and Broca, devote much of their time to pursuits other than operating on patients, are unlikely to be remembered as great *surgeons*. Hence, no operative procedures are among those that bear Broca's name. Nor is it surprising that a journalistic account of his removal of a parotid tumor makes a present day reader's hair stand on end.[10] But the Paris Société de Chirurgie cannot have elected him as their president of 1865 solely on the grounds of his theoretical contributions.

Aside from vascular surgery — where he avoided the scalpel — it was naturally his work on the region of the head which stimulated him to publish.

The treatment of compound depressed fractures of the skull, the removal of bone fragments driven into the brain, was a controversial subject. Broca presented a case in the Société de Chirurgie, giving credit to the interne who had taken the notes under his direction. The indications were well-known: epileptic convulsions starting in the opposite leg. About one month earlier, the fourteen-year-old chimney sweep, probably the victim of his occupation, had been transiently rendered unconscious by a board falling on his head from a third-story window. Broca successfully removed from the brain a 3 by 1½ cm. bone fragment: "a wonderful result for which my congratulations," said

216

M. Legouest, opening the discussion on the 80 to 100 percent mortality of the period.[11]

Not a therapeutic, but a diagnostic triumph was Broca's case of an extradural abscess in 1876.[12] For the first time, a true localization of an invisible intracranial lesion was followed by a neurosurgical intervention. (Macewen in his *Pyogenic Diseases of the Brain and Spinal Cord*, [1893, Maclekose, Glasgow], p. 326, 189, reports a similar case in Broca's convolution. The operation was refused; the abcess verified at autopsy. The year? 1876.) In this patient, the bone, in the left fronto-parietal region, was only laid bare but not fractured by a horse's hoof. About one month later he showed signs of aphemia. On the overlying skull Broca indicated the posterior end of the left third inferior frontal convolution at a point 2 cm. above and 5 cm. behind the orbital process. (He had made extensive post-mortem studies on the correspondence between points on the skull and the underlying convolutions by driving pegs through the bone and identifying the dents these pegs had made in the brain).[13] Through a trephine hole the "abscess situated at the level of the speech area" was evacuated. Already comatose, the patient regained consciousness briefly but succumbed several hours later, although "the interne had remained at his bedside all day."

Might there be other means of localizing brain lesions through the intact skull, even in cases where the site was not determined by a symptom such as aphemia? Broca thought he was well on the way in devising such a method which we might call "thermo-encephalography."

This was the time when thermometry, like microscopy, intermittently forgotten and persistently considered impractical, had finally triumphed: in 1868 Wunderlich had published his sixteen-years' work on body temperature in health and disease.[14] But Broca was not concerned with fevers. Ever since his work on aneurysms had shown him a local rise in temperature due to a change in blood flow, he had found the taking of skin temperatures useful for deciding on amputations of limbs where the pulse was not palpable. Claude Bernard's recent work on the control of blood flow by vasomotor nerves and Brown-Séquard's on capillary congestion were germane to his thinking. From the limbs he transferred his temperature studies to the head.

A "thermoelectrical apparatus" to measure the local temperature rise in inflammatory conditions had been used in France by Breschet and Béquerel senior.[14] To Broca's grief, his own physicists considered his suggestion of using thermocouples impractical; they have been consistently used only since the beginning of our century. Broca had to be satisfied with a "thermometric crown" carrying half a dozen symmetrically arranged instruments, their bulbs containing mercury, shielded with cotton. He also used a spiral mercury thermometer, to improve on the fever thermometers generally employed, but all of them he found too slow.[15]

Even with this equipment, fresh infarcts were shown to be "hot," and in cases of compound depressed fracture and subsequent epilepsy, Broca considered a temperature rise of one to three centigrades over the injured area an additional indication for operative intervention. Cerebral activity, too, must influence scalp temperature; he found it low at rest, also with fasting, but with reading it went up—though only in poor readers. For medical students to get the expected rise in brain heat, mental arithmetic was needed as an extra effort. By and large, the temperature over the frontal lobe was, of course, found the highest.

It may seem farfetched to make this gallant effort the forerunner of electroencephalography, but that this is the case has been shown not too long ago.[16] During the 1860's and '70's Broca had two rivals in this field: Lombard and Schiff. Josiah Stickney Lombard was a former assistant professor of physiology at Harvard. Like most subsequent workers in this field, Lombard went exclusively after psychophysiological correlations—unlike Broca, whose main concern was the thermal diagnosis of cerebral disease. Lombard claimed that, in contrast to Broca's, his apparatus—the first with thermopiles—eliminated the interference by scalp vessels and their temperatures and recorded true brain temperatures.[17] It seems that Broca was not too concerned with this obvious criticism. For his purpose—localizing a focus of disease—the distinction between brain and blood temperature was irrelevant and probably a fallacy in any case.

The other physiologist in the late 1860's who studied "the heating up of nerves and nerve centers as the result of sensory stimulation" was the German expatriate Moritz Schiff, a leading neurophysiologist. He, too, did his finicky experiments with thermocouples, which he embedded in symmetrical points of animal brains, taking great pains to prove that he was recording truly "evoked" (Schiff's new term) cerebral temperature rises, free from vascular interference.[18] It was through Schiff's Italian pupil, the distinguished physiologist Angelo Mosso, that cerebral thermometry passed the turn of the century. Mosso inserted a specially sensitive French mercury thermometer into the brain of Delphina Parodi, a girl with a traumatic "brain fungus." Inspired by Mosso's Die Temperatur des Gehirns, published in 1894,[19] Hans Berger in Jena published his own similar studies as late as 1910,[20] some of them through the intact scalp overlying a bone defect. One day in 1924 this none too rewarding pursuit gave him the idea of using electrodes, and to replace human "thermoencephalography" by the E.E.G.[16]

Localization applied to surgery of the brain, physiology applied to localization—what about pathology of the brain applied to legal medicine? The question was one in general anthropology. Examining the brain of one Lemaire, nineteen years old, executed for murder, Broca found its weight was a mere 1183 grams. In addition, it showed what he took for signs of an old meningitis. The skull that had housed it was conspicuous by an extremely small forehead, asymmetry, and a prematurely closed sagital suture. "In the belief of punishing his guilt," Broca concluded, "they have guillotined a man who was insane."[21]

Lombroso's sensational L'Uomo delinquente—crime a cerebral deformity—was not published until 1876. But criminal anthropology was at home at the Société d'Anthropologie, where Alphonse Bertillon had hatched his practical identification procedures of criminals; Alphonse was the son of Adolphe, the statistician who had cofounded the Society.

Broca contributed several reports on questions of public health,[22] read to the Académie de Médecine where he now was a "discreet and reserved" member.[23]

In a third such report, he convinced his amused audience that the "problem"—surprising in this academic setting—was based on the vested interests of what we might call the French wine lobby. They wished to prohibit the sale of sherry and other strong liquors, called "fortified wines," which were then not being produced in France. The initiative claimed that such beverages contained a "toxic" kind of alcohol. To begin with, prohibition went against Broca's liberal grain. He argued, "This is the answer I propose: Like any other alcoholic beverage, a wine that has been fortified is harmful when used to excess. The fortification of wines in itself presents no particular danger to the consumer."[24] (Two decades later, the French government did forbid the fortification of wines.)

Not at all unexpectedly, Broca drafted the report, in 1864, of an advisory committee to the Assistance Publique, regarding plans for the new Hôtel-Dieu Hospital.[25] The Emperor, about to spend 40 million francs on the new Paris Opera house, felt obliged to match the ungodly expenditure with a virtuous endowment of the ailing poor. The new hospital was again to "rise in the shadow of Notre-Dame."[26] The venerable structure had been waiting for the axe ever since 1785, when

Tenon had written a famous unflattering report about it. Equally un-flattering to the new Hôtel-Dieu, projected on the opposite side of the little island, were most speakers during the Société de Chirurgie's ten sessions devoted to this "most objectionable and inconceivable absurd-ity," as one of them called it.

Criticism concerned mainly overcrowding and lack of air; some innovations were praised. Broca expressed the fear that the city's poor might have to pay for it.[26] Building began four years later. Ten years and 50 million francs finally produced that black, prim, oppressive, pseudo-renaissance item, still in use today.[27]

Broca's concern was with the people, but he was not gregarious. And though he travelled extensively in his own country, he only sparingly sought the limelight of the international congresses that began to multiply. He had been invited to discuss aphasia in Norwich. In the following autumn Broca — together with de Quatrefages and his young anthropological associate Hamy, Franz-Joseph, Emperor of Aus-tria, the gracious Empress of France, and 5,995 other guests from all over the world, people prominent in politics, finance, science, and the arts — was invited, all expenses paid, by the Khedive of Egypt to assist in the grandiose opening of the Suez Canal. After ten years of labor, its sixty-year-old planner and builder, Ferdinand de Lesseps, a second cousin of Empress Eugénie and her protégé, had brought about one of the crowning events in the life of his nation. Here was a symbol of everything the nineteenth century loved and held in awe: things exo-tic and man's indomitable spirit in the face of the heaviest odds, against nature, politics, finance. What investments, what chances of profit, yet what risks! (Eighty-four million francs to compensate the company for giving up forced labor in favor of using modern equip-ment; the total cost was nearly 433 million francs, twice its estimate. Not to speak of losing England's good will: at the opening England was represented chiefly by warships.)[28]

The net gain of this windfall, as brought home by the pioneers of the École Practique in Paris, was the proof that, like the rest of the world, biblical Egypt had known a Stone Age culture.[29] The Egyptians were not "born civilized," their institutions and monuments not, as it was widely asserted, a sudden creation that had come fully made from the hands of the Creator.[30] Hamy showed that flint stones had been used for circumcision in the African Quaternary period.[29] And Broca acquired a set of photographic likenesses[31] to prove that every type of man existed in that oldest, hottest, and most crowded of melting pots.

The Flaws of Evolution

> "Science has so far not given any real
> explanation for the origin of things."

*I*n the modern civilized world, the Story of Evolution has been as triumphant as the Book of Genesis, its one-time rival. While research and revelation have come to coexist quite peacefully, Darwin is by comparison not being read as widely, and the familiar quotations from his works are few. But criticism of Darwinism is apt to be branded as heresy or, worse, treated as simply ridiculous. The popular press, one hundred years ago, enabled an unprecedented number of casual readers to participate in an academic discussion about a biological hypothesis. The scandal of the *Origin of Species* resulted from its impact on an unsuspecting public and its spiritual leaders. Most of the experts were, on the contrary, merely suspicious: evolution had, after all, been on their minds for a long time. We could point to no better example of the prevailing attitude than the struggle Broca had to put up for the survival of his own claim that species are not fixed: the *Memoir on Hybridity*[1] which he managed to make public against odds, the year before the *Origin of Species*[2] came off the press.

"Transformism," as they were calling evolutionary theory in France, had frequently figured in the discussions of the Société d'Anthropologie. But only in the spring of 1870 did the time seem ripe for taking a stand on Darwinism. Broca's opinion, sympathetic but critical, appeared fully formed by 1866, when yet another bone became one of contention: a chinless, massive jaw of the Neanderthal type, found the year before at La Naulette in Belgium.[3] Broca had no doubt that it was human, "quite close, in fact, to the jaws of superior apes." He lined it up in the middle of a series of jaws arranged from ape to man. "But little I care, facts are facts. I have already had occasion to state that I am not a Darwinist . . . Yet I do not hesitate . . . to call this the first link in the chain which, according to the Darwinists, extends from man to ape. . . ."

Pruner-Bey, the Society's president for that year, suddenly claimed he had seen similar jaws in modern Melanesians; the specimen was an example of inverse development, degeneracy, or disease. Broca countered that if such jaws really did exist in modern savages, it would rather strengthen Darwinism. And if, in all fairness, M. Pruner-Bey had had this fact in mind from the start, why had he been so slow in deciding whether to call man or ape the creature leaving a jaw in the Hole of La Naulette?

During the last years Broca had become increasingly involved in the anatomical relationship between man and beast. The work on the nervous system of animals by Leuret and Gratiolet, which had influenced his study of aphasia, bore the sub-title *Considered in Relation to Intelligence*. In 1866 Broca quoted numerous examples where animal intelligence was only a rudimentary form of the human.[4] Three years later he published a 176-page memoir on the analogies and differences within the *Primate Order.*[5] Similar to Huxley's *Evidences as to Man's Place in Nature* of 1863,[6] Broca's main thesis was that, morphologically, man was closer to the anthropoid simians than these were to the lower families of monkeys, tarsiers, and lemurs. His full-scale critique of Darwin's work[7] began with a call for humble self-criticism:

"We are much too fearful of losing the noble halo which we so fondly drape around our cradle. Personally, I am not obsessed by this fear. I am not one to despise upstarts or find more merit in rising than in descending. If I could see a place for sentimentality in science, I would agree with M. Claparède that I'd rather be a perfected ape than a degenerated Adam [presumably suggested by Huxley's preference of having for a father a "miserable ape" rather than Bishop Wilberforce[8]]. . . ."

In the next phrase he summed up the non-credo of the liberal humanist-investigator: "Any philosophical system that enslaves science, no matter how opposed it may be to religious dogma, is just as objectionable as that dogma itself."

He gave a sketch of evolutionary history before Darwin, mainly in France: "The classification of species had to precede the transformist hypothesis. . . . None of the philosophical or theological teachings showed any qualms about accepting the notion of an existing chain or ladder of beings. . . .

"Before the beginning of this century, . . . the fixity of species did not have to take the form of the rigid system required later. It was generally accepted and no great importance attached to it.

"One can see Buffon maintain and reject it in turns. . . . The same Buffon caused not the slightest offense when he ventured the thought that, grouped in one family, all species seem to have a common origin . . . a remark that clearly contained the transformist principle. Buffon did not, however, aspire to an explanation of how the forms of life and the serial disposition of beings have evolved. No threat to any philosophical system was implied, and no person had cause to take umbrage.

"It was a different story when Lamarck, first in 1801, then in 1809, suddenly rose to a much more general and elevated concept. From its height the narrow limits of species, genera, and orders began to look like barely noticeable shadings, as he resolutely denied the fixity of organic types and proclaimed that in nature continuous, limitless change was the law. Pre-established harmony and final cause he replaced by progressive evolution. . . .

"Two things in the Lamarckian doctrine are distinguishable: the general principle of transformism and a theory to explain it.

"The principle, as we have seen, had been envisaged before. But it was not generalized and had not formed the basis for a *scientific* concept about nature. . . . Let us in fairness call it the *principle of Lamarck* —a hypothesis, by the way, that like so many other general statements in science . . . cannot become a *law* until it is proven.

"In our eyes Lamarck would have been an even greater man . . . had he not added those hypothetical explanations that gave his critics such a foothold as to compromise the principle itself. . . . A single formula would have sufficed, to the effect that organisms may change their constitution under the influence of the conditions of life. Today this is called modification due to the *milieu*. . . . Lamarck, who did not know this expression . . . talked about the *reign of circumstances*. It came to the same thing, but among these circumstances he singled out those depending on the animal itself, on its own volition, its needs, and its *habits*. . . . He supposed, for instance, that the interdigital membranes of the aquatic vertebrates were due to their efforts at spreading the toes in swimming, or that the giraffe had lengthened its cervical vertebrae by stretching its neck in order to feed on trees . . . all grist for the mill of his opponents. . . .

"Then he dared to describe the gradual changes leading to the transformation from ape to man. . . . Emotions ran high both outside

223

and inside science. . . . It was easy for naturalists, for physiologists to hit this weak spot. . . . They thought they had killed the very principle of transformism . . . but not to a point of no return. Temporarily threatened, orthodox science needed a more solid wall of protection.

"This consisted in making the immutability and invariability of species absolute. . . . Hybrids were declared infertile . . . at least in the long run. . . . *Sint ut sunt, aut non sint* [They must be as they are, or they must not be at all]. Formulated in Cuvier's famous book, the doctrine of terrestrial upheavals appeared to consolidate this system. Each revolution resulted in the sudden destruction of the old, and the no less sudden creation of the new species. . . .

"Nevertheless, in 1828 a powerful voice arose against the fixity of species: Étienne Geoffroy Saint-Hilaire had rallied to the principle of Lamarck. Two years later, in his memorable discussion with Cuvier before the Académie des Sciences, he upheld the mutability of species. In his *Philosophie Anatomique* . . . he described how often the transitory stages in the development of the embryo resembled the permanent features of animals found at a lower level of the series. Anomalies, called regressive . . . were confirmatory. . . .

"Leaving Lamarck's theory vague, Saint-Hilaire made it unanswerable. . . . But he could give only general reasons to his adversary . . . This grandiose debate held the attention of all Europe for one whole year. . . . It was the struggle of two philosophies: . . . natural causes . . . against supernatural intervention. . . . The majority was on Cuvier's side. . . .

"Meanwhile a problem began to trouble the upholders of fixed species, and nearly threatened to turn them into heretics against their own dogma. Fixity applied to anthropology led straight to polygenism. Already in the eighteenth century . . . one of the reasons Buffon adopted a transformist view was the descent of mankind from a single couple. But if you let the Negro become white, the white man black . . . you can hardly bar other groups in nature from becoming similarly differentiated. Many classical species, animal and vegetable, differ from one another no more than, or even as much as, a Teuton differs from a Negro, a Hottentot from a Polynesian or Australian. The very idea of species being immutable makes for the assumption of several distinct origins of mankind. This notion became particularly suggestive when Cuvier endeavored to prove that man had appeared on earth quite recently, for only a few centuries had gone by between then and the paintings or sculptures displayed on the ancient monuments of Egypt, and these established a neat and faithful distinction between the so-called Caucasian type and the Negro. If only a few hundred years had produced so many divergent features, the fixity of species was done for; if on the other hand, species were immutable, the unity of mankind was done for.

"In Cuvier's time . . . at least in France, most naturalists were polygenists. Cuvier himself, cautious and diplomatic . . . has written nothing openly to oppose monogenism, but neither has he written anything in its favor—a silence which is quite significant on the part of a man who loved to find biblical tradition confirmed by science.

"Now polygenism, although strengthened by the doctrine of permanent species, was nevertheless much attacked because it offended general beliefs. . . . Lamarck was almost forgotten, a remote echo from the past, arousing no more fears. . . . The present danger was polygenism; in order to refute it one might safely invoke an occasional transformist argument without detriment to classical teaching.

"This way it came about that the monogenists unwittingly prepared the way for Darwinism. They showed man all over the world at grips with the most diverse climates. Within a few generations, under the influence of the environment . . . he had become subject to a profound change. For above all, mankind must not have been in existence longer than six thousand years. . . . But it was a slippery slope. . . . Would one eventually have to choose between the heresy of transformism and that of polygenism?

"Such, in brief, was the unsteady march of natural philosophy between Cuvier and Darwin. . . . Over the pursuit of an incidental question—that of the origin of man—the great objective of Lamarck, i.e., the explanation of the series, had been lost sight of. Despite innumerable new discoveries . . . knowledge was not sufficient to attempt a vast synthesis of nature with the rigor required of science. Shall the man be accused of impudence who under these circumstances set out on his bold venture? To judge him in this way is very far from my mind. I am one of those who do not think that Charles Darwin has discovered the true agents of organic evolution; on the other hand I am not one of those who fail to recognize the greatness of his work. . . ."

"Vital competition," Broca agrees, "is a law; the resultant selection is a fact; individual variation, another fact; the eventual transmission of these variations through one or more generations, a possible consequence of the laws of heredity. . . .

"It is wonderful to see with what cleverness Darwin anticipates objections, with what talent he counters them, with what profound knowledge he marshals the enormous material for his indirect demonstration . . . But logic requires direct proof. . . ."

"Now, to Darwin, 'it does not seem incredible' that the main four or five phyla of the animal world and an 'equal or less large' number in the vegetable kingdom, may have descended from a single prototype, a single primitive form between beast and plant. But such a view, he adds, is based on analogy, which is a fallacious guide. . . . In other words, there is nothing to convince him of a limitless application of natural selection. . . . Hence, his doctrine may be called *Oligogenic transformism.*

"Where Darwin himself was hesitant, others went all the way. . . . Especially in Germany a transformism has developed . . . which I shall call monogenic: all the known organic forms are said to be descended from a simple proto-organism—called *monad* by some, *protist* or *proto-zoon* by others—consisting of a single cell or, even less, an element barely resembling a nucleus or nucleolus. . . .

"A third concept that might be called *polygenic transformism,* seems to go back to Buffon. . . . 'The two hundred species described,' he said, talking about the quadrupeds, 'may be reduced to quite a small number of . . . principal stocks that gave issue, not impossibly, to all the others' (*Histoire naturelle,* XIV:358, 1766).

"There is no reason for limiting to a single spot and single moment the spontaneous evolution of matter. . . . To me it seems most likely that centers of organization appeared in very different places and at very different periods. . . . This polygenic transformism is what I would be inclined to accept. . . . My objection against Darwinism would be invalid if it conceded that organized beings have an undetermined but considerable number of distinct origins and if structural analogies were no longer considered sufficient proof for common parentage.

"As to the central question, the permanence of species . . . I did not have to wait for Darwin's book to voice an energetic protest against this classical doctrine. . . . From the first pages of my memoir on hybridity, published in 1858, I have endeavored to show that this doctrine was no longer in keeping with modern science. . . .

"In the argument for or against the permanence of species, . . . the data at first sight seem to favor fixity. We live only such a little while that things less subject to change than ourselves appear permanent to us. . . . What is the value of information going back a few thousand years . . . when we are called upon to evaluate modifications requiring several thousands of centuries? . . .

"Does botany perhaps lead to a different conclusion? . . ." An aster growing wild in the environs of St. Jean de Luz on the Bay of Biscay—*Aster tripolium*—revealed to him on his vacation the most remarkable changes in appearance according to its habitat: on the sea shore, inland, or along the river banks.

"To me this seems a good example to show how some wild vegetable species may vary under the influence of the environment, even beyond the limits ordinarily assigned to the genera. . . ."

Suggestive, yes, but was it proof for the origin and descent of species? Were you allowed, he asked, to extrapolate such observations to animals or to invoke factors other than observable structure?

"Regarding animals, cross-breeding between species that are close to each other . . . testifies to their analogous structure and the similarity between their respective ova and impregnating fluids. Admittedly, transformism gives a very satisfactory explanation for these facts. But is no other interpretation possible? The partisans of transformism seem to think that cross fertility between species is essentially physiological . . . a special case in their favor, based on characteristics other than those of form and structure. I am unable to share this opinion. Physiological manifestations are consequent upon anatomical features. The analogies revealed by the study of hybridity are only the analogies between organs. . . . Because the reproductive system is also involved, one must not imagine that a notion of descent is necessarily implied. These analogies only reflect the great phenomenon that organisms in nature appear in a serial distribution, i.e., a general factor that adds nothing to the degree of probability of the inductions made in support of transformism."

Take the paleontological records, Broca's argument goes on, of the horse, for example, the family *Equidae*, so brilliantly launched by Cuvier. It makes a splendid case in favor of evolution, but it is based on assumption. As to the inevitable confrontation of Creation with Evolution, he criticizes the glibness of Darwinism, in a passage that must have sounded daring, if not outright blasphemous to his listeners. "Let us see if induction and philosophical reasoning will dispel our uncertainty. In essence, the strength of transformism lies in the scientific weakness, I might even say, the impotence, of the doctrine which it opposes. . . . Science has not so far given any real explanation for the origin of things. . . . Hypotheses sustain us for awhile, but there comes a point when the laws as we know them explain nothing. Arrived at this point of powerlessness and darkness, some make life appear on earth; others take a bold step further: to them, it is the separation and condensation of cosmic matter. While the doubters give up and return to objects that are better suited for study, others cannot resign themselves to this uncertainty; they cannot stop at an effect without giving its cause. And when no natural cause turns up, there must be a supernatural one; when no law can be found, all we get is an act of creation.

"In this respect, many transformists differ from their adversaries only in the subtle timing of their miracle or in the degree of its influence. Neither Lamarck, nor Richard Owen, nor Darwin excluded from their doctrine the will of the creator. But once they have accepted the primary phenomenon of germinal organization, of life breathed into matter and of laws to govern it henceforth . . . they insist on science taking over, among the observed facts, chained together by necessary relationships, with no room left for supernatural agents. . . .

"Paleontological forms become extinct after extremely variable periods, one by one, so to speak. Those taking their place have also appeared in a day-by-day succession, a constant renewal of fauna and flora. But if the formation of new species were not due to natural causes, if they were sustained by a supernatural power, we would have to conclude that this intervention is still with us, that the period of creation has never come to an end, that the miracle is in permanence, that nature is subject to a will and not to any laws.

"All right, no more laws, no more science—but then, what are we doing here?

"In the eyes of those who proclaim it, the permanence of species is a law. But why should this law be more valid than any other? The God who has constantly been at work creating and destroying species, why should He not also have power to transform them? If I belonged to the school that explains everything unknown by the intervention of a personal God, I would seek in transformism a refuge against the anxieties caused by the history of this planet. . . .

"When we consider that He could have avoided those awful upheavals, and all that undeserved destruction, simply by allowing the species to fit themselves to their own gradual modifications, we are bound to admit that the doctrine of transformism, more than the permanence of species, is in keeping with the idea which theology gives us about the Lord's kindness and the love for his creatures. . . .

"Now, if you wish to go into details, into all those imperfections and antinomies, the hypothesis of evolution will give you a most satisfactory explanation, whereas the hypothesis of creation implies lapses of memory and blunders unworthy of the creative intelligence. . . . Sham teeth in the fetus of a whale . . . the human vermicular appendix of the cecum . . . wings on birds that cannot fly, toe-webs on those that cannot swim, lateral toes in the Solipedes, no thumb in the Ateles and Colobus monkeys, the abortive clavicle in Acleidian rodents . . . parasites. . . .

"From every point of view, gentlemen . . . the doctrine of permanence only leads to an abyss of confusion and contradiction, to physical and metaphysical impossibilities.

"The only way out is to admit evolution and transformation as a necessary consequence to the way in which species have been distributed and constituted in history.

"But while this conclusion is taking hold of our minds it is not derived from any direct proof. It rests entirely on philosophical induction, and this by itself cannot hold sway over the sciences of observation. . . . Moreover it is not tied to any transformist system in particular. . . . In favor of the theory of natural selection, which is the essence of Darwinism and under discussion here, there is no proof, not even the presumption of one. One may say only that this theory was born out of the need for explaining a mechanism . . . the way emission and wave theories were born in order to explain the path of light rays— with this difference, though, that in physics there has been direct observation. . . . The theory has found a certain number of general facts in nature that are incompatible with the idea of permanent species and go very well with the idea of evolution. Any transformist theory other than Darwin's might explain them equally well, but his explanation is always ingenious, often felicitous and sometimes most attractive. . . ."

The final piece ridicules the presumptive usefulness of preserved variation: "At the banquet of life—in Malthus' phrase—there is no room for everyone born. Hence the survivors must owe this favor to extrinsic factors in their environment or to intrinsic ones in their individual organization. . . . Nature, so to speak, has chosen them for taking care of reproducing their race. This general idea of natural selection is an undeniable fact—quite apart from how this is determined or how it influences evolution. . . .

"In Darwin's natural selection the choice made among the progenitors is based on their innate superior qualities. . . . He makes no secret of his attempt to find in spontaneous evolution a replica of the experiments known from artificial selection. . . . But is this analogy justified?. . . . In it man is made to intervene like the god of finalistic philosophy . . . and nature appears endowed with a personal will—a concept entirely contrary to the whole Darwinian philosophy. . . .

"Does this mean that natural selection is an impossible factor? By no means. But this having some influence does not justify our conclu-

229

sion that it is the sole and universal process leading to evolution, or even that it has ever been capable of producing a single species. In this respect the hypotheses of Darwin and Lamarck are comparable. . . . If one wished to deny any influence which habit and interaction with the environment exert on the structure of an organism one would have to ignore, say, the difference between the hands of a working man and those of an idler. One even might concede that one or the other acquired modification might be transmitted by heredity more or less often or more or less completely. But it is no binding reason for accepting Lamarck's theory; a cause such as this may be real and up to a point efficient without having enough power to transform species.

"Nevertheless, I might be wrong. . . . Yet even if my general objection should be overruled . . . it would be back in force if comparative anatomy presented facts that are incompatible with natural selection. . . .

"Take a natural group, that of the primates, for instance. . . . It has some features . . . that have to do with improvement, others that are simply serial. For the first kind we find a perfectly good explanation in Darwin's hypothesis. Not explained, however, by natural selection and almost opposed to it are such simple serial features as the successively earlier closing of the intermaxillary bone sutures, going from pithecus . . . to man, or the gradual disappearance of a cecal appendix . . . going in the reverse direction. . . ."

He cites many other distinctive features between monkeys and calls them "indifferent," that is, neither advantageous nor disadvantageous. And, "the closer you go into details, the greater becomes the improbability . . . Apply Darwin's thinking to the genus Orang (*Satyrus*). . . . He alone, of all the primates, has no nail on his big toe. Why?. . . . The Darwinists will answer that one day a certain pithecus was born without a big toe nail, and his descendants have perpetuated this variety. . . . Let us call this ape . . . *Prosatyrus I*, as it behooves the founder of a dynasty. . . . While, according to the law of immediate heredity, some of his offspring were like their other ancestors in having a nail on every toe, one or more were deprived of the first nail like their father. . . . Thanks to natural selection, this character finally became constant. . . . But I do not see . . . how this negative characteristic . . . might give him advantage in the struggle for existence. . . ." Broca then discussed two more characteristics of Orang's that are without survival value: absence of the round ligament of the hip and a unilobar lung.

"Thus confronted with the details of this particular case the theory yields a result absolutely contrary to its first principle. And this

is not the only example. . . . I cannot therefore agree with M. Dally
. . . when he says: 'Species are constituted and distributed *as if* they
had been produced by natural selection.' I find on the contrary, that if
species have evolved—which is likely—they are arranged *as if* natural
selection had not been the agent of their transformation.

"I am only too familiar with this manner of reasoning; it already
failed to convince me when our eminent colleague, M. De Quatrefages used it in order to show the unity of the genus Man. 'I find,' he
told us, 'that in time and space the human races behave *as if* they were
all descended from the same progeny.' . . . I then answered, no, to my
mind things looked as if mankind descended from several different
progenies. Thus it goes with all hypotheses, true or false, scientific or
otherwise. They all have their partisans saying *it is as if* and their
opponents saying the opposite. . . .

"For the last ten years transformism has been propagated under
the flag of natural selection. This has given rise to the belief that both
were the same thing and that the only choice for us to make was
between Darwin's hypothesis and the system of permanence. This is a
false alternative. . . .

"The law of serial distribution . . . is manifest everywhere within
the universe. There is a cosmic series as well as an animal and a
vegetable series; there is a chemical series, a series of crystals, and a
series of colors, there is even a sidereal series. . . . One may ask: Is the
series of organisms, while obeying its own laws, not also subject to
some other law that is more general and even more unknown?

"At all times this great problem has obsessed the metaphysicians,
and it suggested to Epicurus his doctrine. What were Epicurus and
Lucretius saying, what their modern followers? They were saying that
in the necessary course of things all possible combinations will
materialize sooner or later, amidst complexities which now will be
more or less favorable and yet, on the contrary, also unfavorable, so
that the results will be as variable as can be, according to time and
place and existing conditions. And as there is always room between
two numbers for a third, one can always, between two effects produced
by the circumstances given, envisage also an intermediate effect,
either already in being, or destined to come into being at some later
date. This is the doctrine of necessity; it is up against the doctrine of
finality, but this is perhaps not much clearer either. All this is
metaphysics, and science ought not to go astray in these hollow
speculations.

"Does this mean that science cannot by itself attain the heights of
a general synthesis? Having failed so far, must we despair of the future?

This is by no means what I think. I prefer to be inspired by the fine words of Buffon: 'The human mind has no limits, it expands in proportion to the unfolding of the universe. Man can, man must attempt everything, and for knowing everything he needs only time.'"

Darwin himself apparently made only one direct reference to Broca's criticism of Natural Selection, the most important of them all: the usefulness of the preserved variation. As the *Origin* kept going through edition after edition, Darwin continued to water down and amend his theory,[9] in order to incorporate, palliate, or refute adverse comment. In the sixth edition, of 1872,[10] he had caught up with the "much more serious objection . . . urged by Bronn and recently by Broca, namely, that many characters appear to be of no service whatever to their possessors, and therefore cannot have been influenced through natural selection. . . . There is much force in the above objection. Nevertheless. . . ." Darwin gives three reasons in his defense. First, how can we know what is, or has been useful to each species? Second, a modification in one part may lead to changes in another, according to a law of growth. Third, while we must allow for "spontaneous variations"—there must be some efficient cause for them. It seems that from "one" to "three" these counter-arguments get progressively weaker.

We cannot expect Broca to have voiced the suspicion that some of the success of Darwin's or rather Herbert Spencer's formula (the survival of the fittest) may be owed to the magic contained in the superlative of the English three-letter word. "Fit" packs a terrific punch for English-speaking people, a mystique neither possessed by any of its blunter synonyms, nor quite translatable into any other language, e.g., *adapté au milieu!* That survival of the fittest "sometimes comes to mean merely the survival of the survivors" was said in 1880. "Natural selection has become widely recognized as an *a posteriori* description of events," say some modern critics.[11] Broca did not criticize the famous formula as a begging of the question, the virtually synonymous terms "fitness," "survival," and "selection." Even stalwart Huxley at one point had to utter the heretic words that "the survival of the fittest . . . failed in application to·specific differences. . . ."[12]

When in 1872 Darwin's *Descent of Man* was translated into French, Broca, reviewing this and Wallace's work, approved of "sexual selection." Yet he still rejected gradual continuous evolution in favor of small abrupt transformations.[13]

In the next year he had occasion to return to the leporids,[14] sixteen years after he had received the curious offspring of a hare mated with a female rabbit.[1] Objections from all sides included those of vociferous breeders unable to confirm the exploit of crafty M. Roux, who was charged with having used Broca's name to mislead the public. Nevertheless, at exhibitions and in zoos, leporids, true to specification, were there for all to see, including Broca's original specimen together with a whole line of leporid descendants.

Modern works are silent about leporids. But in the *Origin of Species* Darwin mentioned them once. Referring not to Broca but to de Quatrefages and "fertility *inter se*," for eight generations of *Bombyx cynthia* and *Arrindia* moths (and a small number of other pertinent examples), he wrote: "It has lately been asserted that two such distinct species as the hare and rabbit, when they can be got to breed together, produce offspring, which are highly fertile when crossed with one of the parent species."[15] A standard work of the latter half of the twentieth century[16] espouses de Quatrefages' classical views rather than Broca's.

Naturally an ocean of data and new terms has come to cover those one hundred years. "Reproductive isolation" is the modern keyword for the concept of species. If there exists a fairly impressive list of interspecies hybrids showing a "breakdown of isolating mechanisms," these occurrences are exceptional and often artificially contrived. But just this very exceptional success of species interbreeding has been declared quite recently—with Broca, so to speak—as possibly having a profound effect on evolution.[17]

Today, a synthetic theory holds the field, compounded of practically every observation and argument that have ever been brought forward in support of evolution from Lamarck on. The greatest single steps in accounting for genetic novelty were, of course, the discovery of the chromosomes and the laws of heredity. By 1873, Mendel's work on plant hybridity had for several years been lying dormant in the bulletin of the *Naturforschender Verein in Brünn*, only in the 1890's was it taken from its shelves and appreciated. Unnoticed in his Moravian monastery garden, Brother Gregor Mendel was not the only one, however, to study plant heredity during the 1860's.[18]

During the same summers we find another amateur botanist bent over plant beds in various hospital gardens of Paris, a surgeon and anthropologist, taking along with him some corn as he moved from his appointment at Bicêtre to that of Saint-Antoine and from Saint-Antoine to the Salpêtrière.[19]

First, in 1861, the aphemia year, Broca set up a modest experiment with cornflowers (bachelor buttons or bluebottles) in his garden at the Bicêtre, with wild seed collected in the fields. Among the blue flowers there were some rather violet ones, others reddish. In the following year seeds from the reddish kind reproduced two-thirds blue: the others were shaded from bluish-purple to pink. Seeds from the lightest varieties sown again in the next year reduced the blue variety to well under one half; most were of an intermediate purple to pink and some almost white. Having to leave Bicêtre, Broca did not continue the experiment but thought it likely that he might finally obtain a "fixed race" of entirely white bluebottles.

He was more methodical, he says, in his experiments with maize (corn). In September, 1866, his farmer at Sainte Foy gave him an all-dark cob picked out of a field of blond maize. Was the dark color a natural variant, spontaneous perhaps, or was it an atavism going back a great many generations? His results of sowing dark maize in successive hospital gardens were as follows:

Before 1866	Cobs constantly blond	
1st Generation, 1866 Ste Foy (Gironde)	Single brown cob, sown at Hôp. St. Antoine in 1867.	
2nd Generation, 1867 (Hôp. St. Antoine)	Plants with blond cobs—21 (i.e. 53%) Plants with brown cobs—19 (i.e. 47%)	
3rd Generation, 1868 (Salpêtrière)	1° Bed sown from one *blond* cob descended from *brown*	Plants with blond cobs, 136 (i.e., 90%) Plants with brown cobs 15 (i.e.10%)
	2° Bed sown from one *brown* cob descended from *brown*.	Plants with blond cobs, 22% Plants with brown cobs, 78%

The "dark" plants in the "blond" bed had fewer cobs: 6 of these plants carried a few blond cobs besides the dark ones; a few were so poorly developed that the color could not be ascertained, hence the figure of all dark plants is less than 15, i.e., only 6 percent.

A number of the dark cobs were also farmed out to friends in various parts of France and to an associated foreign member of the Société d'Anthropologie in Bucharest. In addition, Broca took good care not to disturb or cultivate his maize plot, anxious to let the "struggle for existence" go on between the two races and between them and the weeds, in order to test "natural selection" as well. He hoped to develop two pure strains, two "fixed races," one a reversal to the "predominant" or primary one, the other a dark race "resembling some remote ancestors." How many generations was this going to take, he asked himself. And would he, we may ask, have arrived at the Mendelian "elements," the concept of anatomical particles combining, the stuff of heredity? He was careful enough to establish the exact numerical proportions. His figures were approximately those of Mendel's (who, incidentally, also experimented with maize).[18] In a way they spelled out to Broca that there were dominant and recessive characters. (Darwin, too, had noted the uniformity of F1 as well as the separation in F2 in a ratio approximately 3:1 without getting any closer to Mendel's laws.[20]) But at this point of his report, he was looking only for the ultimate segregation of two races. The war between the French and the Germans interrupted the experiments.

⟿XIII⟻

Group Inhumanity

⟿ | *". . . a big noise about the racial question . . ."*

*W*hat was Broca's role in the bloody events that followed? When he had visited Metz while practically still a boy, he had been fascinated, not only by the many Germans and Jews there, but also by the fortifications bristling with seemingly modern weaponry;[1] later he noted that the citadel had inspired the native young Lallemand to write pacifist poetry.[2] That proud Protestant place in Lorraine, the Divodurum Mediamatricum of Caesar's Gauls, wrested by the Huguenots from the Catholic Hapsburgs in the Renaissance, was to serve France ill in the war of 1870: like the Maginot Line seventy years later, Metz immobilized a sizable portion of the country's striking force; it sealed her defeat by capitulating to the Germans three and a half months after the outbreak of hostilities.

By then Napoleon III had been a German prisoner for eight weeks. But by declaring the war he had already stepped into the trap laid by Bismarck; the famous "Ems Dispatch," which, in the course of finding a king for Spain, had implied a snub of the French ambassador by the King of Prussia! France could take no more humiliations. Her emperor, one-time victor of the Crimea and on the Italian battlefields (for and against the resorgimento), successful conqueror of Indo-China, meddler in China, Syria, and Mexico, had been forced by Bismarck to let down every cause and every friend: Garibaldi in Italy, Maximilian in Mexico, Poland against Russia, Denmark in the matter of Schleswig-Holstein, Austria at Sadowa. And he was powerless to prevent Prussia from occupying or concluding secret military treaties with the rest of the German states.[3]

His own subjects had forced him to let them speak their minds. The irreverent remarks, for instance, that Broca permitted himself in his portrait of Lallemand (1862) or in his discussion of Darwinism would have hardly been wise in the despotic 1850's. The Empress and her entourage feared a revolution and the fall of the dynasty unless some military victory would silence the critics. To elegant gamblers and national snobs alike, war seemed inevitable and desirable. France was ready to be provoked; Prussia was prepared.

The French armies were quickly routed by the invasion from the east, the third in a series of five German invasions during a century and a half. French honor, fear, and cockiness made the people continue the defense of the country, especially Paris, and so, the Bonapartes gone, the Third Republic started out on its shaky beginnings on September 4, 1870, still fighting.

As the German armies were approaching, Broca was put in charge of an *ambulance*: a dozen sheds set up for war casualties, lined up the whole length of the Jardin des Plantes. The recruitment of medical personnel was difficult; we hear that of 24 men scheduled, three refused, and only 16 eventually turned up. In a letter of Broca's dated December 21, 1870, (to Baron Larrey, Junior, chief of the army medical service) we read that "fighting under the walls of Paris has begun this morning." There are four such letters[4] suggesting internes from his service at the Pitié across the street (which occupied the site of the present Mosque) and his own anthropological preparateur Chudzinski to help out, or excusing an interne of Velpeau's who had left to make rounds with that professor. The last letter is dated January 7, 1871; on the next day the first Prussian shells came down on the Jardin des Plantes; ten days later William I of Prussia was crowned Emperor of a unified Germany in Versailles.

Food in the beleaguered and freezing city was extremely scarce. To the horrified astonishment of Edmond Goncourt the people of Paris began to eat canned meat, while the flesh of an elephant and the kidneys of a camel were for sale in a fashionable "English" butcher shop. "Rats are made into *pâté*, quite good, I am told," wrote Victor Hugo. Close to seventy, returned from his exile in the Channel Islands, regaled with joints of bear, deer, and antelope slaughtered at the Jardin des Plantes, yet frustrated, Hugo wrote to one of his young amours:

> Ah, had you come and listened to my wooing,
> I would have served you an unheard of course:
> Of Pegasus, by killing him and stewing,
> I'd given you delicious wing of horse,

237

and a mock will in the same vein:

> Of the most gorgeous thing that I possess,
> When I depart, my country shall partake.
> My ashes? Bah! Inherit me as steak!
> Fair Ladies, there you'll taste my tenderness...[5]

France was going to her doom in questionable taste but still in style.

Anthropologists did not remain aloof. With meetings suspended between July, 1870, and July, 1871, General Faidherbe, advocate of the African Negro, led a small army of resistance in the north. Broca's personal secretary, Léon Guillard,[6] who, like most intelligent Frenchmen, had opposed the war, was killed in action.

Armand de Quatrefages, now in his sixties, chose his own desperate weapon for attacking the enemy. Written at his desk, his 87-page indictment of inhumanity, called *La Race Prussienne*,[7] was published in February, 1871. We must look at it in some detail, as a foil to Broca's stand on the extremes of patriotism. (Passages in quotes are by the original translator.)

Written "to destroy some errors and prejudices," according to the motto, *The Prussian Race* began with the statement: "I have always opposed the application of anthropology to politics." And who had applied anthropology to politics? The Prussians, with their claim that there was an anthropological basis for German unification under Prussian leadership: the fundamental unity of race for all German-speaking peoples. But, according to de Quatrefages, there was no such thing as a Germanic race. The *Pruszi* in particular were descended from Finns and Slavs who, respectively, had exhibited a vicious, unscrupulous tendency to revenge and a treacherous method of guerilla warfare. Both these attitudes were naturally abhorrent to a French aristocrat, steeped in science, Christianity, and humanism. Western civilization had not come to the Finns and Slavs before the early fifteenth century, when they were conquered by Aryan Teutonic Knights and finally joined by Huguenot emigrants in the seventeenth century—Frenchmen who had imposed on the natives their language and culture (Berlin was indeed markedly French in the early eighteenth century). But racially these Aryans were absorbed by the indigenous Finno-Slavs.

So much for chapters I to IX. Chapter X is headed "Bombardment of the Muséum," quite a shock, but the reader has been prepared to expect little good. Like the art objects from the Louvre, "our most precious articles, unique specimens, and entire collections ... had been carried down into the cellars of the various institutes during the preceding three months. ... On the 8th of January between 10 and 11 p.m. and without any summons, there burst upon us this bombardment, which called forth a solemn protest from the central powers. Does one not here recognize the Slav as he is painted by the classical authors? ... Only instead of the javelins of his ancestors, the Prussian sent us, without notice, his shells from a long range.

"Scientists, employees, and their families took shelter in the subterranean galleries of the hothouses. ... Two shells knocked the orchid house to pieces and the house for slips. ... But animals and plants were attended to as usual. ... The moral [demoralizing] effect, so much expected and so loudly proclaimed by the Prussians, was absolutely *nil.* ...

"The havoc was not very great. Some choice plants were destroyed. ... cultivated only by us and intended to be spread over the whole of Europe through us. ... Smashed up, too, were the collections brought from Mexico. ... A stuffed crocodile lost its head, some stuffed lizards were disembowelled. ... Among our living animals, one parrot was killed. None of the employees was wounded."

"Stray shells," the Prussians said: ninety-five of them coming down on the Muséum and its annexes in and around the Jardin des Plantes, between January 8 and 25: forty-seven on the Hôpital de la Pitié, 5 on the Rue Geoffroy Saint-Hilaire (the street between them) —a total of 135 *stray* shells on 50 acres?

De Quatrefages concludes that the Prussians were not really out to kill, uselessly, the sick, the young, and the learned. Their deliberate aim was to annihilate those scientific collections—absolutely unrivalled, consulted, among others, by visitors from Germany, doomed to perish by the men who envy, execrate, and wish to strip of her superiority and lustre, "Paris, the cursed Babylon. ... A crusade, preached in terms ... of the pitiless mysticism and boundless ambition that animated the old knights ..." (i.e. Aryan Teutons, not Finno-Slavs—by now de Quatrefages has almost forgotten his racial argument).

"But the warlike proceedings of Prussia carry us yet farther back into history. ... One would have thought that ... such a state of things was impossible ... that the institution of standing armies ... would leave citizens to their business ... that the general march of civilization might at times be slowed but would not altogether cease.

"Thanks to Prussia, it will be thus no more.

"Warned by our misfortunes, nations will arm from one end to the other. . . . When the next conflicts come . . . men will comprehend that war against civilization was, if not invented, at least revived by the Prussian race.

"Blinded by the joy of an unexampled triumph . . . Germany will undoubtedly read in my words only the resentment of the conquered. . . . Her union with Prussia has been founded by the sword and cemented with blood. . . . How long will it last? . . . Will Russia look on during this triumph of Pan-Germanism without raising her voice in the name of Pan-Slavism? . . . Will the Slavo-Finnic races wish to reign altogether, over the Germanic and the Latin? . . ."

In light of future events, de Quatrefage's rhetoric was perhaps no wider off the mark than those 135 Prussian shells had been in this pilot experiment of total warfare, which killed one parrot, decapitated a stuffed crocodile, and smashed a few hothouses. His anthropological case was really as good as the political, yet to deduce the latter from the former, a ridiculous nonsequitur. But the outcry of the critics was not directed against that. Naturally, the pamphlet—anthropology applied to politics in order to oppose this very same trend—did not fail to hit the Prussians in their most sensitive spot. They could take in their victorious stride all kinds of justified accusations. War is war. But being called Finno-Slavs! Their scientists promptly fell to, not so much to explode the myth of any Finno-Slav inferiority, but to prove that they, of all people, were not so shamefully descended. The refutation, thorough and dignified, came from Rudolf Virchow,[8] Prussia's foremost authority in this as well as many other matters.

Virchow could not disprove the possibility that the Prussians might be part Finns, part Slavs, with an admixture of Germanic and French elements, whatever that may mean in terms of race. What Virchow did was to upgrade the Finns by showing that many of their present-day descendants were blond longheads, as were many Prussians. The issue was not really touched upon by his anthropological survey of five million German school children. In fact, Virchow's study might have served as a death-blow to racialism, but it rather did the contrary. At the International Congress of Anthropology and Prehistoric Archeology in Budapest in 1876,[9] Virchow presented his colored maps to show that dark-haired, dark-eyed school children, if still in a two-third majority, were less common in the north than in the rest of Germany. Far from representing a mongoloid influence, he concluded, the Prussian population had "preserved the Aryan type of the ancient warrior nations in its most perfect purity." Broca said the technique Virchow had used reminded him of his own effort, seventeen years ago, in separating the tall (and blond) from the small (and dark) in France, on colored maps; but he had based them on the size of recruits: adults, not children. Virchow's thesis lacked support, he thought, for the hair is very apt to change color during childhood and adolescence. Virchow had to agree. The two learned men also agreed that in their experience it was impossible to get the recruiting boards to record eye and hair color; expecting cooperation from the military was wishful thinking. Still, "M. Virchow, through his relations in the political world, ought to be in the position . . ." the Frenchman suggested. "Je serais très-heureux si, chez vous, le ministre de la guerre se montrait plus aimable que chez nous," the Prussian replied. (A proposal to introduce any language other than French into the proceedings had failed.)

Virchow, a militant liberal, was far from being a racist. His views in many matters were close to Broca's. For instance, he repeated Broca's statements of 1861 that the Mincopies, i.e., "Negritos," were not Negroes but a separate Oceanic race indigenous to their Andaman Islands south of Burma.[8] The main disagreement between Virchow and Broca was about several prehistoric skeletal remains: Virchow claimed that certain of their characteristics were the result of disease, an erroneous view which Broca took great pains to correct when it was supported by Pruner-Bey.[10] In nearly all of these two scientists' interests and in the pattern of their lives, Broca and Virchow show remarkable parallels. Years after Broca's death, Beddoe, then President of the Royal Anthropological Institute in London, surveying the state of his science outside his country, continued to insist on this parallel.[11]

Virchow's greater fame — comparisons are as inevitable as they are invidious at such junctures — is owed to his theory of cellular pathology, which has naturally prevailed over Broca's views. Ackerknecht calls equally sincere Virchow's admiration for Broca and his naive disappointment that, in 1871, Broca did not help him in his fight against de Quatrefages.[12] When Virchow announced Broca's death to his German colleagues, he was moved to characterize his French counterpart as "a gentle, amiable, and always humane person," also to "put it on record that after the war Herr Broca was one of the first who openly took it upon himself to reestablish contact with our Berlin Society. He was at all times ready to seek an understanding with us. . . ."[13]

Among the numerous reactions to the pamphlet of de Quatrefages there also happened to be an Italian contribution. Professor Mantegazza in the *Archivio per l'Antropologia* drew attention to a German piece called *Die psychische Degeneration des französischen Volkes* by

241

Karl Stark, a psychiatrist. The Italian review triggered a protest by Hamy, one of the professors of the École d'Anthropologie, and to this Broca added:[14]

"Sr. Mantegazza will no doubt understand why his article on the little book by M. de Quatrefages cannot remain unanswered. Without entering into the fundamentals of the debate I must point out that the eminent editor of the *Archivio per l'Antropologia* has drawn a strange parallel between the work of Stark and that of M. de Quatrefages. Voltaire has given publicity to the *mot* of Lord Bolingbroke: 'The French will lock up a few who are lunatic to make you believe that the rest of them are not.' M. Stark has taken this witticism very, very seriously. He proves that, A + B, the French are afflicted with an incurable form of madness called ambitious paralysis. He lets his so-called science play a shameful role and uses it to insult a whole nation in peacetime. Tomorrow a French alienist will most probably pay him back by proving, A + B, according to the rules of science, that all Germans are dipsomaniacs, cleptomaniacs, or idiots. I have heard this said in certain public thoroughfares, and our own exploiter of popular passion will be M. Starks' opposite number here.

"If M. Mantegazza has not grasped the difference between such acrobatic stunts and the little book of M. de Quatrefages, it is no doubt because he felt that for any proper Prussian it must be an insult to see his Germanic origin questioned. But he will agree that some quite estimable nations have existed in history who were not the offspring of the old Germanic tribes. Germany has placed herself under the Prussian flag after a vain attempt to establish her political unity under the leadership of Austria. If those who have prepared it had invoked only political motives, science would be silent, but they have made a big noise about the racial question. A pocket anthropology has been created for the use of the man in the street: Slav races, Germanic races, Latin races — it was all so easy to comprehend. With this sort of thing they have excited a racial patriotism in German speaking countries, which is certainly more dynamic than the ordinary patriotism — if perhaps less durable (unless the republican idea gets to join it some day). Yet once anthropology was involved, there was no reason why a French anthropologist should be disqualified as a chauvinist when he undertook to refute the views of German anthropologists.

"M. Mantegazza has found the word *chauvinist* in the German press, where it has been used and abused in a thousand ways. There, a German who loves his country is a patriot; a Frenchman who loves his, a chauvinist. It seems to me, though, that the ephithet was coined in France. While the species *Chauvin* does exist in all countries with a military legend, it was baptized and ridiculed in French vaudeville; this is where M. Mantegazza might have acquainted himself with it. When pronouncing the word "Français," Chauvin always lets a string of sonorous R's roll from his throat. He will not admit that the French soldier has ever been beaten except when the devil had his hand in it. . . . But Chauvin does not read anthropological papers; to him race is a military uniform, and he troubles himself little to find out anything about the physical characteristics and ethnic affinities possessed by the ancestors of the Prussians.

"For twenty years France has supported a disloyal government which has alienated her from the affections of other nations. Her punishment has been hard. The conduct of this government toward Italy has been particularly odious. By pretending to protect the secular power after rendering it untenable, and by suppressing the surge of Italian unity after having made it a necessity, France has forced Italy to accept the Prussian alliance, and by 1866 Italy saw that her northern frontier had been promised her in vain by the French program of 1859.

"M. Mantegazza's apparent appreciation of Germany cannot diminish mine for his person and his work. But it is not fair to accuse present day France of her solidarity with the perfidious government that put her at a finger's breadth from doom. She rejected that government with almost unparalleled unanimity on the fourth of September, 1870. . . . The moment has come for forgetting the sad day of Mentana." (At Mentana, the French, supporting the Pope, defeated Garibaldi in 1866.)

Broca's defense of de Quatrefages, coupled with an attack on racism and chauvinism, covers the national and, above all, the factual aspects of the case. Fourteen years older, de Quatrefages was Broca's opposite in many ways. They were both Protestants, but de Quatrefages was a conservative, religious man, opposed to Broca's concepts of evolution and polygenism. "No contrast could have been greater: de Quatrefages tall, slender, always calm and reserved, serious and full of kindness; Broca, small, portly, dark and never still, always seemed to be going to war"—according to a eulogist of de Quatrefages.[15]

Naturally, Broca, militant pacifist, blamed "the perfidious government." Like every Frenchman, he had to bear, not only the humiliation of the defeat and the misery of the siege, but the awareness that none of the Second Empire's glitter and prosperity had compensated the nation for being cheated out of the fruits of 1848, when democracy in France was almost established.

This double despair created in some others the crazed hope that now was the moment for violent action, now the opportunity for getting rid of both the Prussians and the new French government, which, under Thiers, threatened to pave the way for an Orleanist restoration. There loomed the threat of a wild class war, to be followed by more despotism and more misery. As in 1848, Broca opposed both extremes and displayed his civic initiative in a rather daring feat.

When in 1870 the defense in the east had crumbled, the Empress-Regent, to meet the emergency, had called up the National Guard and thus given arms to a potentially revolutionary element. By the end of October, 1870, three days after the fall of Metz, the first riot and talk of the Commune swept Paris. From March 1st to 3rd of the following year, the German army staged its brief appearance. Three weeks later Thiers moved the French provisional government back from Bordeaux, not to Paris, which seemed unsafe, but to Versailles, from there to conduct the peace negotiations. Thiers had no illusions about the prevailing desperate and explosive mood in the capital and the unpopularity of his peace dealing.

On March 8, 1871, a small detachment of government troops was to seize a few pieces of cannon the National Guard had placed on the Montmartre. The little coup failed, and two generals were shot in the melee. Thiers transferred the regular troops from Paris to Versailles to prevent fraternizing with the aroused lower classes, as had happened in 1848. A leftist government was immediately set up in Paris to fill the vacancies, for by March 20, a mass exodus of all bourgeois elements, including public servants, had followed the army's move to Versailles.

The name "commune," implying a local unit of self-government, goes back to the revolution of 1789. In 1871 Communism was not yet defined as Marxism and not much more known in France than it had been in 1848. But there was no mistaking the Commune of 1871 for anything other than a proletarian uprising with strong overtones of wounded nationalism. Their war was first and foremost directed against the traitors of Versailles. In numerous sorties many hostages were taken and many were shot on both sides, but by all accounts the inhumanities perpetrated weighed heavier on the "right" side of the scales.

By March 26, with the Commune established in Paris, "civil services worked normally. . . . Six thousand sick, abandoned in the hospitals without attendants, were immediately cared for. . . ." one modern historian says.[16] This means that most doctors had left Paris, while the nursing personnel remained.

With the advent of the Third Republic, back in September, 1870, Broca, Verneuil, and two other surgeons had been appointed to a Council running the Assistance Publique. Its Bonapartist director was made to resign, and the organization was changed to what it had

244

been before 1848. (The measure was again reversed in the following June.) Come March, 1871, the new administrator and several members of the board made off to join the government in Versailles. On April 7, another administrator, the third within these few months, was named by the Commune. This "Citizen" Treilhard duly recorded the assets of the Assistance Publique in the ledger: a pittance of 4,718 francs and 70 centimes.[17] Where had the money gone?

"It is generally unknown," says Pozzi in his obituary,[18] "what an immense service Broca rendered the administration of the Assistance Publique during the Commune. The director of this great institution precipitously left for Versailles without informing Broca, then Vice President of its Council.... Only the cashier was left behind in the building. The Avenue Victoria, together with the adjacent Place de l'Hôtel de Ville, was occupied by the Federates [insurgents]. Broca was without news from Versailles, where functionaries who had remained in Paris were apparently frowned upon. He also got wind that the Federates had designs on the strong box of the hospitals, and he decided to save it, notwithstanding the risk. He stuffed all the valuables into some travelling bags of his and deposited them at the Charité with the concurrence of the administrator of that hospital. Wisely, he left three or four thousand francs in the safe and enjoined the cashier to remain at his post so as not to arouse suspicion. None too soon, for on the next day some armed insurgents turned up in the building, Avenue Victoria ... and found only the insignificant amount instead of the expected fortune.... A supply cart with potatoes, led by a trustworthy man, ostensibly went to the Hospice d'Ivry [outside the guarded fortifications of the city]. Hidden under the potatoes was the precious luggage. The cart passed the outposts safely, took the road to Versailles, arrived there next day.... Broca's travelling bags contained *seventy-five million francs* in cash and bonds.

"After the government's victory and return to Paris, when everyone was holding out his hand to be rewarded for services great and small, Broca kept deliberately silent about his bold action. He seemed to have forgotten. So had the government, which dissolved the Council of the Assistance Publique without a word of thanks to its Vice President. No one should get any mistaken ideas.... Not that he affected disdain for an honor conferred by the Power; he simply did not care...."

No one doubts Pozzi's detailed version of Broca's instigation and handling of the transfer and the reason for his official silence later. He may have rejected the idea of receiving an award from hands even bloodier than those from which he had saved the public funds.

In this second siege of Paris, during the May days of 1871, the cannon of the advancing Versailles troops destroyed much of what the Prussians had hardly touched, and what the Commune had failed to burn down in a final fit of rage. This joint effort of destruction by fratricidal Frenchmen affected an incredibly large part of Paris, historical and new. The regular troops lost about one thousand men. The number of Communards killed (before or after being jailed) has been estimated up to thirty times that figure. The survivors, from the 120,000 either thrown into prisons or deported to penal colonies, were not pardoned until nine years later.[16]

Within weeks after the holocaust, the revived but gutted City of Lights was swarming with sightseers from across the Channel, organized by Cook's Tours, for new thrills among the ruins. Guides were needed: the recent demolitions, added to those going on peacefully for several decades, had made Paris almost unrecognizable.

Among the many streets destroyed by fire was Rue de Lille, a block away from Broca's apartment. His rooms, full of books, manuscripts and specimens collected for half a lifetime, escaped damage. Their owner had stayed in rioting Paris, emptied of nearly all the "better people," to look after his patients, to run the precarious affairs of the Assistance Publique as he saw fit, and to start, with his assistant Chudzinski, a large collection of brain casts.[18]

═XIV═

Around the Great Limbic Lobe of the Mammals

"Otters can be very sentimental. . . ."
Charles Kingsley, The Water Babies

*A*n underpinning, vast in proportion to the rest of the brain, supports the cerebral hemisphere of non-primate mammals. Modified by evolution, the structure plays an important part in man; this is the great limbic lobe of Broca. The subject marks Broca's decided return to studying the brain and its physiology. In his fifties, he was embarking on a venture that gave the lie to a remark he once made, undated but timeless: "Getting on in years makes us unfit for science; the work has to be done while we are young."[1] Yet no other work of his is more strongly linked to recent research. Pozzi, writing an introduction to a reprinting in 1888, rightly guessed that it was "perhaps Broca's greatest claim to admiration by posterity."[2]

Evolution is often discontinuous, progress often "polygenic." Between 1879, when Broca published his work on the great limbic lobe and the olfactory centers,[3] and 1950,[4] the line was broken. Only in the immediately following generation did men, such as Ramon y Cajal, speak of those "memorable works of Broca."[5] Soury, the most comprehensive historian of the nervous system, did not refer to a tomb when, at the turn of the century, he pointed to these works as "an imperishable monument erected to the science of comparative anatomy and functional localization of the brain. . . . This is the manner in which research ought to be done by anyone who still realizes that a fact cannot be considered known unless it is meaningful."[6]

Dormancy is a natural condition for germinal ideas. Posterity is quite commonly incapable of recognizing as its very own the dust it sees clinging to objects of the past. To make the source meaningful, we must start in midstream, in 1937, when the revival occurred, not of Broca's name, but of his concept. In that year J. W. Papez published *A proposed mechanism of emotion,* a paper which created quite a stir.[7] It was a significant step along the "wild goose chase"[8] opened by Gall, another attempt at "localizing" in the brain a psychological function: emotion.

"The ensemble of hypothalamus, gyrus cinguli, hippocampus, and their interconnections," Papez proposed as "representing theoretically the anatomical basis of the emotions. . . . It may elaborate the functions of central emotion as well as participate in emotional expression."[7]

This "ensemble," or functional whole, was Papez' original way of combining these parts; individually most of them were very old anatomical knowledge. To Broca only *hypothalamus* probably was an unknown term for the floor of the third ventricle. Possibly introduced by Edinger in the 1890's,[9] the term quietly made its way into the *Basle Anatomical Nomenclature* of 1895,[10] slipped into Gray's *Anatomy* in 1908, but was taken for granted by Karplus and Kreidel when they began their startling publications on the hypothalamus in 1900.[11] An obvious term, really, for around 1820 Burdach had referred to the structures it subsumes as lying "beneath the thalamus."[12] The hypothalamus eventually came to be looked upon as a cerebral hub and spur for practically every facet of mammalian metabolism and behavior. In bulk it is only a mere cubic centimeter or so. Papez showed how various neighboring structures might share in handling some of its load, forming a "circuit" rather than a "center."

The part of this circuit known as *uncus* had slowly risen into prominence after Hughlings Jackson in 1880 had pointed out the peculiar features of "uncinate fits,"[13] a certain type of nervous attacks first described by Herpin, today usually called "psychomotor" or "temporal lobe" seizures. What, according to Jackson, do the patients experience? "Crude sensations, smell, taste, and the epigastric sensation . . . so to speak with brutal disregard of psychological propriety, crude developments of 'digestive sensations.'"

Unfortunately, microscope, oscilloscope, and experimental excisions have failed to confirm what Jackson and many after him saw so convincingly and intimately connected: the hallucination of odor and the uncinate or hippocampal gyrus from which the phenomenon had taken its name. Papez, like Ramon y Cajal some four decades earlier, found no evidence for the function of smell in this circular system. Olfactory functions are denied to any part posterior to uncus and amygdala, olfactory tubercle, and piriform area[14] (it is pear-shaped in lower animals). An old habit, however, clings to the term *rhinencephalon* ("smell brain," Turner).[15] In 1949, McLean began to call this area the "visceral brain, . . . controlling the activity of the bowels, blood vessels, and such basic drives as obtaining and assimilating food, fleeing from or orally disposing of an enemy, reproducing, and so forth." It might deal with "primitive infantile material . . . oral or oral-anal . . . inclusively visceral. Considered in the light of Freud, the visceral brain has many attributes of the unconscious id. . . . Although it is not unconscious . . . (it) eludes the grasp of the intellect because its animalistic and primitive structure makes it impossible to communicate in verbal terms."

Broca's concepts regarding this region, which he, too, for the first time, had seen as a functional whole, were meanwhile kept trailing, reduced, disfigured, and rather meaningless through the textbooks of anatomy. Neither Papez' paper nor the first one by McLean contained any reference, nor had Hughlings Jackson referred to the limbic lobe when he wrote on uncinate fits. Yakovlev, without referring to Papez, used the term "limbic lobe of Broca" in 1948, but he stripped the classical concept of some of its essentials.[17] The authors of two extensive and copiously documented French surveys of this region[18, 19] in 1952 made no mention of their great compatriot.

Von Bonin, in his *Essay on the Cerebral Cortex* of 1950, may have been the first to point out how "strangely reminiscent of Broca's 'grand lobe limbique'" Papez' "large reverberating circuit" was.[3] Two years later McLean introduced Broca's non-commital term "limbic" to take the place of "visceral" in his system;[20] since 1962 he has headed a "Section on Limbic Integration and Behavior" in the United States National Institutes of Health. As though it had never been eclipsed, "limbic" is now in current use.

Needless to say, yet condescendingly stressed in 1961[21] by Gastaut and Lammers, Broca was working before the era of cytoarchitectonics. The poorly layered character of this cortical portion only confirms Broca's basic contention that this indeed is an old and primitive structure. Gastaut and Lammers also did not believe that, "on an exclusively morphological basis, the concept of a limbic lobe in Broca's sense can be maintained," because "he considered this large limbus to be the cortical center of olfaction," whereas in reality "a large part is non-olfactive." More careful readers of Broca's memoirs, however, cannot fail to see that he had serious doubts about the great limbic ·lobe being exclusively olfactory in function.

While Broca did set out to connect the great limbic lobe with the sense of smell, he felt he ought to go a hesitant step further: "The lobe of the hippocampus and the lobe of the corpus callosum are very unlike each other, in both their structure and their connections. . . . Each must have a special function hitherto unknown. . . . It does by no means follow that these two lobes (convolutions) are *exclusively* concerned with olfaction. . . ."[22] The italics are his; he also said he did not wish to "insist on this somewhat hazardous conjecture, . . . an hypothesis, so devoid of proof." But nothing is dearer to a scientist's heart than a hypothesis.

Odors coming in as sensations via the olfactory tract are split as they travel over two "striae"—"roots," in French, is a better term. (See illustration on p. 259, a-b and f.) The (stronger) lateral root goes to the hippocampal gyrus below, the medial root to the callosal (or cingulate) gyrus above. Broca speculated that "the former gyrus may have the function of distinguishing the odors from one another, while the callosal lobe may appreciate them from the animal's point of view with respect to pleasure and pain. . . ."[22] (This, it turns out, is one of the choice areas that rats, given an implanted electrode and a lever to work it, will stimulate in themselves for their own enjoyment.[24])

For this dual aspect of all sensation—discrimination versus emotion—Broca saw an analogy in the double innervation of the sense of taste (by the fifth and ninth cranial nerves respectively), which was present in other sensory modes, for instance touch: "Touching an object that is too hot, we have a burning sensation; when the object cools down and contact with it is no longer painful, it will reveal its qualities of form, volume, consistency, etc. . . ."[23] (An interesting point, in view of current controversies about pain.)

How far did Broca advance toward the concept of a visceral and emotional brain? "In the life of osmatic animals, the sense of smell is not only the source of highly practical information, but it also is the source of agreeable sensations, to the point of voluptuousness—or disagreeable ones, to the point of suffering. Even in ourselves these sensations remain quite vivid. Far more than the sense of taste, the sense of smell makes us appreciate the qualities of our food, from the kind that may plunge the gourmet into profound pleasure to that which may provoke disgust, nausea, and even vomiting."[22]

It is a strong hint that we must suspect this area to represent a quality other than crude olfaction—as well as what that quality might be. Broca's "unknown special function" has turned out to be a welter of them, for respiration, blood pressure, peristalsis, sexual drive, and memories, every known vegetative function, may be affected by stimulating the limbic lobe. Broca deduced this non-olfactory property from the paradox of a well-developed anterior portion of the cingulate gyrus in the dolphin, an animal totally devoid of the sense of smell. (See illustration on p. 261.)

There was a natural fascination about the subject: "We may well be astonished at the quite extraordinary complexity and the exceptional character of this olfactory apparatus in man. We may ask by what fancy of nature the least useful of our senses has turned out to be precisely the one that disposes of the most numerous special and varied anatomical resources; why the nervous filaments issuing from its sensory membrane remain distinct instead of uniting in a single trunk as do those of vision and hearing and, instead of penetrating the skull by a single foramen, enter it through a great number of holes, a very fragile sieve; why the strength of the cranial wall should thus be sacrificed without compensation.

"I do not invent these questions; they have embarrassed the anatomists for a long time. To escape the issue they have converted the olfactory bulb into a ganglion comparable to those of ordinary sensory nerves, and they have made of the olfactory tract a simple intracranial nerve. In vain, for they had to admit that this so-called nerve — which unlike the others does not branch out, is not round, has no neurilemma, and in the fetus is hollow — that it is an organ without analogy, and that this so-called 'ganglion,' which does not communicate with any others, neither receives nor gives off any anastomotic branches, is lined with pia-arachnoid, and has absolutely nothing in common with nerve ganglia.

"This is not all. We have noted those strange, complex, inexplicable arrangements, all for the benefit of a sense organ which is only an accessory with us. . . . The olfactory system alone proceeds to the cortex directly. It alone has the privilege of ending by three roots, to establish its connections with three distinct centers, all three situated in front of the peduncles. Alone, finally, it has the privilege of a direct insertion in the noble frontal lobe."[25] Clearly, Broca saw in the great limbic lobe more than an olfactory organ, "rhinencephalon," or "smell brain."

This venture into comparative anatomy was neither sudden nor surprising, but part of a plan to give a comprehensive account of nomenclature, form, and functions of the brain. Anatomy was to have physiological as well as evolutionary meaning. Broca's earlier work on disordered speech in relation to a specific convolution was based on Leuret and Gratiolet, the finders of analogous parts in widely different brains, as well as on Gall and Bouillaud, the "localizers." The localization of function in the cerebral convolutions, discredited by the phrenologists, was made respectable by Broca, the anatomist, in 1861. Nine years later, the principle was fully vindicated by physiological experiment: Hitzig and Fritsch in Berlin had set a dog's limbs in motion by stimulating the animal's precentral cortex with electrodes.[26] But the great following gathered around the new German prophets and around Ferrier in England[27] was not to do away with gross anatomy and the classical approach. That field was far from exhausted. Textbooks of the period mirror the ignorance about the cerebral convexity and its nomenclature. And nobody had seriously tried to see any particular meaning in the inferior and medial surface of the cerebral hemispheres. But while breaking new ground, Broca is also on the defensive against all-out experimentation or "vivisection," the term which animal protection societies managed to make abhorrent.

"Experimental method has served physiology so well in our century that all other methods have been virtually eclipsed by it..." Broca conceded. "Supposing you had been successful in producing a limited mutilation of one of these parts without altering the function of others; it still would be impossible to put any question to the animal so as to determine the functional disturbances that you have produced. At the same time the differences in cerebral type and response do not allow us to apply to man the results of experiments made on other animals, even apes."[28]

The truth of this passage is evident, yet Broca does sound a little like a Velpeau depreciating the microscope. Few if any men in science escape this natural trend of clinging to the methods of their youth; most of them will reserve an old man's welcome, cool or worse, for novelty. Equally natural is the corollary of the young discoverer's attitude: "A new truth in conflict with the prejudices of our teachers has no means of overcoming their hostility. Neither reasoning nor facts prevail, only their death will make it succeed. Innovators must be resigned to wait for the arrival of this ally, as the Russians were waiting for the arrival of General Winter."[29] The words are Broca's, date uncertain, but not the approximate time of life when he must have felt them most deeply.

Broca never tired of extolling the clinico-pathological method for localization. In 1879 and 1880 he demonstrated the brains of, respectively, one upper and one lower limb congenital amputee. He showed the corresponding lesions, which we might call porencephalic cysts. They were situated in the precentral region. (No such clinico-pathological association in phocomelia has been recorded in the modern literature, including autopsy reports on the "thalidomide babies." But Gowers has reported such a case: "The brain in congenital absence of one hand." *Brain* 1:388-390, 1878.) In the discussion he said: "The experiments made by Ferrier on monkeys do have real significance. However, the electrical excitation may easily spread beyond the points stimulated, and the animals whose skulls have been opened may be in such a condition as to blur the result a good deal. On the whole, morbid anatomy is always the most solid basis for the study of cerebral localization in man. You observe a disordered function in the living, and you look for the cause post mortem. No doubt this is slow, but it has revealed to us the seat of language; it is the method to which we owe almost all that has since been discovered about the other cortical centers."[30]

An overstatement perhaps, in favor of pathology, but as he continued with his defense of comparative anatomy he seemed to express the uneasiness that students of the brain must have felt before the concepts of the neuron and the synapse became established: "Eighteen years have elapsed [i.e., since aphemia] and despite the greatest perseverance by a great number of observers . . . the questions concerning other cerebral localization have not found their solutions. . . .

"If we have begun to know the morphology of the convolutions rather well, if we have to a small extent been able to follow certain nerve roots in the depth of the brain centers beyond their apparent origins, we must confess that in present-day preparations and dissections we cannot directly demonstrate most of the fiber connections, sensory or motor, as they exist between various parts of the brain, between the transmitting agents [relay stations] and the cortical points where they end. It is the insufficiency of contemporary anatomy that frustrates the physiologists' efforts.

"At first I was impressed by the excessive differences between the cerebral morphology of various groups of mammals. But . . . there remain a certain number of fundamental characteristics which are variable in degree only, not in essence. Each one of the constituent parts of the hemisphere may grow larger or smaller to such an extent that the corresponding region, or even the whole hemisphere, may show a considerable change in shape. Very frequently, therefore, we might miss the analogies if we limit ourselves to comparing the brains taken from only two different groups of animals. On reviewing the whole series, however, we may observe transitions which allow us to determine with confidence analogous parts and their invariable connections. Where the most minute dissections have failed, comparative anatomy of the brain . . . and its interpretation may be of great help in the search for localization.

"Of all the parts of the cerebral hemisphere, the most variable are no doubt those serving olfactory function. The variations are so great as to justify the division of all mammals into two groups . . . which I have distinguished by the terms *osmatic* and *anosmatic*. In the former, this system is very well developed in all its parts; in the latter, it is either considerably diminished or totally abolished."[31]

The osmatic brains which Broca described and pictured were those of marmot, beaver, rabbit, otter, sloth, fox, tapir, horse, deer, pig, boar, and rattler; among the anosmatic were the dolphin, seal, monkey, ape, and man.

"If we consider that . . . the base of the hemisphere remains stationary and imperfectible while the convexity develops in the sense of increasing perfection, if we see how the former is to lose in importance while the latter is to progress, we come to realize that the former is the seat of the lower faculties prevailing in the brute animal (*la brute*) while the latter is the seat of the higher faculties prevailing in the intelligent animal. The mantle of the hemisphere (Burdach) is thus composed of one part that is brute (*brutale*) — represented by the *great limbic lobe* — and another that is intelligent — represented by the rest . . . . The latter may be called the 'convoluted mass' (*masse circonvolutionnaire*) in gyrencephalic species. But this is not applicable to those brains which are devoid of any real convolutions [i.e., the lissencephalic]; here it may be called the 'extralimbic mass'. . . "[32]

If Broca did not quite think in terms of a "visceral brain" or an "unconscious Id," he associated anatomically a primitive sensory organ, that of olfaction, with the lower instincts and set it against the higher functions of the intellect.

Gall had blithely structured the hierarchy of the mind by having excellence increase in the brain from back to front, starting with the cerebellum as the lowliest organ; he made no reference to any sensory function, not to speak of his total lack of proof. Broca's better supported, if similar, scheme was from the bottom up. In it the animal and the spiritual part of man's nature — Faust's "two souls," Schopenhauer's *Will and Idea* — find an anatomic and evolutional basis. (So, in a way, they did in Meynert's "primary" and "secondary" self,[33] an inspiration, no doubt, to his most famous pupil, but Freud went one better by splitting off the super-ego). The dichotomy of man, especially as related by Broca to a hierarchy of man's senses, has not found favor everywhere, and Soury, Broca's admirer in all other respects, was quite outspoken in his criticism: "If such misconceptions surprise us today," he wrote, "we must not forget that nearly all of us have shared them. . . . Why should olfactory impressions be of a less precious essence than those of sight and hearing?... There can be no antagonism between sensation and intelligence. . . . But Gall and his followers, as well as Magendie and the biologists, felt obliged to reject the doctrines of the sensationalists. To them the senses and intelligence, far from engendering one another, were so heterogeneous that even though Spurzheim had increased by six the number of Gall's organs of the soul, he forgot yet the fundamental sense of all mental activity: the sense of touch."[34]

The "sensationalists" to whom Soury alludes are, of course, the radical eighteenth-century philosophers: beginning with Hobbes, Locke, and LaMettrie, followed by Condillac and the "idéologues" (Testutt de Tracy and Cabanis); they rejected primary ideas and had a great influence on early nineteenth-century physiology.[35]

Although on the whole a late product of the school of "ideology," Broca was not entirely free from the conventional separation of reason and sensation and the hierarchical relationship between them. Value judgments had never died out in the biological sciences; "survival value" is one such concept. But Broca frequently stressed that for him anatomical observation was more important and binding than any kind of ideology. "He had not read August Comte or Herbert Spencer," Dally of the Société d'Anthropologie remarked in his eulogy, "for they had no laboratories and had never been *internes de hôpitaux*."[36] While this may be a misleading statement in view of his limitless readings, Broca probably did consider pure philosophy a waste of time, especially in the over-crowded years of his maturity.

Minutely describing the reciprocal changes in morphology — apparent rather than fundamental — Broca saw the functional coherence of the parts and so discovered this entity. The transformation of behavior clinging to the transition of form suggested to him the unity of this region and its uniformity in the evolution of mammals. In his method he brought a new attention to detail and kept a steady eye on the guiding concepts; comparative anatomy of the brain had never been done like this before. It was repeated on a much greater scale,[37] but it has never been surpassed. Comparative anatomy was indeed far from dead. Elliot Smith's later work on the region,[38] mostly in marsupials, is in some ways critical of Broca's, but in 1910 he came to pay this tribute: "It will be observed that we are returning once more to a conception such as the genius of Broca embodied in the idea of a limbic lobe. . . ."[39]

255

While he coined this term and endowed it with special meaning, Broca did not claim priority in seeing a ring of convolutions: "This region was called the 'great aperture of the hemisphere' by [Achille Louis] Foville and Gratiolet. For above, behind, and below the thalamus and the cerebral peduncle, one can see the large opening into the lateral ventricle. Another distinct opening is the foramen of Monro. Yet these two openings are only a minimal portion of the region under scrutiny. It actually takes in the cut surface of the *corpus callosum*, the septum lucidum, the anterior portion of the fornix, the commissures, the cerebral peduncles, the floor and lateral wall of the third ventricle, the border of the dentate gyrus on the inferior edge of the ventricular *cleft of Bichat* [the choroidal fissure],[40] and finally this cleft itself as it leads into the lateral ventricle. It is here that all the convergent fibers pass through as they enter and leave the hemisphere. While that portion of the internal surface which is left uncovered by the cerebral mantle does not represent an actual opening, it is, in a way, the entrance and exit of the hemisphere, a feature which in Latin terminology, much used abroad, may be rendered by the word 'limen.' As it surrounds the threshold of the hemisphere the mantle forms a border which resembles the circular edge of a purse. Hence, I am calling this border the limbus of the hemisphere, and the convolution that forms it the 'limbic convolution.'

"This large convolution consists of two arcs. . . . The distinction usually made between these two arcs is motivated, up to a point, by their location in two different regions (i.e., the fronto-parietal and the temporal) but also the line of demarcation between them which is a prolongation of the calcarine fissure (the little hippocampus of Gratiolet). [*Le petit hippocampe* is the *hippocampus minor* of Vicq d'Azyr; *l'ergot*, the spur, or *calcar avis* of Morand.[41] Its positive aspect forms a ridge inside the ventricle.]

"This dividing line, however, is only a superficial one, not more than a small dent in the thickness of the limbic convolution; in most cases it does not even occupy its whole width or reach its concave border. In any case, between the callosal and hippocampal gyri the continuity is never broken.

"This was perfectly recognized by Gerdy and by Foville. . . ."[42]

Broca pays his critical respects to his forerunners (and teachers), Gerdy, Foville, and Gratiolet, but does not mention Rolando. Ten years before Gerdy and Foville, Rolando described and depicted the continuity of fibers starting with the medial olfactory root and, going through his *processo cristato*, running a full hemicycle to end in the uncus.[43] Also, Theodor Meynert in Vienna was well aware in 1872

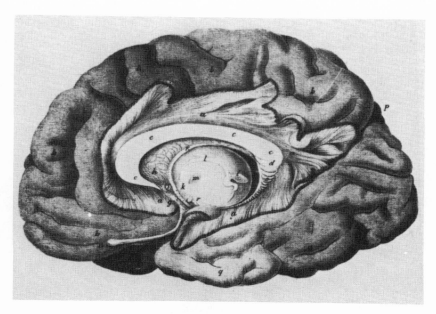

Rolando's illustration of the human brain, right hemisphere, medial surface. Left to right: b-b, superior frontal gyrus—paracentral lobule—praecuneus; a-a, (top) gyrus singuli or callosal gyrus; c-c, corpus callosum; a-a bottom) hippocampus and uncus. This whole ring a-a-a-a was called *processo cristato* by Rolando.

c, cuneus.

Luigi Rolando: "Della struttura degli Emisferi Cerebrali," *Mem. R. Accad. Sci. Torino,* Vol. XXXV, 1830, pp. 103-146.)

that the gyrus fornicatus, under which he understood callosal and hippocampal gyri, constituted the "smell brain."[56]

Limbic, Broca said, "implies no theory, describes no definite shape and is thus applicable to all mammals." The word "lobe" replaced Gerdy's and Foville's "convolution." But while convolution was a term "that once could be used to denote any portion of the folds of the hemisphere," a convolution, or gyrus, could, since Gratiolet, and strictly speaking, not be made to extend beyond the confines of a lobe. Even the callosal gyrus was a "lobe" under this definition as it formed "a very special area which cannot be attached to any of the lobes accepted so far."

Why call the limbic lobe "great"? The illustration of a horse's brain on p. 258, showing enormous olfactory bulges (11, 13) at the base, is an eye-opener. (From Chauveau and Arloing's book on the *Comparative Anatomy of Domestic Animals,* 1871, Broca noted it was "obviously not made up to state my case.") "Poorly developed in pri-

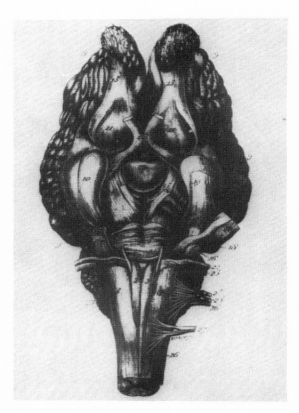

Chauveau and Arloing's illustration of the inferior surface of horse's brain. The spikes on the olfactory bulbs are the cut ends of the olfactory filaments connecting the bulb, through the cribiform plate at the base of the skull, to the mucosal lining of the nose. 11, pyriform lobe, covering quadrilateral, later perforated space 10 and 19, right and left hippocampal gyri. (M.A.P.B. p. 297.)

mates, this system is in other mammals . . . more distinct from the rest of the hemisphere than any of the divisions commonly called *lobes* — it represents a primary division more basic than any lobe; in addition, it actually includes several lobes, hence the word *lobe* does not sufficiently characterize it: therefore I call it the great limbic lobe.[44] . . . In shape it may be compared to a tennis racket."[45]

Broca briefly traced the sub-mammalian development of this system.[46] In amphibians, reptiles, and birds such as fowls and sparrows, the olfactory centers are joined to the rest of the brain as they are in mammals. In birds of prey, however, in ducks, and in most fishes, the system is much larger than the rest of the brain, entirely separate from it, and in direct communication with the motor tracts of the spinal cord. "It draws on itself for all its functions; what notions it may

A page from Broca's manuscript with his drawing of the infero-medial surface of an otter's right cerebral hemisphere: O, olfactory lobe (bulb); a - b, lateral root (stria) of olfactory lobe (tract); f, medial root; F, frontal, P1, parietal lobe; C, origin, C'-C", rest of callosal (cingulate) lobe (gyrus); H-H', hippocampal lobe (gyrus); 1-2-3, corpus callosum; 4, thalamus; 5, cerebral peduncle separated from the great limbic lobe by Bichat's cleft (choroidal fissure); 6, optic tract. (Sketch to M.A.P.B., p. 274.)

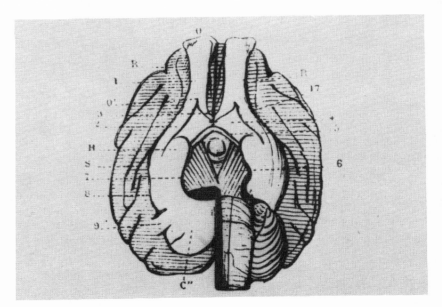

Broca's drawing of the undersurface of the otter's brain. On the right (left of picture) cerebellum and pons have been dissected away.
As in the previous figure, O is the olfactory lobe, H the hippocampal, C″ the posterior end of the callosal "lobe." 1, olfactory tract, 2 and 3, its lateral and medial roots, 4, anterior, perforated space, 5, optic tract, 6, cerebral peduncle. (M.A.P.B., p. 276.)

transmit to the animal are immediately transformed into volition, and it becomes effective without the participation of any other cerebral organ." It is, in other words, an intimate link between smelling and moving, a feature retaining some importance in the osmatic mammalian brain.

As the prototype Broca used the brain of the otter,[47] for it occupies an intermediate position between the osmatic and anosmatic type of great limbic lobe. The aquatic mammals, e.g., the dolphin family, occupy the extreme end of the series. In them the olfactory apparatus is non-existent: "everything has disappeared, not only the olfactory lobe, but even the olfactory nerve fibers, to the point where the *lamina cribrosa* of the ethmoid bone is without perforations; here the great limbic lobe consists only of two parts: the hippocampal and the callosal lobe. . . . Their hippocampal lobe is reduced to a minimum . . . and even smaller than in the primates . . . an olfactory desert. . . ." (see illustration on p. 261).

So much for the lower arc of the ring. As to the upper arc, "I must mention a finding that is rather hard to reconcile with my assumption

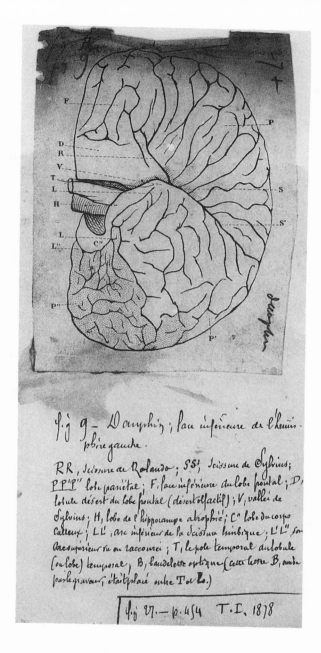

A page from Broca's manuscript with his drawing of the brain of a dolphin, inferior surface of left hemisphere. Note the anterior placement of the Rolandic fissure (R), hence the still relatively small frontal lobe (F) and the large parietal lobe (P). H, atrophic hippocampal lobe; C″, posterior end of callosal lobe; L - L′ - L″, the limbic fissure; D, "olfactory desert"; I, temporal lobe. (M.A.P.B., p. 334, fig. 32D.)

that there must be a close correlation, in other animals, between olfaction and the anterior portion of the callosal lobe. The callosal lobe is wide in osmatic mammals but very narrow in the primates, and so is their medial olfactory root. . . . In the cetaceans . . . it is actually non-existent, except for its anterior portion which . . . indeed is as well developed in them as it is in the osmatic group, and full of grooves—a sign of pronouned functional activity. . . . Has some other function developed here? . . . "[48]

Among those having a primate brain Broca counts "the four hominid families": the anthropoid apes, the pitheci, and the cebine monkeys. Unlike Linnaeus but like Alphonse Milne-Edwards, he excludes the lemurs.[49]

Some lower primates such as the marmoset have very primitive-looking brain mantles. They are without folds, or lissencephalic, similar to many if not all nonprimate mammals. Yet they are undoubtedly primates. "The folding of the mantle is not a primary event. . . . It is *directed* by the connections . . . but it is *determined* by the geometric relation between surface and volume. . . . What distinguishes them from the brains of the nonprimate cat, horse, or elephant, with their heavily folded extra-limbic masses? Certainly not the possession of convolutions. . . . The primary distinction . . . lies in the relationship of the great limbic lobe to the rest of the cerebral cortex. The radical distinction . . . between lissencephalic primates and lissencephalic nonprimates is this: In all nonprimates the olfactory lobe is very well developed; also, the hippocampal lobe, relatively enormous, is separated from the extra-limbic mass by a limbic fissure invariably deep and wide. . . . Lissencephalic primates, like all other primates . . . have no true olfactory lobe but only a tiny rudimentary ganglion. Gone also is the distinct hippocampal lobe, or rather it is now fused with the extra-limbic mass; the corresponding portion of the limbic fissure has completely disappeared."[50]

What are the vestiges of the olfactory lobe in the most intelligent animals? The olfactory nerve is one; there are others to fill—or to emphasize—the void. "In the anosmatic mammals the great limbic lobe appears to be interrupted by the anterior perforated substance of Vicq-d'Azyr—here not even covered by gray matter—but its continuity is in fact preserved by the olfactory roots. Yet there is still another link: *la bandelette diagonale.* "[51] In anosmatic mammals, including man, all that survives of the thickly cellular quadrilateral space of the osmatic group is this diagonal band. The tiny structure is the only remaining link between the callosal and the hippocampal gyrus.

The diagonal band of Broca has survived as such in the literature. Less fit for survival was Broca's *carrefour de l'hémisphère*, situated within

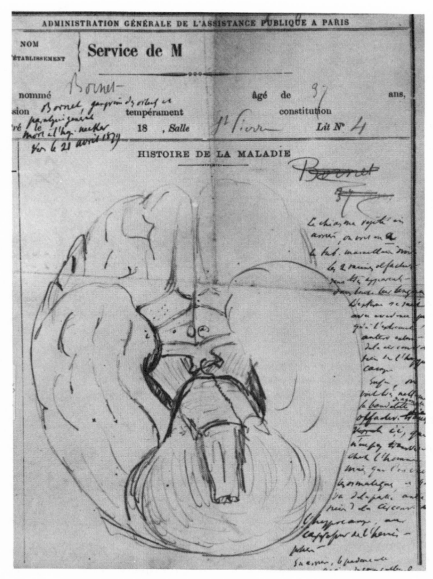

Broca's hand-drawn sketch on a hospital note sheet: *i - i,* diagonal band. His note reads: "Bornet, gangrene of toes and general paresis. Died at Hôp. Necker about 21 April 1879 [aged 37]. With the chiasm drawn back, one sees the right mamillary body at *a*. The two olfactory roots stand out well over their whole length. The lateral one can evidently be followed up to the antero-lateral extremity of the hippocampal gyrus. Finally, one can see the olfactory *diagonal band* quite clearly — *i, i.* It is not horizontal in man as it is in osmatic animals [i.e., not a true *diagonal* across the diamond-shaped *quadrilateral space*]. It runs from the anterior end of the hippocampal gyrus to the *carrefour de l'hémisphère.* . . . (Courtesy Prof. Vallois, Musée de Paléontologie Humaine, Paris.)

the same few square millimeters. A *carrefour*? "Here, i.e., at the origin of the callosal gyrus (c), there is a small flat area which is in communication with the medial surface of the frontal lobe in front, the callosal lobe above, the medial portion of the quadrilateral space below. . . . It is here, finally, where, below and in front, the medial olfactory root (i) comes to an end, as well as, below and behind, the diagonal band, (d) which—as we have seen—extends from the hippocampal lobule to the origin of the callosal gyrus [see illustration on p. 265].

"These multiple communications justify the name, *carrefour of the hemisphere*, which I have given to this tiny area."[52]

Unfortunately, modern scholarship killed Broca's idea of a traffic center in the brain and perverted his novel concept of converging nervous pathways. Instead of preserving "Broca's junction," they lamely dubbed it the "parolfactory area." The great importance he attached to this junction between limbic and extralimbic portions of the brain has been forgotten, and yet it has been endorsed by neurosurgical experience. A disproportionately large clinical deficit results from a small lesion in "Broca's parolfactory area," due to its numerous connections[53] (see illustration on p. 265).

What exactly was the anatomical significance of the great limbic lobe in man? Working on a schematic description of the human brain shortly before his death, Broca almost apologized for applying to the human situation a term taken from comparative anatomy. But the analogies were sufficiently important, he felt, and certain parts of the human brain had so far not been named. "Limbic," moreover, was shorter and more to the point than previous terms had been.[54]

He was convinced that a direct connection existed, at least in osmatic mammals, between the olfactory bulb (or lobe) and the major motor pathway of the cerebral peduncles. He called it the "middle or gray root" and insisted that this was a motor pathway. His evidence was mainly histological.

For the first time since the 1850's, he returned to the tool that had almost been a weapon in the days of campaigning with Lebert, Follin, and Verneuil for the miscroscopic diagnosis of cancer. The sections made by a Doctor Planteau and stained with picro-carmine showed Broca what we call the mitral cells of the sensory organ of olfaction: larger multipolar cells, he said, in the third zone of the olfactory lobe of the dog, with nuclei measuring 10 to 15 microns and bodies up to 50 microns in diameter—indeed, up to 90 microns considering their processes—and he followed these up to a distance of 250 microns. From their resemblance to the motor anterior horn cells of the spinal

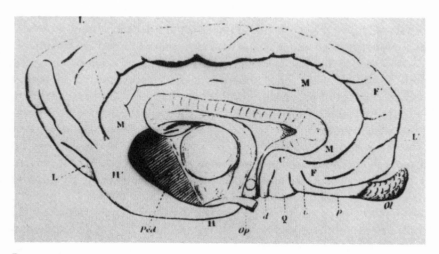

Broca's drawing of the medial surface of the brain of a donkey, left hemisphere, to show the *carrefour* (junction) of the hemisphere, at C, where we see converging: *d*, diagonal band; *Q*, quadrilateral space; *i*, medial olfactory root; and *F*, frontal lobe; M, callosal lobe.

cord and to the cells in the motor cortex of the dog, he inferred them to be motor. He did not find them in the anosmatic olfactory bulb; the large oval cells there he believed to be their rudimentary equivalent—without function, because he could not see any processes.[55]

The histological interpretation was erroneous, but the concept as such is not obsolete. "The anterior perforated substance . . ." Papez said in 1957, "gives rise to . . . a most primitive motor path . . . (going) to the interpeduncular nucleus . . . (and) to the reticular formation. . . . Some primitive and generalized reactions were mediated in premordial vertebrates by this rudimentary system extending from the olfactory brain to the reticular formation."[56] Adey, in the same symposium, reported his new finding of a "direct connection between the entorrhinal (hippocampal) area and the tegmental areas of the midbrain. . . ."[57]

Man, Broca said in closing his second memoir, has three olfactory centers: (1) the anterior, at the orbital surface of the frontal lobe, is supplied by the superior root; (2) the superior, or carrefour of the hemisphere, at the "origin of the callosal gyrus," by the medial root; (3) the posterior, in the hippocampal gyrus, by the lateral root. In the osmatic animals, the olfactory lobe represents a fourth center and has a fourth middle or gray root.[58] The latter allows automatic, immediate transference from sensation to action, a reflex. His concluding exam-

265

ple shows how close he came in regarding the limbic system as we do: as a sensori-motor system acting upon the animal's inner environment.

"Watch a dog out hunting.[59] First, sniffing at random along his path, he inhales a welter of animal, vegetable, and mineral odors that make a number of impressions on his olfactory lobe. At once these are passed on to the sensory center. Here they are transformed to sensations which go on to the frontal lobe by fronto-limbic connections.

"Our dog suddenly stops. One of the scents he has picked up reveals the presence or passage of some animal. Friend, foe, or prey? If a prey, is it worth pursuing and the trail fresh enough to promise success? The dog hesitates, decides it is not a matter for pursuit, saunters on, stops again. This time the matter is more serious. . . . He sniffs attentively, studies his sensation, and finds he is not mistaken: a hare. The hunt is on.

"So far the olfactory apparatus has functioned like any other sensory system. Instead of scenting a hare, the dog might have seen or heard one. . . . But in the hot pursuit of his prey, he must lose no time. For the hare is equipped with his own olfactory sentinel, to scent the enemy, to get a start on him. Success is a matter of speed. Now that the problem is solved, the odor of the trail classified as unmistakable, the sensory center need no longer intervene.

"His mind is made up, the order given: follow the trail! This is a straightforward action, and the nerve cells of the olfactory lobe will do. But they are not equipped to face possible complications . . . and the hare may have suddenly vaulted, turned, made a detour, crossed his own path, gone back (they are clever!), or another game animal may have come through the area to confuse the trail. The dog may hesitate, investigate again, the sensory center come into play, intelligence deliberate once more to modify the plan of the chase. . . .

"Pursuing or pursued, an animal makes use of the olfactory lobe for driving; of the frontal lobe, for control. You may take any animal in any of its other vital performances, such as choosing food, making love, seeking and following the long way home — the olfactory system always functions in two ways: first as a *means of investigation*, second as a *means of action*.

"The first function is called *sniffing*; it takes place in the sensory center to which the olfactory lobe transmits its impressions by means of the medial and lateral roots. . . . By contrast, what we might call *olfactory action* . . . has the simplicity and instantaneity of a reflex. . . . It is the direct transformation of sensation into movement without intervention of the will. . . ."

The vivid passage makes us smile, charmed with its vision on one hand, its naïveté on the other. Its basis — relative size and shape, analogies between these and performance—cannot be wholly accepted. But we also must smile, embarrassed, at ourselves. A whole century of research, inspired by, independent of, or oblivious to this work, uncountable man-hours of experimentation, unfathomable piles of data, have not given us a means for an adequate critical evaluation. But we can appreciate the bold stride from dissection to behavior and the meaning deduced from developmental morphology. Despite some notions that remain unconfirmed or must be discarded, we perceive the direction towards our present-day understanding. Our views on the behavior of the dog—also man's best friend neurologically, from Sechenov to Pavlov, from Descartes to Broca—have acquired more precision and sophistication, and so have reflexes, from Marshall Hall to Sherrington and the writers on the reticular formation. Behavior stratified according to anatomical levels, and according to connections arranged in shorter and longer chains, for immediate instinctive action on one hand, more delayed deliberation on the other: this notion was more thoroughly envisaged a few years later by Hughlings Jackson. We still believe that older and simpler mechanisms coexist in competition with evolutionarily more recent acquisitions. The anatomical notion of a threshold or limbus is, for better or worse, also a foundation stone of modern psychology; it is the threshold that separates, and ties together, unconscious and conscious experience.

In animals, where Broca saw the threshold or wall of the limbic lobe closed on itself, he saw it surrounded by a moat: the limbic fissure. In man, he saw it split up into the rhinal and hippocampal fissures. He asked himself whether the absence of this fissure might confer some hierarchic distinction. Was this distinction applicable to the genus Homo? Perhaps it was not, and at this point the solid notion of "higher" and "lower" races began to show a fine crack.

In osmatic animals, he wrote,[60] the limbic fissure separates an entirely independent gyrus hippocampi from the temporal lobe. In whales and dolphins—in animals, that is, without a sense of smell and yet highly intelligent—the fissure disappears. It forms only a sulcus in monkeys, apes, and seals; it is vestigial in man: "Hence a few years ago, I was led to believe that the absence of a limbic sulcus established a distinction between the brains of man and ape. But then I found that the sulcus was present in all Negro brains that I examined; I found it in the brains of an Annamite, a Chinese, a dark-skinned man from Hindustan and a native of Peru—in short I did not see it lacking in any Non-Caucasian brain. (I did not wish to prejudge possible exceptions, I simply had not encountered any.) I was, therefore, led to consider the presence of this sulcus as a sign of inferiority in the human, an indication of incomplete evolution, an arrest at the simian stage. But pursuing my studies further, I realized that the limbic sulcus exceptionally exists also in some white men—perhaps a little more frequently in brains of an inferior quality than in those richly endowed with convolutions—but sometimes (rarely, it is true) even in the latter kind. On the other hand, it was also absent from the majority of idiots and from microcephalic brains, even those that presented quite a few simian characteristics. All this proves nothing against the idea of evolution; a brain very well developed and perfected as a whole may nonetheless preserve some inferior feature in some of its parts. By the same token, a brain quite inferior as a whole may show signs of superiority somewhere. . . ." In other words, the question of racial inferiority would have to be approached with far greater caution than before. No longer did nature seem to have set those limits to development that a cursory glance at the human—in fact, the racial—condition had led one to take for granted. Earlier in 1872, Broca had already expressed the opinion[61] (based on cranial measurements) that the relative size of the frontal lobes was largely acquired. Like any other part of the anatomy it might increase with activity, training, learning. It was not a distinction of birth or class, and it was not a distinction of race.

"Not only does education," he had then concluded, "make a man superior . . . It even has the wonderful power of raising him above himself, or enlarging his brain, and of perfecting its shape. To ask that instruction ought to be given to everyone is to make a legitimate request in the social and national interest and perhaps in the racial interest, beyond that. Spread education, and you improve the race. If society wants to, society can do it."

The finding or disputing of distinctive features between the brains of man and ape, on the one hand, and the brains of Caucasian and "primitive" man, on the other, was then a fashionable preoccupation. Much argument about this or that minor cerebral sulcus endured well into this century. For serious scientists today, it has lost most of its interest, being too inconstant and prejudicial.

The hope that each convolution may have its individual functional significance has also been disappointed. We can no longer accept Broca's dictum that *"les circonvolutions sont des organes."* He clearly stated, however, that the shape of the convolutions was variable; only their positions and relationships were fixed.[62]

Broca was, of course, not aware of the visual, acoustic, and tactile areas of the cortex and of the role the thalamus played with its projections to these areas, a subject which has so importantly occupied the neuroanatomists of our century. But in *The Great Limbic Lobe*, he did a good deal more than the title indicated. The work really covers the phylogenesis of the whole forebrain, especially with an aspect which we might call "fronto-parietal rivalry." Like Leuret and Gratiolet before him, he pointed to the tremendous increase in growth of the frontal lobe as one goes up in the mammalian class. The fundamental step Broca made beyond his predecessor was to show that increasing frontal predominance proceeded in direct proportion to limbic atrophy, and that this was evolutional.[63] In addition he worked out an interesting mechanical concept regarding the genesis of the other three lobes that form the brain's convexity. Calling "parietal" everything situated behind the coronal sulcus of the carnivores—analogue of the Rolandic or central fissure of the primates—an originally much larger parietal lobe was forced backward as a whole, and downward in part, by the expanding mass of the frontal. This downward trend gave rise to the temporal lobe of the primates, into the vacated space of the shrinking hippocampal lobe of the lower forms. Owing to the limited space and the pressure from in front, the vertically arranged primitive parietal gyri were tilted and folded horizontally, and so formed the grooves of the occipital lobe; its largest transverse fissure, on the medial aspect, became the calcarine.

Broca's main concern was to bridge the apparent gap between the conformations of the primate and that of the nonprimate brain; hence his view of a primate parietal lobe, relatively *reduced* in size due to frontal increment. This view flies in the face of present-day teaching, but the reason for accepting it is partially semantic. The later discoveries of the optic, acoustic, and tactile functions of the cortex have led modern observers to extrapolate from their knowledge of these functional areas, and so they assign the terms temporal, occipital, and parietal to lobes that do not exist in nonprimates. Nonprimates have shallow and short cerebral fissures, and their extra-limbic brain, though convoluted, is not divided into "lobes"—at least not divided in the sense in which the primate brain is. (To call the parietal area, which is not so shaped, a "lobe," is in any case, a semantic inaccuracy, an analogy hallowed by tradition.) Living in trees, as most primates do, may or may not have anything to do with the supposed increase in the size of the tactile, or "parietal," area. But to support the concept of parietal expansion through evolution, it is customary to describe that area as small in the nonprimate brain. The only certain fact is that all parts of the neopallium increase in size, the frontal area showing the greatest relative gain, as Gratiolet had already demonstrated.

Broca's concern with the gross morphology of the cerebral cortex during the last few years of his life crowns the efforts of a century in which "the morphological concept was superseded by the anatomical," as he wrote,[62] or the generic by the individual. Broca wished to standardize and simplify cerebral nomenclature, while preserving generally accepted terms wherever this was feasible. "A name for everything, one name only, and one that stands for nothing else;" this he knew to be a pious postulate, if worth striving for. Thus "fissures" to separate the five lobes of the brain; "sulci" for the grooves between the convolutions; "incisurae," for smaller, less constant folds, buried or superficial, by which all major convolutions are mutually connected. The major convolutions were to be named after the lobes to which they belonged, and listed by numbers. Descriptive terms (Huschke's "lingualis and fusiformis") he criticized for being uncharacteristic for some species and unnecessarily cumbersome in illustrations, and he introduced the temporal and the occipital pole.[64]

Uncertainties that remained regarding differences in the brains of various species were largely a matter of obtaining sufficient material, especially of the hominid apes. It had been a mere three decades since the first gorilla, skin and bones, was brought from equatorial Africa to Boston and described by Dr. Savage, an American missionary.[65] Apes were so rare that Broca presented to his society each new primate brain he received, three gorillas among them.[66] We have his careful instructions for preserving such perishable goods.[67] Gratiolet still had to be content with a gorilla brain arriving much decayed in a keg of tafia (second-rate rum).[68] They came to France from the Gabon, a part of her colonial empire, since 1960 an independent member of her Commonwealth, and best known through the late Albert Schweitzer's Lambarene. In Broca's day, especially in DuChaillu's widely read, spine-tingling *Explorations and Adventures in Equatorial Africa* of 1861,[69] the Gabon literally seemed to beggar description: it was, in the author's involuntary anticlimax, a place "remarkable for its fauna, which is, in many respects, not only extraordinary, but peculiar." Here for the first time the general reader was treated to a witness' account of the gorilla's undeserved reputation for ferocity and sexual insatiability, plagiarized as the King Kong of urban twentieth-century movie-lore. No wonder it had become the rage of late nineteenth-century Caucasian man. Darwin's bestseller was dubbed "The Gorilla Book," and, a real gorilla from Hamburg, on exhibit at the London Zoo, declared "Lion of the Season," by Mr. Punch.[70]

The first well-preserved brain of *Gorilla Savagii*, as it was then called, ever presented in Europe was one that Broca had received from a Dr. Nègre.[71] A little later that year, 1876, the Germans had theirs, too, from a six-month-old infant, kept alive thanks to Herr

Freckmann of Hamburg for three days at the United States Mission in Gabon. Such brains caused much controversy among the cognoscenti: Professors Bischoff and Pansch argued about the ascending and the horizontal branch of the Sylvian fissure, and they were joined, in print, by Broca, Meynert, and others. As this argument also concerned the third (or inferior) frontal convolution, especially its opercular region—the "cape" (*le cap*) he now called it—Broca had this comment to make: "M. Bischoff concludes that . . . (this region) is very rudimentary in the orang and chimpanzee, and almost nonexistent in the gorilla. If true, this conclusion would please me greatly . . . naturally. For if the organ of articulate speech existed only in man it would make a very precious argument in my favor. But although the third frontal convolution is much more developed in man, I am bound to recognize that it is present in simians; in the anthropoid apes its development is even quite marked. . . ."[72]

⇒XV⇐

"*Irremovable*"

France et Science!
Political slogan of the seventies.

*L*uzarches is a place some 25 miles north of Paris where the Broca family—Pauline was now nineteen, Auguste eighteen, André fourteen —spent its vacations. Among French surgeons, little Luzarches has special status, because of a medieval church, believed to harbor the relics of St. Côme, patron saint of surgeons. His name, in the days of Saint Louis and the founding of the Sorbonne, was given to the first surgical college in Paris. Luzarches has remained the annual rallying point of worshipers among the surgical fraternity. It also has a thirteenth-century fortress, or rather its original walls, several feet thick and sufficiently roomy to accommodate a hall and staircase, entered by a nineteenth-century pseudogothic portal and topped by a *pavillon.* This lofty villa provided the Brocas with six rooms, a kitchen, a bathroom, and some utility rooms.

Broca had acquired the property for 60,000 francs in the summer of 1872.[1] For the hot season, according to family tradition, the Brocas, with father Benjamin and the three children, would make their annual carriage trip to Luzarches, the skulls and bones—taken along for study—rattling in their boxes. On weekends, the fortress was alive with students and collaborators. An attractive round turret stood on the landscaped grounds, also intact from the thirteenth century, its top floor converted into a study. *La Tour de Broca* has been a sight-seeing spot since the 1870's: during the summer the light burned until midnight in the old tower, visible from the town below.

Broca was a member of the Luzarches Municipal Council, but his signature appears only twice in the minutes. The city fathers knew

Broca better as "the philanthropist at whose door you could knock any day or night" for a gratis consultation.[2]

In 1877, for the last time, Benjamin Broca made the long, complicated journey back from Luzarches by Paris and Bordeaux, to Saint Foy, and out to Les Bouhets, to be buried under his cypresses, among his vineyards and his family.[3] He had seemed so irremovable from the living.

Irremovable? It is a legal term, which in French public life means "elected for a lifetime." Until 1884, seventy-five of the three hundred members of the French Senate were irremovable as a sign of the special trust the country wished to place in them. In that capacity Broca was to join them in 1880, for a few months only, as if to lend ironic poignancy to the term.

After the fall of the Empire the Senate, with its reactionary tradition, was not reestablished until 1875; not until 1879, when the National Assembly moved back from Versailles to Paris, was it again installed in the spacious halls of the Palais du Luxembourg, built for a Queen of France, with high Renaissance ceilings, soft red carpets, leatherbound volumes, plush fauteuils, wainscoting and Delacroix paintings.

A dozen years before his election, still during the Second Empire, Broca's name had come up in the Senate—not as a candidate but as one of several black sheep. The subject was "Freedom of Higher Education," but the slogan meant its opposite: the return of the universities to Catholic domination.[4] A provincial newspaper published a petition demanding a curb on the "materialism" emanating from several chairs of the École de Médecine. At the Salpêtrière an assistant had allegedly made fun of a religious amulet worn by a patient.[5] Opening the debate, Cardinal Bonnechose quoted a letter to the editors of several newspapers: "Go to the lectures of MM. Vulpian, Sée, Broca, Axenfeld, Robin, and others, and look at the jammed hall: 1500 young men eagerly listening . . . all determined adepts and defenders of science, i.e., materialism. . . ." Monsignor continued, "Materialists go so far as to deny that medicine made any progress as long as it was associated with a philosophical doctrine. I affirm the contrary. . . . A doctor must know about the soul. . . . The scalpel and the microscope alone will never know the true cause of disease, or the art of healing. (Strong approval.) True science is religious. . . ." Teaching materialism was, like advocating civil disobedience, an offense and for weeks the attacks continued on the whole spectrum of evil forces: transformism, Saint-Simon, Fourier, Proudhon, Comte, the Encyclopedists, Lassalle, "those German ideas," Malthus, Flourens, Longet, de Quatrefages, Broca, and Claude Bernard, whose *force créatrice* "ought to be investigated."

Sainte-Beuve, the critic, poet, and biographer, appealed to common sense, which he defined as "a minimum of belief in the supernatural." "It has been shown," he said, "that Professor Broca has not defended Malthusianism and that his phrase was misquoted. . . . [Wealth, Broca had said, increases foresight and restricts procreation in a moral sort of way. Malthus, he later explained, had maintained the opposite. In the French revolution, property was divided, yet the nation grew numerous, disproving Malthus. Nonsense to call him a Malthusian, but little did Broca care.[9]] MM. Vulpian and Charcot have denied the report that one of their assistants had laughed at the patient with the amulet." Professor Sée, famous for his work on the origin of fever, Sainte-Beuve commented, was being vilified because he was a Jew; Broca because he was a Protestant. "Are there perhaps two theories on fever—one Roman Catholic, the other heretic?" The voting was a victory over the heretics,[5] yet in the following year, the last year under the Empire, Claude Bernard was elected to a seat in the Luxembourg.

After the days of the Commune, criticism of the regime was again dangerous. In this first, frankly royalist or "Moral Order" phase of the Third Republic, Raspail, now eighty, people's doctor without a degree, advocate of socialized medicine, scientist, political extremist, was jailed once again, for the fourth time. Professor Robin was crossed off a list of jurors in 1872 and had to weather many riots in his classes,[6] instigated by those students who were not "defenders of science, i.e., materialism."

Animosity against an academic teacher was thus largely political. By the same token, the popularity of Broca and anthropology was not all academic. The figure of "1500 eager listeners" may not have been far from the truth, much as we may wonder what attracted so many young men to lectures about shapes and sizes of skulls. But apart from the dynamic lecturer, his subject was in the news. One can hardly overestimate the impact of anthropology on the French intelligence. The thrill of evolutionary theory reverberated from all sides. Anthropologists were also dealing with a student population steeped in a Celtic and romantic past, saturated with the glory of France, faced with the shattering defeat of 1870. Young Frenchmen wanted to hear what the much-talked-about superiority of one European race over another might amount to. Had the Prussian soldiers won the war because they were drilled early and by better teachers, or had they also been born with better brains? Was the French "race" physically, or even morally, degenerating? Childhood mortality was shocking,[7] but the "so-called degeneracy of the French population" a myth, Broca told the Académie de Médecine in 1876.[8]

Governments are slow to support new lines of research. The new anthropology was framed by two little laboratory rooms, filled with skulls and every instrument for measuring their every dimension, proportion, and angle—ludicrously inadequate. For years these were to cater to members of the Society, visitors, and undergraduates, in addition to Broca himself and his staff. The locale was the attic of a gothic refectory, now part of the École Pratique. Once the Cordelier monks' dormitory, it had served through many vicissitudes, revolutionary and commercial, and as a painter's studio. Danton, Marat, and Desmoulins had made it the headquarters of their Club des Cordeliers, much as the church of St. Jacob had served for the Club des Jacobins. The old Musée Dupuytren was on the ground floor of the refectory. Among its pathological specimens, well known to Parisians out on a Sunday stroll to exercise their goose pimples, the museum also contained Leborgne's and Lelong's pickled brains, contributed by the chief of the premises above. Craniology and comparative anatomy were taught in the attic.[9]

But across the street—Rue des Écoles—the second largest amphitheatre of the Faculté had soon to be opened to anthropology lectures because, as Broca wrote in his report of 1872 to the Minster of Education, "the great majority of the audience are medical students. Anthropology is germane to their studies but not an integral part of the curriculum. Their interest . . . shows that they know how to work for the sole aim of instructing themselves although they are not motivated by the necessity of taking an examination."[10]

Expansion was also needed in research and publications. The Bulletin was bursting at the seams. In 1872, Broca published a new periodical, Revue d'Anthropologie, independent from the Société d'Anthropologie, another province of his growing little empire. Verneuil marvelled at his talents as an organizer: "You had to see this impetuous man line up the items as though he had done ten years of pen-pushing in a government office."[11]

From 1875 on, under the political leadership of Gambetta, Broca could press harder for his great project, a School of Anthropology. Reports, submitted every other year, filling several pages with the imposing work done, not only by the members of the Society, but by Broca's own staff, were one strong influence on the Minister. Others tried to stifle the new science. During the Empire they clamored on

Refectory of the Club des Cordeliers (in the background), with the Musée Dupuytren on the ground-floor; top floors were later occupied by Broca's Institut d'Anthropologie. Ecole de Médecine left foreground. The scene represents the havoc created by the uprising of the Commune in 1871. (Courtesy Bibliothèque Nationale, Paris.)

the floor of the Senate for the "freedom of higher education." In the fall of 1876, yet another vitriolic campaign was launched by the Catholic press against the personalities of the prospective Anthropological School. It seriously imperiled the consent of an intimidated Minister of Education.[12]

In academic circles the anti-scientists had naturally become a minority. The Faculté de Médecine, with Wurtz, its Dean, favored anthropology as a discipline germane to medical teaching and supported Broca's project. But something else was lacking: space and funds. So Broca went out to hunt for space and funds, the *sine qua non* of modern research, the basic quest by the chief investigator.

A chair of anthropology held by de Quatrefages had existed for some time, but it was at the Muséum de l'Histoire Naturelle, not within the Medical School. For the Academic Senate of the Faculté de Médecine, it was therefore "an honor to develop in its bosom this very important branch of research." As a result, the loft in the old Cordeliers refectory was permanently put at the disposal of *"notre éminent collègue, le Dr. Broca."* But to be useful, space must be divided, and where find the funds for making two stories out of one attic, and partition them off?

Within two months "at least" 23 out of the 300-odd members of Broca's Society contributed the first 35 of the 1000-franc shares. Work begun in the summer of 1875 was completed during the next ten months—"with the speed of a *coup de théâtre.*"[12] The eventual cost of remodelling the old gothic dormitory amounted to nearly 100,000 francs[9], a sort of key money, really, paid by the Société d'Anthropologie to the owner, the Ecole de Médecine, which through a grant by the city of Paris was the final beneficiary of the Revolution of 1794.

In 1940 Professor Vallois still could write that every anthropologist would climb undismayed those uncomfortable two flights of high steps and go to the lecture hall through a long, narrow passage, past the Broca Museum, the meeting room of the Society, and five tiny work rooms assigned in 1876 by Broca to accommodate instruments for craniometry, dissection, drawing, plaster casts, chemical and photographic work. "Broca's instruments are still largely in use," Vallois wrote, "not only those that have gradually acquired their definitive shape, but the first models which he conceived and constantly perfected . . . Some of them are forgotten. But what better proof of their usefulness than to find them reinvented by various anthropologists abroad. . . ."

In the Museum, Broca merged the 2500 skulls from his home with the Société's 1200, together with casts of primate brains, human and other, normal and abnormal, casts of other preserved organs, and one of the largest showcases in the world with samples of hair.

With the German armies again approaching in 1940, Vallois' account was written none too soon. Laboratoire and Musée Broca and Musée Dupuytren were hastily evacuated, all floors declared unsafe and closed, books and instruments removed to the Musée de Paléontologie Humaine, including the master's walking cane that concealed a measuring rod, and his Scottish Glengarry cap. The Société d'Anthropologie and the osteological collection went to the Musée de l'Homme. There it has taken three workers two years to install the final 15,000 skulls in eighty-two floor-to-ceiling wall-cupboards, not to speak of the skeletons and individual bones. Broca's own Basque and Breton series are still getting quite a bit of attention. The brain casts are in the Musée Orfila at the new Medical School, the Musée Dupuytren is in the basement of the École de Médecine. At this time of writing the old gothic repository for human remains is still being remodelled.

Broca finally opened his School of Anthropology at the end of 1876, the year in which he was acclaimed at the International Anthropological Congress in Budapest. (French participation in this meeting was about three times that of any except the host country—a measure of Broca's influence. Even the clerk of the court of Luzarches had subscribed to the event; sixteen-year-old Auguste Broca was taken along to the second of the three meetings abroad which his father attended. The first time, in Norwich, Broca had shared the vice-presidency with T. H. Huxley; this time it was with Virchow.) Like other officials before him, the minister yielded to the ardent founder[12] and gave an annual and individual authorization. The appellation School was withheld for a while; each individual course had to receive separate ministerial approval. Anthropology still seemed a little too popular and a trifle subversive. At the same time moral and other support grew; the city of Paris granted an annual subvention of 12,000 francs to the man who had described the basic features of her long dead citizens. By 1878, the Republic, never over-generous, began to give a little more benevolent attention to scientific institutions and decided that the budget of France could afford an annual 20,000 francs for supporting a School of Anthropology. Topinard (who became Broca's successor) taught "biological anthropology"; Dally, ethnology; de Mortillet, prehistory; Hovelacque, linguistics; Adolphe Bertillon, the statistician, "demography"; Bordier, "medical geography." All these men have made anthropological history, together with Hamy and Manouvrier, the teacher of Hrdlička. Broca taught "anatomical," i.e., physical anthropology.[13] School, Laboratory, and Museum now formed an Institute of Anthropology—a triumph, largely of private enterprise, for the profit of science.

Eighteen seventy-eight was also the year of another World Exhibition in Paris. Thanks to their tremendous recuperative power the defeated nation and her capital dazzled the world with such great names as Flaubert and Zola; Manet, Monet, and Degas; Pasteur. By 1872, the French had also launched their Association for the Advancement of Science, with Claude Bernard as president and Broca, one of its "most fervent, zealous, active, energetic, and powerful advocates," as vice president.[28] At the first meeting in Bordeaux Broca pointed out the new trend for French Science: decentralization and freedom from official ties.

The World Exhibition of 1878 included an anthropological pavilion and, coincident with it, an International Congress of the Anthropological Sciences, with Broca as president and the architect Viollet-le-Duc, famous restorer of old Gothic, on its committee. The building for the anthropological exhibits, at the site of the Trocadéro (the present vast Musée de l'Homme), measured 270 by 45 feet—not so modest for the times. Sessions were sensibly scheduled only from 3 to 6 p.m.[14]

At these meetings Broca struck up a friendship with Professor Boghdanov, his opposite number in Moscow. When in the following summer the Russian Imperial Society of Friends of Natural Science, Anthropology, and Ethnography organized a similar venture, Broca, with de Quatrefages, Topinard, Hamy, de Mortillet, and four other French scientists travelled via Leipzig, Dresden, and Breslau (Vroclav) to Warsaw and from there, all expenses paid, in luxury carriages to Moscow, where Russian hospitality in the grand manner was awaiting them. Broca's itinerary notes record, en route and at destination, his visits to museums, galleries, libraries, archeological sites, botanical gardens, medical schools, hospitals, the Kremlin. The Russian hospitality had been "so generous, so cordial" and, as he added in the last of his many toasts, "so brotherly. . . . If this word has sometimes been abused, here we may apply it legitimately, for we are all natural brothers through Science, our common mother."[15] From Moscow to Kiev, and home via Vienna, (where he stopped for little over one day), to Graz over the Semmering, another single day in Venice, and on to Montpellier for another meeting of the Society for the Advancement of Science. Five more days in the countryside, and back to a pursuit perhaps not quite so brotherly.

To be active in the highest echelons of politics was not unusual for men well-known in other fields, especially in the nineteenth century and in France. The medical profession, inspired and divided by politics, took its fair share in parliamentary debate and legislation. Broca had remained alive not only to the irritations by government but also to the challenge of overcoming them. During the first dozen or so years of Louis Napoléon's reign, he would have had to sacrifice all else, had he given vent, in public, to what he wrote privately, in rhymes, about "The Man of the 2nd December . . . the fearless hero and his army! Fearless, as he and his cutthroats mowed down a disarmed crowd, fearless as they left the boulevards littered with the bleeding bodies of women, old men, and children! Let me sing him, Bonaparte, and his execrable clique who sold the Republic for thirty pieces of silver . . ."[16]

Neither a political novice nor an intransigent, Broca refused during the Empire to stand as a candidate for a cowed Chamber of

Deputies.[17] Immediately after the war and Commune, Broca was persuaded to run for deputy on the "republican" list. "Republican", of course, did not mean conservative, rather the opposite. In the United States, whose national identity as a republic was never seriously challenged, "The Republic" is the epitome of hallowed tradition, law, and order. But *"Vive la République!"* meant "down with the old order." It was a cry for a hundred years of foiled attempts to establish a democracy. A "Republican" was simply one opposed to the monarchy, no matter what his allegiance to any one of the fine shadings between left and center. Right of center everything was royalist, Orleanist, or Bonapartist and pro-Church of Rome. Broca raised 60,000 ballots: not enough.[18]

But again, with republicanism gaining ground under Gambetta's leadership, Broca could not resist its call when a permanent seat in the Senate became vacant in January, 1880. "He shared all our struggles for recapturing the confiscated rights of democracy," said a fellow Senator, "but we had to do violence to his modesty. . . . Still, as we were going to regenerate the public school system in France, a place in the Senate was unmistakably his. . . ."[19] The choice of a suitable regular politician seems to have presented some difficulty.[20] Moreover, the Republican Left wished to impress the country with the names of internationally famous men. And *"France et Science!"* was a political slogan of the day.[21]

After 1878 the Republicans gained ascendancy even in the Senate. They formed a spectrum composed of delicate hues. Broca belonged to Gambetta's *Union Républicaine.* Another band, also moderate, called itself "Republican Left," under the leadership of Jules Ferry, Minister of Education. A third, or "Radical Party," of the extreme left was led by Georges Clemenceau, M.D. At one time a teacher in the United States, he had been Mayor of embattled Montmartre for the Commune; later he toppled several cabinets including Gambetta's, played an important part on the liberal side of the Dreyfus affair, and twice became Prime Minister. In his seventies, the "Tiger" of World War I successfully opposed Poincaré, Lloyd George, and President Wilson; with the Versailles Treaty of 1919 he got his revenge for 1871.

Yet a fourth republican party existed, confusingly called *Centre gauche,* as it was far more "center" than "left." Jules Simon, subtle in the shading of his political belief, was its leader; its candidate for the vacant *inamovible* or "irremovable" senator's seat was M. Bétolaud, a lawyer. As his opponent, M. Broca was nominated "enthusiastically and without debate" candidate of the *Union Républicaine.*[22] The press gave its readers their daily ration of party bias; the voting itself was done by the 300 Senate members. On the left, *Le National* (January 20, 1880) featured the sentimental angle:

"'An eighteen-month-old child of a friend of mine', a reader in Batignolles writes, 'suffered from a bony tumor in the temporal region of the skull. The whole faculty had given up the case as hopeless . . . in view of the child's age and the seat of the ailment. . . . Doctor Broca . . . saw the little patient in his home. . . . The operation had proved successful beyond all hope. Overwhelmed by gratitude, the family raised the question of payment, but because my friend is not a rich man the learned professor refused. . . .'"

By contrast, this appeared in the Catholic *Figaro*:

"February 1, 1880 . . . Broca is a second-rate surgeon. In spite of his pretentions concerning a branch of science called anthropology, a field in which he has not distinguished himself by any original work, he must not think that he belongs to the category of a Bichat or a Claude Bernard. These men did not believe themselves to be more than anatomists and physiologists. Above all Mr. Broca is one of the heads of that little church of materialists . . . in the bosom of the Faculté de Médecine where it reigns supreme."

Middle-of-the-road, *Petit Journal du Soir* (February 12, 1880) stressed the candidate's religious dependability beyond the facts:

"Atheist, materialist, radical: that's what most publicists who favor the candidacy of M. Bétolaud call M. Broca. The truth is that not by a single act, not a single written word has M. Broca given anybody the right to apply these epithets to him. A Protestant, scion of one of those old families of the Languedoc who sealed their faith with their blood, M. Broca married a Protestant, Mlle. Lugol, and it was a Protestant minister who blessed their union and baptized their three children. Although belonging to the liberal faction of Protestantism, M. Broca is registered at the Consistory and has taken part in all the votes of the Synod. [See Chapter VIII. His name cannot be found anywhere on the parish register of voters.] This is not exactly the image of a dyed-in-the-wool atheist. . . . Crowned with all the academic laurels . . . he does not belong to the *Institut*. The reason is quite simple. . . . To be an innovator is perhaps not regarded as exactly a merit by the *Institut*. . . .

"He devotes only the strictly necessary time to his practice, enough not to inconvenience people. Then he goes and shuts himself up in his laboratory at the École Pratique together with his most eager assistant, M. Chudzinski, one of those 'rats of the amphitheatre' who, microscope in hand [*sic*], scrutinizes the mysteries of the flesh. . . . At the sight of the lonely glow in his window, friends of the professor, out late in the Rue de Saints-Pères, often exclaim 'Broca has not gone to bed!'" And thus it went on, in good electoral fashion, panegyrics and slander.

As soon as the news of Broca's election was out on February 6, *Le Figaro* (today the only survivor of them all and still fit to print the news) forgot what it had said the week before, dutifully changed the tone and, still a little sour faced, managed to stand to attention: "He has only friends even in the most opposed camps. . . . His great passion, his favorite relaxation is music — good music — the kind played by the marvellous *Orchestre de Conservatoire* of which the doctor is one of the most faithful and enthusiastic patrons.

"In private he has an open character, an upright mind, a solid stomach; he does not despise a joke, nor good food, and he will worry a week in advance what he is going to offer his guests when he invites them for dinner. He is one of the usual guests at the famous Renan dinners which take place at Bréhant's every month, where he has taken the place vacated by Théophile Gautier. . . .

"The son of the obscure country doctor has made his way."

The close call was reported by *Siècle* (February 6): "The ballot was closed at 3 o'clock. Twenty minutes later the president announced its outcome: 275 votes, 2 blanks. The absolute majority was 137. M. Broca got 140, M. Bétolaud 132, and M. Vacheron 1. . . ."

For three days the newspapers could not get the excitement about the controversial senator out of their system. The clippings in Broca's pasted volume go on and on. Nobody had bothered to look up the relatively noncontroversial parts of his work, no one remembered aphemia. The Darwinist angle was endlessly played up. How were they to know the difference or to tell the average reader that the transformist senator-professor had been critical of Darwin? Or that he had not coined but only quoted — and that with some reservation — the saying by the Swiss anatomist Claparède (following in T.H. Huxley's footsteps), that he "would rather be a perfected ape"? Even across the Atlantic, in the medical historian's basic book, the admirable Garrison has through many editions since 1913 credited Broca with this aphorism, in addition to a couple of unfortunate sentences on his racial theories that manage to be contrary to fact, inconsequential, and unintelligible all at once.[23]

The opposition sought to stigmatize the Senator-elect as a materialist. During the nineteenth century it was bad form even among scientists to mention the subject of materialism, and even where conditions had made this more or less safe. Whatever their innermost thoughts — and many scientists have been finding orthodoxy compatible even with atomism — most have quietly aban-

Caricature representing Broca as an ape: "From the rostrum the new lifetime Senator Broca will henceforth give examples of behavior in line with his theories." (*Le Triboulet*, February, 1880. Courtesy Bibliothèque Nationale, Paris.)

doned, simultaneously with their student quarters, the arguments about God and the soul and left the problem to those who make a living by its pursuit. If one sort of materialism was embodied by Sancho Panza, the other sort became more and more an attribute of the questing Don.

This deliberate indifference was essentially Broca's attitude to the problem, an attitude that rejected any dogma in science, materialistic or theological. "M. Broca," said a speaker in the Société d'Anthropologie, "regards the question of another life as insoluble and thinks that wise men should not occupy themselves with it. . . ."[24]

Bold but not foolhardy, radical but not extreme, and fanatic only in his quasi-religious belief that facts were infallible, Broca was an empiricist and a pragmatist. His independent mind combined the spirit of rebellion with the sense of the ridiculous. The speaker just referred to believed in "the explanation of another life by chemistry," one of those confused juxtapositions of incompatible premises: religion and science. Broca never attacked religion *per se* any more than he would have attacked chemistry, but he knew that either foe was too ill-provided with evidence or with competence for solving the problems of the other side.[25] He pleaded for peaceful coexistence. He was no pedant and no zealot, but his moderation could not always be counted on. We hear occasional outbursts of petulance; we see an almost self-destructive drive, side by side with the unheated and honest examination of facts. This blend of intellectual, emotional, and moral assets, the fact that he had rectitude, vision, and charm, enabled him to do great things, to succeed in his world, and still be liked. He seems to have overcome much of the natural hostility the person encounters who grows older and continues to be so right and so successful. What must have endeared him to young and old, partisans and opponents alike, and yet given him authority, was that neither side was ever left in doubt about his motives; the sincerity was accepted even when the message was not.

On February 19, 1880, Broca's friends of the two Chambers of Parliament, all the Societies in Paris whose member he was, the Médecins and Chirurgiens des Hôpitaux, and *Presse Médicale* celebrated his election with a banquet at the customary gala hotel, the Continental, Rue de Rivoli, at 20 francs a plate. In a great round of speeches, two hundred people greeted and toasted the national recognition of the controversial new science in the person of the new *sénateur inamovible*, its founder. "The occasion was without equal among celebrations of this sort,"[26] "remarkably spirited, animated and serene throughout."[27] "If there are so many of us gathered around you here it is because you are always making new friends without ever losing a single one of them," said Verneuil, addressing the man who had been his closest friend since early dissecting days.

In retrospect, the remark which Broca made there in a mood of uncommon elation suggests an intimation of death. It may, of course, have been his ever-present awareness of what his mother would have called "the sin of pride." "If I were superstitious," he is supposed to have said to some friend at the banquet, "my present happiness would make me feel that I am menaced by a great danger."[18] He was.

In the few remaining months of his life Broca did manage to serve "France, Science, and Freedom" in equal shares. His attendance at the Senate was exemplary, and he kept up this neat separation, this nice balance between medicine and politics, to a point so fine that some may have found it hard to agree. When public interest seemed paramount, the vested interests of the medical profession had to take second place, and with it the esprit de corps of the Académie de Médecine, although he was then its vice-president.[28]

The main topic of the Senate sessions was not public health, but the laicization of schools. Jules Ferry, the Minister of Education, proposed the famous controversial *article 7*, a law designed to reverse the *loi Falloux*, in force since 1852, according to which a member of the clergy was entitled to teaching credentials without a qualifying examination. (Amended several times since Jules Ferry's first onslaught, it was not finally repealed until 1904.) On March 9, 1880, the Senate defeated *article 7* by a vast majority. One would expect Broca to have voted for it, but his name is not among those few in favor, the only ones recorded—all of the extreme left.[29] Was this one of the reasons for de Mortillet's snide remark that the world would not remember Broca as a Senator?[30]

Broca's immediate contribution was the report[31] he drafted as member of a legislative committee dealing with another proposal by Jules Ferry. Already adopted by the Chambre des Députés, it concerned the establishment of public secondary schools for girls.

The Second Empire had not supported Duruy, its enlightened Minister of Education, when he, too, had proposed public high school for girls. Hitherto, they might receive such instruction only in convents, or for a fee, in private schools. Even attempts at providing elementary schools for them had always failed—for "lack of funds," Broca recalled—until Guizot, under Louis-Philippe, made such education, "optional" and the Second Republic made it obligatory in 1848.

The thought behind providing high school for all girls, Broca continued, was not political but social. Society was based on the family: "The family is what woman makes it. . . . Entrusted with such a high mission must mothers be ignorant and futile?" And he outlined a detailed curriculum that excluded Latin and Greek, reduced philosophy to a course in ethics, science to an elementary level. Arithmetic should be raised to the boys' level, and they should have some notion of the law. Most important, they ought to learn the principles of hygiene, of infant care in particular. "Our dreadful rate of child mortality is a disgrace to the nation . . . 60,000 infants a year might be saved by better hygiene." On the other hand "moral instruction" should take the place of the religious kind, as it was "expensive" and could be left to the home. . . .

"I have the honor to deposit on the rostrum of the Senate. . . ." The words of this formula, as he was handing over his report on June 21, 1880, were the only recorded ones that Broca ever spoke in a Senate meeting. He had seventeen more days to live.

Considering the tight grip in which the church and tradition held every aspect of a woman's life, Broca's proposal to replace religious by "moral" instruction naturally raised the greatest furor. The debate did not open until November. By December public high schools for girls became law in France.[21]

Coeducation being routine today we may not appreciate the significance of that report; its treatment may seem tame. Summing it up one might say, with a book review in The New Yorker,[32] that "Frenchwomen were [to be] educated but not emancipated" for one or more generations to come. Broca was no doubt more enlightened in this matter than most of his contemporaries, but he was no outright feminist. If greater equality for women was nevertheless on his mind, it would not have been politically sound to voice it here.

The law brought France at last on an equal footing with Germany and other nations. It also made it easier for young women to aim higher. But paradoxically, in contrast to Prussia, one of the last countries to admit women to academic studies such as medicine, France had not in theory excluded women from aspiring to a profession. In practice, the block was usually their inadequate preparation at the high school level, the subject of Broca's report.

It was on Broca's recommendation that already in 1870, perhaps profiting from the war, a Mlle Brés was the first to be admitted as a "substitute interne" at the Pitié. Four years earlier this brave and fortunate young lady had been told by Dean Würtz that there was no law against her studying medicine. But in view of her inadequate high school preparation, she had to work two more years before she could obtain the certificate enabling her to register in a medical school. By then (1868) she was joined by Miss Garrett from England, Miss Putnam from the United States, and Mlle Gontscharoff, presumably from

Russia. Miss Putman might have been able to take her medical degree in her own country, where Elizabeth Blackwell, after many difficulties, had entered the Medical School of Geneva, New York, twenty-four years earlier. In Switzerland, Zurich also had opened its dissecting rooms and patient wards to a number of eager Russian girls, before Paris did.

After Broca had created the precedent, Verneuil, too, was known as one of the few gallant advocates of women's interneships. By 1875, when Mlle. Brés graduated, the École de Médecine listed (not to say boasted) twenty-two female students.[33]

Broca was not to hear the favorable outcome of his report.

A coronary thrombosis? In Broca's day this diagnosis was hardly made. Even the terms *angina, angor pectoris,* or *pectoris dolor* were certainly not in Seneca's medical vocabulary when he complained of an attack which was "like giving up the soul, rightly called *meditatio mortis,*" an exercise in dying.[34] In 1768 Heberden, who coined the term *angina,* considered the condition "not extremely rare"[35] after collecting one hundred cases of it.[35] Yet an English manual on heart disease published one year after Broca's death called it "a by no means common affection."[36]

The French school saw the condition first and foremost as a neuralgia involving the vagus, the nerve of the heart, a thoracobrachial or intercostal (sympathetic) neuralgia, according to Trousseau. Cardiac pathology had been frequently noted but was disregarded.[37]

"The Diagnosis of a Case of Thrombotic Occlusion of a Coronary Artery Made at the Bedside," proudly proclaimed in 1878 by Adam Hammer (a German-American), was not apt to arouse much of a following.[38] Electrocardiography was unknown in the nineteenth century. In 1880 cardiac death in France was still a "paralysis of the heart nerve."

The tensions of the twentieth century, the real or imaginary worries of people with great responsibilities, are said to cause angina and fatal necrosis of the heart muscle; heavy smoking and overeating make for sclerosis of the coronary arteries. All these, including heavy cigar smoking (although probably not cigarettes, which Napoleon III had made fashionable), were part of Broca's avant-garde life. "He made a cult of his duties . . . burdened his shoulders out of all proportion," according to his friend Verneuil;[11] the curtains in his study were saturated with cigar smoke, according to one of his granddaughters; "these feverish movements of the man for whom there will not be enough time to bring forth all that fermenting, boiling life trying to take shape within, of the man who knows this and drives himself to crowd several lives into the one that is too short," were remembered nearly thirty years later.[39]

The last photograph taken of Broca, the Senator, is in sharp contrast to earlier ones. It is a shock to see his remaining hair quite white, his features drawn and somewhat flabby, his eyes veiled with what must be fatigue.

Family tradition speaks of Augustine's concern for her husband all through the preceding years. If we believe *Le Temps* and *Le Figaro*,[40] Broca's fatal illness — apparently so very brief and sudden — was in fact neither. According to these two leading dailies, he thought himself subject to "intercostal neuralgia."

On July 7, in the week following his fifty-sixth birthday, he had some pain in the left shoulder. But he made light of it, his friends said, and spent the day "in the usual manner: at the hospital among his students and in the laboratory with his collaborators; in the evening he worked on a paper about the torsion of the humerus,"[41] that interesting phenomenon of comparative anatomy, related to the upright posture which the higher primates have acquired in the course of evolution. Next day ("hot and sultry, with thunder storms")[42] "after giving one of his scrupulously prepared lectures,"[11] he went to the Senate. The chest pain became such that he had to leave. "Returning home he could not sit down at his desk — quite a frustration for him. Death took him by surprise as he was stretching out on his bed to catch some sleep. Peacefully, without a struggle — unaware, so to speak — he left this life."[41] "Yes, I am still in pain. But I hope I shall be able to sleep," were supposedly his last words, according to *Journal des Connaissances Médicales*.[43] *Le Temps* has him leaving the session, "for a few moments to rest in one of the rooms reserved for Senators, but he returned to the assembly. As his pain continued he went home. In the evening he retired while his pain was causing no alarm among his friends. Towards midnight he was unable to stay in bed; he felt as though he were suffocating. Lying down on a couch he died a little later."[40]

Le Figaro, who like the *Journal des Connaissances Médicales* and *Le Temps*, knew every grisly detail, some of them contradictory, added that "according to all probability, Dr. Paul Broca has succumbed to a bulbar hemorrhage, caused by excessive work. . . ." *Le Temps* had him die of an aneurysm, the subject of his book of 1856.

Paul Reclus and Samuel Pozzi, who with two other doctors undertook the autopsy — presumably in the deceased man's home, as was the custom — spoke of an attack of angina that felled him, yet, "the heart was sound, the brain intact, the viscera normal."[43] No post-mortem protocol was left. Chudzinski made a cast of the brain.[44]

Broca's brain, undersurface of left hemisphere. The inscription is on the inferior (third) temporal gyrus. Olfactory nerve to the left. Cast by Chudzinski. (Courtesy École de Médecine, Department of Anatomy, Rue des Saints-Pères.)

On the morning following Broca's death President Say addressed the Senate: "In the midst of his immense labor and the passionate polemics which he aroused, he had that equanimity, that youthful heart and gaiety which only strong minds and good men possess. . . . Thanks to them he disarmed the most violent adversaries of his theories. (Very good! Very good!) He also had only friends in the Senate; his death causes grief to us all. (Strong approbation and applause.)"[45] Senators will be Senators. Next day the obituaries appeared on the front pages.

On July 11, a Sunday, he was buried at the southeast corner of the Montparnasse cemetery, in a grave that now holds his wife, his children, and some members of their families. There were close to 2000 people; most of them following the hearse, on foot, the two miles or so from his home. It ought to have been a state funeral, *Tribune Médicale* observed. The first precedent of this kind had occurred at Claude Bernard's death two years before; the writer of the obituary felt he ought to couple the two names.[46]

The pallbearers were Jules Ferry, Minister of Education, and Pelletan, vice-president of the Senate; Vulpian, Dean of the Medical School; the President of the Académie de Médecine; the President of the Société d'Anthropologie, the Secretary-General of the French Association for the Advancement of Science; a Chirurgien des hôpitaux; and an interne.[43]

Epilogue: The Statue

> As long as he is not fully formed, as each
> day adds something essentially new, we
> follow him step by step, event by decisive
> event; as he gets to be a man, allow him
> more freedom; as he is about to deal with
> things, consider those in themselves; but
> rejoin him as we take his measure at the
> end.
>
> Sainte-Beuve, on writing a biography

A vital organ fails; in the middle of life an organism has ceased to function. Any other moment lived gives birth and owes its existence to one essentially similar; only first and last events stand out emphatically against the surrounding nothingness. A confrontation of fundamental contrasts, but beyond that the poignance of dying combines with the thwarted plan and the lost memory, the withdrawn promise. To have, except in utter senility, another day to live is to remember and still be young; to die is to be robbed of past and future, no matter how well family and friends treasure a shadowy inheritance.

These are private matters. In the telescopic view and the cold light of history, the death of a public figure takes another dimension, for we must add the timelessness intended by those who have erected a solid monument for the man. As to Paul Broca, followed here, first "step by step," how are we to "rejoin him as we take his measure in the end"? The modern reader finds such an abstract evaluation at the beginning, in the Introduction. But this biographer's, this student's, first real encounter with Broca was in Paris, with his statue. Trying now to "rejoin" it, he finds that it, too, is only a memory.

When nineteenth-century man began to question his origins and to worship the future, he left as a symbolic by-product those innumerable stone or bronze images, contemporary supermen who had toiled successfully and hard to bring that future about. "Erecting statues has been our latest mania," reminisced Jules Simon, a liberal politician, once premier of the Third Republic, at the turn of that century. Take Paul Broca standing on the Place de l'École de Médecine, heart of the Left Bank, center of its Quartier Latin. No site could have been more prominent; hence, it was just right for "the founder of anthropology," as Simon calls him. Appropriately measuring a skull with a craniometer of his invention, he also was "a statue for peace." (Only some hundred yards away they had brazenly emplaced another national hero—bloody Danton—"terror openly glorified!") As to the fate to befall the Broca statue, Simon had no illusion: "Quite likely they'll put him in storage some day. . . ."[1]

Cynical, political, and on the whole correct, the prediction was still an understatement. Two world wars later a compliant "de facto Vichy government, at the behest of the German authorities of occupation," had the statue melted down, one among 130 in Paris "of copper alloy and not representing any true artistic or historic interest." (Danton was spared.)

That was 1941. Twenty years later, a medical library attendant, quite an old man, looking down with me on the spot where the Broca statue had been standing, could not remember it. At Sainte-Foy-la-Grande, Broca's birthplace where a replica was similarly razed, a barber said: "We don't care that much for monuments. . . ."

Not so the biographer: an avid collector of all palpable evidence, he is also afflicted with something called "agalmatophilia,"[2] or monumentomania. He even dreams of having his idol over for supper, complete with Leporello's list of references—"son già mille e tre."

Folklore may be revealing. In a 1917 vaudeville show the playwright, a wine merchant of Sainte Foy, had Broca literally step down from his pedestal to seek revenge for that scandalously "modest" unveiling of 1887, seven years after his death.[3] The Catholic city fathers had resented that statue. Protestant money and the Prefect of the Département finally managed to emplace it, apparently with little fanfare, at the city periphery.[4] There had been no funds for a monument to honor a Catholic native son of Sainte Foy: Pierre Gratiolet, who also happened to be a meritorious neuroanatomist. He had only a Boulevard named after him. It runs into Place Broca, now graced by a café and a garage of this name.

291

The statue of Broca, Place de l'École de Médecine (1887–1942), Boulevard St. Germain, by Choppin. The inscription reads: Paul Broca, Fondateur de la Société d'Anthropologie, Professeur à la Faculté de Médecine de Paris, Sénateur, 1824–1880. (Courtesy Viollet, 6 Rue de Seine, Paris.)

Also scandalously "modest," the Paris unveiling aroused some furious comment. Gabriel de Mortillet, a distinguished archeologist, a former collaborator of the "founder," and politically far left, accused Broca's own family of having shamefully soft-pedalled the event. Sending out a minimum of invitations, they had scheduled it during the summer vacation at 9:30 a.m. to keep away the students and nearly everybody else: "the hour of executing criminals . . . to execute scientific truth, yes, to kill the free spirit of Paul Broca!!!" Police agents "teeming both in the audience and in the buildings around . . . Yesterday's *Figaro* expressed concern as to possible incidents, regrettable protests against the materialistic doctrine of the late scientist. . . ."[5]
. . ."[5]

No doubt Mme. Broca, far more conservative than her late husband had been, was only too anxious to prevent any flare-up of the partisan passions she had known only too well. And had he not hated crowds, abhorred ostentation? Had he not once groaned "that man will wreck everything," meaning the same de Mortillet, who had advertised Broca's School of Anthropology, just about to be opened, as a "School for Free Thought"?[6]

Of the fifty sculptors competing, a deaf-mute artist named Choppin was given the prize contributed, on the initiative of the Société d'Anthropologie, by official subscription. Choppin's work was chosen because the jury thought, "the thinker, the scientist, the unpretentious and good-natured man whose memory was to be perpetuated ought to be shown the way we so often had seen him work in his laboratory, in his everyday clothes and unposed . . . his head bare . . . inclined . . . meditative. . . ." Duly reported in the medical press the low-keyed, semi-private ceremony taking place, after all, in the heart of academic Paris, acquired a touch of color from the presence of a Russian: Anatole Boghdanov. The professor had expressly come all the way from Moscow bearing two wreaths, one of his own, the other on behalf of the Imperial Society of Friends of the Natural Sciences and Ethnography, Section of Anthropology, to honor "'the savant of genius, the eminent man and founder . . .' Too moved to offer his reminiscences of their long and lasting friendship himself, he asked M. de Quatrefages to be his interpreter."

Broca was also survived by a daughter, Pauline, and two sons. Auguste, author of an early text on pediatric neurosurgery,[7] was one of the leading pediatric surgeons of his time; André, Professor of Medical Physics at the Paris Faculté de Médecine. Two dozen great-grandchildren live in Paris, with their respective multiple offspring, who rightly can and, with the appropriate smile, do call Paul Broca their "ancestor" in a mixture of pride and modesty. Alive also, but in the public domain, are two monuments he himself created: the French Society and the French Institute of Anthropology, the latter recently celebrating its hundredth anniversary.

This tribute has testified to the many "areas" that have remained associated with his name. May it be worthy of its subject.

References to Bibliography
(by chapter)

KEY TO ABBREVIATIONS

C I   Paul Broca Correspondence 1841– 1857, Vol. I
C II   Ibid., Vol. II
P.B.No.   Pozzi — Bibliographie *Rev. d'Anthropologie,* 2e sér. Vol. 2
           pp. 595– 608. (Numbered by F. S.)
B.S.A.   Bulletin de la Société d'Anthropologie (Paris)
T. & T.   Paul Broca: Exposition des Titres et Travaux
           Paris, April, 1862
M.A.P.B.   Mémoires d'Anthropologie de Paul Broca, Vol. 5

INTRODUCTION
(pages 1– 6)

1. Tillaux, 1880.
2. Beddoe, 1891.
3. Gardner, 1957, p. 158.
4. Critchley, 1961.
5. Garrison, 1929, p. 493.
6. Laborde, 1880.
7. Cornil, 1880.
8. See Ch. VII, below.
9. See Ch. XII, below.
10. See Ch. IX, below.
11. Bernard, 1865 (1957), p. 111.
12. See Ch. XIV, below.
13. P.B. No. 195, 1855.
14. P.B. No. 338, 1870.
15. Horteloup, 1884.
16. P.B. No. 203, 230 . . . 1857 and 1875.
17. Schreider, 1963.
18. Leguèbe, 1977.
19. Boymier, 1880.

CHAPTER I. SAINTE-FOY-LA-GRANDE
(pages 7– 15)

1. Isaac and Bonifacio, 1952.
2. Maurois, 1947.
3. Musée de l'Assistance Publique, Paris, Exhibit No. 573.
4. Corriger, 1950.
5. Cordier, Mlle., no date.
6. Palay, 1932.
7. Gagnebin, 1879.
8. Corriger, 1950.
9. Boymier, 1880.
10. Genty, 1935.
11. Reclus, 1880.
12. Broca, P.J.B., 1816.
13. M. S. Broca family
14. Faure, 1935.
15. Eschenauer, 1882.
16. Pennyman, 1952.
17. Sénet, 1956.
18. Nouvel, 1948.

CHAPTER II. CARABIN
(pages 16– 34)

1. Simond, 1900.
2. C I, 3/15/1842, p. 50.
3. C I, 11/5/41, p. 17.
4. C I, 10/25/1841, p. 6.
5. C I, 12/25/41, p. 26.
6. C I, 11/5/41, p. 18.

7. C I, 5/4/42, p. 80.
8. C I, 10/17/41, p. 3.
9. C I, 10/17/41, p. 2.
10. C I, 10/25/41, p. 8.
11. C I, 10/22/41, p. 5.
12. C I, 11/5/41, p. 16.
13. C I, 12/41, p. 25.
14. C I, 1/21/42, p. 30.
15. C I, 1/21/42, p. 31.
16. C I, 3/21/42, p. 51.
17. C I, 3/30/42, p. 57.
18. C I, 4/13/42, p. 62–63.
19. C I, 4/24/42, p. 65–66.
20. C I, 5/1/42, p. 69.
21. C I, 6/29/42, p. 82.
22. C I, 5/18/42, p. 76.
23. C I, 6/29/42, p. 84–85.
24. C I, 11/25/42, p. 100.
25. C I, 12/19/42, p. 107.
26. C I, 12/29/42, p. 110.
27. C I, 4/22/1844, p. 211.
28. C I, 3/19/1843, p. 122.
29. C I, 4/22/1844, p. 209.
30. C I, 12/12/42, p. 105.
31. C I, 4/2/43, p. 129.
32. C I, 5/15/43, p. 147.
33. C I, 11/25/43, p. 180.
34. C I, 12/17/43, p. 183.
35. C I, 1/11/44, p. 187.

36. C I, 2/10/44, p. 196.
37. C I, 3/6/44, p. 197.
38. C I, 5/5/44, p. 213.
39. C I, 5/26/44, p. 218.
40. C I, 6/13/44, p. 226.
41. C I, 7/3/44, p. 228.
42. C I, 1/11/44, p. 188.
43. C I, 4/22/44, p. 210.
44. C I, 3/31/44, p. 205.
45. C I, 10/12/44, p. 241.
46. C I, 6/19/44, p. 203.
47. C I, 11/10/44, p. 247.
48. C I, 12/21/44, p. 255.
49. C I, 12/28/44, p. 257.
50. C I, 1/29/45, p. 265.
51. C I, 4/4/45, p. 281.
52. C I, 4/6/45, p. 287.
53. C I, 5/21/45, p. 292.
54. C I, 5/30/45, p. 295.
55. Hunter and Macalpine, 1963, p. 106.
56. C I, 7/11/45, p. 298.
57. C I, 1/30/46, p. 337.
58. C I, 7/25/45, p. 301.
59. C I, 11/9/45, p. 309.
60. C I, 11/25/45, p. 314.
61. C I, no date (end 1845 or early 1846), p. 334.

CHAPTER III. UPHEAVAL ONE

(pages 35–46)

1. C I, 1/28/1844, p. 191.
2. C I, 11/25/45, p. 317.
3. C Cabanès, 1913, p. 453.
4. P.B.: Poems, M.S. private collection.
5. C I, "end 1845,", p. 321–323.
6. C I, 11/9/45, p. 312.
7. C I, 1/2/46, p. 331.
8. C I, January, 46, p. 335.
9. C I, 12/8/45, p. 319.
10. Les Écoles, 1845–1846, pp. 212–222.
11. Ibid., pp. 258–260.
12. Ibid., pp. 273–279.
13. C I, 1/12/47, p. 374.
14. Prigent, 1962, pp. 8, 21.
15. P.B., Gaz. Hebd. 1854.
16. C I, 1/30/46, p. 336.
17. C I, 11/25/45, p. 316.
18. C I, 3/14/46, p. 345.
19. C I, "June 47," (probably 1846), p. 405.

20. C I, 7/28/46, p. 348.
21. C I, 8/5/46, p. 349.
22. C I, 11/4/46, p. 353.
23. Delauney, P., 1912.
24. C I, 12/28/46, p. 367.
25. C I, December 1846, pp. 362–366.
26. C I, no date—December 1847, pp. 415–419.
27. C I, January 1847, p. 369.
28. C I, 2/1/47, p. 383.
29. C I, 3/24/47, p. 385.
30. Lameyre, 1958, pp. 16, 33, 34.
31. Paris, Guide Michelin.
32. P.B. No. 293, 1850.
33. C I, 4/23/47, p. 389.
34. C II, 1/25/49, p. 88.
35. C I, 1/12/47, pp. 373–379.
36. C I, 8/13/47, p. 412.
37. C I, No date, (December 47?), pp. 441–46.
38. C I, 4/11/46, p. 356.
39. Guillain, 1959, p. 9.

40. C I, No date (December 47?),
p. 416.
41. C I, No date (November 47?),
p. 430.

42. C II, No date, (July or August
1850?), p. 199.

CHAPTER IV. UPHEAVAL TWO
(pages 47– 58)

1. C II, 2/23/48, p. 3.
2. C II, 2/25/48, p. 5.
3. Jarry, 1945.
4. Postgate, 1920.
5. Jackson J.H., 1958.
6. Wilson E., 1940.
7. Prudhommeaux.
8. C I, February, 47, p. 383.
9. Wilson E., 1940.
10. C II, 2/25?/48, pp. 5– 8.
11. C II, early March, 48?, p. 9.
12. C II, March 48, p. 18.
13. C II, 3/11/48, pp. 12– 18.
14. C II, 3/27/48, p. 19.
15. C II, March– April 48, pp. 24– 27.
16. C II, 4/15/48, p. 28.

17. C II, 4/27/48, p. 34.
18. Wolf, J.B., 1963, pp. 202– 211.
19. C II, 5/16?/48, p. 41.
20. C II, 6/1/48, p. 42.
21. C II, 6/14/48, p. 43.
22. C II, 6/27?/48, p. 44.
23. C II, End of January, 48, p. 45.
24. C II, 7/18/48, p. 47.
25. C II, 8/21/48, p. 52.
26. C II, 9/21/48, p. 57.
27. P.B. No. 238, 1867.
28. C II, 1/11/49, p. 79.
29. C II, 9/21/48, p. 56.
30. C II, 12/30/48, p. 76.
31. C II, 1/25/49, p. 88.
32. Achard, 1924.

CHAPTER V. CANCER AND THE MICROSCOPE
(pages 59– 76)

1. Lebert H., 1845.
2. Rooseboom, M., 1956.
3. Lebert Biog., 1869.
4. Ackerknecht, 1958.
5. Liddell, 1960.
6. Ackerknecht, 1953. p. 53.
7. Cole, 1962.
8. P.B. No. 9, 1849.
9. C I, 7/2/45, p. 302.
10. C II, 12/27/48, p. 72.
11. C II, February 49, p. 94.
12. C II, December 49, p. 162.
13. Des Granges, 1938.
14. C II, End February 50, p. 170.
15. C II, 11/26/50, p. 221.
16. P.B. No. 57, 1852. p. 457.
17. Ibid., p. 458.
18. Ibid., p. 460.
19. Ibid., p. 463.
20. Ibid., p. 474.
21. Garrison, 1929, p. 454.
22. Ibid., pp. 520, 459, 510, 523.
23. Weiner, 1968.
24. P.B. No. 57, 1852, p. 470.
25. P.B. No. 57, 1852, p. 474.
26. Ibid., pp. 474– 483.

27. Ibid., p. 480.
28. Ibid., pp. 482– 483.
29. Ibid., p. 494.
30. Ibid., p. 495.
31. Ibid., p. 496.
32. Ackerknecht, 1958.
33. Ibid., p. 504.
34. Ibid., p. 515.
35. Ibid., pp. 517– 519.
36. Ibid., pp. 522– 523.
37. Ibid., p. 525.
38. Ackerknecht, 1953, p. 96.
39. Wilson, W., 1944.
40. P.B. No. 57, 1852, pp. 539– 40.
41. Ibid., 1852, pp. 603– 620.
42. Ibid., 1852, pp. 724– 731.
43. Garrison, 1929, p. 560.
44. Watson, 1844, p. 912.
45. P.B. No. 151, 1866, p. 370.
46. Clemenceau, 1867.
47. C II, 12/18 or 20, 50, p. 227.
48. C II, 1/20/51, p. 237.
49. Horteloup, 1884.
50. C II, 3/15/55, p. 361.
51. Velpeau, 1858, p. IX– LVII.
52. P.B. Moniteur des Hôp., 10/16/54.

53. P.B. No. 119, 1861.
54. P.B. No. 151, 1866 and 1869.
55. Ibid. Vol. 1, pp. 360– 370.
56. C II, 5/29/55, p. 370.

57. Moissenet, *Gaz. Hebd.* 3, 5/9/56, pp. 324– 330.
58. Cabanès, 1917, p. 80.

CHAPTER VI. TRIFLES AND TRIBULATIONS
(pages 77– 89)

1. Sterne, ed. 1941, p. 133.
2. C II, 9/21/48, p. 57.
3. C II, 12/28/48, p. 74.
4. C II, 12/27/48, p. 73.
5. Pozzi, Rev. Sci., 1882.
6. C II, 1/25/49, p. 85.
7. C II, 4/9/49, pp. 106– 108.
8. C II, 4/15/49, p. 109.
9. C II, 4/20/49, pp. 110– 112.
10. Lebert., Biog., 1869.
11. C II, 5/22/49, p. 122.
12. C II, 5/25/49, p. 127.
13. C II, 5/27/49, p. 128.
14. Aubrey, 1938.
15. Billy, 1954, p. 239.
16. Jarry, 1945.
17. C II, 12/8/51, p. 273.
18. C II, 12/28/51, p. 274.
19. P.B. No. 239, 1879.
20. M.S. Wellcome Library Hist. Med., London.
21. M.S. Archives Nationales de France, Paris 51HP2.
22. C II, 4/19/50, pp. 180– 185.
23. C I, 11/21/47, p. 433.
24. C II, 6/6/51, p. 256.
25. C II, 6/16/51, p. 258.
26. C II, 12/30/49, p. 164.
27. C II, April, 1851 (?), p. 248.
28. C II, July, 1850, p. 194.
29. C II, 11/14/50, p. 213.
30. Huard, 1961.
31. Reclus, P., 1880.
32. Horteloup, 1884.
33. C I, 11/25/43, p. 180.
34. Pozzi, *Rev. Sci.*, 1882.
35. C II, November 1851, p. 271.
36. C II, 3/9/53 to 6/7/53, pp. 279– 303.
37. C II, July 1851, p. 263.

CHAPTER VII. RICKETS TO ROTIFERS
(pages 90– 119)

1. Ornstein, 1928, p. 257– 263.
2. Richard, 1875, p. 1– 10.
3. Delauney, H., 1902.
4. Lebert, 1869.
5. P.B. No. 235, 1861.
6. C I, April or May, 1847, p. 394.
7. C I, June, 1847, p. 397.
8. P.B. No. 45, 1852.
9. Ackerknecht, 1953, p. 78.
10. Virchow, 1853.
11. P.B. No. 30, 1850.
12. P.B. No. 1, 1847; No. 5, 1848; No. 14, 1850.
13. C II, February 1851, p. 239.
14. Adams and Denny-Brown, 1954.
15. P.B. No. 3a, 1850.
16. Ibid., 1852.
17. Valentin, 1961, p. 188.
18. P.B. No. 62, 1852.
19. P.B. No. 63, 1852.
20. P.B. No. 56, 1852.
    See Debout, 1868, p. 65, fig. 28.
    See Weber, 1834, pp. 44– 73.
21 P.B. Bull. Soc. Anat., 27:533, 544, 1852.
22. Ibid., 1850.
23. P.B. Bull. Soc. Anat., IV:265– 268; 1853 VI:211, 1855; X:25, pp. 32– 37, 1859.
24. P.B. No. 43, 1852.
25. P.B. Costello, 1861.
26. P.B. No. 58, 1852.
27. P.B. No. 105, 1850.
28. P.B. No. 90, 1855.
29. P.B. 89, 1855.
30. P.B. No. 8, 1849.
31. P.B. No. 18, 1850.
32. Gray, 1973, p. 1330. Kistner, 1965, p. 25.
33. P.B. No. 34, 1851.
34. C II, 5/14/49, pp. 119– 121.
35. Hirschfeld, 1866.
36. Bull. Soc. Cl, 3:235, 1852.
37. P.B. No. 70, 1853.
38. P.B. No. 63, 1852.
39. Rochard, 1875, pp. 428– 432.

40. P.B, No. 70, 1853.
41. C II, 12/28/55, p. 393.
42. C II, 8/11/55, p. 380.
43. P.B. No. 203, 204, 1857.
44. C II, 1853, pp. 307–09.
45. P.B. No. 65b, 1853.
46. P.B. No. 98, 1857.
47. Wangensteen, 1962.
48. P.B. No. 143, 1864.
49. T & T. No. 40, 1868.
50. Rochard, 1875.
51. C II, 1854, p. 327.
52. Belina, 1870.
53. P.B. No. 213, 1863/4.
54. Ricord, 1838, pp. 87–94,
   133–134, 200 ff.
   Proksch, 1895 v. 2, p. 731 ff.
55. P.B. No. 69, 1853.
56. McIntyre, 1947, p. 1 ff.
57. Chassaignac, 1859–1860.
58. Goodman and Gillman, 1955,
   p. 596.
59. Eckman, 1963, p. 2.
60. P.B. No. 111, 1859.
61. P.B. No. 212, 1859.
62. Braid, 1843 (1960).
63. P.B. 109, 109a, 109b., 1859 (1860).

64. Boring, 1957, pp. 116–133.
65. P.B. No. 93, 1856.
66. T. & T. (1) Gaz. Hebd.,
   December 1853 to January 1855.
67. Willius and Dry, 1948.
68. Matas, 1914–1921, Vol. 5, p. 228.
69. Allen, Barker and Hines, 1955.
70. P.B. No. 157, 1866.
71. Garrison, 1929, p. 109.
72. P.B. No. 217, 1866.
73. P.B. No. 233, 1856 (1863).
74. DeCastelnau Mon. des Hôp.,
   July 1856.
75. Gley, 1899.
76. Olmsted, 1946, pp. 34, 40, 80.
77. P.B. No. 82, 1855.
78. Olmsted, 1946, pp. 9, 13–15, 35.
79. C II, 8/11/55, p. 377.
80. P.B. Letter in Mon. des Hôp., 1856,
   p. 833.
81. P.B. No. 116, 1860.
82. (a) Oparin, 1968.
   (b) Beadle & Beadle, 1966,
   pp. 13, 180.
83. (a) Keilin, 1958 (1959).
   (b). Hinton and Blum, 1965.
84. Magath, 1937.

CHAPTER VIII. FOUNDING, FATHERING, FEUDING
(pages 120–135)

1. C II, 4/10/1851, p. 252.
2. C II, 3/3/1854, p. 325ff.
3. Prigent, 1962, p. 35.
4. C II, 12/28/1844, p. 392ff.
5. C II, 12/5/1854, p. 345ff.
6. C II, 9/1/1854, p. 337ff.
7. C II, 2/10/1854, p. 320ff.
8. C II, 9/1/1854, p. 339ff.
9. C II, 1/3/1855, p. 316.
10. C II, January, 1855, p. 354ff.
11. Aubry, 1938, p. 184.
12. Sachaile, 1845.
13. P.B. No. 104, 1858.
14. C II, February, 1857, p. 436ff; 440ff.
15. C II, October, 1855, p. 386.
16. Archives Nationales, Paris.
17. Family possession.
18. B.P. No. 501, 1864 and Consistoire

   Genéral de Paris, Régistre Paroissial
   et Electoral, 1852–1879; Délibera-
   tions July to November, 1864 pp.
   65–70.
19. Gley, 1899.
20. P.B. No. 82, 1855.
21. P.B. No. 116, 1859 (1860).
22. P.B. No. 295 to 298, 1858–1859.
23. Vallois, 1940.
24. Pozzi, 1880.
25. Penniman, 1952.
26. Balzac, 1836 (1837?), last page.
27. Count, 1946; Penniman, 1952.
28. P.B. No. 293, 1850 (1848).
29. Pozzi, 1880.
   Fletcher, 1913 (1882).
   Bull. Soc. d'Anthrop., 1:1ff, 1859.
30. Baillarger, 1840.

CHAPTER IX. THE HUMAN GROUP
(pages 136–164)

1. P.B. No. 325, 1866.
2. B.S.A. 2e ser. J.Z., 1879,
   pp. 708–712.

3. P.B. No. 469, 1859/1860.
4. P.B. No. 295, 1858/1859, p. 514.
5. Ibid., pp. 601–625

6. Lincoln, 1858, pp. 369– 370; 457– 458.
7. Coon, 1963, p. 658.
8. P.B. No. 298, 1860, pp.292– 293.
9. P.B. No. 469, 1859/1860, p.
10. Schaefer, 1931 and 1932.
11. Pruner-Bey, 1865 and 1868.
12. Ibid., 1862, B.S.A.3:238– 242.
13. P.B. No. 306, 1862.
14. Pruner-Bey, 1862, B.S.A.3:332– 228.
15. Discussion, Ibid., 1862, 374– 457.
16. P.B. No. 474, 1862.
17. P.B. No. 477, 1864.
18. Billy, 1954.
19. P.B. No. 478, 1864.
20. P.B. No. 476, 1864, 1866, 1869.
21. Meillet and Cohen, 1952.
22. P.B. No. 440, 1862.
23. P.B. No. 436, 1861.
24. P.B. No. 317, 1863 (1865).
25. P.B. No. 449, 1866 and 1867.
26. Penniman, 1952.
    Sénet, 1956.
    Boule and Vallois, 1957.
27. Prestwich, 1901, pp. 73– 92.
28. Boule & Vallois, 1957.
29. B.S.A., 1859/1860, pp. 58– 60.
30. Penniman, 1952, p. 222.

31. P.B. No. 302, 1859.
32. Boule and Vallois, 1957, p.1ff, p. 195ff.
33. Penniman, 1952, p. 69.
34. Lartet, 1868, B.S.A. 2e sér. v. 3:334– 349.
35. P.B. No. 452, 1868.
36. P.B. No. 454, 1868.
37. Morton, 1839, p. 131 and plate XI-D.
38. P.B. No. 451, 1867.
39. Lastres and Cabiezes, 1960, p. 56ff 87, 96– 98.
40. Prunières, 1874, B.S.A. 2e sér. v.9:185– 189.
41. Ibid., 1874, p. 494– 495.
42. P.B. No. 356, 1874.
43. Walker, 1951, pp. 285– 286.
44. P.B.No. 376, 1876 and 1877.
45. P.B. No. 465, 1876.
46. Bataillard, 1876, pp. 321– 385.
47. P.B. No. 470, 1860.
48. P.B. No. 305, 1862.
49. P.B. No. 330, 1867.
50. P.B. No. 416, 1873.
51. P.B. No. 318, 1879 (2nd ed.)
52. P.B. No. 318, 1865 (1st ed.).
53. Fletcher, 1882.
54. Hoyme, 1953.

CHAPTER X. A MANNER OF NOT SPEAKING
(pages 165– 211)

1. Schenck (ius), 1585, p. 180.
2. Leuret and Gratiolet, 1839 [1857] v. 1, pp. 399.
3. P.B. No. 271, 1876.
4. P.B. No. 496, 1865.
5. Gratiolet, 1854.
6. Ackerknecht and Vallois, 1956.
7. Temkin, 1947.
8. Boring, 1957, Ch. 7.
9. Gratiolet, 1854, pp. 101– 102.
10. Foville and Pinel-Granchamps, 1823.
11. Meynert, 1885 (1892), p. 86ff.
12. Gratiolet, 1854, pp. 10ff, 58.
13. Ibid., 1854, p. 65ff.
14. Pozzi, 1880.
15. B.S.A., 1869, 2e sér., V.4, p. 570.
16. Lutaud, 1925.
17. Sachaile, 1845.
18. Bouillaud, 1825.
19. Ibid., 1839.
20. Ibid., 1848.
21. B.S.A., V.2, pp. 84– 86.

22. Ibid, pp. 465ff.
23. Ibid., p. 286.
24. P.B. No. 240a, B.S.A., vol. 2, pp. 301– 309.
25. B.S.A., 1861, V.2, pp. 429– 430.
26. Gratiolet B.S.A., 1861, V.2, pp. 66– 81.
27. Auburtin, B.S.A. 1861, V.2, pp. 139– 204.
28. Ibid., V.2, p. 435.
29. Ibid., pp. 139– 204.
30. Ibid., p. 301.
31. Ibid., p. 422.
32. P.B. No. 240, 1861, pp. 313– 319.
33. Bonin, 1960, p. XI.
34. Goldstein, 1970, p. 259– 263.
35. P.B. No. 241, 1861.
36. P.B. No. 245, 1861. Bonin (English translation, only partly followed here): 1960, pp. 49– 72.
37. Foville, 1844.
38. Marie, 1906.

39. Joynt, 1961.
   Schiller, 1963.
40. Fritsch and Hitzig, 1870.
41. P.B. No. 247, 1861.
42. Schiller, 1970.
43. Marie, 1906.
44. P.B. No. 248, 1863.
45. P.B. No. 249, 1863.
46. P.B. T. & T., "April, 1862" (1863), p. 67.
47. Bull. Acad. Méd. 28:497, 1863, March, 24, No. VI (correspondence manus.).
48. Souques, 1928.
49. Dax, 1865 (1836).
50. Ombredane, 1951, p. 48.
51. P.B. Bull. Soc. Anat., 37:1862.
52. P.B. No. 253, 1864.
53. Bouchard, 1864.
54. C II, December 18 or 20, 1850, pp. 227.
55. P.B. 255a, 1865.
56. Bull. Acad. Méd. V. 30, 1865, pp. 173– 175. (Lélut)
57. Ibid. V. 30 pp. 575– 600, 604– 638.
58. P.B. B.S.A., 1865, V.6, pp. 493– 494.
59. Bull. Acad. Méd. (Trousseau), 1665, V.30 pp. 658– 675.
60. Trousseau, 1865, pp. 571– 626.
61. P.B. No. 252, 1864.
62. P.B. No. 277, 1877.
63. Stookey, 1963.
64. Boring, 1963, pp. 37,58,59.
65. Critchley, 1964.
66. Family letters, 1865.
67. P.B. No. 256, 1866, pp. 383– 384.
68. P.B. Sur le siège de la faculté du langage articulé (1868)
   Trib. méd. 1869, pp. 254– 256, 265– 269.
69. Bateman, 1865.
70. P.B., Wellcome Library, London, 4/20/68.
71. Lancet II, 1868, pp. 226.
72. Ibid., pp. 259– 260.
73. Ibid., p. 386.
74. Jackson, H. (Brain, 1879– 1880, Vol. 2), pp. 203– 222. Also Selected Writings, 1931, Vol. 2, p. 171.
75. Baillarger, Bull Acad. Med., 1865, Vol. 30, pp. 816– 832; 840– 853.
76. Jackson, (Med. Times & Gazette 1868– 69 and Selected Wr. 1931) Vol. 2, p. 223 fn.
77. Ibid., p. 123.
78. Brain, R., 1961, p. 147.
79. Moutier, Head, Brain, etc.
80. Baginsky, 1871.
81. Wernicke, 1874.
82. Papez in Haymaker & Schiller, 1970, p. 57.
83. Freud, 1891.
84. Jones, 1953, Vol. 1. pp. 65, 189, 212– 214.
85. Marie, 1906.
86. Chevalier, 1959, p. 36.
87. Rev. Neurol. (Paris), 1908, W. 16 pp. 611– 636, 974– 1047.
88. Head, 1926.
89. Moutier, 1908.
90. Penfield and Roberts, 1959.
91. Rasmussen & Milner, 1977, p. 238– 257.
92. Zangwill, 1977, p. 258– 263.

CHAPTER XI. PORTRAITS AND PROJECTS
(pages 212– 220)

1. Dureau, 1880.
2. P.B. T. & T, 1863.
   All obituarists, 1880,1882.
3. Reclus, P., 1880.
4. Pozzi, 1880.
5. d'Écherac, 1909.
6. Cornil, 1880.
7. P.B. No. 236, 1868.
8. C II 1/29/49, pp. 91– 92.
9. Temkin, 1947.
10. Rey, 1895.
11. P.B. 155, 1866 (1867).
12. P.B. No. 270, 1876.
13. P.B. No. 264, 1876.
14. Wunderlich, 1868.
15. P.B. No. 231, 1879.
16. Fishgold, 1963.
17. Lombard, 1878.
18. Schiff, 1870.
19. Mosso, 1894.
20. Berger, 1910, pp. 120,121,123.
21. P.B. No. 258, 1867.
22. P.B. No. 218 & 219, 1866– 1880.
23. Trélat, 1880.
24. P.B. No. 225, 1870.
25. Lancet II, 1868.
26. Bull. Soc. Chir., 1864 (1865) 2e sér. V.5, 571– 582.

27. Assistance Publique,
undated pamphlet.
28. Beatty, 1956.

29. Beatty et al, B.S.A., 1869, 2e sér.
V.4, 685– 688, 705– 717.
30. White, 1894 (1955), Vol. 1, p. 296ff.

CHAPTER XII. THE FLAWS OF EVOLUTION
(pages 221– 235)

1. P.B. No. 295– 298, 1858– 1859.
2. Darwin, 1859 (1872 and 1958).
3. P.B. No. 328, 1867.
and B.S.A., 1866, 2e s'r.
Vol. 1.:593– 603.
4. P.B. No. 321,322, 1865 and 1866.
5. P.B. No. 336, 1869.
6. Huxley, 1863.
7. P.B. No. 338, 1870.
8. Blinderman, 1959.
9. Darlington, 1959.
10. Darwin, 1872 (1958), p. 194.

11. Baildon (Butler), 1880, p. 146.
Ehrlich and Holm, 1962.
12. Huxley (Dampier), 1952, p. 280.
13. P.B. No. 343, 1872.
14. P.B. No. 350, 1873, Discussion,
pp. 268– 293.
15. Darwin, 1872 (1958), p. 263.
16. Mayr, 1963.
17. Ibid. (Stebbins), 1963, p. 168.
18. Iltis, 1932, pp. 127,155.
19. P.B. No. 334, 1869.
20. Darwin, 1872 (1958), p. 280.

CHAPTER XIII. GROUP INHUMANITY
(pages 236– 246)

1. C I, Easter, 1843, p.133ff.
2. P.B. No. 236, 1862.
3. Aubry.
4. M.S. Hôpital Val-de-Grâce
Museum (Paris), 1870.
5. Maurois, 1956.
6. de Quatrefages, B.S.A., 1871
2eme sér, 6:182– 185.
7. Ibid., 1872 (1871).
8. Ackerknecht, 1953, pp.209– 217.
9. P.B. No. 365, 1876.
10. P.B. No. 454, 1868.

11. Beddoe, 1891.
12. Ackerknecht, 1953, p. 234.
13. Virchow, 1880.
14. P.B. No. 484, 1872.
15. Perrier, 1909.
16. Jellinek.
17. Assistance Publique.
Archives, 1871,
MS No. 187: 1,2.
Napias, 1900, pp.32,145.
18. Pozzi, 1880.

CHAPTER XIV. AROUND THE GREAT LIMBIC LOBE OF THE MAMMALS
(pages 247– 271)

1. Achard, 1924.
2. P.B. (Pozzi), 1888, p. XXII.
3. P.B. No. 280, 288, 1878– 1879.
and M.A. P.B., 1888, Vol. 5 pp.
259– 382.
4. Bonin, 1950, p. 123.
5. Ramon & Cajal, 1955 (1901– 02),
p. 117, p. VII.
6. Soury, 1899, p. 883.
7. Papez, 1937.
8. Lewes (Brazier), 1876 (1963).
9. Edinger, 1899 (1896).
10. Barker, 1907.
11. Karplus and Kreidel, 1909 ff.
12. Burdach, 1819– 1826, Col. 2, p. 108.
13. Jackson, 1931, Vol. 1, p. 468.
14. Brodal, 1947.
15. Turner, 1890– 1891.

16. MacLean, 1949.
17. Yakovlev, 1948.
18. Gastaut, 1952.
19. Dell, 1952.
20. McLean, 1952.
21. Gastaut and Lammers, 1961, p. 39.
22. M.A.P.B., 1888, Vol. 5, p. 452.
23. Ibid., p. 451.
24. Olds, 1958.
25. M.A.B.P., 1888, Vol. 5, p. 457.
26. Fritsch and Hitzig, 1870.
27. Ferrier, 1890.
28. M.A.P.B., 1888, Vol. 5, p. 383ff.
29. Achard, 1924.
30. P.B. No. 290, 1880.
31. M.A.P.B. 1888, Vol. 5,
p. 383ff.
32. Ibid., p. 298.

33. Meynert, 1884, Vol. 1, p. 162.
34. Soury, 1899, p. 908.
35. Temkin, 1963.
36. Dally, 1884.
37. Herrick, 1933.
    Ariëns Kappers et al., 1936.
    Tilney and Riley, 1938.
38. Smith, 1896.
39. Ibid., 1910.
40. Bichat, 1802, pp. 88–89.
41. Morand, 1748.
42. M.A.P.B., 1888, Vol. 5,
    pp. 260–265.
43. Rolando, 1830.
44. M.A.P.B., 1888, Vol. 5, p. 266ff.
45. Ibid., p. 273.
46. Ibid., p. 269ff.
47. Ibid., p. 332.
48. Ibid., pp. 334–337.
49. Ibid., p. 343.
50. Ibid., p. 344.
51. Ibid, pp. 399–404.

52. Ibid, pp. 430–431.
53. Taren, 1965.
54. M.A.P.B., 1888, Vol. 5,
    p. 425.
55. Ibid., pp. 404–416.
56. Papez, 1958.
57. Adey, 1958.
58. M.A.P.B., 1888, pp. 460–461.
59. Ibid., pp. 445–449.
60. Ibid., pp. 454–455.
61. P.B. No. 346, 1872.
62. P.B. No. 279, 1878, pp. 211 and 205.
63. M.A.P.B., 1888, pp. 348, 380.
64. P.B. No. 279, 1878, p. 205.
65. Savage and Wyman, 1847.
66. P.B. No. 269,274,281, 1876–1879.
67. P.B. No. 336, 1869, p. 228.
68. P.B. No. 269, 1876.
69. Du Chaillu, 1861.
70. Bartlett, 1899, p. 141.
71. P.B. No. 269, 1876.
72. P.B. No. 278, 1878.

CHAPTER XV. "IRREMOVABLE"
(pages 272–289)

1. Sales document, with the present owner, 1872.
2. Régistre des Délibérations, Mairie, Luzarches, S.et O.
3. Dureau, 1880.
4. Pozzi, 1880.
5. Official Record of the French Senate, 3/27/68, p. 731.
6. Haberling, etc., v. 4, p. 838/9, 1932.
7. P.B. No. 219, 1867.
8. P.B. No. 481, 1867.
9. Vallois, 1940.
10. P.B.Rev. d'Anthro., 1872, Vol. 1., p. 349.
11. Verneuil, 1880.
12. Pozzi, 1880.
13. B.S.A., 1879, 2e sér. Vol. 2, p. 610.
14. DeMortillet,B.S.A., 5/2/78, 3e sér Vol. 1. p. 185.
15. Vallois, 1964.
16. P.B. Poésies, M.S., (family).
17. P.B. M.S., Wellcome Museum, London, 1863.
18. Reclus, P., 1880.
19. Pelletan, 1880.
20. Horteloup, 1884.
21. Bourgin, 1950.
22. XIXe Siècle (daily), 1/22/80.
23. Garrison, 1929, p. 493.

24. Couderau, 1866, p. 335.
25. P.B. No. 193, 1855.
26. Laborde, 1880.
27. Richelot, 1880.
28. Latour, 1880.
29. Le Figaro, 3/10/80.
30. DeMortillet, 1887.
31. Record of the Senate, No. 384, 6/21/80.
32. Unsigned. The New Yorker, 7/8/67, p. 75.
33. Lipinska, 1900, p. 358ff. and 1930, p. 125ff.
34. Seneca, 65 (1917), Ep. 54.
35. Heberden, 1807, pp. 306–314.
36. Sansom, 1881.
37. Jaccoud, 1887.
38. Hammer, 1887.
    Leibowitz, 1970, p. 135ff.
39. d'Écherac, 1909.
40. Le Temps,
    Le Figaro, 7/10/1880.
41. Pozzi, 1882.
42. Le Figaro, 7/8/1880.
43. Cornil, 7/15/1880.
44. Musée Orfila, École de Médecine, Rue des Saints-Pèters Paris VIe
45. Official Records of the French Senate, 7/9/1880.
46. Laborde, 7/11/1880, 7/18/1880.

REFERENCES TO BIBLIOGRAPHY

CHAPTER XVI. EPILOGUE: THE STATUE

(pages 290– 294)

1. Simon, 1901, pp. 257– 258.
2. Scobie and Taylor, 1975.
3. Grenouilleau, 1911.
4. Ste. Foy. Minutes of the City Council, 6/26/1888 (Courtesy M. J. Corriger).
5. DeMortillet, 1887.
6. Topinard, 1890.
7. Broca, A. and Maubrac, 1896.
8. Inauguration de Broca, *Gazette hebd. de Méd. et Chir.* 24: 1887, pp. 511– 512.

304

Broca Bibliography

(From Pozzi, S.: "Paul Broca", *Rev. d'Anthropol.* 2e Sér. Vol. 2: 593-608. With a few corrections and numbers added for reference by the author.) Pozzi points out that he has not included some unsigned journal articles and several proceedings in learned societies where Broca was a discussant, also that care was taken to keep the categories at a minimum and to indicate the chronological order within them: "to follow, at a glance, year by year, the preoccupations of that vast mind."

§I. SCIENCES MÉDICALES
Anatomie et Physiologie Normales et Pathologiques —Chirurgie
1847

1. Recherches sur l'arthrite sèche et les corps étrangers articulaires. (*Bull. Soc. anatom.*, 1847, p. 271; 1848, p. 141; 1850, p. 69, 91, 197, 239– 243; 1852, p. 49– 124. — Description didactique de l'arthrite sèche, 1850, p. 435– 455.)
2. Diverticulum de l'intestin grêle. (*Soc. anatom.* 1847, juin.)
3. Recherches sur l'anatomie pathologique des pieds-bots. (*Bull. Soc. anatom.*, 1847, p. 102 et 168. Voy. 1849, p. 265– 271 et 327– 342; 1852, p. 118 et 396– 405). — Produits par l'altération graisseuse des muscles.
3a. (*Bull. Soc. anatom.*, 1850, t. XXV, p. 40. Voy. 1851, t. XXVI, p. 50-64.)
4. Cancer du maxillaire supérieur, hyperesthésie du nerf sous-orbitaire. (*Soc. anatom.*, 1847, juin.)

1848

5. Recherches sur la pathologie des cartilages articulaires. (Dans les *Bull. Soc. anatom.*, 1848 à 1851. Voyez surtout: Sur le mode de nutrition des cartilages articulaires, 1850, p. 444– 449; sur leur cicatrisation, 1851, p. 106, 182; sur leur nécrose, p. 109, 165, 184; sur leur ossification, 1851, p. 167, 183 et 1850, p. 241; sur leur altération fibreuse, p. 169; sur leur absorption ulcéröide, p. 170, 173; sur leur altération velvétique, p. 172 et 1850, p. 240; sur les adhérences fibreuses des cartilages dans certains cas d'ankylose fibreuse, p. 363.)

1849

6. Sur les anomalies arterielles du membre thoracique. (*Bull. Soc. anatom.*, 1849, t. XXIV, p. 49, 67 et janv. 1850.)
7. Études sur les doigts et orteils surnuméraires. (*Bull. Soc. anatom.*, 1849, 1re série, t. XXIV, p. 336– 342.)
8. Description des arcades artérielles gingivales. (*Bull. Soc. anatom.*, 1849, t. XXIV, p. 282– 285.)
9. De la propagation de l'inflammation. — Quelques propositions sur les tumeurs dites cancéreuses. (Thése inaugurale, Paris, 1849, in-4°, 64 pages.)
10. Rapport sur plusieurs monstruosités présentées à la Société anatomique par M. Collin. (*Bull. Soc. anat.*, 1849, t. XXIV, p. 292– 305.) Pieds-bots voir 1847.

1850

11. Sur les kystes de l'organe de Rosenmuller. (*Bull. Soc. anatom.*, 1850, t. XXV, p. 45–47.)

12. Note sur une anomalie du rein. (*Bull. Soc. anatom.*, 1850, t. XXV, p. 165.)

13. Recherches sur les ruptures de l'aorte. (*Bull. Soc. anatom.*, 1850, t. XXV, p. 246.)

14. Notes sur la pénétration du cancer dans les veines. (*Bull. Soc. anatom.*, 1850, t. XXV, p. 45. — Voy. aussi 1852, t. XXVII, p. 272 et 470.)

15. Trois observations de véritable luxation spontanée de la hanche. (*Bull. Soc. anatom.*, 1850, t. XXV, p. 179 et 183, et 1853, t. XXVIII, p. 47.)

16. Description et interprétation d'un cas d'inversion des membres inférieurs. (*Bull. Soc. anatom.*, 1850, t. XXV, p. 185.)

17. Sur une fistule vésico-utérine produite par un calcul vésical. (*Bull. Soc. d'anatom.*, 1850, t. XXV, p. 328.)

18. Note sur l'état de la circulation capillaire du rein dans les deux premières périodes de la néphrite albumineuse. (*Bull. Soc. anatom.*, 1850, t. XXV, p. 368.)

19. Mémoire sur la pleurésie secondaire consécutive aux inflammations du sein et de l'aisselle. (*Arch. gén. de méd.*, avril 1850, 4e série, t. XXII, p. 385–422.)

20. Diminution du volume de la rate pendant la digestion stomacale. (*Soc. anatom.* 1850, nov.) — Tendon perforant le nerf médian. (*Soc. anatom.* 1850, juin).

21. Ectopie d'un rein. (*Soc. anatom.* 1850, janv.)

22. Artère thyroïdienne fournie par la mammaire interne. (*Soc. anatom.* 1850, mars.)

23. Deux uretères dans le rein gauche, le rein et l'uterère droits étant normaux. (*Soc. anatom.* 1850, juin.)

24. Inversion des membres inférieurs. (*Soc. anatom.* 1850, juin.)

25. Atrophie d'une vésicule séminale correspondant à un testicule atrophié. (*Soc. anatom.* 1850, juillet.)

26. Cancer des os iliaques fréquent chez les jeunes mères. (*Soc. anatom.* 1850, septembre.)

27. Sur l'hypertrophie partielle de la mamelle. Rapport sur un mémoire de M. Lebert. (*Bull. Soc. anatom.*, 1850, t. XXV, p. 54–58.)

28. Recherches sur les dépôts blancs qui s'observent sur les cartilages articulaires chez les gotteux. (*Bull. Soc. anatom.*, 1850, t. XXV), p. 200; 1852, XXVII, p. 172.)

29. Note sur la gangrène spontanée des tumeurs cancéreuses. (*Bull. Soc. anatom.*, 1850, t. XXV, p. 203.)

30. Sur le ramollissement des os dans la partie du squelette qui est située au-dessous des tumeurs blanches. (*Bull. Soc. anatom.*, 1850, t. XXV, p. 232–234.)

Arthrite sèche, voir 1847.

Pieds-bots, voir 1847.

Cartilages articulaires, voir 1848.

Anomalies artérielles du membre thoracique, voir 1848.

Oblitération des bourses muqueuses, voir 1852.

1851

31. Sur la consolidation des fractures des cartilages costaux. (*Bull. Soc. anatom.*, 1851, t. XXVI, p. 184, et 1855, t. XXX, p. 336.)

32. Nouvelles observations sur l'altération graisseuse des muscles et sur leur prétendue transformation fibreuse. (*Bull. Soc. anatom.*, décembre 1851, t. XXVI, p. 379–390.)

33. Sur un mode de guérison des tubercules de l'appareil testiculaire. (*Bull. Soc. anat.*, 1851, t. XXVI, p. 375.)

34. Description du sac dartoïque de la femme. (*Bull. Soc. anatom.*, 1851, t. XXVI, p. 92–98.)

35. Sur un point de l'anatomie de la rotule. (*Bull. Soc. anatom.*, 1851, t. XXVI, p. 164.)

36. Note sur l'ossification prématurée des épiphyses dans les articulations atteintes de tumeurs blanches, chez les enfants. (*Bull. Soc. anatom.*, 1851, t. XXVI, p. 245, et 1855, t. XXV, p. 39.)

37. Amputation congénitale en voie d'exécution. (*Bull. Soc. anat.*, 1851, t. XXVI, p. 250.)

38. Double pied-bot varus-équin, coïncidant avec une déviation des deux genoux. (*Soc. anatom.*, 1851, t. XXVI, p. 111. Voir aussi p. 234.)

39. Pièces relatives à la prétendue transformation fibreuse des muscles: 1° Tumeur fibreuse du biceps, 2ᵉ Atrophie du grand pectoral simulant une transformation fibreuse. (*Soc. anatom.*, 1851, t. XXVI, p. 379).

40. Anomalies des reins et des uretères. (*Soc. anatom.* 1851, mars.)

41. Muscles transverse périnéal surnuméraire. (*Soc. anatom.* 1851, juillet.)

REVUE D'ANTHROPOLOGIE 2ᵉ SÉRIE. T. III.

Pieds-bots, voir 1847.

Cartilages articulaires, voir 1848.

Cancer dans les veines, voir 1850.

1852

42. Sur l'inégal accroissement des os longs par leurs deux extrémités. (*Bull. Soc. anat.*, 1852, p. 555–557 et 576; voy. aussi p. 546–553, et Lebert, *Traité d'anat. pathol. gén. et spéc.*, in-fol., t. II, p. 587–588.)

43. Sur une luxation spontanée congénitale de la hanche. (*Bull. Soc. anat.*, 1852, t. XXVII, p. 10.)

44. État biloculaire de l'estomac chez les individus décapités pendant la digestion stomacale. (*Bull. Soc. anat.*, 1852, t. XXVII, p. 25.)

45. Mémoire sur l'anatomie pathologique du rachitisme. (*Bull. Soc. anatom.*, 1852, p. 141 et 542. — Récompensé par l'Académie des sciences en 1854.)

46. Notes sur deux abcès creusés dans l'épaisseur du cartilage épiphysaire du fémur, chez un enfant rachitique. (*Bull. Soc. anatom.*, 1852, t. XXVII, p. 183.)

47. Anomalie des quatre membres par défaut. Amputation congénitale des auteurs. (*Bull. Soc. anatom.*, 1852, t. XXVII. p. 275–294.)

48. Rapport sur un cas d'anomalies multiples des muscles et des os des quatre membres. (*Bull. Soc. anatom.*, 1852, t. XXVII, p. 390–405.)

49. Atrophie sans altération graisseuse des muscles d'un membre paralysé. (*Soc. anatom.*, 1852, t. XXVII, p. 43.)

50. Sur la gravité considérable des tumeurs fibro-plastiques. (*Soc. anatom.* 1852 janv.)

51. Période préulcérative du cancer. (*Soc. anatom.* 1852, janv.)

52. Sur les kystes des tumeurs cancéreuses. (*Soc. anatom.*, 1852, mars.)

53. Sur la forme des tubercules superficiels des muqueuses. (*Soc. anatom.* 1852, mars.)

54. Poumons en 2 lobes complètement séparés. (*Soc. anatom.*, 1852, janv.)

55. Testicule arrêté dans l'abdomen, épidydime et canal déférent descendus dans le scrotum (*Soc. anatom.*, 1852, fev.)

56. Ectromélie des quatre membres. (*Bull. Soc. anatom.*, 1852, t. XXVII, p. 275–294.)

57. Mémoire sur l'anatomie pathologique du cancer. (*Mém. Acad. méd.*, t. XVI, p. 453–820, avec 1 planche. Paris, 1852, in-4°.)

58. De l'extirpation de l'astragale. (*Gaz. des Hôpit.*, juillet, 22 juillet et 7 août 1852. — Voy. aussi *Bull. Soc. chirurg.*, 2ᵉ série, 1860, t. I, p. 281–311.)

59. Note sur l'oblitération naturelle des bourses muqueuses. (*Bull. Soc. anatom.*, 1852, t. XXVII, p. 50. — Voy. aussi 1851, t. XXVI, p. 23.)

60. Description du tissu chondroïde normal et du tissu spongoïde normal. (*Bull. Soc. anatom.*, 1852, t. XXVII, p. 542–562.)

61. Sur le ramollissement des os des membres paralysés. (*Bull Soc. anatom.*, 1852. t. XXVII, p. 119.)

62. Des difformites de la partie antérieure du pied produites par l'action des chaussures. (*Bull. Soc. anatom.*, 1852, t. XXVII, p. 60.)

63. Sur les tumeurs connues sous le nom d'oignons. (*Bull. Soc. anatom.*, 1852, t XXVII. p. 67, 232 et 461.)

1853

64. Mémoire sur la nature des affections connues sous les noms vicieux de capsulite et de kératite. (*Bull. Soc. anatom.*, 1853, t. XXVIII, p. 451–476.)

65. Recherches sur les vaisseaux de la cornée. (*Bull. Soc. anatom.*, 1853, t. XXVIII, p. 459–467, avec une figure.)

65a. Sur la thérapeutique des maladies articulaires. (*Monit. des Hôpit.*, numéros des 9, 11, et 13 août 1853.)

65b. Sur la nature des accidents produits par l'inhalation du chloroforme. (*Gaz. hebdom.*, 28 octobre, 4 et 25 novembre 1853.)

66. De la luxation des phalanges des orteils; lettre à M. le professeur Malgaigne. (*Revue médico-chirurgicale*, 1853, t. XIV, p. 153–158, — *Monit. des Hôpit.*, 11 octobre 1853.)

67. Sur l'adénopathie épithéliale. (*Bull. Soc. anatom.*, 1853, t. XXVIII, p. 379–391.)

68. Mémoire sur la cataracte capsulaire. (*Bull. Soc. anatom.*, 1853, t. XXVIII, p. 423–451).

69. Sur les effets immédiats de la syphilisation. (*Bull. Soc. chirurg.*, 1853, t. IV, p. 321 et 324.)

70. Mémoires sur les luxations sous-astragaliennes. (*Mém Soc. chirurg.*, Paris, 1853, in-4°, p. 566–646.)

71. De l'étranglement dans les hernies abdominales et des affections qui peuvent le simuler. (Thèse de concours pour l'agrégation. Paris, 1853, in-4°, 180 pages. Une seconde édition de cette thèse a été publiée en 1856. 1 vol. in-18, 270 pages. V. Masson, édit.)

Consolidation des fractures des cartilages, voir 1851.

Ossification prématurée des épiphyses, voir 1851.

1854

72. Observations relatives à l'action de la congélation sur les artères et sur les parois de l'uréthre. (*Bull. Soc. anatom.*, 1854, t. XXIX, p. 298.)

73. Sur une fracture incomplètement consolidée du fémur. (*Bull. Soc. anatom.*, 1854, t. XXIX, p. 306.)

74. Mémoire sur un cas de mort survenu à la suite du cathétérisme utérin, lu à l'Académie impériale de médecine le 31 janvier 1854.

75. Sur la structure intime du tubercule. (*Gaz. hebdom.*, 14 avril 1854, t. I, p. 453. — Lettre sur le même sujet, en réponse à M. Mandl; même volume, p. 495 et 526.)

76. Mémoire sur la nécrose des cartilages articulaires, lu à la Société médicale allemande de Paris le 11 mai 1854. (*Denkschrift zur Feier des zehnjahrigen Stiftungsfestes des Verein deutscher Ærzte in Paris*. Paris, 154, in-4°, p. 34–45. Reproduit dans le *Moniteur des Hôpitaux*, 2, 4 et 6 juillet 1855. — *The Cyclopedia of Practical Surgery*, vol. III, p. 294–298. Londres, 1861, grand in-8°.)

77. Des tumeurs fibro-plastiques. — Classification des tumeurs réputées cancéreuses. (*Monit. des hôpit.*, 7 et 9 décembre 1854.)

78. Sur la cure radicale des hernies inguinales. — Rapport lu à la Société de chirurgie (*Bull.*, 1854, t. V, p. 163–173.)

79. Sur la nature du cancroïde épithélial. — Rapport sur un mémoire de M. Oscar Heyfelder, lu à la Société de chirurgie le 16 août 1854. (*Bull. Soc. chirurg.*, t. X, p. 352–384. Voyez aussi t. VI, p. 82.)

80. Sur la réduction de la luxation de la hanche par la méthode de la flexion. (*Gazette hebdomadaire*, 3 février 1854, t. I, p. 267.)

81. Sur le traitement des hernies étranglées par les réfrigérants et la compression. (*Gazette hebdomadaire*, 9 juin 1854, t. I p. 582.)

1855

82. Propriétés et fonctions de la moelle épinière. Rapport sur quelques expériences de M. Brown-Séquard. (Société de biologie, 21 juillet 1855, *Mémoires* de cette Société, 2ᵐᵉ série, t. II, p. 23–50.) — Ce travail a été reproduit dans plusieurs journaux.

83. Observation de fracture de trois cartilages costaux produite par l'action musculaire. (*Bull. Soc. anatom.*, 1855, t. XXX, p. 338.)

84. Exostose ostéo cartilagineuse. (*Bull. Soc. chirurg.*, avant 1856.)

85. Sur le chondrome et sur la généralisation des tumeurs. (*Bull. Soc. chirurg.*, 1855, t. VI, p. 88–96.)

86. Sur le traitement des anévrysmes cirsoïdes du cuir chevelu et des tumeurs érectiles cutanées, par la méthode endermique. (*Bull. Soc. chirurg.*, 1855, t. VI, p. 148.)

87. Nouveau procédé pour l'opération du bec de lièvre compliqué. (*Bull. Soc. chirurg.*, 1855, t. VI, p. 266.)

88. Sur l'occlusion des plaies par le procédé de M. Laugier, employé comme préservatif de la pourriture d'hôpital. (*Bull. Soc. chirurg.*, 1855, t. VI, p. 279.)

89. Notes sur la structure du foie. (*Bull. Soc. anatom.*, 1855, t. XXX, p. 479.)

90. Note sur la structure de la rate. (*Bull. Soc. anatom.*, 1855, t. XXX, p. 530–533.)

91. Sur la nature épithéliale des ulcères rongeants. (*Bull. Soc. anat.*, 1855, t. XXX, p. 446.)

92. Remarques sur quelques phénomènes que l'on attribue à tort à l'inflammation. Mémoire lu à l'Académie impériale de médecine, le 17 juillet 1855. (*Bull. Acad. méd.*, t. XX, p. 1131–1151.)

1856

93. Des anévrysmes et de leur traitement. (Paris, 1856, in-8°, 1 vol. de 930 pages. Labé et Asselin, éditeurs).

94. Du traitement abortif des bubons vénériens suppurés. Mémoire lu à l'Académie impériale de médecine, le 9 septembre 1856. (*Bull. thérap.*, 1856, t. LI, p. 208–222.)

95. Sur une tumeur fibro-plastique du pied ayant récidivé dans les tendons. (*Bull. Soc. chirurg.*, 1856, t. VII, p. 114.)

96. Sur la possibilité de conserver les mouvements du genou après l'amputation de la jambe au lien d'élection. (*Bull. Soc. chirurg.*, 1856, t. VII, p. 145.)

97. Du cancer et des pseudo-cancers. (Paris, 1856, t. III. *Dict. méd. et chirurg. vértér.* de MM. Bouley et Reynal.)

1857

98. Des injections de gaz acide carbonique dans la vessie comme moyen anesthésique dans les cas d'affections douloureuses de cet organe. (*Monit. des hôpit.*, 4 août, 1857.)

99. Sur une modification de l'appareil galvanocaustique. (Lettre adressée le 10 novembre 1857 à M. le président de l'Académie impériale de médecine, dans le *Monit. des hôpit.*, 12 novembre 1857, p. 1085).

100. Ancienne luxation en arrière de la phalangette du pouce droit (le moule est au musée Dupuytren). (*Bull. Soc. chirurg.*, 13° série, t. VII, p. 80.)

101. Sur un anévrysme cirsoïde de l'artère temporale, guéri par une injection de perchlorure de fer. (*Bull. Soc. chirurg.*, 1857, t. VIII, p. 227–230.)

101a. Rapport sur une varice anévrysmale profonde, suivi de recherches sur la circulation et la nutrition des membres atteints de phlébarterie. (Lu à la Société de chirurgie, le 4 mars 1857, et *Soc. chirurg.*, t. V, p. 209–226, in-4°.)

1858

102. Des différences qui existent entre les deux principales espèces du mal vertébral. (*Bull. Soc. chirurg.*, 1858, t. VIII, p. 421 à 444.)

103. Nouvel appareil prothétique pour les cas de rupture du tendon rotulien sans cicatrisation. (*Bull. Soc. chirurg.*, 1858, t. VIII, p. 441.)

104. Sur un vaste abcès par congestion de la fosse iliaque, du pli de l'aine et de la fesse, guéri par une seule injection iodée. (*Monit. des hôpit.*, 25 février 1858.)

1859

105. Description du muscle amygdalo-glosse. (*Bull. Soc. anatom.*, 1850, t. XXV, p. 362.)

106. Reproduit dans l'Atlas d'anatomie descriptive par MM. Bonamy, Broca, et Beau dessinateur. (Grand in-8°, Victor Masson éditeur, 1866.)

107. Note sur les trois modes de l'ossification. Publiée dans le *Traité d'anatomie pathologique générale et spéciale* de M. Lebert (t. II, p. 589, in-fol.)

108. Inégalité congénitale des deux moitiés du corps. — Singulière conséquence physiologique, (*Mém. Soc. Biol.*, 1859, 3° série, t. I, p. 15–19.)

109. Sur l'anesthésie chirurgicale hypnotique. Note communiquée par M. Velpeau à l'Académie des sciences, 5 décembre 1859. — Reproduite dans le *Moniteur des sciences médicales*, 1859, t. I, p. 404, avec une lettre de rectification. Communication sur le même sujet à la Société de chirurgie. (*Bull.* de cette Société, 7 décembre 1859, t. X, p. 247–270.)

110. Mémoires sur les tumeurs myéloïdes. (*Bull. Soc. chirurg.*, 1859, t. X, p. 390–404.)

111. Sur le traitement du tétanos par le curare. (*Bull. Soc. chirurg.*, 19 oct. 1859, t. X, p. 159 à 175.)

112. Remarques sur les fractures spiroïdes et sur les régénérations osseuses. (*Bull. Soc. anat.*, 1859, t. XXIV, p. 141–159.)

113. Abcès chronique simple du canal médullaire de l'humérus, traité avec succès par la trépanation. (*Bull. Soc. chirurg.*, 26 oct, 1859, t. X, p. 187 à 197.)

114. Sur la nature du fongus du testicule. (*Bull. Soc. chirurg.*, 1859, t. IX, p. 424–428.)

115. Kystes congéniaux du cou. (*Soc. de chirurg.*, 1859, 169.)

1860

116. Étude sur les animaux ressuscitants. Paris, 1860, in-8, 150 p. avec pl. Adrien Delahaye, édit: et (*Mém. Soc. biol.*, 3° série, t. II, p. 1–140, 1860.)

117. Sur une tumeur myéloïde de la main, indépendante du squelette. (*Bull. Soc. chirurg.*, 1860, 2° série, t. I, p. 342.)

118. Remarques sur l'étiologie, la propagation et la récidive de l'épithéliôme. (*Bull. Soc. chirurg.*, 1860, 2e série, t. I, p. 597–602.) Extirpation de l'astragale, voir 1852.

1861

119. Article Tumors du *Dictionnaire de chirurgie* de Costello. (Dans *The Cyclopedia of Practical Surgery*. London, 1861, gr. in-8°, vol. IV, p. 286–522.)

120. Necrosis of Bones and of articular Cartilages (Nécrose des os et des cartilages articulaires). (*Dictionnaire de chirurgie* de Costello. *The Cyclopedia of practical surgery*, vol. III, p. 248–305, London, 1861, grand in-8° à 2 col.)

121. Osteitis ostéite). (*Dictionnaire de chirurgie* de Costello. *The Cyclopedia of practical Surgery*, vol. III, p. 377–430, London 1861, grand in-8°.)

122. Osteophymy (Tubercule des os). (*Dictionnaire de chirurgie de Costello. The Cyclopedia of practical Surgery*, vol. III, p. 431–447. London, 1861, in-8°.)

123. Perchloride of Iron (perchlorure de fer.) (*Dictionnaire de chirurgie* de Costello. *The Cyclopedia of practical Surgery*, vol. III, p. 605, London, 1861, gr. in-8°.)

124. Observation et discussion d'un cas de rachitisme. (*Anatom. pathol. gén. et spéc.* de M. Lebert, 39e livraison. Paris, 1861, in-fol., t. II, p. 585–590, pl. CLXVIII et CLXIX.)

125. Sur les concrétions intracrâniennes dites pétrifications du cerveau. (*Bull. Soc. anatom.*, 1861 ou 1862.)

126. Recherches thermométriques applicables au diagnostic des oblitérations artérielles. (*Bull. Soc. chirurg.*, 1861, 2e série, t. II, p. 334–346, p. 441–450, p. 632–634, t. III, p. 125.)

127. Recherches sphygmographiques applicables au diagnostic des anévrysmes. (*Bull. Soc. chirurg.*, 1861, 2e série, t. II, p. 346.)

128. Nécrose des cartilages articulaires, voir 1854.

1862

129. Sur un nouveau signe des abcès qui communiquent avec l'intérieur du canal médullaire. (*Bull. Soc. chirurg.*, 1862, 2e série t. III, p. 300 et 345.)

130. Sur le traitement des adénômes et des tumeurs irritables de la mamelle par la compression. (*Bull. gén. de thérap.*, février et mars 1862.)

131. Sur un bec-de-lièvre, qui remontait jusqu'au grand angle de l'œil. Autoplastie pratiquée avec succès. (*Bull. Soc. chirurg.* 1862, 2e série, t. III, p. 92–101.)

132. Sur un cas de tétanos traumatique traité sans succès par le curare. (*Bull. Soc. chirurg*, 1862, 2e série, t. III, p. 176–179.)

133. Expériences sur l'incubation des œufs à deux jaunes. (Comptes rend. *Soc. biolog.*, t. III, p. 154–161 et *Annales des sciences naturelles*, 1862, 4e série, t. XVII, 1e cahier.)

134. Sur la méningite et la phlébite rachidiennes consécutives aux eschares du sacrum. (*Bull. Soc. chirurg.*, 1862, 2e série, t. III, p. 51.)

135. Sur la lésion de la moelle dans le tétanos traumatique. (*Bull. Soc. chirurg.*, 1862, 2e série, t. III, p. 173.)

136. Sur un cas de lipômes généralisés. (*Bull. Soc. chirurg.*, 1862, t. III, p. 243–255.)

137. Sur deux cas d'épithéliômes consécutifs de très anciens ulcères de la jambe. (*Bull. Soc. chirurg.*, 1862, t. III, p. 493.)

1863

138. Sur une nouvelle variété d'anévrysme artério-veineux et sur un nouveau procédé hémostatique applicable à la ligature des artères très dilatées. (*Bull. Soc. chirurg.*, 1863 2e série, t. IV, p. 392–402.)

139. Sur une tumeur du maxillaire inférieur constituée par une hypergénèse des éléments du bulbe dentaire. (*Bull. Soc. chirurg.*, 1863, 2e série, t. IV, p. 233.)

140. Sur la structure des tumeurs érectiles. (*Bull. Soc. chirurg.*, 1863, 2e série, t. IV, p. 466.)

1864

141. Adénomes. (*Dictionn. encyclopédique des sciences médicales.* Paris, 1864.)

142. Sur les tumeurs hypertrophiques de la pulpe dentaire. (*Bull. Soc. chirurg.,* 1864, 2ᵉ série, t. V, p. 271.)

143. Sur un cas de nymphomanie invétérée traitée par l'infibulation. (*Bull. Soc. chirurg.,* 1864, 2ᵉ série, t. V, page 10.)

144. Expériences sur la cicatrisation des plaies des nerfs. — Influence de la suppression de l'action nerveuse sur l'inflammation et la cicatrisation. (*Bull. Soc. chirurg.,* 1864, 2ᵉ série, t. V, p. 295–296.)

1865

145. Sur un adénome de la lèvre inférieure. (*Bull. Soc. chirurg.* 1865, 2ᵉ série, t. IV, p. 298.)

146. Sur les brûlures de la muqueuse pulmonaire par la vapeur d'eau bouillante. (*Bull. Soc. chirurg.,* 1865, 2ᵉ série, t. VI, p. 322.)

147. Sur un kyste volumineux de la cuisse développé autour d'une exostose de croissance. (*Bull. Soc. chirurg.,* 1865, 2ᵉ série, t. VI, p. 200.)

148. Sur une nouvelle espèce d'exostoses appelés par l'auteur exostoses de croissance. (*Bull. Soc. chirurg.,* 1865, 2ᵉ série, t. VI, p. 200, et 1866, t, VII, p. 295.)

149. Sur deux complications nouvelles de l'anthrax de la nuque. (*Bull. Soc. chirurg.,* 1865, 2ᵉ série, t. VI, p. 447.)

1866

150. Sur l'origine des luxations congénitales de la hanche. (*Bull. Soc. chirurg.,* 1866, 2ᵉ série, t. VII, p. 329–334.)

151. Traité des tumeurs. (Deux volumes in-8° de 600 et de 540 pages avec figures. Paris, 1866 et 69, Asselin, éditeur.) Vol. I.

152. Sur un polype naso-pharyngien opéré par la ligature. (*Bull. Soc. chirurg.,* 1866, t. VII, p. 93.)

153. Sur une tumeur sous-cutanée du doigt constituée par du tissu unguéal. (*Bull. Soc. chirurg.,* 1866, 2ᵉ série, t. VII, p. 403.)

154. Sur une palatoplastie complète pratiquée avec succès dans un cas de division congénitale de la voûte palatine et du voile du palais. (*Bull. Soc. chirurg.,* 1866, 2ᵉ série t. VII, p. 433.)

155. Trépanation du crâne pratiquée avec succès dans un cas de fracture avec enfoncement et enclavement. (*Bull. Soc. chirurg.,* 1866, 2ᵉ série, t. VII, p. 508; t. VIII.)

156. Sur une luxation sous-glénoïdienne de l'humérus. (*Bull. Soc. chirurg.* 1866, 2ᵉ série, t. VII, p. 48.)

157. Sur un cas d'ulcération interne dans la caisse du tympan, traitée avec succès par la ligature de la carotide primitive. (*Bull. Soc. chirurg.,* 1886, 2ᵉ série, t. VII p. 172.) Voyez aussi t. VIII, p. 70.

1867

158. Recherches sur un nouveau groupe de tumeurs désignées sous le nom d'odontômes. Brochure in-4° de 103 pages avec figures. Décembre 1867. Un extrait de ce travail a été lu à l'Académie des sciences en décembre 1867.

159. Sur la nature et le diagnostic de la polyarthrite vertébrale. (*Tribune médic,* 22 décembre 1867. *Bull. Soc. chirurg.,* décembre 1867.)

160. Nouvelle canule pour le traitement des individus qui ont subi l'opération de la trachéotomie. (*Bull. Soc. chirurg.,* 1867, 2ᵉ série, t. VIII, p. 110, et *Bull. Soc. anatom.,* avril 1867.)

1868

161. Résection de l'articulation tibio-tarsienne pratiquée avec succès dans un cas de luxation compliquée. (*Bull. Soc. chirurg.*, séance du 22 janvier 1868.)

162. Sur le mal perforant. Deux observations avec réflexions dans un article de Lucas Championnière. (*Journal de méd. et de chir. pratiques*, 1868, t. XXXIX, p. 155–158.)

163. Traitement de la gueule-de-loup par la suture osseuse; conservation et consolidation du tubercule intermaxillaire. (*Bull. Soc. chirurg.*, 1868, 2e série, t. IX, p. 147–160.)

164. Sur l'application de la suture osseuse au traitement du bec-de-lièvre double compliqué de saillie de l'os intermaxillaire 5 et 7 mai, 2 observ. (*Gaz. des hôp.*, 1868.)

165. Sur la pilimiction et le trichiasis des voies urinaires. (*Bull. Soc. chirurg.*, 1868, 2e série t. IX, p. 260–266.)

1869

166. Sur le pansement amovo-inamovible des moignons d'amputation. (*Journal de médec. et de chirurg. pratiques*, 1869, t. XL, p. 393–396.)

167. Sur la polyarthrite vertébrale. (*Tribune médicale*, 1869.)

168. Traitement des rétrécissements spasmodiques de l'œsophage par la dilation instantanée. (*Bull. Soc. chirurg.*, 1869, 2e série, t. X, p. 280.)

169. Sur le traitement des anévrysmes cirsoïdes. (*Bull. Soc. chirurg.*, 1869, 2e série, t. X, p. 376.)

Traité des tumeurs, voir 1866. Vol. II.

1870

170. Sur le retard de la consolidation des fractures et le traitement par la suppression des appareils. (*Journal de médec. et de chirurg. pratiques*, 1870, t. XLI, p. 62–65.)

1872

171. De la déformation du crâne sous l'influence du torticolis chronique. (*Bull. Soc. d'anth.*, 1872, 2e série, t. VII, p. 21–23.)

Histoire Et Critique.
1846

172. Suppression des cliniques libres — Le Congrès médical — M. Orfila dans l'exercice de ses fonctions — Salles de dissection — Un échec de M. Orfila — M. Massiat et son cours. — Règlement des internes (Articles publiés dans le journal *les Écoles*, 1846).

1848

173. Rapport sur une observation de M. Corvisart intitulée: Cancer du foie, tubercules pulmonaires (*Soc. anatom.* 1848, t. XXIII, p. 46).

1850

174. Compte rendu des travaux de la Société anatomique pour 1850. (*Bull. Soc. anatom.*, 1850, t. XXV, p. 398 à 455. Tiré à part, broché, in-8° de 62 pages.)

175. Sur les prétendus follicules clos de la vessie (*Soc. anatom.* 1850, février).

1851

176. Rapport sur une observation de kystes de la mamelle de M. Baungarten (*Soc. anatom* 1851, t. XXVI, p. 271).

1852

177. Rapport sur un cas d'anomalie des membres supérieurs. — Réunion des deux reins en un seul par M. Blin Louis (*Soc. anatom.* 1852, t. XXVIII, p. 390).

1853

178. Analyse critique de l'anatomie pathologique de Forster (*Monit. des hôp.*, 1853, mars).

179. Sur une prétendue grossesse extra-utérine traitée par l'électro-poncture (*Monit. des hôp.* 1853, 25 juin).

180. Sur la thérapeutique des maladies articulaires (à propos du livre de M. Bonnet) (*Mon. des hôp.* 1853, 9 août, 11 août et 13 août).

181. Sur les prétendues fractures intra-utérines. (*Bull. Soc. chirurg.*, 1853, t. IV, p. 265, 267 et 268, et 1855, t. VI, p. 211. — Voy. aussi 1859, t. X, p. 23, 32 et 37.)

Traitement des anévrysmes, voir 1855.

1854

182. Le musée de Guy's hospital; — le droit scientifique international (*Monit. des hôp.*, 1854, 14 janvier).

183. Analyse en vers de l'ouvrage poétique de M. Piorry, *Dieu, l'âme, la nature* (*Gazette hebdomadaire*, 1854, 3 fév. T. I, p. 267 feuilleton signé Bap. Lacour).

184. Sur l'application des études microscopiques à l'anatomie pathologique. (*Gaz. hebdom.*, 7 avril 1854, t. I, p. 129.)

185. Discussion sur le microscope et le cancer (à l'occasion de la discussion de l'Académie de médecine). Quatorze articles publiés dans le *Monit. des hôpit.*, 5, 14, 19 et 26 octobre; 9, 14, et 25 novembre; 2 et 12 décembre 1854; 6, 16, 23, 25 Janvier et 8, 9, 15 mars 1855.

186. La microscopie pathologique est-elle utile? (*Monit. des hôpit.*, 17 octobre 1854.)

Qu'est-ce que le cancer? (*Monit. des hôpit.*, 4 novembre 1854.)

187. Rapport sur le procédé de périnéorhaphie de M. Langenbeck, et sur les accidents tardifs du chloroforme. (*Bull. Soc. chirurg.*, 1854, t. IV, p. 368—374. Voyez aussi, pour les accidents tardifs du chloroforme, p. 338.)

1855

188. Réfutation de la théorie de M. Paget, sur la génération des adénomes de la mamelle, par les kystes proligères. (*Bull. Soc. chirurg.*, 1855, t. V, p. 373.)

189. De la prétendue syphilis vaccinale. Rapport lu à la Société de chirurgie, le 11 juillet 1855 (dans les *Mém. Soc. chirurg.*, t. V, p. 578—597, in-4.)

190. Remarques sur le traitement des anévrysmes par la compression indirecte (en réponse à quelques objections). (*Monit. des hôp.*, 12 octobre 1855; additional dans le numéro du 15 octobre 1855 et onze articles publiés dans la *Gaz. hebdom.* de décembre 1853 à janvier 1855.)

191. Analyse de la chirurgie pratique de Gerdy (*Monit. des hôp.*, 1855, 26 avril).

192. Traitement du cancer par le caustique de Landolfi (*Monit. des hôp.*, 1856, 6 juillet), et polémique avec Mousnier, signé Dr Mahieux, ex-interne des hôp. civils de Paris.

193. Examen critique de l'ouvrage de M. Marmisse intitulé: Merveilles médicales de l'Évangile. (*Moniteur des hôpitaux*, numéros des 10, 14, 17, 19 septembre 1855.)

194. Lettre erratum sur l'orthographe du mot anévrysme (*Monit. des hôpit.*, 1855, 15 oct.).

195. Sur le progrès et le doute en matière de science. (*Moniteur des hôpitaux*, 17 août, 1855.)

Prétendues fractures intra-utérines, voir 1853.

Discussion sur le microscope et le cancer, voir 1854.

1856

196. Quelques documents sur la vie de Desault et sur l'histoire chirurgicale des anévrysmes. (*Moniteur des hôpitaux,* 18 mars 1856.)

197. Remarques sur le procédé de rhinoplastie de Sédillot. (*Monit. des hôp.,* 1856, 31 juillet.)

198. Sur les anévrysmes des os, sur les kystes congéniaux du cou et sur la peau bronzée. (Premier Paris). (*Monit. des hôp.,* 1856, 28 aoit.)

199. Sur la ligature de l'œsophage et sur la circoncision. (Premier Paris). (*Monit. des hôp.,* 1856, 4 septembre.)

200. Polémique sur le travail: du traitement abortif des bubons vénériens, 2 lettres (*Monit. des hôp.,* 1856, 25 et 27 septembre).

201. Rapport sur la galvano-caustique. (*Monit. des hôp.,* 1856, 8 novembre.)

202. Sur la méthode galvano-caustique de M. Middeldorpf. Rapport à la Société de chirurgie (5 novembre 1856, t. VII, p. 205–213). Reproduit par un grand nombre de journaux.

1857

203. Du degré d'utilité de la statistique. (*Moniteur des hôpitaux,* numéros des 10 et 13 janvier 1857.)

204. Sur les origines de la méthode sous-cutanée (*Moniteur des hôpitaux,* 24 février 1857.) Sur Descartes et le cartésianisme (5 mars 1857). La méthode sous-cutanée en Allemagne, (16 mai 1857.) 193/4, 217/9, 241/3, 248, 265/6, 297/8, 313/5, 369/70, 409/10, 465/9.

205. Le premier cas de mort par l'amylène, suivi de la traduction de l'article de Snow. (*Monit. des hôp.,* 1857, 23 avril.)

206. Discours sur le concours de l'internat. (Paris, 1857, 26 décembre.)

207. De la cautérisation électrique du galvanocaustique. (*Bull. général de thérap.,* 1857.)

Éloge de Gerdy, voir 1856. [233.]

1859

208. Note sur l'anesthésie chirurgicale hypnotique. (*Acad. des sciences,* 1859, 5 décembre)

209. Sur l'anesthésie chirurgicale provoquée par l'hypnotisme. (*Soc. de chirurg.,* 1859, 7 décembre.)

210. Hypnotisme, lettre adressée au réd. en chef du *Moniteur des sciences médicales.* (*Monit. des hôp.,* 1859, 10 décembre.)

211. Hypnotisme (rectification). (*Soc. de chirurg.,* 1859, 14 décembre.)

212. Suite de la discussion sur le curare (mœurs anglaises) on the treatment of tetanus by worara. (*The Lancet,* 1859, déc.)

Prétendues fractures intra-utérines, voir 1853. [181.]

1863

213. Rapport sur la transfusion du sang. (*Bull., Soc. chirurg.,* 1863, 2ᵉ série, t. IV, p. 321.)

1864

214. Rapport sur le choix du lien constricteur dans les ligatures d'artères. (*Bull. Soc. chirurg.,* 1864, 2ᵉ série, t. V, p. 106–114.)

215. Rapport au directeur de l'Assistance publique sur le plan du nouvel Hôtel-Dieu, 1864, novembre.

216. Sur le nouvel Hôtel-Dieu, et sur l'hygiène hospitalière. (*Bull. Soc. chirurg.,* 1864, 2ᵉ série, t. V, p. 578–582.)

1865

217. Celse et la chirurgie romaine. Conférence faite à la Faculté de médecine le 2 juillet, 1865. Publiée dans le volume intitulé: *Conférences historiques de la Faculté de médecine,* Paris 1866, in-8°, p. 445–457.

1866

218. Institution du concours de Vulfranc Gerdy pour la nomination des stagiaires aux eaux minérales. (*Bull. Acad. de médecine,* 1866, 27 juin.)

1867

219. Sur la mortalité des jeunes enfants. (*Bull. Acad. méd.* 1867.)

1868

220. Rectification et éclaircissement sur la théorie de Malthus. (*Gazette des hôp.,* 1868 du 28 mai.)

221. Rapport sur le système de bandages herniaires de M. le Dr Dupré. (*Acad. de méd.,* 1868.)

1869

222. Rapport sur le prix d'Argenteuil. (*Bull. Académ. de médec.,* 1869.)

223. Rapport sur la prothèse du membre supérieur. (*Bull. Académ. de médec.,* 1869.)

1870

224. Sur la seringue à aspiration de Dieulaloy. (*Bull. Acad. méd.* 1870.)

225. Sur le vinage des vins. (*Bull. Acad. méd.* 1870.)

1871

226. Sur l'alcoolisme. (*Bull. Acad. méd.,* 1871.)

1872

227. Rapport sur le Prix Godard. (*Bull. Acad. méd.,* 1872.)

1873

228. Sur l'organisation du service de santé militaire. (*Bull. Acad. méd.* 1873.)

1874

229. Rapport du Conseil d'administration de l'Association française. Status et règlements. (*Assoc. française,* 1874, Lille.)

1875

230. Rapport sur les travaux de statistique du Dr Bertillon. (*Bull. Acad. méd.* 1875.)

See 217. Préface du traité de médecine de Celse par Vedrennes. (Paris, 1875, G. Masson.)

1879

231. Sur les températures morbides locales. (*Bull. Acad. méd.* 1879.)

1880

232. Fait de syphilis vaccinale. (*Bull. Acad. méd.,* 1880.)

ÉLOGES HISTORIQUES ET ARTICLES
NÉCROLOGIQUES.
1856

233. Eloge de P. N. Gerdy. Lu à la Société de chirurgie dans la séance solennelle du 2 juillet 1856. (*Mém. Soc. chirur.*, t. V, in-4° 1863, et *Moniteur des hôpitaux* juillet/1856). — Traduit en danois et reproduit dans le *Fœdrelandel Copenhague* (du 2 au 10 juin 1857).

1859

234. Eloge d'Amédée Bonnet de Lyon. Lu à la Société de chirurgie dans la séance solennelle du 13 juillet 1859. (*Mém. Soc. chirurg.*, t. VI in-4°.)

1861

235. Eloge d'Adolphe Lenoir. Lu à la Société de chirurgie dans la séance solennelle du 9 janvier 1861. (*Mém. Soc. chirurg.* t. VI, in-4°, et *Monit, des sciences méd.* janvier 1861.)

1862

236. Eloge de François Lallemand. Lu à la Société de chirurgie dans la séance solennelle du 22 janvier 1862. (*Mém. Soc. chirurg.*, p. LVII– XCVI 1868, t. VI et *Monit. des sciences méd.*, janvier et février 1862.) Reproduit dans plusieurs journaux.

1867

237. Discours prononcé sur la tombe de Lagneau. (*Gaz. hebdom.*, 1867, p. 831–832.)

238. Follin. (*Bull. Acad. de médecine*, 1867 t. XXXII, p. 724–729.)

1879

239. Amédée Deville (nécrologie). *Gazette hebdomadaire*, 1879, p. 675–676.)

P. Broca a préstidé à la publication posthume de l'ouvrage de Roux: Quarante annécs de pratique chirurgicale, et à la réimpression des oeuvres de Gerdy.

§II. CERVEAU
Anatomie, Morphologie, Développement, Localisations
1861

240. Sur la structure spéciale des circonvolutions inférieures du lobe occipital du cerveau. (*Bull. Soc. d'Anthrop.*, 1861, t. II, p. 313–319.)
    Sur le volume et la forme du cerveau suivant les individus et suivant les races. (*Bull. Soc. d'Anthrop.*, 1861, t. II, p. 139–204 et 301–321.

241. Perte de la parole, ramollissement chronique et destruction partielle du lobe artérieur gauche. [Sur le siège de la faculté du langage]. (*Bull. Soc. d'Anthrop.*, 1861, t. II, p. 235–238)

242. Sur les rapports anatomiques des divers points de la surface du crâne et des diverses parties des hémisphères cérébraux. (*Bull. Soc. d'Anth.*, 1861, t. II, p. 340).

243. Sur la distinction et la disposition des circonvolutions frontales des hémisphères cérébraux. (*Bull. soc. d'Anth.*, 1861 t. II, p. 196, et *Bull. Soc. anatom.*, 1861, t. XXXVI, p. 151.)

244. Sur le principe des localisations cérébrales. (*Bull. Soc. d'Anth.*, 1861 t. II, 190–204 et 309–321.)

245. Remarques sur le siège de la faculté du langage articulé, suivies d'une observation d'aphémie. (*Bull. Soc. Anatom.*, 1861, t. XXXVI, p. 330–357.)

246. Sur le poids relatif du cerveau des Français et des Allemands. (*Bull. Soc. d'Anth.*, 1861, t. II, p. 441–446.)

247. Nouvelle observation d'aphémie produite par une lésion de la moitié postérieure des deuxième et troisième circonvolutions frontales gauches. (*Bull. Soc. Anatom.*, 1861, XXXVI, p. 398–407.)

1863

248. Localisation des fonctions cérébrales. Siège de la faculté du langage articulé. (*Bull. Soc. d'Anth.*, 1863, t. IV, p. 200–208.)

249. Remarques sur le siège, le diagnostic et la nature de l'aphémie. (*Bull. Soc. Anatom.*, 1863, 2ᵉ série, t. VIII, p. 379–385 et 393–399.)

250. Sur un cas d'altération profonde de la 3ᵉ circonvolution frontale droite sans aphémie. (*Bull. Soc. Anatom.*, 2ᵉ série, 1863, t. VIII, p. 169.)

251. Sur les empreintes cérébrales de la face interne du crâne. (*Bull. Soc. d'Anth.*, 1863, t. IV, p. 199.)

1864

252. Lettre à M. Trousseau sur les mots aphémie, aphasie et aphrasie. (*Gaz. des hôp.*, 23 janv., 1864, p. 35–36.)

253. Note sur deux cas d'aphémie traumatique, produite par des lésions de la 3ᵉ circonvolution frontale gauche. (*Bull. Soc. d'Anth.*, 1864, t. V, p. 213–217, et *Bull. Soc. chirurg.*, 1864, 2ᵉ série, t. V, p. 51.)

254. Sur un cas d'aphémie produite par une lésion traumatique de la 3ᵉ circonvolution frontal gauche. (*Bull. Soc. d'Anth.*, 1864, t. V, p. 362–365.)

1865

255. Procédé pour la momification des cerveaux. (*Bull. soc. d'Anth.*, 1865, t. VI, p. 26.)

255a. Du siège de la faculté du langage articulé dans l'hémisphère gauche du cerveau. (*Bull. Soc. d'Anth.*, 1865, t. VI, p. 377–393.)

1866

Sur la faculté générale du langage, dans ses rapports avec la faculté du langage articulé. (*Bull. Soc. d'Anth.*, 1866, 2ᵉ série, t. I, p. 377–382.)

257. Nouveau cas d'aphémie traumatique. (*Bull. Soc. d'Anth.*, 1866, 2ᵉ série, t. I, p. 396–399.)

1867

258. Sur le crâne et le cerveau de l'assassin Lemaire. (*Bull. Soc. d'Anth.*, 1867, 2ᵉ série, t. II, p. 347.)

1870

259. Réponse aux observations de M. le professeur Owen, sur les caractères distinctifs du cerveau de l'homme. (*Bull. Soc. d'Anth.*, 1870, 2ᵉ série, t. V, p. 592–605.)

1871

260. Sur la déformation toulousaine du crâne (*cerveau*) (*Bull. Soc. d'anth.*, 1871, 2ᵉ série, t. VI, p. 100–120.)

1873

261. Sur le bec de l'encéphale. (*Bull. Soc. d'Anth.*, 1873, 2ᵉ série, t. VIII, p. 356–359.)

1875

262. Sur un crâne microcéphale (*cerveau.*) (*Bull. Soc. d'Anth.*, 1875, 2ᵉ série, t. X, p. 375–76.).

263. Sur le poids relatif des deux hémisphères cérébraux et de leurs lobes frontaux. (*Bull. Soc. d'Anth.*, 1875, 2ᵉ série, t. X, p. 534–536.)

1876

264. Sur la topographie crânio-cérébrale ou sur les rapports anatomiques du crâne et du cerveau. (*Revue d'Anth.*, 1876, t. V, p. 193–248 et 278.)

265. On the relations of the convolutions of the human cerebrum to the outer surface of the skull and head, par W. TURNER. (Revue critique, *Revue d'Anth.*, 1876, t. V, p. 285–289.)

266. Revue critique sur un cas de lésion probable du pli courbe. (Comptes rendus de la Société de biologie du 26 février 1876. (*Revue d'Anth.*, 1876, t. V, p. 295–296.

267. Die topographischen Beziehungen zwischen Schädel und Gehirn, im normalen Zustand, par A. ECKER. (*Revue d'Anth.*, 1876, t. V, p. 296–298; Revue critique.)

268. Sur un cas excessif de microcéphalie (encéphale de 104 grammes). (*Bull. Soc. d'Anth.*, 1876, t. XI, p. 85–92.)

269. Présentation d'un cerveau de gorille mâle et adulte. (*Bull. Soc. d'Anth.*, 1876, 2ᵉ série, t. XI, p. 426–431.)

270. Diagnostic d'un abcès situé au niveau de la région du langage; trépanation de cet abcès. (*Rev. d'Anthrop.*, 5:244–248, 1876.)

271. Note sur la topographie cérébrale. (*Bull. Acad. de méd.*, 1876.)

1877

272. Discussion sur le cerveau à l'état fœtal. (*Bull. Soc. d'Anth.*, 1877, 2ᵉ série, t. XII, p. 217–222.)

273. Sur la topographie cérébrale comparée de l'homme et du cynocéphale sphinx. (*Bull. Soc. d'Anth.*, 1877, 2ᵉ série, t. XII, p. 262–267.)

274. Sur le cerveau du gorille. (*Bull. Soc. d'Anth.*, 1877, 2ᵉ série, t. XII, p. 432–439.)

275. Sur la nomenclature cérébrale. (*Bull. Soc. d'Anth.*, 1877, 2ᵉ série, t. XII, p. 614–618.)

276. Sur la circonvolution limbique et la scissure limbique. (*Bull. Soc. d'Anth.*, 1877, 2ᵉ série, t. XII, p. 646–657.)

277. Rapport sur un Mémoire de Armand de Fleury sur l'inégalité dynamique des deux hémisphères cérébraux. (*Bull. Acad. de méd.*, 1877.) p. 508–539.

1878

278. Étude sur le cerveau du gorille. (*Revue*, 1878, 2ᵉ série, t. I, p. 1–45.)

279. Nomenclature cérébrale: dénomination et subdivision des hémisphères et des anfractuosités de la surface. (*Revue*, 1878, 2ᵉ série, t. I, p. 193–236.)

280. Le grand lobe limbique et la scissure limbique dans le série des mammifères. (*Revue*, 1878, 2ᵉ série, t. I, p. 385–498.)

1879

281. Sur le cerveau d'un gorille de deux ans et demi. (*Bull. Soc. d'Anth.*, 1879, 3ᵉ série, t. II, p. 114–116.)

282. Moyen de conserver les cerveaux destinés à effectuer de longs voyages. (*Bull. Soc. d'Anth.*, 1879, 3ᵉ série, t. II, p. 175–177.)

283. Déformation congénitale du crâne et de la face. Microcéphalie frontale. (*Bull. Soc. d'Anth.*, 1879, 3ᵉ série, t. II, p. 256–259.)

284. Crâne et cerveau d'on homme atteint de déformation toulousaine. (*Bull. Soc. d'Anth.*, 1879, 3ᵉ série, t. II, p. 417–419.)

285. Sur un fœtus exencéphale. (*Bull. Soc. d'Anth.*, 1879, 3ᵉ série, t. II, p. 467–468.)

286. Sur trois cerveaux d'orang. (*Bull. Soc. d'Anth.*, 1879, 3ᵉ série, t. II, p. 607–608.)

287. Sur le cerveau d'un Ectromélien. Localisations cérébrales. (*Bull. Soc. d'Anth.*, 1879, 3ᵉ série, t. II, p. 669–672.)

288. Recherches sur les centres olfactifs. (*Revue d'Anth.*, 1879, 2ᵉ série, t. II, p. 385–455.)

289. Sur un cerveau incomplètement divisé en deux hémisphères, par TURNER. (*Revue d'Anth.*, 1879, 2ᵉ série, t. II, p. 538–546; Revue anglaise.)

1880

290. Localisations cérébrales; sur le cerveau d'un cul-de-jatte. (*Bull. Soc. d'Anth.*, 1880, 3ᵉ série, t. III, p. 410–411.)

291. Moule d'un cerveau de Toulousain. (*Bull. Soc. d'Anth.*, 1880, 3ᵉ série, t. III, p. 165–167.)

292. Sur le cerveau de l'assassin Prévost. (*Bull. Soc. d'Anth.*, 1880, 3ᵉ série, t. II, p. 233–243.

292a. P. Broca a laissé un manuscrit, malheureusement inachevé, sur la morphologie du cerveau. La fin seule manque; il pourra être complété à l'aide de ses notes et sera publié. [Description élémentaire des circonvolutions cérébrales de l'homme d'après le cerveau schématique. *Rev. d'Anth.*, 2ᵉ série, t. 6: 1–34, 193–210, 385–405, 1883. t. 7: 1–21, 1884. — M.A.P.B. V: 707–812.]

§III. ANTHROPOLOGIE
Anatomie Comparée et Anthropologie Générale

1850

293. Rapport sur les fouilles pratiquées dans l'ancien cimetière des Célestins. (*Publié par la ville de Paris*, 1850, in-4°; 19 pages.)

1854

294. Couleur des cicatrices des nègres, voir 1866.

1858

295. Mémoire sur l'hybridité et sur la distinction des espèces animales. (*Journal de physiologie*, 1858, t. I, p. 432–471, p. 684–729; 1859, t. II, p. 218–250, et p. 345–390.)

1859

296. Sur les principaux hybrides du genre equus; sur l'hérédité des caractèrs chez les métis et sur la fécondité des mules. (*Journal de physiologie*, 1859, t. II, p. 250–258.)

297. Résumé des faits relatifs aux croisements des chiens, des loups, des chacals et des renards. (*Journal de physiologie*, 1859, t. II, p. 390–396.)

298. Mémoire sur les phénomènes d'hybridité dans le genre humain. (*Jour. de physiol.*, 1859, t. II, p. 601–625, et 1860, t. III, p. 392–439.)

299. Sur l'influence durable de certains croisements de races (*Bull. Soc. d'anth.*, 1859, t. I, p. 19–26.)

300. Sur les capsules surrénales d'un nègre. (*Bull. Soc. d'anth.*, 1859, t. I, p. 30.)

301. Instructions pour le Sénégal. (*Bull. Soc. d'anth.*, 1859, t. I, p. 121–137.)

302. Sur les races primitives contemporaines de l'époque dite du Diluvium. (*Bull. Soc. d'anth.*, 1859, t. I, p. 70–76 et 86–92.)

303. Documents relatifs aux croisements de races très différentes. (*Bull. Soc. d'anth.*, 1859, t. I, p. 255–264.)
Sur l'hybridité, voir 1858. [295.]

1860

Sur l'hybridité humaine, voir 1859. [298, 299, 303.]

1861

304. Sur la prétendue hérédité des caractèrs accidentels. (*Bull. Soc. d'anth.*, 1861, t. II, p. 41–46.)

1862

305. Sur les proportions relatives du bras, de l'avant-bras, et de la clavicule chez les nègres et les Européens. (*Bull. Soc. d'anth.*, 1862, t. III, p. 162–172.)
306. La linguistique et l'anthropologie. Mémoire lu à la Société d'anthropologie, le 5 juin 1862. (*Bull. Soc. d'anth.*, 1862, t. III, p. 264–319. Traduit en russe par M. Fedtchenko, et publié dans les *Actes de la section d'anthropologie de Moscou*, 11 mars 1865.)

1863

307. Sur les léporides ou métis du lièvre et de la lapine (*Journal d'agriculture pratique*, 5 août 1863, p. 154–156.)
308. Sur les fouilles du mont Berny. (*Bull. Soc. d'anth.*, 1863, t. IV, p. 75–78.)
309. Sur la perforation de la fosse olécrânienne de l'humérus. (*Bull. Soc. d'anth.*, 1863, t. IV, p. 510–513. Voyez aussi t. VI, p. 83, 397, 469 et 711.)
310. Echelle chromatique des yeux. (*Bull. Soc. d'anth.*, 1863, t. IV, p. 592–605 et t. V, p. 767–773).
311. Sur la couleur de la peau des Nègres à la naissance. (*Bull. Soc. d'anth.*, 1863, t. IV, p. 612.)
312. Fouilles de Chamant; sépultures de l'âge de pierre. (*Bull. Soc. d'anth.*, 1863, t. IV, p. 652–656.)
Ossements de Mont-Maigre et d'Orrouy, voir 1864.

1864

313. Sur les ossements extraits de la caverne sépulcrale du Mont-Maigre, près Orrouy (Oise). (*Bull. Soc. d'anth.*, 1864, t. V, p. 56–62 et p. 718–722. Voyez aussi, t. IV, p. 510–713.)
314. Tableau chromatique de la chevelure et de la peau. (*Bull. Soc. d'anth.*, 1864, t. V, p. 138–140 et p. 767–773.)
315. Sur un œil d'Albinos. (*Bull. Soc. d'anth.* 1864, t. V, p. 141–145 et *Bull. Soc. anatom.*, 1864, p. 258.)
316. Sur l'état des crânes et des squelettes dans les anciennes sépultures. (*Bull. Soc. d'anth.*, 1864, t. V, p. 642–653.)
Échelle chromatique des yeux, voir 1863.

1865

317. Histoire des travaux de la Société d'anthropologie de 1859 à 1863, lue dans la séance solennelle du 4 juin 1863. (*Mém. Soc. d'anth.*, 1865, t. II, p. VII–LI. Reproduit dans les *Archives générales de médecine*, dans la *Presse scientifique des Deux Mondes*, et dans *The anthropological Review.*
318. Instructions générales pour les recherches et observations anthropologiques (anatomie et physiologie). (*Mém. Soc. d'anth.*, 1865, t. II, p. 69–204 et pl. V. Reproduit en entier dans les *Archives de médecine navale*, 1865, p. 369–504. Traduit

en russe par M. Fedtchenko, et publié par la section d'anthropologie de Moscou. (2ᵉ édition très augmentée), 1879, un vol. in-16 de XIV– 290 pages, 26 figures et 2 planches chromo-litho.)

319. Sur les sillons observés à la surface des crânes et des ossements qui ont séjourné très longtemps dans le sol. (*Bull. Soc. d'anth.*, 1865, t. VI, p. 54– 58 et p. 255.)

320. Fouilles pratiquées dans l'une des grottes de Menton (*Bull. Soc. d'anth.*, 1865, t. VI, p. 221.)

321. L'intelligence des animaux et le règne humain. Brochure in 8° de 46 pages. (*Bull. Soc. d'anth.*, 1865, t. VI, p. 656– 670; et 1866, 2ᵉ série, t. I, p. 53– 79.)

La linguistique et l'anthropologie, voir 1862. [306.]

Perforation de la fosse olécrânienne, voir 1863. [309.]

1866

322. Discours sur l'homme et les animaux. (*Bull. Soc. d'anth.*, 1866, 2ᵉ série, t. I, p. 53– 79.)

323. Sur la couleur des cicatrices des Nègres. (*Bull. Soc. d'anth.*, 1866, 2ᵉ série, t. I, p. 509, Voyez aussi 1ʳᵉ série, t. III, p. 137 et *Bull. Soc. anatom.*, 1854, t. XX, p. 167 et 198.)

324. Sur l'exposition anthropologique égyptienne (*Bull. Soc. d'anth.*, 1866, 2ᵉ série, t. I, p. 574– 580.)

325. L'anthropologie, son but, son programme, ses divisions et ses méthodes. Article Anthropologie du *Dictionnaire encyclopédique des sciences médicales*, 1866, t. V, p. 275– 300. — Reproduit dans *The anthropol. Review*, 1867.

Intelligence des animaux, voir 1865. [321.]

1867

326. Sur les caractères anatomiques de l'homme préhistorique. (*Comptes rendus du congrès d'anth. et d'arch. préhistoriques*, Paris, 1867, p. 367– 402.)

327. L'antiquité de l'homme et la prosopopée de M. le Dʳ Robert, directeur *des Mondes*. (*Pensée nouvelle*, 1867, 15 décembre.)

328. Sur la mâchoire de la Naulette et sur la question darwinienne. (*Congrès d'anth. et d'arch. prehistor.*, Paris, 1867, p. 362– 402.)

329. Sur les cavernes et la perforation de la fosse olécrânienne (*idem*, p. 144– 147.)

330. Sur les proportions relatives des membres supérieurs et des membres inférieurs chez les Nègres et les Européens. (*Bull. Soc. d'anth.*, 1867, 2ᵉ série, t. II, p. 641– 653.)

L'Anthropologie, voir 1866. [325.]

1868

331. Histoire des progrès des études anthropologiques depuis la fondation de la Société en 1859. Compte rendu décennal 1859– 1869. (*Mém. de la Soc. d'anth.*, 1868, t. III, p. CV– CXXV.)

332. Histoire des travaux de la Société d'anthropologie de 1865 à 1867. Lue dans la séance solennelle du 20 juin, 1867. (*Soc. d'anth.* 1868, t. III, p. 1. Reproduit dans la *Revue des cours scientifiques* et dans *The Anthrop. Review.*)

333. Nouvelles recherches sur l'anthropologie de la France en général et de la Basse-Bretagne en particulier. (*Mém. Soc. d'anth.*, 1868. t. III. p. 147– 209.)

Couleur des cicatrices des nègres, voir 1866 [323.]

1869

334. Expériences sur les phénomènes de l'hérédité et de l'atavisme. Etude sur la formation des races. (*Bull. Soc. d'anth.*, 1869, 2ᵉ série, t. IV. p. 79– 86.)

335. Sur les ossements des cavernes de Gibraltar. (*Bull. Soc. d'anth.*, 1869, 2ᵉ série t. IV. p. 146– 158.)

336. L'ordre des primates. Parallèle anatomique de l'homme et des singes. (*Bull. Soc. d'anth.* 1869, 2ᵉ série, t. IV p. 228– 401.

1870

337. Sur l'origine de l'art de faire le feu. (*Bull. Soc. d'anth.* 1870. 2ᵉ série, t. V p. 76– 84.)

338. Sur le transformisme. (*Bull. Soc. d'anth.* 1870 2ᵉ série, t. V, p. 168– 242. Reproduit dans la *Revue scientifique.*)

1871

339. Sur la déformation toulousaine du crâne (*Bull. Soc. d'anth.* 1871, 2ᵉ série, t. VI, p. 100– 120.)

1872

340. Les Troglodytes de la Vézère. (*Association française, Bordeaux* 1872. t. I. p. 1199– 1237). Reproduit dans la *Revue scientifique.*

341. Sur la classification et la nomenclature craniologique d'après les indices céphaliques. (*Revue d'anth.* 1872, t. I. p. 385– 423.)

342. Études sur la constitution des vertèbres caudales chez les primates sans queue. (*Revue d'anth.* 1872, t. I. p. 577– 605.)

343. Les sélections, la descendance de l'homme, la sélection sexuelle de Darwin et la sélection naturelle de Wallace (revue critique) (*Revue d'anth.* 1872 t. I. p. 683– 710.)

344. De la déformation du crâne sous l'influence du torticolis chronique. (*Bull Soc. d'anth.* 1872, 2ᵉ série, t. 8 p. 21– 15.)

345. Excursion anthropologique dans la Lozère. La caverne sépulcrale de l'Homme mort. (*Bull. Soc. d'anth,* 1872. 2ᵉ série, t. VII, p. 523– 526.)

346. De l'influence de l'éducation sur la forme et le volume de la tête. (*Bull. Soc. d'anth.,* 1872. 2ᵉ série, t. VII. p. 879– 896.)

346a. Le Laboratoire d'anthropologie de l'École des Hautes Etudes. *Rev. d'anthrop.* 1: 349– 354, 1872.

1873

347. Les temps préhistoriques dans le sud-est de la France. L'homme dans la vallée du Gardon; allées couvertes de Provence. Revue des livres. (*Revue d'anth.* 1873. t. II p. 503– 508.)

348. Rapport annuel du laboratoire d'anthropologie de l'école des hautes études (*Minist. Inst. publ.,* 1871– 72, p. 26– 32. — 1872– 73, p. 40– 46. — 1873– 74, p. 50– 55. — 1874– 75, p. 57– 61. — 1875– 76, p. 86– 88. — 1876– 77, p. 81– 85. — 1877– 78, p. 125– 129. *Revue d'anth.,* 1873, t. II, p. 559– 566.)

349. Sur les Celtes (discussion) (*Bull. Soc. d'anth.* 1873. 2ᵉ série, t. VIII, p. 247– 252.)

350. Sur les léporides, (*Bull. Soc. d'anth.* 1873 2ᵉ série, t. VIII, p. 268– 278 et 280– 285.)

351. Sur les monstres doubles (discussion) (*Bull. Soc. d'anth.* 1873, 2ᵉ série t. VIII. p. 884– 889 et 892– 893.)

1874

352. De l'influence de l'humidité sur la capacité du crâne. (*Bull. Soc. d'anth.* 1874, 2ᵉ série, t. IX p. 63– 98.)

353. Sur les doctrines de la diplogénèse. (*Bull. Soc. d'anth.,* 1874, 2ᵉ série, t. IX, p. 156– 180.)

354. Sur les crânes perforés (discussion), (*Bull. Soc. d'anth.* 1874, 2ᵉ série, t. IX p. 189– 205).

356. Sur les trépanations préhistoriques. (*Bull. Soc. d'anth.* 1874, 2ᵉ série, t. IX. p. 542– 555 et 1876, 2ᵉ série, t. XI, p. 236– 251 et 431– 440).

357. Discussion sur les Celtes; le nom des Celtes. (*Bull. Soc. d'anth.* 1874, 2ᵉ série t. IX p. 658–663.)

358. Discussion sur Millie-Christine. (*Acad. de méd.*, 1874).

1875

359. Instructions craniologiques et craniométriques. (*Mém. Soc. d'anth.* 1875, 2ᵉ série, t. II, p. 196.)

360. Sur l'origine et la répartition de la langue basque (Basques français et Basques espagnols). (*Revue d'anth.*, 1875, t. II, p. 1–53.)

361. Discussion sur les microcéphales. (*Bull. Soc. anth.*, 1875, 2ᵉ série, t. X, p. 56–60 et 69.)

362. Sur une momie de fœtus péruvien et sur le prétendu os de l'Inca. (*Bull. Soc. d'anth.*, 1875, 2ᵉ série, t. X, p. 133–139.)

363. Monstre ischiopage ayant vécu cinq mois et demi. (*Bull. Soc. d'anth.*, 1875, 2ᵉ série, t. X, p. 274–75.)

364. Sur un enfant microcéphale vivant présenté à la Société. (*Bull. Soc. d'anth.*, 1875, 2ᵉ série, t. X, p. 541, 542.)

Instructions générales, voir 1865.

1876

365. Le Congrès international d'anthropologie et d'archéologie préhistoriques (session de Budapest). (*Revue d'anth.*, 1876, t. V, p. 733–736.)

366. Discussion sur le gisement néolithique de Moret (Seine-et-Marne). (*Bull. Soc. d'anth.*, 1876, 2ᵉ série, t. XI, p. 279–285.)

367. Sur de prétendues amulettes crâniennes. (*Bull. Soc. d'anth.*, 1876, 2ᵉ série, t. XI, p. 461–463.)

368. Trépanations préhistoriques. — Crânes trépanés à l'aide d'un éclat de verre. (*Bull. Soc. d'anth.*, 1876, 2ᵉ série, t. XI, p. 512–513.)

369. Sur l'âge des sujets soumis à la trépanation chirurgicale néolithique. (*Bull. Soc. d'anth.*, 1876, 2ᵉ série, t. XI, p. 572–576.)

370. Le programme de l'anthropologie. Leçon d'ouverture des cours (broch. in-8 de 15 p. 1876.)

371. Rapport du conseil sur la proposition relative à l'article additionnel présenté pendant la session de Budapest (*Cong. inter. d'anth. et d'arch. préhis.*, Budapest, 1876, p. 23–25.)

372. Sur une nécropole de l'âge de fer en Italie (*idem*, p. 407–110).

Trépanations préhistoriques, voir 1874. [356.]

Trépanations et amulettes crâniennes, voir 1876. [367.]

1877

373. Sur les apophyses styloides lombaires. (*Bull. Soc. d'anth.*, 1877, 2ᵉ série, t. XII, p. 633–637.)

374. Sur la maladie des Scythes. (*Bull. Soc. d'anth.* 1877, 2ᵉ série, t. XII, p. 537, 538.)

375. Les races fossiles de l'Europe occidentale (*Association française*, Havre, 1877, t. VI, p. 10–25.)

376. Sur la trépanation du crâne et les amulettes crâniennes à l'époque néolithique. (*Revue d'anth.*, 1877, t. VI, p. 1–42 et 193–225, et *Congrès d'anth. et d'arch. préhist.* Budapest, 1876, p. 101–192.)

377. Rapport sur un squelette envoyé par le président de la Société Borda de Dax. (*Bull. Soc. d'anth.*, 1877, 2ᵉ série, t. XII, p. 200–203.)

378. Sur la généalogie de l'homme d'aprés M. Haeckel. Le placenta des Lémuriens. (*Bull. Soc. d'anth.*, 1877, 2ᵉ série, t. XII, p. 276–270.)

379. Sur la trépanation néolithique (*Acad. de méd.*, 1877).

380. De la trépanation du crâne pratiquée sur un chien vivant par la méthode néolithique. (*Bull. Soc. d'anth.*, 1877, 2ᵉ sér., t. XII, p. 400.)

381. De la plagiocéphalie chez le singe. (*Bull. Soc. d'anth.*, 1877, 2ᵉ série, t. XII, p. 402.)

382. Sur l'apophyse mastoïde et la station bipède. (*Bull. Soc. d'anth.*, 1877, 2ᵉ série, t. XII, p. 411–413.)

383. Le pli transversal du singe dans la main de l'homme. (*Bull. Soc. d'anth.*, 1877, 2ᵉ série, t. XII, p. 431–432.)

1878

384. Squelettes de deux Hindous noirs des environs de Madras. (*Bull. Soc. d'anth*, 1878, 3ᵉ série, t. I. p. 47–53.)

385. Sur les indices de largeur de l'omoplate chez l'homme, les singes et dans la série des mammifères. (*Bull. Soc. d'anth.*, 1878, 3ᵉ série, t. I, p. 66–92.)

386. Sur deux cas où un doigt surnuméraire s'est développé à l'âge adulte. (*Bull. Soc. d'anth.*, 1878, 3ᵉ série, t. I, p. 283–285.)

1879

387. Sur la fausseté des résultats céphalométriques obtenus à l'aide du conformateur des chapeliers. (*Bull. Soc. d'anth.*, 1879, 3ᵉ série, t. II, p. 101–106.)

388. Sur la détermination de l'âge moyen. (*Bull. Soc. d'anth.*, 1879, 3ᵉ série, t. II, p. 298–317.)

389. Sur la faculté que présente un jeune magot de reconnaître les représentations artistiques des animaux de son espèce. (*Bull. Soc. d'anth.*, 1879. 3ᵉ série, t. II, p. 441–443.)

390. Tête de deux Néo-Calédoniens (Ataï et le Sorcier). (*Bull. Soc. d'anth.*, 1879, 3ᵉ série, t. II, p. 616–617.)

391. Méthode des moyennes. —Étude sur les variations craniométriques et de leur influence sur les moyennes; détermination de la série suffisante. (*Bull. Soc. d'anth.*, 1879, t. II, p. 756–820.)

392. Rapport des directeurs de laboratoires (anthropologie). (Paris, 1879, *minist. de l'inst. publiq.*, 1868 à 1879.)

1880

393. Sur les moyennes (discussion) (*Bull. Soc. d'Anth.*, 1880, 3ᵉ série. t. III, p. 119.)

394. Sur un microcéphale âgé de deux ans et demi; anomalies viscérales régressives. (*Bull. Soc. d'anth.*, 1880, 3ᵉ série, t. III, p. 387–388.)

394a. Discours d'ouverture du congrès international des sciences anthropologiques en 1878. (Paris, 1880, Imprimerie nationale, p. 17 à 23.)

395. Sur le buste d'une jeune fille zoulou. (*Bull. Soc. d'anth.*, 1880, 3ᵉ série, t. III, p. 227–228.)

396. Sur un enfant illettré doué de la faculté de faire mentalement des calculs trés compliqués. (*Bull. Soc. d'anth.*, 1880, 3ᵉ série, t. III, p. 244–269.)

Une œuvre considérable de P. Broca a été traduite et publiée en Russie par la Société impériale des amis des sciences naturelles, d'anthropologie et d'ethnologie de Moscou. C'est un BAREME ANTHROPOLOGIQUE qui permet d'établir rapidement les divers indices, de réduire toutes les mesures étrangères en mesures françaises, d'utiliser le cyclomètre, de rectifier l'ellipse. Il renferme, en outre, des tableaux pour l'application de la méthode trigonométrique à la craniologie et un tableau des *numéros descriptifs* de l'usure des dents, de la glabelle, de la protubérance occipitale, de l'épine nasale, de l'état des sutures, etc. (Moscou, 1879, in-folio, 29 pages.) L'ouvrage est précédé d'une notice étendue sur l'emploi du barème et de la méthode trigonométrique. (Moscou, 1879, in-folio, 36 pages.)

Le manuscrit français existe et sera publié.

Craniolgie Générale.

1860

397. Mémoire sur le Craniographe et sur quelques-unes de ses applications. (*Mém. Soc. d'anth.*, 1860–63, t. I, p. 348–378.)

1861

398. Sur le Craniographe et sur la détermination de plusieurs angles nouveaux nommés angles auriculaires. (*Bull. Soc. d'anth.*, 1861, t. II, p. 673–686.)

1862

399. Sur la détermination des points singuliers de la voûte du crâne qui limitent les angles auriculaires. (*Bull. Soc. d'anth.*, 1862, t. III, p. 17–24.)

400. Sur la situation relative du trou occipital chez les nègres et chez les Européens. (*Bull. Soc. d'anth.*, 1862, t. III, p. 524–530.)

401. Sou les projections de la tête et sur un nouveau procédé de céphalométrie. (*Bull. Soc. d'anth.*, 1862, t. III, p. 534–544.)

402. Sur l'inion ou point iniaque, et ses variations suivant les races. (*Bull. Soc. d'anth.*, 1862, t. III, p. 18–20 et p. 589–591.)

1864

403. Sur le crâne de Schiller et sur l'indice cubique des crânes. (*Bull. Soc. d'anth.*, 1864, t. V, p. 253–260.)

404. Incertitudes des mesures prises sur les crânes moulés en plâtre. (*Bull. Soc. d'anth.*, 1864, t. V, p. 435–437 et p. 449–455.)

405. Sur un nouveau goniométre. (*Bull. Soc. d'anth.*, 1864, t. V, p. 943–946.)

1865

406. Procédé géométrique pour mesurer l'angle sphénoidal sans ouvrir le cràne. (*Bull. Soc. d'anth.*, 1865, t. VI, p. 564–572.)

1866

407. Description of a new goniometer. (*Mémoires read before the Anthropological Society of London*, vol. II, p. 82–91. Londres, 1866.)

1868

408. Sur le stéréographe, nouvel instrument craniographique destiné à dessiner tous les détails du relief des corps solides (*Mém. Soc. d'anth.*, 1868, t, III, p. 99–126.)

409. Comparaison des indices céphaliques sur le vivant et sur le squelette. (*Bull. Soc. d'anth.*, 1868, 2e série, t. III, p. 25–32.)

1869

410. La cadre *a maxima* et le compas micrométrique. (*Bull. Soc. d'anth.*, 1869, 2e série, t. IV, p. 101–104.)

1872

411. Sur l'angle orbito occipital. (*Revue d'anth.* 1872, 2e série, t. VI, p. 305–432.)

412. Recherche sur l'indice nasal. (*Revue d'anth.*, 1872, t, I, p. 1–35, et *Bull. Soc. d'anth.*, 1872, 2e série, t. VII, p. 25–39.)

413. De la classification et de la nomenclature craniologiques d'après les indices céphaliques. (*Revue d'anth.*, 1872, t. I, p. 385–423.)

414. Le goniomètre occipital. (*Bull. Soc. d'anth.*, 1872, 2e série, t. VII, p. 634–638.)

415. Sur la direction du trou occipital, description du niveau occipital et du goniomètre occipital. (*Bull. Soc. d'anth.*, 1872, 2e série, t. VII, p. 649–668.)

1873

416. Recherches sur la direction du trou occipital et sur les angles occipitaux et basilaires. (*Revue d'anth.*, 1873, t. II, p. 193–234.)

417. Sur la mensuration de la capacité du crâne. (*Mém. de la Soc. d'anth.*, 1873, 2ᵉ série, t, I, p. 63–152.)

418. Sur le plan horizontal de la tête et sur la méthode trigonométrique. (*Bull. Soc. d'anth.*, 2ᵉ série, 1873, t. VIII, p. 48–92.)

419. Quelques résultats de la détermination trigonométrique de l'angle alvéolo-condylien et de l'angle biorbitaire. (*Bull. Soc. d'anth.* 1873, 2ᵉ série, t. VIII, p. 150–179.)

420. L'équerre flexible auriculaire et le goniomètre auriculaire. (*Bull. Soc. d'anth.*, 1873, 2ᵉ série, t. VIII, p. 147–150.)

421. Le demi-goniomètre facial. (*Bull. Soc. d'anth.*, 1873, 2ᵉ série, t, VIII, p. 233–236.)

422. Sur le trapèze intracrânien. (*Bull. Soc. d'anth.*, 1873, 2ᵉ série, t. VIII, p. 359–363.)

423. Sur l'endocrâne. Nouveaux instruments destinés à étudier la cavité crânienne sans ouvrir le crâne. (*Bull. Soc. d'anth.*, 1873, 2ᵉ série, t. VIII, p. 352–383.)

424. Nouvelles recherches sur le plan horizonta de la tête et sur le degré d'inclinaison des divers plans crâniens (*Bull. Soc. d'anth.* 1873, 2ᵉ série, t. VIII, p. 542–563.)

1874

415. Études sur les propriétés hygrométriques des crânes, considérés dans leurs rapports avec la crâniométrie. (*Revue d'anth.*, 1874, t. III, p. 385–444.)

416. De l'influence de l'état hygrométrique des crânes sur leur capacité. (*Bull. Soc. d'anth.*, 1874, t. IX, p. 63–98.)

417. Sur la valeur des divers angles faciaux et sur un nouveau goniomètre facial, appelé le goniomètre facial médian. (*Bull. Soc. d'anth.* 1874 2ᵉ série, t. IX, p. 358–384.)

418. Cubage des crânes. —Révision et correction des résultats stéréométriques publiés avant 1872. (*Bull. Soc. d'anth.*, 1874, 2ᵉ série t. IX, p. 563–573.)

419. Sur le Cyclométre, instrument destiné à déterminer la courbure des divers points du crâne. (*Bull. Soc. d'anth.*, 1874, 2ᵉ série, t. IX, p. 676–686.)

1875

420. Recherches sur l'indice orbitaire. (*Revue d'anth.*, 1875, t. IV, p. 577–616.)

421. Sur la scaphocéphalie. (*Bull. Soc. d'anth.*, 1875 2ᵉ série, t. X p. 23–28.)

423. Sur un crâne microcéphale. (*Bull. Soc. d'anth.*, 1875, 2ᵉ série, t. X p. 75–76.)

424. Sur la perforation congénitale et symétrique de deux pariétaux. (*Bull. Soc. d'anth.*, 1875, 2ᵉ série, t. X, p. 192–199.)

425. Sur les accidents produits par la pratique des déformations artificielles du crâne. (*Bull. Soc. d'anth.*, 1875, 2ᵉ série, t. X, p. 199–205.)

426. Sur les trous pariétaux et sur la perforation congénitale double et symétrique des pariétaux. (*Bull. Soc. d'anth.*, 1875, 2ᵉ série, t. X, p. 326–336.)

426. Notions complémentaires sur l'ostéologie du crâne. Détermination et dénominations nouvelles de certains points de repères. —Nomenclature crâniologique. (*Bull. Soc. d'anth.*, 1875, 2ᵉ série, t. X, p. 337–366.)

1877

427. Sur l'angle orbito occipital. (*Bull. Soc. d'anth.*, 1877, 2ᵉ série, t. XII, p. 325–333.)

1878

428. Sur le plan horizontal du crâne. (*Bull. Soc. d'anth.*, 1878, 3e série, t. I. p. 345–359.)

1879

429. Sur les crânes de diverses races que M. Hortus a recueillis à Cayenne. (*Bull. Soc. d'anth.*, 1879, 3e série, t. II, p. 177–179.)

1880

430. Méthode trigonométrique; le goniomètre d'inclinaison et l'orthogone. (*Bull. Soc. d'anth.*, 1880, 3e série, t. III, p. 132–159.)

431. Sur le goniomètre flexible. (*Bull. Soc. d'anth.*, 1880, t. III, p. 183–192.)

432. Sur la méthode orthogonale de M. Ihering. (*Bull. Soc. d'anth.*, 1880, 3e série, t. III, p. 357–362.)

433. Préparation des crânes d'enfants à fontanelles non ossifiées. (*Bull. Soc. d'anth.*, 1880, 3e série, t. III, p. 385–386.)

Craniologie Spéciale.

1855

434. Étude anthropologique sur le crâne du Manni-Beker-Nos. (*Bull. Soc. polym. du Morbihan.* Vannes, 1855, gr. in-8°. — Tiré à part à la suite de la brochure de M. de Closmadeuc sur le tombeau de Quiberon. (*Bull. Soc. d'anth.*, 1865, t. VI, p. 73–78.)

1861

435. Observations anthropologiques sur les habitants de la Basse-Bretagne. (*Bull. Soc. d'anth.*, 1861, t. II, p. 413–417.)

436. Sur des crânes provenant d'un cimetière de la Cité, antérieur au treizième siècle. (*Bull. Soc. d'anth.*, 1861, t. II, p. 501–513.)

1862

437. Sur les crânes basques de Saint-Jean-de-Luz. (*Bull. Soc. d'anth.*, 1862, t. III, p. 43–101 et 1868, 2e série, t. III, p. 9–20.)

438. Sur la capacité des crânes parisiens des diverses époques. (Bull. Soc. d'anth., 1862, t. III, p. 102–116.)

439. Sur les crânes du dolmen de Meudon. (*Bull. Soc. d'anth.*, 1862, t. III, p. 320.)

440. Sur les caractères du crâne des Basques. (*Bull. Soc. d'anth.*, 1862, t. III, p. 579–591, et 1863, t. IV, p. 39–62.)

1864

441. Description du crâne déformé de Voiteur (Jura). Bull. Soc. d'anth., 1864, t. V, p. 385–392.)

442. Sur les crânes d'Orrouy. (*Bull. Soc. d'anth.*, 1864, t. V, p. 718–722.)

1865

443. Sur les crânes des tumuli de Maintenon (Eure-et-Loir) et de Méloisy (Côte-d'Or). (*Bull. Soc. d'anth.*, 1865, t. VI, p. 23–26.)

444. Crâne de l'âge de pierre de Quiberon. (*Bull. Soc. d'anth.*, 1865, t. VI, p. 75–78.)

445. Crânes de la rue des Écuries-d'Artois, et crânes de Parthenay (Deux-Sèvres). (*Bull. Soc. d'anth.*, 1865, t. VI, p. 78–79.)

446. Sur les crânes de l'ossuaire de Saint-Arnould (Calvados). (*Bull. Soc. d'anth.*, 1865, t. VI, p. 511–514.)

Crâne de Manni-Becker-Nos, voir 1855. [434.]

1866

447. Sur les fouilles de la caverne abri de Lafaille à Bruniquel. (*Bull. Soc. d'anth.*, 1866, 2ᵉ série, t. I, p. 48– 52.)

448. Sur le crâne de Dante Alighieri. (*Bull. Soc. d'anth.*, 1866, 2ᵉ série, t. I, p. 206– 210.)

449. Sur une seconde série de crânes basques du Guipuzcoa. (*Bull. Soc. d'anth.*, 1866, 2ᵉ série, t. I, p. 470– 473. Voy. aussi 1867, 2ᵉ série, t. II, p. 18– 21.)

1867

450. Sur les fragments de crâne humain d'Éguishem. (*Bull. Soc. d'anth.*, 1867, 2ᵉ série, t. II, p. 129– 131.)

451. Sur la trépanation chez les Incas. (*Bull. Soc. d'anth.*, 1867, 2ᵉ série, t. II, p. 403– 408.)

Crânes basques du Guipuzcoa, voir 1866.

1868

452. Sur les crânes et ossements des Eyzies. (*Bull. Soc. d'anth.*, 1868, 2ᵉ série, t. III, p. 350– 392.)

453. Sur le crâne des Meyrueis (Lozère). (*Bull. Soc. d'anth.*, 1868, 2ᵉ série, t. III, p. 129– 134.)

454. Sur le prétendu rachitisme des ossements des Eyzies. (*Bull. Soc. d'anth.*, 1868, 2ᵉ sér, t. III, p. 432– 446.)

455. Les crânes des Eyzies et la thèorie esthonienne. (*Bull. Soc. d'anth.*, 1868, 2ᵉ série, t. III, p. 454– 510.)

Crânes basques de St-Jean de Luz, voir 1862. [437.]

1872

456. Sur la caverne de l'Homme-Mort près St-Pierre-les-Tripiés (Lozère). (*Cong. inter. d'anth. et d'arch. préhist.* Bruxelles, 1872, p. 182– 198.)

1873

457. Sur les crânes de la caverne de l'Homme-Mort. (*Rev. d'anth.*, 1873, t. II, p. 1– 53.)

458. Sur les crânes de Laugerie-Basse (Époque du renne). (*Bull. Soc. d'anth.*, 1873, 2ᵉ série, t. VIII, p. 217– 221.)

459. Anciens crânes déformés macrocéphales des environs de Tiflis (région du Caucase). (*Bull. Soc. d'anth.*, 1875, 2ᵉ série, t. VIII, p. 572– 578.)

460. Sur les crânes de Solutré. (*Bull. Soc. d'anth.*, 1873; 2ᵉ série, t. VIII, p. 819– 836.)

1874

461. Crânes plagiocéphales des grottes de Baye. (*Bull. Soc. d'anth.*, 1874, 2ᵉ série, t. IX, p. 266.)

462. Crâne scaphocéphale d'une négresse du Sénégal. (*Bull. Soc. d'anth.*, 1874, 2ᵉ série, t. XI, p. 349– 358.)

1875

463. Sur les crânes des grottes de Baye. (*Bull. Soc. d'anth.*, 1875 2ᵉ série, t. X, p. 28– 32.)

1876

464. Sur deux séries de crânes provenant d'anciennes sépultures indiennes des environs de Bogota. (*Bull. Soc. d'anth.*, 1876; 2ᵉ série, t. XI, p. 359– 373.)

465. Sur un crâne macrocéphale déformé de l'époque barbare en Hongrie. (*Cong. inter d'anth. et d'arch. préhis.*, Budapest, p. 561–572.)

466. Sur les traces de l'homme pliocène en Toscane (*idem*, p. 57–59.)

1879

467. Sur un mode peu connu de déformation toulousaine. (*Bull. Soc. d'anth.*, 1879, 3ᵉ série t. II, p. 699–700.)

468. Sur un crâne de fellah et sur l'usure des dents. (*Bull. Soc. d'anth.*, 1879, 3ᵉ série, t. II, p. 342–344.)

Ethnologie
1860

469. Recherches sur l'ethnologie de la France. (*Mém. Soc. d'anth.*, 1860–61, t. I, p. 1–56.)

470. Sur les kabyles blonds de l'Auress. (*Bull. Soc. d'anth.*, 1860, t. I, p. 162–165 et 179.)

471. Remarques sur les langues polynésiennes (*Bull. Soc. d'anth.*, 1860, t. I, p. 250–255.)

472. Sur le défaut de perfectibilité de certaines races. (*Bull. Soc. d'anth.*, 1860, t. I, p. 337–342, p. 368–376.)

1861

473. Sur l'origine des races d'Égypte et de leur civilisation. (*Bull. Soc. d'anth.*, 1861, t. II, p. 550–555.)

1862

474. Sur la diversité des types des Indiens d'Amérique. (*Bull. Soc. d'anth.*, 1862, t. III, p. 408–410, 423 et 433.)

1863

475. Sur les caractères physiques des Mincopies, ou habitants des iles Andaman. (*Bull. Soc. d'anth.*, 1863, t. IV, p. 497–508.)

1864

476. Recherches sur l'ethnologie de la Basse-Bretagne. (*Bull. Soc. d'anth.*, 1864, t. V. p. 146–155; 1866, 2ᵉ série, t. I, p. 700–702.) (*Mém. Soc. d'anth.*, t. III, fasicule II, avec une carte cantonale.)

477. Qu'est-ceque les Celtes? (*Bull. Soc. d'anth.*, 1864, t. V, p. 557–562.)

478. Sur les origines des races d'Europe. (*Bull. Soc. d'anth.*, 1864, t. V, p. 305–315; p. 557–562; p. 569–573. Voy. p. 193–196.)

479. Carte de la répartition de la langue basque. (*Bull. Soc. d'anth.*, 1864, t. V, p. 819–822 et 1868, 2ᵉ, série, t. III, p. 7–8.)

1866

480. Notes et instructions anthropologiques relatives à l'Exposition égyptienne. (*Bull. Soc. d'anth.*, 1866, 2ᵉ série, t. I, 574–580.)

Ethnologie de la Basse-Bretagne, voir 1864. [476.]

1867

219. Sur la mortalité des jeunes enfants. (*Bull. Acad. de méd.*, 1867, t. XXXII, p. 351–367.)

481. Sur la prétendue dégénérescence de la population française. (*Bull. Acad. de méd.*, 1867, t. XXXII, p. 547–603 et p. 830–862.)

Répartition de la langue basque, voir 1864. [479.]

1869

482. L'ethnologie de la France au point de vue de infirmités. (*Bull. Acad. méd.*, 1869.)

483. Sur l'ethnologie de l'Abyssinie. (*Bull. Soc. d'anth.*, 1869, 2ᵉ série, t. IV, p. 65–72.)

1872

484. La race prussienne et Signor Mantegazza. (Rev. d'Anth. 1:163/4, 1872.

1873

485. La race celtique ancienne et moderne; Arvernes et Armoricains, Auvergnats et Bas-Bretons. (*Rev. d'anth.*, 1873, t. II, p. 577–628.)

486. Sur la question celtique. Crânes des Bas-Bretons et des Auvergnats. (*Bull. Soc. d'anth.*, 1873, 2ᵉ série, t. VIII, p. 313–328.)

1874

487. Les Akka, race pygmée de l'Afrique centrale (*Rev. d'anth.*, 1874, t. III, p. 279–287.)

488. Ethnogénie italienne. — Les Ombres et les Etrusques. (*Rev. d'anth.*, 1874, t. III, p. 288–297.)

489. Nouveaux renseignements sur les Akka. (*Rev. d'anth.*, 1874, t. III, p. 462–470.)

490. Sur l'ethnologie de la France. (*Bull. Soc. d'anth.*, 1874, 2ᵉ série, t. IX, p. 593–594.)

1876

491. Les peuples blonds et les monuments mégalithiques dans l'Afrique septentrionale. — Les Vandales en Afrique. (*Rev. d'anth.*, 1876, t. V, p. 293–404)

492. La race brune et la race blonde en Allemagne (*Cong. inter. d'anth. et d'arch. préhis.* Budapest, 1876, p. 581–584.)

1877

493. Sur les textes relatifs aux Celtes dans la Grande-Bretagne. (*Bull. Soc. d'anth.*, 1877, 2ᵉ série, t. XII, p. 509–511.)

1879

494. Sur une carte de la langue bretonne de M. Mauricet. (*Bull. Soc. d'anth.*, 1879, 3ᵉ série, t. II, p. 22–25.)

495. Sur les prétendus énarés du Caucase. (*Bull. Soc. d'anth.*, 1879, 3ᵉ série, t. II, p. 73–76.)

Articles nécrologiques

496. Discours prononcé sur la tombe d'Antelme. (*Bull. Soc. d'anth.*, 1864, t. V, p. 574–577.)

496a. Éloge funèbre de Pierre Gratiolet. (*Mém. Soc. d'anth.*, 1865, t. II, p. CXII–CXVIII.)

497. Discours prononcé sur la tombe de Morpain. (*Bull. Soc. d'anth.*, 1870, t. V, p. 159–162.)

498. Léon Guillard. (*Rev. d'anth.*, 1872, t. I, p. 357, 358.)

499. Jules Assézat. (*Rev. d'anth.*, 1876, t. V, p. 744–746.)

500. Discours prononcé sur la tombe de M. Périer, le 15 mai 1880. (*Bull. Soc. d'anth.*, 1880, 3ᵉ série, t. III, p. 400–404.)

Appendice

Liberté Électorale. — Affaire Du Conseil Presbytéral de L'Église Réformé de Paris.

501. Mémoire présenté à M. le ministre de la justice et des cultes sur un fait relatif à l'inscription des électeurs paroissiaux dans l'Église réformée de Paris (Paris, 1864. Juillet). Appendice. — lettre donnée le 18 juillet 1864, par ministère d'huissier à M. le président du Conseil presbytéral.

Appel au Consistoire de l'Église réformée de Paris coutre une décision du conseil presbytéral de la même Église (1864).

Affaire du registre paroissial de Paris, 2 lettres (Arcachon, 1864, 4 et 13 septembre).

Le règlement électoral du Consistoire de Paris. 1re lettre (Arcachon, 1864, 17 septembre; 2e lettre (Sainte-Foy, 1864, 25 septembre); 3e lettre (Sainte-Foy, 1864, 3 octobre); dernière lettre (1864, 22 octobre 1864.)

A Monsieur le pasteur Louis Vernes (Sainte-Foy, 1864, 21 septembre).

A Monsieur le rédacteur de l'*Espérance* 2 lettres (Arcachon, 1864, 5 septembre) et Sainte-Foy-la-Grande, 1864, 19 septembre). (Tous ces articles ont été publiés dans le journal religieux *Le Lien.*)

502. Exposition des Titres et Travaux (Paris, Avril 1862.)

Samuel Pozzi

General Bibliography

Achard, Charles. "Paul Broca (1824-1880)." *Bull. Acad. Méd.* 3ᵉ sér. 92 (1924): 1347—1366.

Ackerknecht, E.H. *Rudolf Virchow, Doctor, Statesman, Anthropologist.* Madison, Wisc. University Press, 1953.

—————."Historical Notes on Cancer," *Med. Hist.* 2 (1958): 114—119

—————, and Vallois, H.V. "Franz Joseph Gall, inventor of phrenology, and his collection," (transl.). *Wisconsin Studies in Medical History,* 1, 1956.

Adams, R.D., Denny-Brown, D., and Pearson, C.M. *Diseases of Muscle.* New York: Hoeber, 1954.

Adey, W.R. "Organization of the Rhinencephalon," in *Reticular Formation of the Brain.* H.H. Jasper et al., ed. Boston: Little, Brown, 621—644 (630), 1958.

Allen, E.V., Barker, N.W., and Hines, E.A. *Peripheral Vascular Disease.* 2nd ed. Philadelphia: Saunders, 1955.

Ariëns Kappers, C.U., Huber, G.C., and Crosby, E.C. *The Comparative Anatomy of the Nervous System of Vertebrates, Including Man.* New York: Macmillan, 1936.

Aubry, O. *Le Second Empire.* Paris: Fayard, 1938.

Auburtin, Ernest. "Sur les fonctions cérébrales et sur la faculté du langage articulé." *Bull. Soc. d'anthropol* 2 (1861): 209—220.

Baginsky, A. "Aphasie in Folge Schwerer Nierenerkrankungen, Uraemie," *Berlin Klin. Wsehr.* 8 (1871): 428—431, 439—443.

Baillarger, J.G. François. "Recherches sur la structure de la couche corticale des circonvolutions du cerveau," *Mém. Acad. Roy. Méd.* 8 (1840): 149—183. (English transl. in G. von Bonin. *The Cerebral Cortex.* Springfield, Ill: Thomas, 22—48, 1960.

Baldick, R. *Pages from the Goncourt Journal.* London: Oxford University Press, 54, 1962.

Balzac, Honoré de. *La Vieille Fille.* Paris: Simon, no date.

Barker, L.F. *Anatomical Terminology.* (BNA). Philadelphia: Blakiston, 1907.

Bartlett, A.D. *Wild Animals in Captivity.* London: Chapman Hall, 1899.

Bataillard, P. "Etat de la question de l'ancienneté des tsiganes en Europe," *Congrès International d'Anthropologie et d'Archéologie Préhistorique* (8), Budapest: (1876) 321—385.

Bateman, Frederic. "On aphasia, or loss of the power of speech," *Lancet I* (1865): 532—533.

Beadle, G. and Beadle, M. *The language of life. An Introduction to the Science of Genetics.* New York: Doubleday, 1966.

Beatty, C. *Ferdinand de Lesseps.* London: Eyre and Spottiswode, 1956.

Beddoe, J. "Anniversary Address by the President," *J. Anthropol. Hist.* 20 (1891): 348—359.

Belina, Ladislas de. "De la transfusion du sang au point de vue physiologique et médical," *Arch. Physiol. Norm. Path.,* 1ᵉʳᵉ sér. 3 (1870): 43—63, 355—383, 463—472.

Benedict, Ruth. *Race: Science and Politics.* New York: Viking Press, (1940) 1959, pp. 119, 129, 130.

Berger, Hans. *Untersuchungen über die Temperatur des Gehirns.* Jena: Fischer, 1910.

Bernard, C. *An Introduction to the Study of Experimental Medicine (1865)* (transl. H.C. Greene). New York: Dover, 1957

Bertogne, M. *L'Administration Générale de l'Assistance Publique à Paris.* Paris: Donnat-Montchrestien, 1935.

Bibby, G. "The Celts," *Horizon* 7 (1965): 21—30.

Bichat, Xavier. *Traité d'anatomie descriptive.* vol. III. Paris: F.R. Buisson, 1802.

Billy, A. *Les Frères Goncourt.* Paris: Flammarion, 1954.

Blinderman, C.S. "Thomas Henry Huxley," *Scientific Monthly.* April, 1959, 171—182.

Bonin, G. von. "European races of the Upper Paleolithic," *Human Biology* 7 (1935): 196—221.

_____. *Essay on the Cerebral Cortex.* Springfield, Ill.: C.C. Thomas, 1950.

_____. *Some Papers on the Cerebral Cortex.* Springfield, Ill.: C.C. Thomas, 1960.

Boring, E.G. *A History of Experimental Psychology.* 2nd ed., Ch. 7, New York: Appelton, 1957.

_____. *History, Psychology and Science: Selected Papers.* Watson, R.I. and Campbell, D.T., ed. New York (1963): Wiley, 37, 58, 59.

Bouchard, Ch. "Aphasie sans lésion de la troisième circonvolution frontale gauche," *Comptes rend. Soc. Biol.*, 4ᵉ sér. 1(16) (1864, 65): 111—116.

Bouillaud, J.B. "Recherches cliniques propres à démontrer que la perte de la parole correspond à la lésion des lobules antérieurs du cerveau, et à confirmer l'opinion de M. Gall, sur le siège de l'organe du langage articulé." *Arch. Gén. de Méd.*, Feb. 21, 1825, 3ᵉ année t. VIII: 25—45.

_____. "Exposition de nouveaux faits à l'appui de l'opinion qui localise dans les lobules antérieurs de cerveau, le principe législateur de la parole," *Bull. Acad. Méd.*, IV, 1839.

_____. "Recherches cliniques propres a démontrer que la sense du langage articulé et le principe coordinateur des mouvements de la parole résident dans les lobules antérieurs du cerveau," *Bull. Acad. Roy. Méd.* Feb. 22, 13: 699—719; *ibid.* 778—808, Discussion: 808—816. March 7, 1848.

_____. "Recherches expérimentales sur les fonctions du cerveau," *J. de Physiol.* 10 (1830): 36. Magendie.

Boule, M. and Vallois, H.V. *Fossil Men.* (transl. M. Bullock) New York: Dryden Press, 1957.

Bourgin, G. *La Troisième République.* 2nd. ed. Paris: Colin, 1950.

Boymier. "Notice sur Gratiolet et P. Broca," *J. de Méd. Bordeaux* 10 (1880): 159—161, 173—174.

Braid, James. (Neurypnology, etc., London, 1843) in *Braid on Hypnotism.* A.E. Waite, ed. (biography). New York: Julian Press, 1960.

Brain (Lord) Russel. *Speech Disorders.* Washington: Butterworth, 1961.

_____. "The neurology of language," *Brain* 84 2 (1961): 145—166.

Brazier, M.A.B. The history of the electrical activity of the brain [etc] *Med. Hist.* (1963): 202.

Brissaud, E. *Histoire des expressions populaires relatives . . . à la médecine.* Paris: Masson, 139, 1892.

Broca, A. and Maubrac, P. *Traité de Chirurgie Cérébrale.* Paris: Masson, 1896.

Broca, P. For Broca's writings, see separate bibliography.

Broca, P. *Paul Broca, Correspondence 1841—1857.* 2 vol. Paris: Schmidt, 1886.

_____. *Mémoires d'anthropologie de* (1871—1888). 5 vol. Paris: Reinwald.

Broca, P.J.B. *Aperçu succinct . . . sur les ganglions lymphatiques, et leurs principales maladies,* Thèse 28 pp. Paris: Didot, 1816.

Buffon, George Louis Leclerc, Comte de. "Discourse on Style, given at the Académie Française on the day of this Acceptance," August 27, 1753, at 3 p.m., p. 21—22, Paris, Hachette, 1921.

Burdach, K.F. *Vom Baue und Leben des Gehirns*. 3 vol., Leipzig, 1819—1826.

Butler, S. *Unconscious memory* (1880). London: Fiefield, 1910.

Cabanès. *Moeurs intimes du passé 4ème sér*. La vie d'étudiant. Paris: Michel, 1913.

Cabanès. *La Salle de Garde*. Paris (1917): Montagu, 80.

Chassaignac. *Bull. Soc. Chir*. 10: 137ff., Oct. 5, 1859—1860.

Chevalier, J. *Entretiens avec Bergson*. Paris: Plon, 1959.

Clemenceau, Georges. *De la génération des éléments anatomiques*. Thèses, Paris, reprinted, 1867.

Cole, W.H. "The significance of cancer cells in the blood," *Journal of the American Medical Association* 181 (1962): 434.

Coon, C.S. *The Origin of Races*. New York: Knopf, 1963.

Cordier, "Mlle." *Sainte-Foy-la-Grande au temps des guerres de religion (1541—1622)*, unpublished thesis in Archives Départmentales de la Gironde, Bordeaux.

Cornil, V. (editor and most likely author). "Paul Broca," *Journal des connaissances méd. prat.*, Paris 47 (July 15, 1880): 225—226.

Corriger, J. *Sainte-Foy-la-Grande (Gironde) et ses environs*. Guide illustré, 1950

Costello, W. *Cyclopedia of practical surgery*, 4 vol. London, Taylor, and Greening, 1841-1861.

Couderau. "Sur la religiosité comme caractéristique," *Bull. Soc. d'Anthropol*. 2ᵉ sér. 1 (1866): 329—340.

Count, Earl W. "The evolution of the race idea in modern Western culture during the period of the pre-Darwinian nineteenth century." *Trans. New York Acad. Sci.*, Ser. 2, 8 (1946): 139—165.

Critchley, McD. "Broca's contribution to aphasia reviewed a century later," in Garland, H. *Scientific Aspects of Neurology*. London: Livingstone, (1961) 131—141.

Critchley, McD. "La controverse de Dax et Broca." *Rev. neurol*. Paris 110 (1964): 553—557.

Cruveilhier, Jean. "Sur la paralysie musculaire, progressive, atrophique." (Discussion) *Bull. Acad. Nat. Méd*. 18 (1852): 490—501, 546—583, 590—605, 623—644.

Dally, E. "Eloge de Paul Broca," *Bull. Soc. d'Anthropol.*, 3ᵉ sér. 7 (1884): 921—956.

Dampier, Sir William C. *A History of Science and its Relation with Philosophy and Religion*. 4th ed. Cambridge University Press, 1952 (1929).

Darlington, C.D. *Darwin's Place in History*. Oxford: Blackwell, 1959.

Darwin, Charles. *The Origin of Species by Means of Natural Selection or the Preservation of Favoured Races in the Struggle for Life*. 6th ed., Jan. 1872. New York: Mentor Book, 1958.

Dax, Marc. "Lésion de la moitié gauche de l'encéphale coïncidant avec l'oubli des signes de la pensée," (lu a Montpellier en 1836), *Gaz. hebd.*, 2ᵉ ser., 2: 259—260 (1865): Dax G., Jr. 260—262.

Debout. "Coup d'oeil sur les vices de conformation . . . des membres et . . . ressources mécaniques, etc." *Mém. Soc. Chir*. Paris, 6 (1868): 1—196.

Delauney, H. *Les sociétés savantes de France*. Paris: Lahure, 1902.

Delauney, P. "L'école militaire renoueuse et la dynastie médicale des Valdajou," *Bull. Soc. Fr. Hist. Méd*. 11 (1912): 204—257.

Dell, P. "Correlations entre la système végétatif et le système de la vie de relation. Mesencéphale, diencéphale et cortex cérébral," *J. de Physiol*. 44 (1952): 471—557.

Des Granges, Ch. M. *Histoire de la littérature française*. 33ᵉ ed., Paris: Hatier, 1938.

Du Chaillu, Paul Belloni. *Explorations and Adventures in Equatorial Africa*. London: Murray, 1861

Dureau. "Professor Paul Broca," (transl. fr. *Gaz. Méd.*, Paris), *Med. Times and Gaz.*, London (Sept. 4, 1880): 283-284.

d'Écherac. "Jubilé du cinquantenaire de la Société d'Anthropologie 7/7/1909," *Bull. et Mém. Soc. d'Anthropol.*, 5ᵉ sér. 10 (1909): 299 — 301.

Eckman, L. *Tetanus, Prophylaxis and Therapy.* New York: Grune, Stratton, 1963.

Edinger, L. *The Anatomy of the Central Nervous System of Man and of Vertebrates in General.* transl. by W.S. Hall. Philadelphia: Davis, 1899; based on the 5th German edition, 1896.

Ehrlich, P.R. and Holm, R.W. "Patterns and Populations," *Science*, 137 (1962): 652 — 657.

Eschenauer, (Pastor). "Paul Broca au Collège," *Bull. Soc. d'Anthropol.*, 3ᵉ sér, 5 (1882): 675 — 679.

Faure, J.L. "Manifestations en l'honneur du Professeur Jean-Louis Faure à Sainte-Foy-la-Grande 14 5 sept., 1935," *J. de Méd.* Bordeaux, 6 — 7. 20/10/1935.

Ferrier, Sir D. *The Croonian Lectures on Cerebral Localisation.* London: Smith, Elder, 1890.

Fischgold, H. "D'Angelo Mosso à Hans Berger: Comment est née l'electroencéphalographie (1961)," in *Essays on the History of Italian Neurology.* L. Belloni, ed., Univ. Milano (1963), 232 — 254.

Fletcher, R. "Paul Broca and the French School of Anthropology," a lecture delivered in the National Museum, Washington, D.C., April 15, 1882, *Saturday Lectures*, No. 6 (July 24, 1913), Judd and Detweiler from *Miscellaneous Papers*, 1882 — 1912. Library, Surgeon General's Office.

Foville, A. Louis. *Traité complet de l'anatomie, de la physiologie et de la pathologie du système nerveux.* Part 1 and Atlas by E. Beau and F. Bion. Paris: Fortin, 1844.

_____, and Pinel-Grandchamps, F. *Recherches sur le siège spécial de différentes fonctions du système nerveux.* Paris: Bovee, 1823.

Freud, Sigmund. *On Aphasia* (1891) transl. E. Stengel. New York: Internat. Univ. Press, 1953.

Fritsch, G. and Hitzig, E. "Über die elektrische Erregbarkeit des Grosshirns," *Archiv. Anat., Physiol., und wissenschaftl. Med.*, Leipzig (1870), 300 — 332; transl. G. von Bonin in *The Cerebral Cortex.* Springfield, Ill. (1960): C.C. Thomas, 73 — 96.

Gagnebin, F.H. Lettre de J.F. Arnaud, chapelain de l'Ambassade de Hollande & Paris, *Bull. Soc. Hist. Protestantisme Français*, 28 (1879): 381 — 383.

Gardner, M. *Fads and Fallacies in the Name of Science.* 158, New York, 1957.

Garrison, F.H. *An Introduction to the History of Medicine.* 4th ed. Philadelphia: Saunders, 1929.

Gastaut, H. "Correlations entre le système nerveux végétatif et le système de la vie de relation dans le rhinencéphale," *J. de Physiol.* 44 (1952): 431—470.

_____, & Lammers, H.J.: Anatomie du Rhinencéphale. In Alajouanine, Th.: *Les Grandes Activités du Rhinencéphale.* vol. 1. Paris: Masson, 1961.

Genty. *Les Biographies Médicales.* Paris: Baillière, 1935.

Gley. "Discours" (on the 50th anniversary of the Société de Biologie), *Comptes rendus séances et mém. de biol.*, 11e sér., vol. 1 (1899): 1011 — 1080.

Goldstein, K. "Pierre Paul Broca" in W. Haymaker & Schiller, ed. *The Founders of Neurology* 2nd ed. Springfield, Ill. (1970): C.C. Thomas, 259 — 263.

Goodman, L.S. and Gilman, A. *The Pharmacological Basis of Therapeutics.* New York: Macmillan, 1955.

Gray, H. *Anatomy of the human body.* Philadelphia: Lee & Febiger, 1973.

Gratiolet, P. *Mémoire sur les Plis Cérébraux de l'Homme et des Primates.* Paris: Bertrand, 1854.

_____, "Note sur les expansions des racines cérébrales du nerf optique et sur leur terminaison dans une région déterminée de l'écorce des hémisphères," *Compt. rend. Acad. Sci.* Paris, 39 (1854): 274 — 278.

Grenouilleau, A. *Ste.-Foy Défile*; Ste.-Foy-la-Grande. 1911.

Guillain, G. J.-M. *Charcot, 1825–1893, His Life—His Work.* ed. and transl. Pierre Bailey. New York: Horber, 1959.

Haberling, Hübotter, and Vierordt. *Biographisches Lexikon der hervorragenden Artzte aller Zeiten und Völker.* Berlin: Urban und Schwarzenberg, 2nd ed. 1932.

Hammer, A. *Wien. med. Wschr.* 28: 97–102, 1878, and *Canad. J. Med. Sci.* (Toronto) 3:353–357, 1878.

Head, Henry (1861–1940). *Aphasia and Kindred Disorders of Speech.* 2 vol. New York: Macmillan, 1926.

Heberden, G. (Wm.). *Commentarii de morborum historia et curatione.* 2nd ed. London: Payne, 1907. Ch. 70: *de Dolore Pectoris,* 306–314.

Herrick, C.J. "The Amphibian Forebrain," *J. Comp. Neurol.,* 58 (1933): 1–288.

Hinton, H.E. and Blum, M.S. "Suspended animation and the origin of life," *New Scientist* 28 (1965): 270–271.

Hirschfeld, L.M. *Névrologie et esthésiologie. Traité et iconographie du système nerveux et des organes des sens de l'homme, etc.,* Atlas par J.B. Leveillé, 2nd ed. Paris: Masson, 1866.

Horteloup. "Eloge de M. le docteur Paul Broca," *Bull. et Mém. de la Soc. de Chir. de Paris* 10 (Jan. 30, 1884): 122–142.

Hoyme, L.E. "Physical anthropology and its instruments: an historical study," *Southern J. Anthropol.* 9 (1953): 408–430.

Huard, P. "Paul Broca (1824–1880)," *Rev. d'hist. des Sciences,* 14 (1961): 47–86.

Hunter, R. and Macalpine, I. *Three Hundred Years of Psychiatry: 1535–1860.* London (1963): Oxford, 106.

Huxley, L. *Life and Letters of Thomas Henry Huxley, by his son,* N.Y. (1902) Appleton, 1: 294–295.

Huxley, T.H. "On the brain of Ateles Paniscus," *Proc. Zool. Soc.,* (June 11, 1861), 247–260.

—————. *Evidences as to Man's Place in Nature.* London: Williams and Norgate, 1863.

Iltis. H. *Life of Mendel.* transl. E. and C. Paul. New York: Norton, 1932.

Isaac, J. and Bonifacio, A. *XVIIe et XVIIIe Siècles.* Paris: Hachette, 1952.

Jaccoud. "Angine de poitrine" in *Nouveau Dictionnaire de Méd. et Chir.* vol. 2 (1887), 489–510.

Jackson, J. Hampden. *Marx, Proudhon, and European Socialism.* New York: Macmillan, 1958.

Jackson, J. Hughlings. *Selected Writings.* J. Taylor, ed., vol. I London (1931): Hodder and Stoughton, 385–411.

—————. "On the physiology of language." *Brit. Assn. for Advance. Sci.; Med. Times and Gaz.* (Sept. 5, 1868), 275–276.

Jarry, E. *Débuts de l'Histoire Contemporaine* (1789–1851) Paris: Ed. de l'Ecole, 1945.

Jellinek, Frank. *The Paris Commune of 1871.* London: Gollancz, 1937.

Jones, E. *The Life and Work of Sigmund Freud.* vol. 1 (1856–1900). New York: Basic Books, 1953.

Joynt, R.J. "Centenary of patient 'Tan.' His contribution to the problems of aphasia," *Arch. Int. Med.* 108 (1961): 933–956.

Karplus, J.P. and Kreidl, A. "Gehirn und Sympathicus," *Pflüger's Arch. f.d. ges. Physiol.* (1909) 129: 138–144; 1910. 135: 401–416; 1912. 143: 109–127.

Keilin, D. "The problem of anabiosis or latent life: history and current concept." *Proc. Roy. Soc.* London: Ser. B, 150 (1959): 149–191.

Kistner, R.W. *Gynecology, principles and practice.* Chicago: Year Book Med. Pub., 1955.

Kohn, H. "Zur Geschichte der Angina pectoris: Heberden oder Rougnon?" *Zeitschr. f. klin. Med.* 106 (1927): 1–20.

Laborde, J.V. "Broca sénateur; banquet en l'honneur de sa nomination, le 10 février dernier," *Tribune méd.* (1880) 11–13, 97–105, 291.

_____. "Mort du Professeur Broca," *Trib. méd.* 7/11/1880, 13:336; *ibid.* (July 18, 1880), 337-340; *ibid.* (Roger, H.), 345.

Lameyre, G. *Haussmann, Préfet de Paris.* Paris: Flammarion, 1958.

Lastres, J.B. and Cabieses, F. *La trepanación del cráneo en el antiguo Perú,* Imprenta de la Univ. Nac. Mayor de San Marcos de Lima. 1960.

Latour, A. "L'Académie de médecine et le Sénat," *Union méd.,* 3ᵉ sér. 29: 261—263, 313—314, 325—326, 1880.

Lebert, H. *Physiologie pathologique, ou recherches cliniques, expérimentales et microscopiques sur l'inflammation, la tuberculisation, les tumeurs. etc.* 2 vol. Paris: Bailliére, 1845.

_____. *Biographische Notizen.* Breslau: Korn, 1869.

Leguèbe, André. "Les méthodes statistiques de Paul Broca." *Bull. et Mém. de la Soc. d'Anthrop. de Paris.* vol 4, sér. XIII (1977), p. 23—30.

Leibowitz, J.O. *The History of Coronary heart disease,* London: Wellcome Institute, 1970.

Leuret, F. and Gratiolet, P. *Anatomie comparée du système nerveux considéré dans ses rapports avec l'intelligence.* 2 vol. and atlas, vol. 1 by Leuret. Paris: Didot, 1839—1857.

Lewes, G.H. Review of *The functions of the brain* by D. Ferrier, *Nature* 25 (1876): 73—74; 93—95.

Lincoln, Abraham. *Complete Works.* Ed. J.G. Nicolay and J. Hay. New York: Century, 1894. vol. 1, 369—70; 457/8, 1858.

Lipinska, Melanie. *Histoire des femmes médecins depuis l'antiquite jusqu'a nos jours.* Paris: Jacques, 1900.

_____. *Les Femmes et le progrès des sciences médicales.* Paris: Masson, 1930.

Lombard, J.S. *Proc. Roy. Soc. London* XXVII B (1878): 166—177.

Lutaud, A. "Les médecins dans Balzac," *Bull. Soc. Franc. d'Hist. Med.* 19 (1925): 145—158.

Macewen. *Pyogenic Diseases of the Brain and Spinal Cord.* Glasgow, 1893.

McIntyre, A.R. *Curare, Its History, Nature, and Clinical Use.* Chicago: University of Chicago Press, 1947.

MacLean, P.D. "Psychosomatic disease and the 'visceral brain.' Recent developments bearing on the Papez theory of emotion," *Psychom. Med.* 11 (1949): 338—353.

_____. "Some psychiatric implications of physiological studies on frontotemporal portion of limbic system (visceral brain)," *EEG Clin. Neurophysiol.* 4 (1952): 407—418.

Magath, T.B. "The History of Steam Sterilization," *Am. Med. Hist.* 8 (1937): 338—344.

Marie, Pierre. "Révision de la question de l'aphasie," *Semaine méd.* (1906). 241—247, 493—500, 565—571.

Matas. R. "Surgery of the Vascular System," in Keen. W.W. *Surgery* (1914—1921). vol. 5: 228—229.

Maurois, A. *Histoire de la France.* vol. I. Michel, 1947.

_____. *Olympio, The Life of Victor Hugo.* (Trans. by G. Hopkins) N.Y.: Harper, 1956.

Mayr, E. *Animal Species and Evolution.* Cambridge, Mass. Harvard, 1963.

Meynert, Th. *Psychiatrie.* Wien, Braumüller, part 1: 162, 1884.

_____, "Über den Wahn (1885) *Samml. von populär-wissenschaftichen Vorträgen über dem Bau und die Leistungen des Gehrins.* Wien 1892 p. 86ff.

Michelin. *Guide du Pneu: Paris.* 10th ed. Paris, 1959.

Moissenet. "Extrait du rapport sur le traitment . . . du docteur Landolfi . . ." *Gaz. hebd.* 3 (1856): 324-330.

Morand, F.S. "Sur quelques parties du cerveau," *Hist. de l'Acad. Roy. des Sci.,* Paris, 1744 5—7. 1748.

Mortillet, G. de. "La Statue de Broca," *L'Homme.* 4(1887): 449– 455.

Morton, S.G. *Crania Americana.* Philadelphia: Dobson, 1839.

Mosso, Angelo. *Die Temperatur des Gehirns.* Leipzig: Veit, 1894.

Moutier, François. *L'Aphasie de Broca.* Thèse, Paris, 1908.

Napias, H. *L'Assistance Publique en 1900.* pp. 32, 145.

Nouvel, Ed. *Le Collège Sainte-Barbe.* Paris (1948) pp. 21– 23.

Olds, J. "Self-stimulation experiments and differentiated reward systems." in *Reticular Formations of the Brain.* H.H. Jasper et al., ed. Boston: Little, Brown, 1958

Olmsted, J.M.D. *Charles-Edouard Brown-Séquard.* Baltimore (1946): Johns Hopkins Press, 34, 40, 80.

Ombredane, A. *L'Aphasie et l'élaboration de la pensée explicite.* Presses Univ. de France, 1951.

Oparin, A.I. *Genesis and evolutionary development of life.* New York: Academic Press, 1968.

Ornstein, M. *The role of scientific societies in the seventeenth century.* Chicago: University of Chicago Press, 1928.

Palay, S. *Dictionnaire du béarnais et du gascon modernes.* Pau, Marrimponey (1932), p. 191.

Papez, J.W. "A proposed mechanism of emotion," *Arch. Neurol. Psychiat.* 38 (1937): 725– 743.

—————. "The visceral brain, its components and connections," in *Reticular Formations of the Brain.* H.H. Jasper et al., ed. Boston (1958): Little, Brown, 591– 605.

Pelletan. Funeral speech: Paul Broca, *Bull. Soc. d'Anthropol.,* 3e sér. 3 (1880): 497 ff.

Penfield, W. and Roberts, L. *Speech and Brain Mechanisms.* Princeton Univ. Press, 1959.

Penniman, T.K. *A Hundred Years of Anthropology.* 2nd ed. London, Duckworth, 1952.

Perrier, E. "On Broca and de Quatrefages," *Bull. et Mém. Soc. d'Anthropol.,* 5e sér 10 (1909): 305– 328.

Postgate, R.W. *Revolutions from 1789 to 1906.* London: Richards, 1920.

Pozzi, S. "Paul Broca," *Revue d'Anthropol.,* 2e sér, vol. 2, (1880) 577– 608.

—————. "Paul Broca," *Rev. Scientifique:* 33e sér 2: 2– 12, 1882.

Prestwich, Grace Anne (Milne) M'Call, Lady. *Essays Descriptive and Biographical.* Edinburgh: Blackwood, pp. 73– 92, 1901.

Prigent, J.M. *Contributions a l'etude du journalisme médical francais.* These, Rennes, 1962.

Proksch, J.K. *Die Geschichte der venerischen Krankheiten.* vol. 2, Hanstein, Bonn, 1895.

Prudhommeaux, J.J. *Icarie et son Fondateur Étienne Cabet.* Paris: Rider, 1926.

Pruner-Bey, F. "De la chevelure comme caractéristique des races humaines d'après des recherches microscopiques." *Mém. Soc. d'Anthropol.,* sér 1, vol. 2: 1– 35, 1865; *id.*: "Deuxième série d'observations microscopiques de la chevelure," *ibid.* vol. 3 (1868): 77– 98.

Quatrefages, J. L.A. de. *The Prussian Race, Ethnologically Considered.* (transl. I. Innes) London: Virtue. 1872.

Ramon y Cajal, S. *Studies on the Cerebral Cortex (Limbic Structures).* (transl. L. M. Kraft) London: Lloyd-Luke, 1955.

Rasmussen, T. and Milner, B.: "Clinical and surgical studies of the cerebral speech areas in man." In *Cerebral Localization.* Ed. K.J. Zülch, O. Creutzfeld, G.C. Galbraith. Springer, Hiedelberg-Berlin (1977), p238– 257.

Reclus, Paul. "Paul Broca," *Rev. mens. de méd. et chir.* 4 (1880): 745– 764.

Reclus, Maurice. *Monsieur Thiers.* Paris: Plon, 1929.

Rey, P. "Une opération de Broca," *Chron. méd.* (1895) 584– 591.

Richelot, G. senior. "Banquet offert à M. Broca," *Union Méd.,* 3e sér 29: 301– 306, Feb. 24 1880.

Ricord, Ph. *Traité pratique des maladies vénériennes, etc.* Paris: Rouvier et Bouvier, (1838) 87– 94, 133– 134, 200.

Rochard, J.: *Histoire de la chirurgie française au XIXe siècle.* Paris: Baillière, 1875.

Rolando, L. "Della Struttura degli Emispheri cerebrali," *Memorie Real Acad. Sci.* Torino, (1830) 35, 103– 146.

Rooseboom, M. *Microscopium.* Leyden, 1956.

Sachaile (anagr. Lachaise, C.) *Les médecins de Paris jugés par leurs oeuvres, ou statistique scientifique et morale des médecins de Paris.* Paris, 1845.

Sansom, A.E. *Manual of the Physical Diagnosis of Diseases of the Heart.* 3rd ed., London: Churchill, 1881.

Savage, T.S. and Wyman, J.M.S. *Boston J. of Nat. Hist.* 5 (Aug 18, 1847): 417– 441.

Schaefer, A. "Leben und Wirken des Arztes Franz Pruner-Bey." *Janus* 35: 249– 277, 297– 311, 335– 343, 360– 375, 1931. *ibid.* 36: 59– 70, 114– 127, 1932.

Schenck (ius) J. *Observationes medicae,* Leyden, 1585, [quoted by Dax Trousseau, Benton & Joynt; Brain.]

Schiff, Moritz. "Recherches sur l'échauffement des nerfs et des centres nerveux à la suite des irritations sensorielles et sensitives," *Arch. physiol. norm. et pathol.,* 1ère sér. 3 (1870): 5– 25, 198– 214, 323– 333, 451– 462.

Schiller, F. "Leborgne— In Memoriam," *Med. Hist.* (1963) 79– 81.

_____. "Concepts of stroke before and after Virchow." *Med. Hist.* (1970) 115– 132.

Schonberg, H.C. *The Great Pianists.* New York: Simon and Schuster, 122, 1963.

Schreider, E. "Les liaisons anthropométriques dans l'espèce humaine," *L'Anthropologie* 67:49– 84.

Scobie A. & Taylor J.W. "Perversions ancient & modern. I. Agalmatophilia, the statue syndrome," *J. Hist. Behav. Sci.* XI (1975): 49– 54.

Seneca. *Ad Lucilium Epistulae Morales.* (65 A.D.) Epistle *LIV.* London: Kernemain, 1917.

Sénet, Andrew. *Man in Search of His Ancestors (The Romance of Paleontology).* (transl. Maledin Barnes) New York: McGraw-Hill, 1956.

Simon, Jules. *Le soir de ma journée.* Paris, Flammarion (1901): 2, 257– 258.

Simond, Ch. *Paris de 1800 à 1900.* Paris (1900): Plon, 193– 208.

Smith, Grafton Eliot. "The morphology of the true 'limbic lobe,' etc.," *J. Anat. Physiol.,* 30 (1896): 157– 167, 185– 205.

_____. "Some problems relating to the evolution of the human brain," *Anat. Anzeiger,* 24 (1904): 74– 83.

Souques, A. "Quelques cas d'anarthrie de Pierre Marie: Aperçu historique sur la localisation du language," *Rev. neurol.* 2 (1928): 319– 368.

Soury, J. *Le système nerveux central . . . Histoire critique des théories et des doctrines.* Paris: Carré et Naud, 1899.

Sterne, L. *The Life and Opinions of Tristram Shandy, Gentleman* (1759– 1767). London (1941): Oxford University Press, 133.

Taren, J.A. "Anatomical pathways, etc." *Neurology* 15 (1965): 228– 234.

Temkin, D. "Gall and the phrenological movement," *Bull. Hist. Med.* 21 (1947): 275– 321.

_____. "Basic science, medicine and the romantic era," *Bull. Hist. Med.* 37 (1963): 97– 129 (124).

Tillaux. Funeral speech for P. Broca, *Bull. Soc. d'Anthropol.* 3e sér., 3 (1880): 497 ff.

Tilney, F. and Riley, H.A. *The Form and Functions of the Central Nervous System.* New York: Hoeber, 1938.

Topinard, P. *"La société, l'école, le laboratoire et le musée Broca,"* (à la mémoire de Broca) pamphlet, Paris, 1890.

Trélat, Wysse. Funeral speech for P. Broca, *Bull. Soc. d'Anthropol.,* Paris, 3e sér., vol. 3: 496ff. Aug. 5, 1880.

Trousseau, Armand. *De L'Aphasie (Clinique Médicale de l'Hôtel-Dieu de Paris)*. 2nd ed., vol. 2. Paris (1865): Bailliére Fils 571– 626.

Turner, W. "The convolutions of the brain: A study in comparative anatomy," *J. Anat. and Physiol.* 25 (1890– 1891): 105– 153.

Valentin, B. *Geschichte der Orthopädie*. Thieme, Stuttgart, 1961.

Vallois, H.V. "Le laboratoire Broca," *Bull. et Mém. d'Anthropol.*, Paris, 11 (9ᵉ sér) (1940): 1– 18.

——————. "Un manuscrit inédit de Broca: Voyage en Russie en 1879," *Ethnografiia Sovietskaia*, 2 (1964): 70– 77.

Velpeau, A. "Discussion académique (1854)," in *Traité des maladies du sein*. Paris: Masson, IX– LVII, 1858.

Verneuil. Funeral speech for P. Broca, *Bull. Soc. d'Anthropol.*, 3ᵉ sér. 3 (1880): 497ff.

Véron, Louis. *Mémoires d'un Bourgeois de Paris, I*. Paris, 1856.

Virchow, R. "Das Normale Knochenwachstum und die rachitischen Störungen desselben," *Arch. f. path. Anat. & Physiol., etc.* 5 (1853): 409– 507.

——————. *Gesammelte Abhandlungen zur wissenschaftlichen Medizin* Frankfurt, Meidinger (1856), pp. 380– 450, 478– 504.

——————. "Broca," *Deutsche Gesellsch. f. Anthropol., Ethnol. u. u. Urgesch.*, Berlin, 11 (Aug., 1880): 23– 24.

Walker, Earl. *A History of Neurosurgery*. Baltimore: Williams & Wilkins, 1951.

Wangensteen, D.H. et al. "Achieving 'physiological gastrectomy' by gastric freezing," *J. Amer. Med. Assn.* 180 (1962): 439– 444.

Watson, T. *Lectures on the Principles and Practice of Physics*. Philadelphia (1844), 912.

Weber, Ernst Heinrich. *De pulsu, resorptione, auditu et tactu (De subtilitate tactus)*. Lipsiae (1834), 45– 77.

Weiner, Dora B.: *Raspail, Scientist and Reformer* with a chapter by Simone Raspail. New York: Columbia University Press, 1968.

Wernicke, Carl. *Der Aphasische Symptomenkomplex. Eine psychologische Studie auf anatomischer Basis*. Breslau: Cohn & Weigert, 1874.

White, Andrew D. *A History of the Warfare of Science with Theology in Christendom* (1894) New York: Braziller, 296. ff. 1955.

Willius, F.A. and Dry, T.J. *A History of the Heart and Circulation*. Philadelphia: Saunders, 1948.

Wilson, Edmund. *To the Finland Station*. New York: Harcourt, Brace, 1940.

Wilson, W. "Cellular tissue and the dawn of the theory." *Isis* 35 (1944), 168– 173.

Wolf, J.B. *France 1814– 1919*. New York: Harper Torchbook, 1963.

Wunderlich, C. A. and Seguin, E. *Medical Thermometry and Human Temperature*. (1868). New York: Wood, 1871 (transl.)

Yakovlev, P.: "Motility, Behavior and Brain, etc." *J. Nerv. and Ment. Dis.* 107: 313, 335, 1948.

Zangwill, O.L.: "Excision of Broca's area without persistent aphasia." In *Cerebral Localization*. Ed. K.J. Zülch, O. Creutzfeld, G.C. Galbraith. Heidelberg-Berlin, Springer, 1977. p. 258– 263.

Index